The Migration
of British Capital
to 1875

Leland H. Jenks

PROFESSOR EMERITUS OF SOCIOLOGY
Wellesley College, Massachusetts

BOOKS
10 East 53d St., New York 10022
(a division of Harper & Row Publishers, Inc.)

This edition published in the U.S.A. 1973 by
HARPER & ROW PUBLISHERS, INC.
BARNES & NOBLE IMPORT DIVISION

Copyright © Leland H. Jenks 1927

ISBN 06-493314-8

Printed in Great Britain by The Camelot Press
London and Southampton

52336

Contents

CONTENTS

CONTENTS

The Migration of British Capital to 1875

CHAPTER I

FINANCIAL SOCIETY AT THE END OF THE EIGHTEENTH CENTURY

"I reap where I sowed not, and gather where I did not scatter."
—Matthew, xxv, 26.

SETTING FORTH THE THEME

What is endeavored in this study is to set forth some of the principal ways in which the migration of capital has influenced the rise of an invisible empire of which London is the metropolis—the empire of British enterprise—the overseas extension of the British economic system.

It is not an attempt to find out all about the economics of the British Empire. We have not sought to trim the ungainly limbs of economic life to the Procrustean bed of the modern state-system. Nor have we given that life a character with its wanton conduct toward the political nursemaids alone in view. The story is one of a function, of which the British people have been largely the performers, by which modes of thought and action the world around have been shaped to a pattern; by which areas politically and geographically remote have been stirred to the rhythm of a common effort.

In the present volume we have sought to follow British capital for the fifty years during which it was transmitting the direct effects of the Industrial Revolution to the Continent and elsewhere. An encyclopaedia could not relate the multitude of these activities, and we promise no encyclopaedia. There is no pretense of telling all of the things that are true and ascertainable about British foreign investment. There were important movements of British capital before 1875 which this study will not seek to trace. Our concern is to portray the migration in some typical manifestations, in conduct which was of moment in its time. Our story is not so much of where the money went as of how it got there. Our quest is less for what happened than for the mechanisms, the habitudes, the animating spirit which arose in the migration of British capital. For it is not the least impressive thing about activity that it leaves a path. And paths are themselves determinants of further action. They beckon as invitingly even when the sign-posts change.

Mechanisms of finance, habitudes of business relationship, the spirit of enterprise and of venture upon alien soil—these all took form in the movement of British capital abroad. Once formed they became the carriers of activities which, achieving continuity, made the British Isles a part of an ever-widening economic whole. Out of those activities there arose structures vital to the people of the British Isles, but with only casual relation to the political conglomeration of which those islands formed a part.

IN LIEU OF DEFINITION

The investment of capital is no strange phenomenon. It is the essential act of faith of every man who enters business, buys a farm, or employs a laborer. Nor is it new. It was commonplace to the peasant folk to whom Jesus preached his gospel. In a sense every expenditure not directed to the immediate gratification of a want, every purchase which bears the prospect of gain, is an investment. There need be no question of intent in such a purchase. There was investment before there were investors. The man who employs his resources deliberately to secure a maximum return is the artificial product of a sophisticated age. But acquisitive capitalism is not the only form of economy under which investment would arise. The employment of purchasing power to procure an income, no matter by whom performed, or where, or for what purpose, is an investment of capital.

Familiar and inescapable as this operation is, there is reason to recall that in the economy of western civilization it has come to hold a crucial position. Seeking the most profitable methods, our diversified productive systems have come to depend to an increasing degree upon the use of loan capital drawn from a common source. Merchant and manufacturer, farmer and cooperative,—none can direct his enterprise to the greatest advantage without a continual expansion of his resources. Each draws from a common pool of capital, which springs in part from bank credit. The nature of this reservoir is such that its repletion depends upon the continued fruitfulness of the streams which it supplies. Hence the available resources of all are staked upon the productivity of each. And the administration of the flow of this mass investment has become one of the most vital functions of social control. It is one element of discipline amid the riotous anarchy of modern business.

No aspect of the policy of this administration presents problems of greater concern and delicacy than the matter of foreign investment.[1] For there is a discongruity between productive systems and the national states in which they arise which seems to grow rather than abate in distinctness. On the one hand there is an unreadiness of the home market to absorb industrial products which persuades manufacturers, especially of steel and other capital goods, to place them abroad by means of credit operations in the development of backward countries. There is an inadequacy in most countries of essential raw materials, foodstuffs and tropical produce, whose cheapness and abundance at home may be promoted by an application of capital abroad. More generally there are recurring inequalities in the international trade balance which may be adjusted to the profit of foreign banking specialists by large transactions in foreign securities. At the same time there is a friction in this capitalistic mechanism occasioned by the political frontier and the discordant policies of alien governments. It would seem at times that the investor's vision is distorted at the boundary line. He acts not in a real world, but in one colored red, black and yellow upon a map. Economic man is something of a nationalist, and those who would like to use his money upon easy terms at home are ready to acclaim his sentiment. Thus emigrating capital often passes the frontier with friction. Yet it as often becomes a force tending to draw the frontier after it. And so manifold have been the political consequences of its movements that foreign loans and concessions have been handled as essential factors in the balance of power, the cementing link of military understandings.

Thus it is not possible to view foreign investment merely as a factor in the national balance-sheet. It is not enough to speak of it as the use of purchasing power to procure an income from abroad.[2] More too is involved than the distribution of capital goods and the classified lists of the Stock Exchange. There is implied the creation of property rights which may involve governments in action beyond their boundaries. And there are suggested sanctions and forms of social control which beneath the consciousness of law transform economic processes and the very motivation of economic life. It is by investment, among other channels, that industrialism itself has been transmitted to distant parts of the world. Age-old systems of culture and reflection may at long last owe survival or decay to the manner in which the invested capital is applied. A civilization already old when England was a forest, may be altered or destroyed by the action of foreign capital at Shanghai. More distinctly than investments within the orbit of an accepted economic order, the migration of capital beyond its pale implies valuations not readily charted in a statistical scheme. Nor are such implications exhausted in a far land. Specialization and dependence are mutual qualities. The movements of capital which doom one people to the production of frozen beef and hard wheat if they will live, sentence another as certainly to export calico and to live in Bethnal Green. In ignorance or design the pecuniary reckonings which direct the migration of capital chart a course for modern history.

BEFORE THE POUND WAS SOVEREIGN

Thru the nineteenth century and down to 1914 the country whose foreign investments occupied the most vital relation to her productive system was Great Britain. In volume her capital exports distanced those of her nearest competitors. London was the money capital of the world, even tho British predominance in international trade was modified toward the end of the century by the emergence of Germany and the United States. The latter country alone was indebted to Great Britain for nearly five billion dollars of capital at the outbreak of the war. British investments in Central and South America were fully as great. The English·

speaking dominions taken together and India had absorbed from four to five hundred million pounds apiece. Holdings elsewhere, in Europe, Egypt and the Far East, exceeded the latter sum.[3] Twenty per cent of the British national income came from abroad, and in good years the same proportion was annually reinvested. Four billion pounds invested beyond the seas were the guarantee, with command of those seas, that in emergency an industrial population of fifty millions would be fed.

How far the war may prove to have permanently altered this position can not now be predicted with confidence. It seems certain, however, that New York in the next generation will be at least a close competitor to London for financial leadership. And it is not untimely to recall that Great Britain has not always been the chief source of capital for the exploitation of the world.

To the age of Walpole and Chatham the picture of agriculturally dependent Britain employing a considerable portion of its wealth abroad, to ensure raw materials and subsistence and markets for its population and industries, would have seemed highly incongruous. Holland occupied in the seventeenth and eighteenth centuries preeminently this position.[4] Unable to live on the produce of the land, the Dutch citizens had taken to sea. The profits of an immense carrying trade and the position of Amsterdam as the leading exchange in Europe brought surpluses to Holland which her merchants did not hesitate to lend to political and commercial rivals. Moreover, the religious liberty extended by the Dutch and the comparative freedom of the Amsterdam bourse drew heretic and Jewish capitalists from less tolerant communities. With them came the business of purveyance to the needs of impecunious sovereigns—a hazardous trade which Florence and Genoa, Augsburg and Antwerp had conducted in earlier generations. At Amsterdam it was reduced to order. By 1672 the Dutch were familiar with negotiable public securities binding not only upon a sovereign but upon his state.[5] They had a market in which such instruments were actively bought and sold, with professional speculators ever ready to augment the supply of counters with which they played. England and Austria, France and the Continental Congress in turn sought Amsterdam with their public obligations. About 1760 the Dutch held in their own names some twenty million pounds in consols, besides shares in the stock of the Bank of England and the East India Company.[6] This was approximately one-seventh of the National Debt. Contemporaries believed that much larger sums were normally advanced to British merchants and gentry upon the mortgage of consols and real property.[7] Indeed in 1773 a special act of Parliament validated the claims of alien mortgagees in the West Indies, to enable sugar planters to borrow more extensively in Holland.[8] The European world looked to Amsterdam as its financial metropolis.

The main features of the British economic position at this time may be set forth in a few words. England was a nearly self-sufficient state, of the early capitalistic type, managed by a landed aristocracy.[9] The basis of her economy consisted in agriculture and domestic manufactures. The lower classes produced enough products from these to supply the needs of the metropolis as well as their own; and their landlords employed their revenues in enjoying the expensive pleasures of Westminster. There was also an exportable surplus of textiles and grain, sufficient to supply the nation with naval stores, colonial goods and precious metals, to keep up the interest on England's foreign debt, and to pay the expenses of her subsidized foreign legions. These demands tended to increase rather than diminish. Overseas a portion of the British people in the colonies formed an expanding market, and at home the population grew which was engaged in implementing the resultant trade. From early in the eighteenth century a perceptible movement was under way to stimulate the productivity of the country. Scientific agriculture made its appearance; and to provide auspices favorable for its application primitive village economies were invaded by act of Parliament. Where communal slackness had browsed, now bristled the hedgerows of the Enclosure Acts. By their means the productivity of the land kept pace with the rapidly growing demands of the metropolis. But it remained for technical discoveries in the coal, iron and textile industries to augment the exportable surplus and the manner of its supply, and for the canal, turnpike and coach-, ing movements to incite the process of industrial concentration. Meanwhile the aim of policy, so far as British statesmen had formulated it, was simply to maintain as wide a margin as possible between the produce Great Britain could export and the articles she must buy abroad. Accordingly the foreign trade of England, which was then a highly self-sufficient country, was smaller than that of France and Holland which were then less so.[10]

England had been protected by the Navigation Acts from dependence on the Dutch carrying trade. During the eighteenth century there began a concentration of capital which gave promise of financial independence as well. On the one hand there was an adventitious accumulation of wealth arising from certain inexpensive foreign ventures, notably the West Indian sugar trade, the traffic in African slaves, and the spoliation of India.[11] On the other there was a steady redistribution of indigenous wealth, implemented by jobbery in the funds, loan and subsistence contracts, the administration of patronage and the Enclosure Acts.[12] If England was affected largely by reason of these conditions it was by no means because her position was peculiar as compared with that of France. It was rather that having more money in their hands than they knew how to spend, the nabobs and the contractors and the opulescent classes generally placed it for safety and advantage with banks, whence it could be drawn to extend the operations of farmers and grain dealers, clothing factors and miners, merchants and shipbuilders,—of all whose undertakings promised to pay for its use. The eighteenth century was not preeminently a century of thrift and economy, if attention be directed to the principal cities. The age of rococo and baroque, of flamboyant fashion, of elaborate speech, could not be accused of miserliness.[13] Nor will the candid historian insist that it was industrious. Yet under the fermenting influence of the newly discovered note and deposit system the capital resources of Great Britain grew by leaps and bounds during the closing decades of the century.

Thus the outbreak of protracted war upon the Continent could serve as stimulus to processes that were already in motion, and transform the commercial position of Great Britain by disabling the rivals whose functions she was now prepared to perform. To comprehend a complex era of rapid and momentous change, historians are pleased to ticket it with the label "revolution." Not one but a dozen revolutions swept western Europe from 1783 to 1815. It was a revolution in industry, mining and transportation which was under way in the England of the younger Pitt. There was a series of French Revolutions which, summoning England to war, welded her into an economic society. These great processes cradled a Commercial Revolution which placed the carrying trade of Europe and her colonies in the hands of English merchantmen. And fleeing the tide of Napoleon's invasion

came Financial Revolution, the migration of capitalists and
money market from Amsterdam to London.

THE MONEY MARKET AT LONDON

The money market at London which came thus to commanding importance at the beginning of the nineteenth century was not much more than one hundred years old.   It may
be said to have come over the Channel with William of
Orange.   The successive wars of William and of Anne
fostered a loosely associated "City," which derived its profits
from war contracts and dealings in the public debt and from
the perquisites of a rapidly expanding trade.   By the last
quarter of the eighteenth century its main constituents were
well-defined.

There was a Bank of England, owned and operated by the
leading merchants of London, which enjoyed a monopoly of
issuing notes payable on demand in London.   It managed
the public debt, receiving the revenues assigned to the Consolidated Fund and keeping the principal and interest books
of the fundholders.   It marketed the short term bills of the
government in their various forms, holding many of them as
an investment.   And it served the banking and mercantile
interests as well.   Thru its agency commercial paper was
frequently discounted before its maturity for Bank notes and
deposit accounts.   Thus the velocity at which merchants could
turn over their capital was enhanced, and business credit was
buttressed by an institution whose stability and strength were
already legendary.

There were merchants too with branch houses in the
"provinces,"—in commercial centers outside of London from
which many of them had their rise, and with regular cor-

respondents abroad. Their acceptances circulated in payment for the goods they bought, and they drew upon foreign markets at sixty or ninety days as their merchandise found customers. Book credits like cash payments were not the rule. The whole volume of trade, domestic as well as foreign, was paralleled by a structure of bills whose manipulation formed the principal business of the money market, narrowly conceived.[14] Upon their own account the leading mercantile houses dealt extensively in this paper and performed many functions later to be consigned to banks.

There were private bankers already, antedating as a class, and in the case of Childs and Hoares, as individuals, the establishment of the Bank.[15] As "goldsmiths" during the struggles of the Stuarts with their Parliaments they had become caretakers for the valuables of country gentlemen and city merchants engrossed in politics. They kept "running cash" to meet the needs of these persons, issued "running cash notes" in payment for confiscated lands their customers were purchasing, and undertook the collection of rent rolls. They performed these services free and even paid for the privilege; for they did not allow the money deposited in their care to corrode from lack of use. And they used it without allowing it to leave their possession. Instead of lending the actual specie and plate with which they were entrusted to the government departments, navy contractors and City merchants who would pay them handsomely for its use, they made their loans in notes—promises to pay specie upon demand. As confidence spread in the ability of the goldsmiths to fulfil their promises they were less frequently called upon to do so. And they made the discovery, apparently original with them, that they could safely issue notes exceeding by many times the amount of money actually left with them upon deposit. Their discovery may be regarded

as scarcely less momentous than the invention of the print-
ing press or of the steam engine. The notes which they issued so plentifully passed into circulation and augmented the
monetary funds of the business community. Eventually the
notes returned to the firm which issued them for redemption;
but by arranging loans so that some of them were constantly
coming due, the goldsmith-banker was assured of being able
to meet all the notes that were likely to be presented for payment at any one time. Thus he earned interest upon several
times the amount of his actual monetary resources, and in doing so quickened the spread of capitalistic traits through English society. These characteristics did not disappear from
English banking. To the note-method of pyramiding loans,
was added the device of multiplying them by the cash-account,
a book-credit with the banker which could be drawn upon by
personal check for the benefit of third parties. And if these
services were made use of principally by mercantile classes,
they were at the more general disposal of the British community. The deposit of agricultural revenues and the personal account carried for non-mercantile classes were the distinctive features of British banking to continental observers
in the eighteenth century.[16] They had much to do with the
comparative cultural breadth of which many bankers were
already proud and their rapid assimilation to the social status
of the landowning aristocracy. They had much to do with
the first steps toward the financial integration of English
society.

In the course of time the London bankers had found their
position enhanced by the rise of country banks with which
they were in regular correspondence. These financed the
domestic trade which grew as city and country became increasingly interdependent.[17] The provincial banks rose particularly to facilitate payments in this trade. A wholesale

draper at Nottingham offered his services to tradesmen and corn factors in his locality to handle all their accounts with London. The side-line became central; and *Smith, Payne & Smiths* became in London the headquarters of a series of Midland banks performing remittances. Deposits came to their care from farmers, especially in Lincolnshire, who did not go up with frequency to London. And their profits augmented as they imitated in their localities the note-issuing activities of the Bank in the metropolis. At Lincoln, they maintained for fifty years a bank of deposit and circulation second only in size to the Bank of England. A marriage with the Wilberforces brought them to Hull. Smiths carried the account of Arkwright, inventor of the factory system; and the hosiery trade revolved about their credits.[18] It was ability to cause their promises to pay to circulate in limited areas as money that helped the number of these "country rag merchants" (in Cobbett's phrase) to swell from a scant dozen in 1750 to nearly four hundred by the end of the century. The monetary system of whole areas depended upon bank paper whose principal basis consisted in bills drawn at sixty days upon the correspondent bank in London and constantly renewed.[19] The business life of the entire country was in position to circulate upon a diminishing proportion of metallic currency. And middlemen in the corn and wool trades were able to extend larger credits to producers. Thus the City found root in the soil of England and nourished its fertility.

And there was the National Debt, the "funds" in which gentlemen in eighteenth century fiction bestowed their property for the benefit of their lovely daughters.[20] Product, too, of the Whig Revolution, it exceeded fifty million pounds by 1714. The Seven Years' War brought the total to £132,-000,000; and the wars begun at Lexington and Concord added a hundred millions to this sum. Evidence of British wealth, the growth of the National Debt was the prime agent in its concentration. Three-fourths of the annual budget of the government in 1783 were absorbed in dividends. Nine million pounds were paid to rentiers when the entire annual turnover of British foreign trade did not exceed thirty-five millions. Hume reports that in his time this enormous claim upon the taxpaying ability of the British Isles was held by only seventeen thousand fundholders. Their property was readily transferable, relatively stable in value, a sure and frequent basis of credit extension by bankers in London and Amsterdam.

Mediating the transfers of public stocks and speculating heavily in their fluctuations in value, there were the brokers and jobbers of Jonathan's Coffee House—after 1773, of the Stock Exchange.[21] They were not numerous, nor were they highly regarded socially before the Napoleonic wars brought them the business of a continent and shrined their labors in a classic temple. As the concern of London merchants was with foreign markets, theirs was with government credit. Their fortunes rose and fell with the political news rather than with the woolen market. From any important connection with the industrial life of Great Britain the stock market was entirely divorced. Canals and turnpikes and docks were promoted in the eighteenth century by joint-stock subscription, in spite of the fact that the companies could not limit the liability of their shareholders. But they were not floated in a public market before the "canal mania" of the early nineties. There was no market for the shares until the enterprises were well established and proprietors sought loans upon their property. In the first decade of the nineteenth century these stocks with those of some coal mining companies began to be dealt with in a corner of the room devoted to foreign government stocks.

But the transformation of industry (the machine) and of conveyance (the coaching business) did not receive even this indirect support. The industrial enterprises which commenced in the early eighties to transform Great Britain began with individual savings or advances from local banks and financed their expansion out of their own earnings. It was mainly at the market end, thru advances of London merchants and bankers to buyers at home and abroad, that the financial system was of service to the productive movement. And when the wealth which accrued from the industrial transformations flowed to London, it was not for many generations sent up by the manufacturers, but by the landed proprietors and middlemen to whom also the Machine paid toll. Thus there was a business as well as a social cleavage between industry and finance which did not begin to be bridged until the rise of railways.[22] Money market and factory were at opposite ends of the pecuniary chain which was linking British society into new relations.

Nevertheless the structures essential to a vigorous money market were in existence by 1783. And the funds at their disposal, if not adequate to English needs, were at least more plentiful than most European capitals could command. By the close of the American war money was so easy in London by comparison with France that rentes were being bought upon speculation.[23] One feature of the Anglo-French Commercial Treaty of 1786 was the anticipation that the financial difficulties of the Bourbons would be still further relieved by British capital. There were investments dating from this period which received special treatment in the treaty of November 20, 1815, which ended England's wars against the Revolution.[24]   What connection the market at London had with those absentee investors who were attracted to the American interior before and after independence is not certain.[25]   There were Englishmen, however, who were so fortunately placed as to be able to arrange land grants.   And it was no small thing that the leading private banking house of Amsterdam at the close of the century was owned by the Hopes, a Scotch family, most of whose members resided in England.[26]

THE STIMULUS OF WAR

The loosely connected dealers in pecuniary wealth at London were transformed into a financial society, just as technique was altered, agriculture commercialized, and British economy made industrial, under the stimulus of war.   Napoleon's continental system no less than the progress of French arms disrupted the trade in which the prosperity of old commercial centers consisted.[27]   English and American ships inherited that colonial trade for which two centuries of statesmen had schemed.   England alone could supply the arms and military stores upon which continuance of the war depended.   And if the purchasing power of the Continent was decimated, its demand was exclusively directed to the London market.   England, untouched by invasion or blockade, undrained until 1808 even of human resources, became a closely integrated economic organism.   Industry and agriculture were quickened by the demands which their government made upon them; their production was multiplied by increased application of capital and their reorganization under the enclosure movement and the factory system.   The trade of the world revolved about London, and to its center came capitalists from Germany, Spain and Holland, seeking the security of a stable government and a share in the profits of its undertakings.

Expanding trade and productivity supplied the means by which Great Britain financed the successive coalitions against Napoleon. Between 1793 and 1816, £1,573,000,000 were raised by the British government in loans and taxes to meet expenses occasioned by the war. £652,000,000 were raised in taxes levied from 1798 to 1815 over and above those required to meet the civil expenses of the government and the charges upon the pre-war debt. This sum paid the entire direct costs of the war during that period. The balance was raised by public borrowing in London. It covered the cost of the first five years of war, and compounded the interest upon the borrowings which had been necessary to meet it. When the war ended in 1815 the British government was raising seventy millions a year in taxation, largely expended upon the products of British industry and agriculture for delivery to the troops abroad, and was borrowing thirty millions net a year to meet the interest upon the debt already incurred. This sudden display of financial power was not the consequence of any bookkeeping hocus-pocus. Neither the flight of capital from Europe nor the plunder of the colonies of France and Holland and Spain made it possible. The people of England paid for the war as it was waged by working harder and, thanks to the changing technique, more efficiently. However, Pitt's financing down to 1798 had been vicious; by sparing the taxpayer then, it imposed multiplied burdens later. And in sequel the nation was mortgaged to a new class in its society, the rentiers, the fundholders, for an annual sum of thirty million pounds, three times the public revenue before the revolutionary wars.[28] The bulk of this sum was being collected in customs, excise and stamp duties, and constituted an engine by which wealth was transferred from a large consuming public to the much smaller number who owned consols. These were to constitute the first investing public.

Upon the rise of funded wealth, the focussing of the processes of production upon governmental war demand, the domination of movements of money and goods by contracts and licenses issued in London, the City grew and came to solidarity. The resources of the Bank had been strained to their limit almost from the first. And the government was obliged to turn more confidingly to the private banks and those merchants of London that began to be known as "merchant-bankers." Among their private depositors, their country correspondents, with their ability to give indefinite currency to their short-time acceptances, the private banks commanded the market for the loans which the government had to issue. The merchant-bankers were yet more indispensable. Nearly the entire cost of the war was to be met abroad. In gold or supplies the proceeds of loans and taxes must be at the disposal of Great Britain and her Allies in the field. Only merchants thru their foreign correspondents were able to perform this service. They could meet pay-rolls in Flanders out of Mexican dollars coming in payment for calico delivered in Spain. They could assemble cloths from Yorkshire, sabres and muskets from Sheffield, and horses from Ireland, and deliver them in Trieste for an Austrian campaign. And as they would contract for the employment of the government's money, their aid was invaluable in providing it. With the bankers they made up groups to bid in the public loans, and when successful had the entire proceeds at their disposal.[29] The loan-contracting business led to the Stock Exchange. Leading partners sometimes qualified as members. And on the other hand such prominent firms of stock-jobbers as Goldsmids and Ricardos found their business approximating that of merchant-bankers and entailing a corresponding social status. Sir Francis Baring and Abraham Goldsmid were mentioned together as "the Pillars of the City." [30] The business of foreign remittance moreover merged in that of domestic. Both became continuous with the movement of merchandise upon contract or commission in a market in which war demand was the decisive factor. And this was knit up with the movement of the exchanges, the circulation of paper money, and all with the rise and fall of the funds. There was solidarity of interest in the City.

Yet every transaction involved a separate arrangement. The activity of London was individual, not corporate. Sixty odd merchants and bankers competed in ever shifting combinations to derive their maximum advantage from the public needs. It was eloquent of the spirit of the time that they received a crown of civic virtue for their efforts. In the rapidly growing caste of "made men," bankers and brokers found themselves aristocrats.[31] Politicians sought their favors and bestrewed them with honors. Great Whigs were complaining in 1798 of the rise of a "bourgeois upstart aristocracy." [32] In 1801 the active head of the leading firm of private bankers, William Smith, was elevated to the peerage as Lord Carrington. The Barings who had migrated from Germany two generations before blossomed into the baronetage with an Anglo-Saxon pedigree.[33] And King George himself in a lucid moment with Charlotte his Queen, honored the Brothers Goldsmid with a call.[34] Rentier and squire were assimilated to their financial intermediaries in a new social and political alignment. The City gave its complexion to the New Toryism. And policy which had guided the price of the funds now sought its orders from them.[35]

New life has its counterpart in new disease. As the

pecuniary integration of England proceeded there flourished a new phenomenon which men sought variously to ascribe to the wickedness of the Whigs, the malevolence of the money-power, the war, the armistices, the gold standard and paper money. Crisis was a chronic malady in changing England.[36] The first symptom of interdependence between the parts of British economic life was the chaos which followed their frequent lack of coordination. Active as the government was in claiming the output of its people's increased exertions, the extension of credit and production in some branches of national economy was continually exceeding immediate demand. Money as well as goods followed British policy to the Continent. Trade came increasingly to depend upon credits extended upon an ever-narrowing monetary base. And credit swayed to a dozen winds. The frustration of a market hope, the curtailment of hostilities, the accomplishment of a hostile blockade, the failure of a crop, the collapse of prices before a glut of merchandise, meant catastrophe to the entire society. Bankers demanded payment upon their bills receivable, merchants were bankrupted and disgraced, factories brought to a stand, while everyone with paper currency sought cash or Bank of England notes from his banker. Foreign exchanges soared as London sought to recoup its monetary position and strained in the slender credit facilities of its continental customers. In 1793, in 1797, in 1803, in 1810, in 1815 trade and finance sustained depression. English economy resembled its most characteristic form of commercial organization, the partnership, in which the resources of all members were at all times imperilled by the possible follies of each. It is not to be wondered that it was those business men who like the Quakers and the Jews most tempered their individualism with an older economic tradition, the community of the family, who most persistently throve.

About the economic and personal relations of one such group there developed a new institution in the money market which foreshadowed to a remarkable degree more centralized control of the investment of banking funds. The partnership of Overend, Gurney & Co., bill-brokers, dated from 1807; but the business which it handled had been developed during the preceding decade by the silent partner, Thomas Richardson.[37] In origin this business consisted in bringing together sellers and purchasers of commercial paper. Its opportunity lay in the chaotic condition of the English banking system and the uneven geographical distribution of loanable funds. In the agricultural areas of southeast England, in Norfolk and Suffolk, and in Somersetshire, bankers accumulated deposits which they did not see their way to lay out locally to advantage. Notes had replaced specie in their local trade, and the accessibility of London by mail-coach after 1784 made it convenient to carry their reserves there for more remote investment. At the same time, the resources of banks in Lancashire and Yorkshire were continually strained by the demands of their local merchants and manufacturers for loans. And they sought constant relief in seeking to discount their commercial paper in London. It required specialized knowledge to enable London merchants to distinguish between good and bad bills from this source; and the men who became the first bill-brokers had been clerks detailed to do this work in London houses of more varied activities. Ultimately they set up a specialized business on their own account, and provided what was essentially a clearing-house for domestic bills. Their recommendation enabled banks in Lancashire to liquidate their

outstanding loans for London paper of a quality which circulated as money in the provinces and could be the means of
further loans.   The bill-brokers found purchasers of Lancashire paper among their clients in Norfolk.   Thus the
agricultural counties were brought to share in the development of their industrial rivals.   In another generation from
mere brokers Overend, Gurney & Co. were to develop into a
bankers' bank.   Their recommendation was to become a
guarantee.   They were to carry the demand deposits of half
England and in paying interest for their use virtually to fix
the market rate of discount.   They would discount outright
commercial bills from banks all over England in need of more
liquid assets.   And their judgment was to be a power in the
direction of more permanent British investments.   Their
standing in the money market in 1810 was in no small measure
due to connections with the Gurneys of Norwich and with
the Quaker houses of Barclay and Fry and Buxton in London.

ENGLAND FACES OUTWARD

Thus England tended to become a mechanism of interacting
parts habituated to a high rate of activity and the transmis-
sion of a great surplus of energy abroad.   A pauperized fifth
of the population had been put to work; untilled land had been
brought under the plow; new instruments of production
dotted the land in the form of steam engines and machines.
A nation had adapted itself to production for market under
individual contract, expressed in pecuniary terms.   And its
pecuniary relations were grouped about London as a magnetic
pole.

Great Britain had learned in war to produce a surplus.

She had in doing so not only developed new processes, new instruments, new economic relations; she had released new motives, the aspirations of thousands of individuals who had glimpsed a path to personal achievement and social elevation. For many these aspirations led through the application of work in manufacture to the augmentation of the material products of the land. For others they were directly centered in a money market which not only played with the counters of credit, but functioned as a conduit for the delivery of surplus produce over-sea. And for the rapidity of these developments, the war-time market concentrated in the government demand was responsible.

Not because she must, but because she was used to doing it Great Britain after the war sought to continue to produce at the old speed. And because of the same habituation, she sought outlet for her energies in seeking another foreign market to replace that which government contracts had provided abroad. Foreign investment throve as a means to foreign trade. It blazed the trail for cosmopolitan specialization, for the extension of the Industrial Revolution, the expansion of British economy to embrace the world.

There was an alternative. A transformation of the distributive processes as radical as that of technique might have involved such a proportioning of British resources as would have developed a home market instead of one abroad. The income accumulating to the classes who during the war paid taxes and bought consols, might have found its way to laborers in wages, to small farmers in liquidation of the overcapitalization of their land. That would have meant social revolution. It would have meant a different nineteenth century. It might have implied an abatement of that mingled spirit of calculation and adventure which animated the new economic leviathan. And it would have required a set of historical antecedents with which Great Britain was at the beginning of the nineteenth century not equipped. William Spence, raising the lone cry in 1807 of "Britain Independent of Commerce," was shouted down by the City, which was not so independent, and by the economists, who were fascinated by the stir of the machine and the strong, sure strokes of the piston.[38] The gaze of the money market was outward, and the movement of England followed the gaze.

CHAPTER II

FOREIGN INVESTMENT AFTER WAR

"Who hold the balance of the world? Who reign
O'er congress, whether royalist or liberal?
Who rouse the shirtless patriots of Spain?
(That make old Europe's journals 'squeak and gibber' all)
Who keep the World, both old and new, in pain
Or pleasure? Who make politics run glibber all?
The shade of Buonaparte's noble daring? —
Jew Rothschild, and his fellow-Christian, Baring."
                              —Byron, *Don Juan*, canto xii.

THE POST-WAR DEPRESSION

The Napoleonic wars had given England prosperity, and peace seemed likely to deprive her of their fruits. For Britain's agriculture and her industry had received a stimulus from the war which found no immediate counterpart in a world at peace. As government orders for military stores fell off, merchants found themselves loaded with goods for which there was no market. They were operating upon credits which were not likely to be renewed. It was necessary to sell even goods for which demand at a good price might soon be expected. British manufactures were dumped in every port of the Atlantic and its adjacent waters and sold at sacrifice prices. This carried ruin to foreign industries, and brought little benefit to the exporters. It did little to promote stable trade connections.

At the same time British agriculture approached collapse, for its output was no longer required for Wellington's armies.

Doubtless a demobilized man will eat as much as a soldier, but no Waterloos depend upon his nourishment. Domestic trade moved in rhythm with agriculture. Thousands of traders found oblivion in bankruptcy. Credit was abruptly curtailed. Country bankers closed their doors by the hundred. The commercial discounts of the Bank of England, which had amounted to twenty million pounds in 1810 and had been fifteen million in 1815, fell to four million by 1817. In conformity to the usury laws, interest rates held firm; money simply was not loaned. Industrial shutdowns coupled with demobilization brought into being an army of unemployed estimated at half a million, and threw into high relief social inequalities which war-time prosperity had concealed.

But the lapse of government contracts was not the only reason for the depression which followed the war. There was also a currency situation.[1] Since 1798 England had been virtually upon a paper-money basis. The Bank of England had not been redeeming its notes in gold; and the figure of 211 in ratio to the price level of 1790 taken as 100, is a fair index of the degree to which the monetary circulation of the country had been inflated. A venturesome spirit may be a more essential factor in progressive business periods than the mere augmentation of media of exchange. But when men believe firmly that prices rise and fall in ratio with the quantity of money, such a belief is likely to control their adventure. Prices respond to anticipation as well as to demand. And since the war was at an end, it was anticipated that inflation would stop. The early resumption of specie payments by the Bank was promised by the government and insistently demanded by important elements of public opinion. Fundholders, who were nearly synonymous with the governing classes, could not be expected to oppose a step which it was expected would add to the purchasing power of their incomes. Cobbett, "tribune of the people," was of one voice with the fundholders, though he joined with it a demand that all debts public and private be reduced by fifty per cent. The stockjobbers, headed by the Ricardos, who had been playing the market for a fall against firms more successful in securing government contracts, had long been for resumption. The Bullion Report of 1810, prepared, according to Siberling, under their auspices, furnished apparently scientific proof that the money market could be stabilized upon a gold basis; and economists broadcasted the demonstration. Resumption seemed inevitable, and with it contraction. And although the date was not set and specie payments were not actually resumed until 1821, deflation proceeded by anticipation and with cumulative velocity as it caught the country bankers who had issued the major part of the depreciated currency. Thus the fall of general commodity prices from an index number of 211 in the first quarter of 1814 to 130 in the third quarter of 1816 was an irrevocable one.

Moreover, all Europe was trying to get back to specie payments at the same time, and the United States as well. Gold and silver in vaults and hoards were in active demand, with slight prospect of their early increment. For the mines of Mexico and Peru, which had been for three centuries the principal source of supply of the precious metals, had been disorganized by revolutionary disorders in those countries. Mines had been abandoned, capital withdrawn, mining villages depopulated, the whole apparatus of mining operations fallen to decay. The production of gold and silver in the western world, which between 1800 and 1810 had reached an annual average of ten million pounds, declined in the next decade to six millions.[2] With Russia and the Far East draining the precious metals out of circulation, the stock of money available for the commercial countries ceased to grow in proportion to population and trade. Indeed, according to Del Mar, it absolutely declined from £380,000,000 in 1808 to £313,000,000 in 1829, and to £270,000,000 in 1838.[3]

This dwindling stock of the precious metals was of immediate and persistent importance for the foreign if not the domestic trade of Great Britain. For international trade, with the domestic trade of most commercial countries, was to a relatively high degree upon a money basis. In default of a credit organization of greater complexity and elasticity, the decline in the stock of precious metals imposed a downward trend upon commodity prices throughout the western world.

The movement was continuous. The post-war depression was but the first phase of a regressive trend that dominated business cycles until the middle of the century. Price levels, which according to Siberling's indices stood at 130 in 1816, sank successively to 91 by 1830, to 84 in 1843, and reached the low point of the century at 79 in the third quarter of 1849 about the time that emigrants were beginning to leave England for the California gold fields. Thru the intervening years there were price rebounds as the rhythm of confidence and despair moved in the markets and stirred the pulses of dealers in credit. But definite reversal of the general downward trend of prices awaited restored productivity of the precious metals or the elaboration of stable credit mechanisms for the conduct of international trade.

For the generation during which Great Britain was becoming definitely industrialized the secular regression of prices was of moment. To those manufacturers to whom it did not bring failure it commended technical refinements in the direction of reduced costs. In rural areas where valuations did not respond willingly to downward phases of the price cycle it provoked malaise; and it had the same effects in the labor market generally. To the rentier it worked continued advantage, as his predetermined income meant progressively more in terms of goods. And it placed a premium upon saving for investment in securities which bore a fixed rate of interest, which assured the investor an unearned increment at the expense of the societies which used his capital. The subjects of the late Hanoverians had not made the acquaintance of statistical graphs, and were but dimly conscious of these trends. General price recessions were ascribed to specific technical improvements. But the rentier's increment assured him twice yearly of his sagacity.

OPPORTUNITY

With these general economic conditions which underlay the activities of British investors from 1815 to 1850 there must be recalled the geographical distribution of economic opportunity. The outstanding circumstance was that the world was not equally commercialized. This was not in the early part of the nineteenth century so much a matter of different resources, as it was a difference in the degree to which capitalism, not to say industrial capitalism, was the prevailing mode of economic activity. "The rational exploitation of economically active men for the purpose of making as large a profit as possible" (paraphrasing Sombart), prevailed only sporadically outside the British Isles. Moreover there were wide differences in the degree of political stability, indeed of the entire orientation of political society with respect to business, with corresponding differences in status and freedom of investment. These were elements in an economic differentiation which were reflected tho not measured by interest premiums upon foreign investment.

The mass of Europe was in 1815 still prevailingly agricultural. Serfdom, feudal relations, self-sufficing estates, commercial and industrial mores of the gild type subsisted over wide areas—at least over those not conquered by Napoleon. In such regions there was no prospect of a sudden market, no leverage to economic endeavor other than the slowly rising consumption standards of the all-powerful baronage and the military aspirations of the more westernized rulers. Where Napoleon's arms had carried some of the social and legal consequences of the French Revolution, commerce and industry had been burdened with the costs of conquest, credit abused by forced loans. New life had been given to the authoritarian state, protector but even more regulator of business life in the interests of its own power. Mining codes regularized the conditions under which mineral deposits could be exploited, but compelled all who would mine, even upon their own land, to obtain special license and conform to the conditions of the government. Impulse to economic development in France and Spain and Holland, Italy and the Germanies could be imparted only thru the governments of those countries. Their public finances were corrupt, and disorganized by war.

East of the Suez and the Bosphorus lay a bottomless pit of household economy and slave labor into which money flowed with little chance of recovery. Only political conquest, as in the case of India, has checked the flow of precious metals from West to East. And economically the East was actually in a phase of retrogression as the goods of Manchester and Sheffield undermined the industrial preeminence of Mohammedan centers.

There were finally the European settlements of the New World, experimenting with a variety of economic systems, from towns of seagoing freemen to slave-manned haciendas, all endowed with uncharted land and unappraised resources, but whose very existence depended upon the importation of labor and capital.

Here was a field for activity; and there was also one in the reorganizing of Europe's finances. The way to an expansion of England's foreign markets, like the road to her political security, seemed to lie thru the stabilizing of conditions in Europe and the development of the New World. The activities of the representative merchant of the post-Napoleonic period, Alexander Baring, reflect some realization of these relations. Scarcely had the post-war slump spent its initial force, when in 1817 the firm of Baring Brothers was lending gold to the Second Bank of the United States and had plunged into the intricacies of the financial reconstruction of Europe.

FINANCING THE FRENCH INDEMNITY

The overthrow of Napoleon had brought its reparations problem. Its solution was the prerequisite to the political settlement and economic recovery of the Continent. From the monarchy which they had restored in France the victorious Allies had exacted a pecuniary indemnity of 700,000,000 francs, to be paid in five annual instalments. Pending the fulfilment of this duty a considerable army of occupation was left in the country under command of the Duke of Wellington, toward the support of which France was bound to pay an agreed sum of 150,000,000 francs a year more than the indemnity. In addition the Allies stood sponsor for private claims of their subjects against France to an amount which no one seemed anxious to ascertain with exactitude.[4]

France was not lacking in resources. She emerged from

the war comparatively scatheless. Her public debt was relatively small, only fifty francs per capita as compared with a British per capita debt of nearly a thousand. But, as in 1789, the wealth of France was not the wealth of her government. Her public credit had not recovered from the bankruptcy of the old régime and the drastic policies of the revolutionary assemblies. The measures of the *Chambre Introuvable* did nothing to brighten this tarnished reputation. Effective capital was scarce and capitalists were suspicious. In the first three years of its existence the restored monarchy pawned a large part of the royal forests for the benefit of emigré nobles and tampered with the security of the floating debt.[5] Allied diplomatists privately expressed the opinion that the indemnity payments could never be made. Metternich is said to have been willing to discount Austria's portion thirty per cent for cash.[6] The sentiment was expressed that the Allies had "demanded the impossible in order to obtain something." But unless the indemnity were paid, the occupation of France was likely to continue indefinitely, a condition which few statesmen contemplated with the open satisfaction of the representatives of Prussia. The trade of France was sluggish; nothing could be procured by high taxes; Napoleon's hoarded gold had been drained by initial payments.

There seemed but one way to finance the reparation. That was for France to float a large foreign loan. It was reasoned that the mere flotation of such a loan would enhance French credit, cause rentes to rise, and ensure the success of the venture to those who undertook it. The evidence of French credit abroad would rouse capitalists at home from their lethargy and draw out the hoards of the bourgeoisie to share in the benefits of a rising market.[7] Thus France could be brought to make the reparation which she was abundantly qualified to do only by showing individual Frenchmen how they might gain important advantages over other Frenchmen in the process.

There was no question as to the firm to be entrusted with the management of the reparations loan. Not even the Rothschilds occupied the commanding position then held among moneyed men by Baring Brothers and Co. This firm of merchant-bankers had developed out of a wool manufacturing business of the "putting-out" type in Devon, founded early in the eighteenth century by an immigrant from Bremen, Germany. In the third quarter the woolen factors were merchants trading from London overseas. Their interests extended rapidly to include Russian furs and Chinese silks. A family alliance with the Binghams of Philadelphia enhanced the Baring wealth and brought the firm leadership in the Anglo-American trade. In the Baltic too it had primacy among remittance houses. During the wars it was entrusted by opposing combatants with important tasks of commercial diplomacy. Of many firms which flourished upon the loan and subsistence contracts of Pitt and Liverpool, none did so well. A junior partner sat in the court of directors of the Bank of England. The head, Alexander Baring, "a heavy-looking young man, with a hesitating manner; but very clear in his ideas," was member of Parliament. In 1814 the famous house of Hope and Co. of Amsterdam came under its control thru Alexander Baring and his brother-in-law, P. C. Labouchère.[8] During the Hundred Days, Baring Brothers, with Smith, Payne & Smiths, marketed a loan of £30,000,000 for Great Britain, finding customers in St. Petersburg, Amsterdam, Hamburg, Vienna, Basel and Frankfurt, to all of which cities portions of the proceeds were to be remitted as subsidies to the Allies of Great Britain. In France Barings were specifically interested in provision contracts for the armies of occupation thru the agency of Ouvrard, an indefatigable Paris banker with whom they had been associated in gold transactions for Napoleon.[9] The prestige and facilities of this firm were essential for the reparations loan to have the contemplated success.

When the project was first considered in 1815, the British government discountenanced it on the ground that it would interfere with its own borrowing plans.[10] But when at the end of 1816 France stopped payment upon indemnity instalments this opposition was withdrawn, upon the understanding that Barings were to manage the loan. Castlereagh, as British Foreign Secretary, assumed a fine neutrality. His government could not encourage the loan, he explained, lest it be in some way compromised and involved in financial liability. On the other hand, he would agree to place no obstacles in its path.[11] Unofficially his government found a way to be of considerable assistance. For the Duke of Wellington as commander-in-chief of the army of occupation could employ all the prestige of his victorious empire without committing it to anything. Concern for the subsistence of the troops prevailed upon him to take active charge of loan negotiations.[12] French opinion had been clamoring for a reduction of his army. And to furnish favorable conditions for the issue of a loan, Wellington agreed to reduce his establishment by one-fifth. But the Duke refused flatly to urge upon the French minister Richelieu a contract for rentes at five points below the market price, and advised Castlereagh that it was a bad bargain for France.[13] These were the auspices under which the first important foreign loan contract was made by a British house.[14]

The contract arranged by Baring and Labouchère in February, 1817, put them in possession of a 5% loan to produce one hundred million francs at a net price of about 53, on the nominal value of which they were to receive a commission of 2½%. That is to say, the loan would be issued for forty million dollars, would realize nineteen millions to the French treasury and one million to the contractors, who would be in a position moreover to make all they could by selling rentes above 53. The proceeds of the loan, it was agreed with the conference of ambassadors, were to be applied to the maintenance of the army of occupation. At the same time a second loan upon identical terms was arranged for, which Barings might issue at their option within four months, or which the Powers would market themselves with Barings as agents if rentes should fall. This loan would provide indemnity payments to March 31, 1817. The balance of the indemnity for 1817 was to be made the object of a third loan and a separate bargain.[15]

The anticipated rise in the market took place without delay, and both loans sold rapidly. By July, Alexander Baring was disposing of the third loan which at 65 realized 115,000,000 francs to France. French bankers underwrote all of these loans for one-third of their sum, but the initial subscriptions came almost entirely from London. Nevertheless the French public was becoming interested. In the spring of 1818 its government ventured to open a loan for popular subscription in Paris at 66½, and the loan was oversubscribed fifteen times. When another offering was made thru Barings a week later, to be devoted specifically to the indemnity payments outside of France, the Paris press teemed with articles suggesting the readiness of local bankers to handle such contracts. It was necessary for Wellington to speak quite bluntly to the ministry upon this occasion to cause it to realize the great importance of leaving everything to Baring. Great Britain was contemplating specie payments that year and did not care to see the money market played upon by too many agencies. But the market for rentes developed so favorably that during the summer of 1818 the Allies agreed to compound the private claims for a fixed sum, and to arrange a final contract which would enable the indemnity payments to be completed thru Barings early in 1819.[16] Never had market predictions been more brilliantly verified by their results. The French government had gained a credit with its subjects which it had not possessed for decades. The Allies were securing their reparations. And the managers of the loans had reaped their reward in profits which contemporaries estimated with conservatism at a million pounds and a half. "There are Six Powers in Europe," the Duc de Richelieu is reported to have said, "Great Britain, France, Russia, Austria, Prussia and Baring Brothers." And Barings were a synonym for the investment market at London.

Certainly the Baring loans were achieving "political advantages of great importance."[17]   Contemporaries were less of one mind with regard to their economic consequences for England. The London press denounced the "base and wretched avidity of the Monied Interest, which at the prospect of gain, is ready to forget all the claims of patriotism." When England's agriculture and manufactures were at their lowest ebb, it was no time to transfer capital to enrich her most dangerous rival.[18]   The law interfered to prevent a poor artisan from leaving the country, declared Lauderdale in the House of Lords. Was it to be endured that the law should be powerless with regard to the rich capitalist, and that he should be encouraged to export the money of the country, the main nerve of all our resoures?[19]   "The profitable employment of our own, and not foreign people nor slaves, constitutes the wealth and prosperity of the British

Empire," declared a spokesman of the country interest.[20]

This was the age of the economists, however, and their logic overbore dissenting opinion. A writer in the *Times* set forth with precision the economic theory of the export of capital.[21] Loans to foreign governments, he explained, could be effected by an export of gold, of bills of exchange, or of merchandise to the borrowing country. If it were gold that was exported, that gold must have been secured from the Spanish Main by equivalent exports of merchandise. Bills of exchange in turn represented exports of merchandise either to the borrowing country or to some other. In short a loan to a foreign government could be neither more nor less than "the exportation of a certain quantity of the industry of one country, either directly or circuitously, to another country, whose government borrows." The inference drawn was that such loans would stimulate the export trade and would thereby prove highly beneficial to English industry at large.

There was truth in the analysis, if not in the inference. Nevertheless the manner in which loans were remitted did make a great deal of temporary difference. The proceeds of the first Baring loans were paid to France in the form of Paris acceptances. The sale of rentes abroad was in fact a mobilization of mercantile credits against France from all over the world. Manchester men shipping cotton goods to New York, for example, received in payment bills on Paris for tobacco shipments from Virginia, and discounted them with Barings to speculate in rentes.[22] France received her loans in the form of increased imports. Not a sou entered France in the form of specie; while the British trade balance for 1817 shows no fluctuation. That is to say, the capital invested corresponded closely to the indemnity payments and army contracts which were to be fulfilled.[23]

But France was not the only European government in need

of funds. Russia, Austria and Prussia were also confronted with a post-war budget problem. During 1817 and 1818 these powers resorted to borrowing, both internal and external, in the effort to obtain a diplomatic free hand by its solution. In the cases of Russia and Austria the borrowing was specifically to secure bullion with which to retire part of a heavily inflated currency, with which those governments had financed their final efforts against Napoleon. During the summer of 1818, Prussia negotiated a loan of five million pounds thru N. M. Rothschild, the first unguaranteed foreign loan to make its formal appearance in London, and the first to do homage to the pound sterling.[24] Altho Prussia had not the remotest intention of retiring her paper currency, she too required remittance in gold. At the same time specie was moving willingly to eastern Europe in anticipation of a grain shortage in France and the United Kingdom. The premium upon gold in the Baltic ports rose so high in the course of 1818 (above 10%) that merchants bought gold wherever they could find it to ship to St. Petersburg for investment in "metallic inscriptions." [25] Now the gold with which these remittances were made came out of reserves which were actively employed as the basis of commercial credit in England, France and Holland. The shipments did not amount to a large proportion of the commercial capital of those countries, but they did absorb a staggering proportion of their bank reserves. In midsummer the British government abandoned plans for immediate resumption of specie payments. In the fall the Bank of England raised its discount rate, and the Bank of France, with reserves dwindled to 37,000,000 francs, withdrew the support by which the Paris bourse had been able to exaggerate the patriotic enthusiasm for rentes. And in October, November and December a financial panic swept the money market, imperilling the loans which France had contracted to terminate her indemnity obligations, and threatening to wipe out the advantages which various parties had gained from the earlier operations.[26]

It was upon this occasion that the important principle received demonstration that while a loan contractor is bound to make all that he can out of a successful operation, he can not be compelled to stand the losses of failure. Under contracts concluded on October 9, 1818, the Baring Brothers and their associates were bound to make payments upon a loan of 179,000,000 francs net, to be issued at 75 during the first nine months of 1819. Moreover as agents for the Powers they had the same period in which to market rentes valued at 100,000,000 francs for which sum the private claims had been compounded. As the monetary stringency developed it became clear that the contractors could not perform either obligation without ruin. And ruin meant that the powers would get little or nothing, that French credit would be wrecked and all the hopeful owners of French investments, that ambassadorial heads would fall in witness to their bungling, while the new state-system being so cautiously launched at Aix-la-Chapelle would embark most inauspiciously. So the Quadruple Alliance listened to the appeals of Baring and helped him out of his bad bargain. Not once, but twice at Aix-la-Chapelle, and once again at Paris, the time limit upon the operations was extended and terms adjusted to a steadily falling market.[27] The last change was wrested by Wellington from the conference of ambassadors in Paris in December, after the Congress had broken up. And the Duke wrote Metternich to explain it when it was all over. It was agreement, or nothing, declared Wellington. The time-limit was finally extended to eighteen months; France made a generous contract; and the

Allies agreed that the rentes to be issued upon their behalf should be calculated at rates which prevailed before the panic, and sold for what they would bring.[28] The risks faced by post-Napoleonic financiers thus do not seem to have been overwhelming.

But the Quadruple Alliance was not at hand to rescue debtors whose contracts were not underwritten by political exigency. Doubtless the panic of 1818 and the consequent depression in England were not due wholly to the gold loans to the "northern powers." The grain shortage was also important, and in many respects operated in the same manner. Like the loans, it carried gold from England to a country that was heavily her creditor on account of naval stores and furs. And Russia, moreover, at this time exported far more than she received from all countries put together. Hence no indirect adjustment of the payments for grain or for metallic inscriptions was possible. Specie must be procured. And in 1818 it was increasingly hard to come by. Revolution had resurged in the Spanish and Portuguese colonies; American production of gold was at its lowest ebb. To restore gold reserves to their former condition of plenitude was not quickly to be accomplished. There was tension in London, and murmurings in the provinces. And confronted with disorder at home, Castlereagh made no pretense of neutrality.

THE FINANCIER OF LEGITIMACY

But the interest of English merchants in the chances to lend money abroad was checked neither by the panic, nor by the domestic depression. Adjustment was easy to a more permanent investment of capital in foreign securities than British capitalists had contemplated at first. They had been invited to share in the Baring operations definitely as a speculation. As rentes advanced they sold out their purchases to the French. But the crisis of 1818 left them with stocks of a market value of over ten million pounds still in their hands. From 1819 this amount steadily increased.[29] "Few gentlemen return from Paris," declared the merchant-banker Haldimand before a parliamentary committee, "without having made a small investment in French stock." Rentes paid better interest than consols, pointed out Nathan Rothschild, "besides its being a growing passion at the present time."[30] The alarm created by disorders in the industrial districts in the fall of 1819 rendered this passion more general. There never was a time, declared Baring in the House of Commons, when so much money was withdrawn from enterprise at home to invest in foreign funds. "There was a general *sauve qui peut* among monied men."[31]

In view of this hospitable attitude on the part of Englishmen with money to lend, almost every power in Europe found itself suddenly short of funds and in the course of a few years followed the example of Prussia in negotiating a sterling loan in London.[32] And like Prussia many of them sought not Barings with their commissions but the man whose successful operations for a fall in 1818 had impressed statesmen with his power.

The story of the Rothschilds has been frequently told.[33] Until recently it was all apocryphal. No canonical revelation had been vouchsafed. In detail it was filled with signs and wonders. It began with the goldsmith of Frankfurt, Meyer Amschel Rothschild, usurer to various mid-European princelings, to whom a landgrave in flight from Napoleon entrusted the accumulated profits of his traffic in mercenary soldiers. The money was sent to London, so the story went, in care of Meyer's son Nathan, who was doing well in the calico trade; and there it furnished the basis for dealings upon a large and profitable scale in the European exchanges.

A recent biography of the Frankfurt goldsmith, based partly upon the archives of Hesse-Cassel, partly upon those of the Rothschilds, brands this story of beginnings as definitely legendary. It enables the historian to do more justice to the business acumen of the thrifty landgrave, who had his savings invested in first-class mortgages, in British consols, and in personal loans to the Royal Dukes. And it enables the historian to trace a different connection between the Rothschild fortune and its legend than the one usually narrated. Meyer Amschel waxed prosperous not on the savings of the fugitive landgrave, but on the rumor that he had been entrusted with them.

Son Nathan, who came to England in 1798, had his way to make alone with neither savings nor rumor to help. He was even forbidden the pleasure of dunning the Royal Dukes. But war-time England presented opportunities of which, in default of data, it is quite safe to assume that young Nathan took full advantage. By 1812, the British government desirous of remitting quantities of gold to Wellesley's armies in Spain found Rothschild's connections the most serviceable in procuring the gold and in forwarding it most expeditiously. And rumors began to circulate of Nathan's prowess, greatly to the advantage of his own speculations in the exchanges and in consols.

By the Congress of Aix-la-Chappelle in 1818, the Rothschilds had saved Europe more than once by their skill in rounding up the claims of the pettier German states and in discriminating what their princelings asked from what they would be content to receive. Prussia and Austria were already insisting that all remittances made to them be handled by Rothschilds. Nathan's brother Salomon had settled at Vienna in response to Metternich's new policy of permitting Jewish immigration. Another brother, James, had come to Paris. While London hummed with anecdotes of Nathan's prodigious coups.

How the bold market-raider became loan-specialist dealing in the promises only of governments of the most approved legitimacy and won for his firm the nick-name of High Treasury of the Holy Alliance, is a story related by Cape-figue.[34] At the Congress of Laibach, so the story goes, the Northern Powers faced a series of revolutions along the Mediterranean which threatened the political system they had devised for Europe. They needed money with which to finance the requisite military gestures. Barings were involved, money was tight, England and Holland unresponsive to their proposals. Castlereagh, less alarmed by revolution than by mobile armies, was dissociating himself from the policies of the Quadruple Alliance. To establish financial independence of England, Metternich turned to a house which seemed more cosmopolitan than English. Three loans must be floated with the utmost discretion and success. There must be one of a hundred million florins for Austria for military purposes, one of forty million rubles for Russia to continue the retirement of her paper money, and one of forty million thalers for Prussia for armaments. The loans were floated in 1822, the Austrian outside of London, where long-continued default upon the Boyd-Benfield loans of a generation before had left her credit in as low esteem as the policies of Metternich. The Rothschild brothers won great prestige from their success. Four of them were straightway made barons of the Austrian empire. Baron James was made Austrian consul-general at Paris; and Baron Nathan soon received the like distinction at London. Gentz hymned their praises as "the Phidias and Praxiteles of loans." And in the following year they were entrusted with an important share in the conversion into three per cent rentes of the French five per cent indemnity loans.

Henceforth the position of Rothschilds in the public finance of the Continent was fixed. For a generation to come the public loan business of legitimate governments upon the Continent was all but a Rothschild monopoly. By their manipulation of the exchanges in 1831 the Austrian government was brought to terms.[35]   In 1836 Baring Brothers refused to handle even the British West India Emancipation loan unless Rothschild neutrality were ensured; and the Bank of England hesitated to give unusual accommodation to any rival.[36]   Naples, Brazil, Holland and Belgium as well as the four leading continental powers were regular Rothschild customers. Between 1822 and 1825 they floated loans in London which secured an actual investment of twelve million pounds, and private investments in foreign currencies which Rothschilds handled represented a placement of British capital of unknown dimensions.

LOAN MANAGERS AND REVOLUTION

Doubtless it was the higher interest and the "growing passion" which sold bonds in London to finance the frustration of British foreign policy upon the Continent. But the bulk of the foreign loans which from 1822 to 1825 flashed in continuous display upon the Stock Exchange appealed to that blend of political idealism and commercial strategy which was the dominant tone of British public opinion for

the better part of the century. They were loans in support
of revolution rather than legitimacy. They were inspired by
the necessities of the revolutionary government of Spain and
those of her revolted provinces.

Spain's case is representative. Confronted by a large
deficit in revenue when it came into power in 1820, her
constitutional government contracted a loan for ten million
dollars in Paris, which was underwritten in London and
which found subscribers chiefly there. In the following
year the deficit was twice as large and a larger loan was
necessary. Loans and deficits continued to soar in geometri-
cal ratio. During the three years that the constitutional
government prevailed, it raised abroad loans to the nominal
amount of more than sixteen million pounds. Not so much
as this reached the Spanish Treasury. By 1823 the stock
was selling as issued for thirty cents on the dollar; the proceeds were largely absorbed in the purchase of military
supplies in Great Britain and in efforts to keep up the
market price of the successive loans.[37]

At the same time the revolted colonies of Spain were
besieging the London money market for means of defending
themselves from reconquest. The British government still
professed complete neutrality on the question of South
American independence. It was by no means certain of the
success of the movement, and it had no intention of throwing
the peninsula of Spain into the hands of the French by open
advocacy of a separation for which it profoundly hoped,
but whose republican tendencies it as strongly mistrusted.[38]
But patriotism is a virtue which in England is not confined to
the precincts of Downing Street. The foreign policy of
Englishmen is something more and something less than the
foreign policy of their ministers of state. Whatever the

motives which impelled the Foreign Office to cloak its mixed
emotions in correct aloofness, their jurisdiction did not
extend beyond Temple Bar. English merchants and officers
had been already engaged in activities which can with difficulty be described as neutral. Begun under Admiralty
patronage in the later stages of the Napolenic wars, they
continued in crescendo after the Congress of Vienna had
removed their shadow of justification. In the three years
following 1817 six expeditions sailed from London for
Venezuela alone, and at least two others for New Granada,
to assist Bolivar and other revolutionary leaders. English
officers and English men made up the detachments, and
the accompanying ships were fully armed. The officers
paid the expenses of their recruits; merchants ventured the
ships and supplies.[39] For these and other services the Latin
republics came into existence under heavy obligations to
Englishmen.

Colombia led the way in the settlement of her accounts.
In June, 1820 her vice-president, Zea, appeared in London
with powers as minister plenipotentiary. Castlereagh would
have nothing to do with him officially.[40] But the creditors
to the number of two hundred were glad to make his acquaintance. He assured them that the dignity of his government
would not permit it to look closely into the origin and nature
of claims against it. With little question he consolidated
all claims presented at their face value into debentures bearing interest at ten per cent.[41] This interest was not paid,
but in March, 1822 a formal loan of two million pounds was
arranged in London thru Herring, Powles & Graham, a
firm of merchants trading to the Caribbean. The debentures
with interest due were accepted in part payment and when
commissions and interest for two years in advance had been
deducted from the proceeds of the loan, there were about

£640,000 left for Colombia. This sum was laid out thru the contractors in the purchase of a toy navy and military stores.[42]

Other American republics were roused to emulation, hopeful that by engaging the Briton's money his political sympathies would be secured. In rapid succession Chile, Peru, Buenos Ayres, Mexico, Guatemala sought loans in London to supply their miniature armies with uniforms and ammunition and to secure a ship or so as an appropriate background for their respective admirals. Nor would a single loan suffice. The more a country borrowed the better its credit, it seemed. Colombia and Mexico borrowed twice, Peru three times, and the now independent monarchy of Brazil as many. The comedy turned burlesque when a loan was eagerly taken up for the "Kingdom of Poyais," a fictitious political entity on the Mosquito coast of which a Scotch officer had assumed the title of "Cazique." Within the three years 1823, 1824 and 1825, £17,500,000 were actually paid in to contractors upon the securities of the new Latin American states.

The negotiation of the loans followed well-defined lines. An agent of the borrowing government appeared in London, a high official or private persons operating on a commission. The agent approached one or more issuing houses and arranged a contract with one of them embodying the terms upon which the loan was to be issued. Thenceforth the arrangements were in charge of the contractor. Usually he sought the influence and cooperation of other parties with whom he shared the risk and profits. Prospectuses were prepared, often only in manuscript, and sent around to brokers and wealthy clients. Newspapers were supplied with reading matter extolling political conditions in the borrowing state. In the case of the South American republics, pamphleteers were engaged to prepare elaborate studies of their resources, topography and customs.[43]   When a selected list of subscribers had been provided with portions of the loan, a day was set for its issue, a few shares were allotted to new applicants, and an announcement was made that the entire loan had been disposed of. Disappointed applicants found plenty of stock for sale upon the Exchange in a rapidly rising market, and their purchases at the enhanced price brought the chief profits to the contractor and his friends.

There were not many firms engaged in this issuing business, altho more participated in what was later called the "underwriting."   Baring Brothers and N. M. Rothschild were of course of first importance, and their issues were first in quality as well as in volume.   Their historic connection with the Argentine and Brazil respectively dates from this period.   But upon ordinary securities they neither frowned nor smiled.   A. L. Haldimand, B. A. Goldschmidt, Barclay, Herring & Richardson, Frys & Co., J. & S. Ricardo, Thomas Wilson, Hullett Brothers and Reid, Irving & Co. contracted for most of the loans to minor states.   These houses were not banks.   They did not issue notes or keep current accounts, altho some of them accepted deposits. Ricardos excepted, they were not stock-brokers.   They were mercantile firms engaged in a large way in foreign trade with resources and connections which made possible an active business in acceptances and exchange.   It was their importance in the remittance market, the mobile character of their assets, the extent of their connections more than their intrinsic wealth that made the business of foreign loans available for them.   They seem to have had no sales organization.   Their success depended upon their friends and the manipulation of crowd psychology upon the Stock Exchange.

The terms of the loans varied widely. In general governments preferred to borrow at a low interest no matter how large the discount at which their loan was issued. There was in this nothing to displease the investor who thereby was promised a large bonus when his principal was repaid. Nor was the contractor averse, his commission being computed upon the nominal rather than the real amount of the loan. There was another bonus extended for immediate payment of subscriptions in full, the loans being payable in instalments over periods varying from six months to a year. And a third bonus was frequently arranged by ante-dating the time from which interest was to run upon the loan. However even with these conditions the profits promised to investors were not exorbitant. They ranged from 5½% to 8% when consols were paying three and four. The real profits of the loan business went to the contractors. Controlling all the stock they had an excellent chance to play the market in it for a rise. But they were not dependent upon such maneuvers for remuneration. There was an immediate commission of from two to five per cent upon the nominal amount of the loan. There were the possible profits of undisposed interest and principal balances left in their hands sometimes for months. There was an agency fee for many years to come for handling dividend payments and the operations of the sinking fund.[44] Nor was this all. In accepting the Colombian loan of 1824, Goldschmidts secured a two-year option on all loans to be contracted and were appointed agents for all mercantile transactions in England on behalf of the Colombian government. They received a commission for raising the money, a commission for spending it, and a commission for paying it back.[45]

HOW THE PHILHELLENES HELPED THE GREEKS

The Greek loans of 1824 and 1825 furnish a striking illustration of what may be termed the "realities" of revolutionary finance.   In the spring of 1821, the great powers in congress assembled at Laibach were startled by the news of the outbreak of a Greek insurrection.   The powers were discreetly horrified; but the movement spread rapidly, and under the cautiously benevolent rivalry of Alexander I and George Canning the semblance of a government came into being.   It sent its agents here and there thru western Europe in search of more active sympathy and funds.   In London the representatives were welcomed with open arms by the entire Whig aristocracy, which were at the time at a loss for a club to belabor the Tories.   A Philhellenic committee was materialized which included every distinguished liberal of the day from Jeremy Bentham to Lord John Russell. Its object was avowedly to provide supplies and to raise a loan   for   the   struggling   nationality.   Political   idealism proved equal to the test imposed upon it.   The loan was launched at a banquet in the Guildhall, presided over by the Lord Mayor of London, February 21, 1824.   Oxford and Edinburgh, Manchester, Liverpool and Aberdeen responded, and the loan of eight hundred thousand pounds at 59 bearing 5% interest was heavily oversubscribed.   Remittances were made to an English committee in Greece of which Lord Byron was the most notable member, and the money was put to timely use in the preservation of Greek maritime cities.

In 1825 a second loan was called for.   The stockjobbers were by this time deeply interested, and the loan was entrusted to the Ricardos who brought out bonds for two million pounds at 56½. The enthusiasm of the politicians meanwhile had turned to other channels and it was fifteen months before anyone began to ask what had been done with the money. The revelations as they transpired consumed columns of newspaper space. It appeared that only £275,000 of the second loan had been sent to Greece, £182,000 in specie, £60,000 in stores, and £33,000 in bills accepted. Of the balance not a penny had as yet come to the assistance of the revolution. Little of it ever did. £200,000 had been held out for interest payments. An equal sum had been spent in keeping up the price of Greek stock so that subscribers would pay up their instalments in full. Liberal sums had lined the pockets of the Greek commissioners, and more had gone to rescue such distinguished Philhellenes as Joseph Hume and John Bowring from losses on a falling market. £160,000 were set aside for a naval expedition to proceed to Greece under the command of Lord Cochrane. The noble and gallant lord had stipulated for enough of this sum to make him independent for life, and the balance had been dissipated in disastrous experiments in auxiliary steamships in the contract for which another Philhellene was heavily interested. Another £160,000 was sent to the United States for the purchase of two frigates and to materialize American good-will. The expenses of supervising the construction of these vessels ran up so high in the hands of an eminent French colonel of dragoons and a liberty-loving American officer that one frigate had to be sold to the federal government to pay for the completion of the other. It was not until 1828 that two small ships and Lord Cochrane finally appeared off the coast of Greece.[46] It was half a century before the Greek government evinced its gratitude by paying interest upon these loans.

THE MACHINE IN QUEST OF GOLD

The migration of British capital reached its maximum activity in the twenties upon a wave of business elation which swept England in 1824 and 1825. The launching of the Alliance Assurance Company early in the former year under the combined patronage of Nathan Rothschild and Samuel Gurney was an initial event in a speculative mania as exciting as the South Sea Bubble. The deflation of values incident to the post-war collapse had entirely run its course. The business life of the country had become more or less stabilized with reference to a scale of values whose further decline would be slow and at the time invisible, corollary of the diminishing supplies of the precious metals. The effects of resumption of specie payment had been discounted in advance. They had been overcompensated. And the long-leashed hopes of the business community were ready to spring at any game that offered. Consols had reached their low point of 66 at the end of 1820 and had been rising almost continuously since. The note circulation of country banks had doubled since 1821. The cost of living had reached its low point in 1822. A movement upward of general price levels followed. Industry and commerce gave such abundant employment that political agitation almost ceased. Industrial disturbance proved more effective and won the repeal of the Combination Acts in 1824.

Cotton and other raw materials were in demand and were objects of eager speculation. But enthusiasm gathered about the belief, kindled by the promoters of a few assurance and mining companies, that it was possible to make a great deal of money quickly by forming joint-stock companies. It mattered not the purpose, tho many projectors simultaneously conceived the idea that many investors would be allured by the possibility of doing something with steam engines. Within less than two years prospectuses were published calling for a total capital of £150,000,000. There were companies to build railways in England, of which the Stockton & Darlington had substance, companies to build canals in the Suez and Nicaragua, to delve for coal in Wales and iron in Staffordshire, companies to supply water, gas and milk, to fetch wool from Australia and to encircle Europe with steamships. Most of these concerns had neither concessions nor practicable plans. They were lost to view after the first deposit of reckless subscribers had been converted to the benefit of the solicitors who had aided in their concoction.[47] But among them were some enterprises which reached the stage of actual operations. The Canada Company and the Australian Agricultural Company were real estate undertakings that were to be of moment in the history of the respective colonies. The Continental Gas Company was to continue extending its business of illuminating German cities to the outbreak of the World War. But at the time the companies which most stirred the markets were the group brought into being under the encouragement of Canning's American policy, and which contemplated sending the steam engine and the machine to delve for American gold.

The economy of the South American colonies prior to 1806 had revolved about their production of the precious metals. Revolution and war had checked their production. But now that the independence of the colonies was in a fair way to recognition it appealed to many that the best way to give this independence a firm economic basis was to aid in the reopening of the disordered mines.[48] And Englishmen would not only be "patronizing infant liberty and liberal principles" by investing their money in this endeavor In the development of Latin America was the prospect of permanent markets for British goods independent of the hostile tariffs of the Continent and the United States. This would not only assist Canning to "redress the balance of the Old World." It would accomplish what seemed to British statesmen no less essential, it would establish a salutary commercial and political balance between the new republics and the less friendly United States. It would also go far to supply that precious metal whose absence had been the cause of monetary distress. Moreover there was wealth in it beyond belief. If the Valencianas and Reglas had made fortunes with their primitive technique, what could not be accomplished by a really superior craft? [49]

The new countries displayed no reluctance to part with their treasures. Their agents in London proffered concessions with the loan contracts. Roving adventurers in the Andes were showered with leases from local authorities. Companies multiplied to exploit the grants and rival promoters quarrelled over the allotment of shares.

At the end of 1824 a sudden furore swept the City and invaded Westminister Hall. The shares of the recently launched Real del Monte Company, whose concession was believed to be especially well-selected and well-managed, climbed to a premium of 1200 and more within a few days. Other shares followed, and companies with and without concessions poured into the market to the number of more than thirty, demanding more than two million pounds of capital at once. Their boards of directors contained among them the names of practically every well-known firm in the City with the exception of Baring and Rothschild.[50] The Quaker banking and mercantile families were especially conspicuous among them. There was no question of the success of the companies as a matter of promotion. Dazzled by sudden visions of wealth, the West End broke thru the barriers of social disesteem which had restrained it from the stock market. The wealthiest peer in England, Lord Grosvenor; the leading King's Counsel, Adam; the Lord Chancellor himself, were speculating in American mines. A young man named Benjamin Disraeli was writing, as broker's clerk, pamphlets demonstrating the wisdom of these gentlemen.

Returns must be unusually ample and quick to satisfy all anticipations. Cornish miners were hastily collected, steam engines purchased, and they were dispatched to commence operations in the spring. All parties awaited the golden harvest which this combination of Cornish science with the power of steam could not fail to realize. So certain was London of the result that thoughtful articles appeared expressing apprehension lest the sudden increase in the supply of gold raise prices and injure the fundholders. It might even, feared some, enable the Chancellor of the Exchequer to pay off the National Debt! [51]

British merchants interested in South American trade found other opportunities, meanwhile, to exploit the friendship which Canning's diplomacy was exciting. At Buenos Ayres they founded a bank with $2,000,000 capital which paid 20% in its first year. Another was projected in Chile where among other manifestations of British enterprise Bolivar proposed to introduce the Lancastrian school system. In Colombia a more elaborate program was under way. One Englishman contracted for the state salt farm. Another had the exclusive concession for rolling copper. A third formed a company to lease Bolivar's private estates, including silver. Two companies had pearl fishing concessions. Herring, Powles & Graham (a firm in which Thomas Richardson, backer of Overend, Gurney & Co. and of the *Stockton & Darlington Railway* was a silent partner) in addition to contracting a loan secured grants of land for mining and for emigrant colonies, and they maintained weekly newspapers at Bogota and Caracas to advocate British interests.[52]   They projected a canal across Nicaragua. Young Robert Stephenson, sent out by them as engineer in charge of their mines, was in 1825 surveying a railway to Caracas from the coast before "The Rocket" had been dreamed of.[53]

Stephenson's experience was typical of the fortune of most of these early adventures in international enterprise. His Cornish workmen could not adapt their methods to the strange conditions of a silver mine; they grew rebellious at their north country superintendent; they succumbed to South American beverages and to the climate. The machinery sent out from England, while excellent, was too bulky to transport into the mountains on mule-back. Nor were the mine-locations happily chosen. They required long and expensive drainage operations at best. Natives were suspicious and obstructive; their labor could not be depended upon. No quick returns were possible.

But the mining companies had been formed to earn dividends and premiums. And stockholders grew impatient when instead they were called on for further payments upon their capital, to enable operations to continue. The prices of their shares which had soared to irrational heights came tumbling down. In the case of most companies, shareholders refused to meet further calls. One after another the mining and associated projects were abandoned. Some eight or nine of them continued to operate, absorbing an annual investment of about half a million pounds for a number of years as they tried to get on a paying basis. Up to the middle of the century only the Anglo-Mexican, the Real del Monte and the Imperial Brazilian are known to have returned anything like their original capital to the participants in the form of dividends.[54] The machine did not bring gold to England.

THE FOREIGN LOAN MANIA ENDS

The collapse of the South American mining speculations was the most striking of the reverses which the money market encountered toward the end of 1825. Alarmed at the progress of the speculative movement the Bank of England ceased to discount commercial paper, in hope of maintaining its reserves. And country banks found themselves encumbered with mortgages and worthless stocks upon which they had made advances, their notes coming back to them for payment and with no place to turn for help. A recession set in involving the bulk of small merchants who had been venturing in foreign trade in ultimate ruin. Some dramatic bank failures drained out gold from the Bank of England. In December the country was "within twenty-four hours of barter." Only the agreement of government and the Court of Directors that the Bank might exceed the legal limit of its note issue and expand its commercial discounts, saved the situation.[55] But it did not do so until much working capital had been extinguished and many business anticipations thwarted; and the appetite for foreign loans as well as for joint-stock ventures had turned to distaste. Consols fell steadily during 1825 and foreign government stocks followed them down. Rumors of political dissensions in many of the borrowing countries aided the fall. In January, 1826, B. A. Goldschmidt & Co., then agents for Colombia, suspended payment, with the current interest instalment upon the Colombian loans still in their possession.[56] And the bubble burst. Investors came to a sudden realization that the only interest they had received had come out of the principal of successive loans, that they were likely to obtain more only by advancing it. And the South American republics suddenly discovered that they had borrowed beyond their means, that they could expect no more assistance in the immediate future, and they faced their first lesson in public finance,—that while financiers can divest themselves of their obligations by bankruptcy, governments have no such refuge.

WHAT THE MONEY ACCOMPLISHED

It would be agreeable to record that the early ventures abroad of the British investor proved as profitable to himself as to the plausible contractors; that they gave a profound stimulus to British trade and industry, improving employment and the standards of living; and that they promoted prosperity abroad and political well-being without compensating disadvantages for Great Britain. But such a record would bear little relation to the facts. Not only the South American mines proved a graveyard for British fortunes. Within two years of the panic of 1825, Spain, Portugal, Greece, and every country in South America to which money had been lent—except Brazil—were in default upon their interest payments. For thirty years their financial affairs were in hopeless confusion. An even longer period elapsed before some of these states approached solvency. Their stocks passed from the hands of the original purchasers at nominal prices, a shilling or two upon the pound, into the hands of professional speculators and were for half a century the football of the stock exchanges.

The effect upon British trade and industry is less easy to

determine. The remittance of loans to the revolutionary governments, at all events, was in the form of merchandise. Possibly two-thirds of the amount actually remitted made a direct demand upon various industries concerned in military and naval stores. The balance was consigned in cotton goods and hardware. The British customs returns, which do not include the sale of ships, show a distinct increase in value as well as in volume in the South American trade between 1815 and 1825. For the five-year period ending 1818 the average declared value of exports to the Latin American countries was £2,800,000. The average for the next five years was £3,120,-000. In 1824 the exports were valued at £5,572,579; in the following year at £6,425,715. After that date British trade with those countries continued to grow in volume as it did to most other parts of the world, its money value remaining constant at between four and five million pounds. This increase in trade could only have been financed by British credits in some form or another, at least until the mine output revived, and until sheep- and cattle-raising and sugar plantations could market a more ample surplus. It meant that for a generation ten per cent of all British and Irish produce exported went to Latin American countries, in contrast to the five per cent which was its proportion in 1815. But since the credits were extended but once, and rarely after 1825 except on mercantile bills, the maintenance of this trade volume was due not to the investor but to many small enterprises conducted by Irishmen and others with very little capital, which developed an exportable surplus from South America. The interest due Great Britain upon the government loans was an obstacle to this continued trade. There were frequent clashes between merchants resident in South America and the bondholders.

Of the relation of the continental loans in support of

legitimacy to foreign trade a precise statement is even less possible. Import returns are inadequate. The value of exports from the United Kingdom to European ports steadily dwindled through the twenties despite large loans to Spain, Naples, France, Prussia and Russia. This was especially true of the item of reexports, consisting principally of goods from India and West Indian possessions. It is not to be believed that Europe during this period found less need for tropical produce or improved her facilities for obtaining it independent of the British market. Hence the conjecture is reasonable that Englishmen made their European investments largely in the form of Indian revenue remitted directly to European ports in the form of merchandise, and by the reinvestment of the increasing dividends arising from the loans already made.

It is difficult to see how these movements worked materially either to the benefit or disadvantage of the British workingman or of British economy as a whole. Some of the investments clearly stimulated a demand upon industry for exportable goods. But investments at home might have stimulated an equivalent demand. The fact that a loan will be supplied in merchandise exports is no argument in its favor. It must be shown that in such a transaction the merchandise will command a higher price, or capital higher interest in proportion to security. Whatever benefits prevailed in these respects accrued to the contractors and their friends; and of them only to the more prudent. The transactions as a whole may be said to have been a loss to British economy for more than a generation, and then to have been given value only because no statute of limitations runs with respect to the debts of minor states.

But this was a risk commensurate with the profits investors and business men hoped to gain. And it may be questioned whether anticipations less dazzling would have aroused any comparable financial effort. Credit capital is not a fund, supplied by streams of calculable volume, exerting continuous pressure of the hydraulic type in search of the weakest outlet. It does not accumulate in proportion to disuse; it does not exist for all purposes alike. In some degree the hopes entertained with respect to South America created the resources with which it was sought to realize them. And it is by no means certain that more credit capital could have been found in 1825 for home development than was being extended to manufacturers by their banks, to a handful of sound transportation projects by retired manufacturers. A housing policy for industrial areas supported by public and parochial loans would have meant much to the well-being of the British population, and in the long run to the prosperity of her economy. But neither government nor bankers then conceived of their function in such positive terms. The theory of "the greatest good to the greatest number" did not prevail with respect to the employment of credit.

The most certain consequence of the first period of British loans to foreign governments was the accumulation of assets readily negotiable abroad. And to a country rapidly becoming unable in emergency to feed her growing population from her own harvests this proved to be of almost immediate importance. In 1828, 1829 and 1831 occurred a series of short harvests in Great Britain, sending grain prices above the Corn Law maximum, and requiring considerable importations of grain from Poland, Prussia and Hungary.[57] These imports were sudden and extraordinary. They came from regions cultivated under servile tenure, which normally absorbed little in the way of British manufactures and could not rapidly assimilate more. Banking facilities were scant. Payment must be made immediately and in a medium which would circulate readily. Bullion and specie went in large quantities for this purpose as they had gone in 1818. But the securities of continental governments which had not been disturbed by revolution were found equally usable, and a cheaper mode of remittance. By the end of 1828 practically all Austrian securities had left England. Russian, Prussian and French stocks followed. If their purchase had been of doubtful advantage for British agriculture, they proved to be an international currency of the first importance in financing the corn trade.[58] For although their sale involved a real loss of national wealth for the purpose of immediate consumption, it did this without deranging the monetary system and price levels. In due time gold, had more been required, would have returned to England by way of France and Italy to which it might have been sent in payment for luxury articles for the feudal proprietors of eastern Europe. But in the meantime the losses in the fall of prices, stoppages and shutdowns, large as they were, would have been much greater. The discontent of which the reform movement, the Birmingham paper currency agitation, and the precursors of Chartism were symptoms might well have swollen into full revolution and have altered the whole trend of English development in the nineteenth century. Such an alteration would not necessarily have been for the better.

Some of the effects abroad of the loan investment may be briefly indicated. The loans to the legitimate governments certainly stimulated European economic life. They called into activity local capital, liberated it for employment more remunerative than the public debt, and expended in bonuses behind tariff walls they helped to create new textile industries in Holland, France, Prussia and Russia. The exports of British machinery had not been large.[59] More British foremen than capitalists became directly interested in factories on the Continent. And in countries where mercantilism was still the dominant mode of economic thought, the financial help of governments facilitated by foreign borrowings was very important. Within two decades after Waterloo, England was no longer sending cloth to the Continent. Her function was to supply yarn to the weaving and clothing mills of Belgium and France, Saxony and Prussia. The investment of her capital had given wing to the migration of the industrial arts.

The effects upon South America, on the other hand, seem to have been vicious. The armaments secured for defense against a decadent mother country were turned to weapons of aggression against neighboring republics and weapons of partisan aggrandizement within the several states. The revolt from Spain had been in part a revolt of the mestizo against an alien culture. The activities of British merchants in support of politicians of unblemished descent seemed only to fasten in more plausible form the European ascendancy upon the native. Moreover the ample revenue which they could at any time secure in London tended to make the first revolutionary governments indifferent to the opinion of their people at the very time when it was of prime importance that they reflect it. It encouraged that unblushing confusion of the business of government with the promotion of private fortune which is a notable characteristic of undeveloped political societies. The violence, the corruption, the instability, the financial recklessness which characterized most of the South American republics during a large part of the century are in no small way attributable to the early laxity of the London money market.[61]

Thus the migration of capital from Great Britain began as a function of the activity of a handful of merchant-bankers interested primarily in keeping alive the foreign connections which were the basis of their business life. Between 1815 and 1830 at least fifty million pounds had been invested more or less permanently in the securities of the most stable European governments, more than twenty million had been invested in one form or another in Latin America, and five or six millions had very quietly found their way to the United States.[62] The movement provided employment for British industry and enterprise. It was an export from a surplus of potential economic power which the leaders of the movement did not have wit enough to engage in activity at home. It had consequences, both political and economic, at home and abroad. These were not so momentous as participants in the movement expected. And it was with the United States which had attracted the least capital that in 1830 the economic relations of Great Britain were developing most favorably.

CHAPTER III

A CYCLE OF ANGLO-AMERICAN FINANCE

"What aristocratic privilege was ever equal to that of controlling the currency of seventeen millions of people, and making money plenty or scarce at pleasure?"
—Illinois Senate and House Reports (1842).

WE BALANCE MERCHANDISE WITH SECURITIES

In the days of the Reform Bill and of Andrew Jackson and Nicholas Biddle, the purchase of American stocks for investment was no untried fancy with British merchants. According to John Gladstone, it was already in 1819 a practice "of many years standing, and therefore escapes observation."[1] Indeed one of the earliest manifestations of the Financial Revolution had been the transfer to London of the United States securities which the Dutch once held. The States had taken them to Versailles and Amsterdam in payment for revolutionary supplies; and Dutch capitalists relieved the exigencies of the French Treasury after 1783 in buying up its shares. Amsterdam made further advances in 1791 when the American domestic debt was funded; and in 1803 the purchase of Louisiana was financed by a loan made in Holland. But already the major portion of American securities held in Europe had crossed the Channel. As early as 1791 several million dollars of the debt had been placed by Bird, Savage & Bird, London stockbrokers, among

their customers.[2]   Ten years later the coupons upon bonds
in excess of four million pounds were paid through Baring
Brothers.   This alone was more than all the holdings of the
Dutch and Swiss.[3]   By 1805 the coupons paid through Barings represented a nominal capital of £5,747,283.   This sum
included, besides the unpaid debt of the United States abroad,
at least seven million dollars in the stock of the First Bank
of the United States.[4]   As the debt, foreign and domestic,
was paid off British holdings diminished.   The extinction
of the Bank in 1811 and the War of 1812 reduced to £1,500,-
000 the amount upon which Barings paid dividends.   The
balance had been reabsorbed in the United States.

A more progressive movement set in after the war.   In
1817 and 1818 temporary loans of bullion were made to the
Second Bank of the United States.   They became the basis
of a permanent investment in the stock of that institution
which in 1820 amounted to nearly three million dollars.   Another million was added to this amount by 1828, and the total
was doubled during the next three years.   Out of 300,000
shares in private hands in July, 1831, 79,159 were held abroad
by 466 shareholders, largely men who had invested more than
ten thousand pounds apiece.[5]   Meanwhile part of the American public debt had returned abroad.   Fourteen million dollars of it were owned by British investors in 1828, five millions by other European creditors.[6]   Beyond possibility of
statistical appraisal were also lands in Maine and Pennsylvania
and Virginia.   There were properties such as Alexander Baring acquired during that sojourn in America that won him a
wife and a mobile fortune.[7]   It had not been uncommon
for wealthy aristocrats to ask such firms as Barings to invest
some money for them in those uncultivated lands which
the tide of westward migration seemed likely to appreciate.
And the property of the Marquis of Caermarthen in the Man-

hattan Banking Company was doubtless not the only venture into business which had been made before 1830.[8]

These movements of capital, especially in their earlier phases, had a marked relation to the balance of trade between the United States and Great Britain. But they were petty affairs, of more moment in the financial history of the United States than in that of the British people. They were probably not greater than the amount of British capital engaged in American trade, if as great. Investment in the United States in considerable volume dated from a significant change in the financial organization of the American trade, the building of a "credit bridge" which involved the commerce of Brazil, the Far East and the colonies of Spain, as well as that of the United States.

In spite of political differences and tariff walls, the United States after their Independence were still the principal customers of Great Britain and looked to that country for their chief market. Thirty-six per cent of the domestic exports of the United States went to the British Isles between 1820 and 1830. Eighty per cent of the cotton supplies of Lancashire came from the South. Sixteen per cent of the domestic produce and manufactures of the United Kingdom between 1820 and 1830 were shipped to American ports; and this merchandise formed forty-three per cent in value of the total imports into the United States.[9] For the first decade after the War of 1812 British manufacturers endeavored to drive this export trade upon their own account. They shipped directly to agents or customers on the Atlantic seaboard, dumped unassorted goods in New York to be sold at auction, paying import duties in advance and taking long bills for their sales, which they discounted with provincial bankers in England.[10]

A variety of circumstances broke down this system of trading which was, nevertheless, essentially that pursued recently in the Manchester trade with backward countries. Goods which were most in demand tended to be shipped to excess. Staple lines were wanting. The turnover of capital was slow. The general bankruptcy of American merchants in 1825 completed the wreck of the consignment system. It became the policy of English manufacturers to reduce their stocks, narrow the margin of trading, and shorten the period between production and sale. American bills disappeared from the market. Not only exchange but shipments came to be concentrated on either side of the Atlantic in the hands of a few banking and mercantile houses, having implicit confidence in one another, mainly interested in the cotton trade.[11] On the American side the Bank of the United States became the dominant factor in the exchanges about 1826 thru its branch banking facilities.[12] In London and Liverpool a group of eight houses, of which Baring Brothers and Brown Brothers were the most active, handled practically all of the exchange and credit relations with America.[13]

The business dealings of banker and commission merchant were closely interwoven. Baring Brothers did little trading upon their own account. They handled cotton as agents for Southern factors and New York exporters; and they purchased British goods upon account of American firms for export to New York. Wholesale merchants, the Yankee dry-goods houses which were the pillars of American respectability in the ante-bellum period, now handled the import trade at the Atlantic ports. But they could not trade adequately with their own capital. The Yankee firms depended to a large extent in their buying upon credits which came, directly or indirectly, from such firms as Barings themselves.[14] The Bank of the United States and other seaboard banks had correspondence with one or another of the English merchant-bankers, with drawing accounts running into the millions of dollars. At the low interest rates prevailing in London from 1828 to 1834 it became very profitable to sell bills against these credits to American importers. The Bank paid two or three per cent for its money, and could easily secure seven in the United States.

The bills drawn by Americans upon London were in addition to the documents arising from the cotton trade, and were not solely in payment for British manufactures. Wines from France, coffee from Brazil, sugar from the West Indies, tea and silk from Hong Kong were paid alike with bills on London.[15] But sooner or later the credits which they represented must be covered. And so far as British exports to the United States were concerned, American cotton and other produce were usually sufficient to balance the account. The adverse balances in the China and colonial trade were met for a number of years by the export of specie and from the profits of the New England carrying trade. Prior to 1830, ninety per cent of the foreign trade of the United States was carried under the American flag; Yankee ships competed successfully in the direct trade from China, Brazil and the West Indies to Europe. The net result of Jackson's West India policy, however, was to increase the handicaps under which American ships engaged in the direct trade between those islands and the United States, and virtually to exclude American ships from the circuitous trade by way of British North America and Europe.[16] The abolition of the East India Company's monopoly in 1834 brought similar advantages to British merchantmen in the Far East. Hence during the early thirties the profits of the American carrying trade fell off, while the volume of American shipping to and from the United States sank to seventy-five per cent of the total.[17]

Under these circumstances American securities came to occupy a more important rôle in the international balance of payments.

British exports settled the balances against the United States wherever they arose thruout the world; and to cover the large overdrafts which the luxurious tastes of Uncle Sam were continually running up, the merchant-bankers took his stocks. Thus the bulk of the foreign trade of the United States came to depend upon a system of banking kept in motion by an increasing willingness of Englishmen to buy American securities. The interests of Anglo-American trade harmonized happily with the desires of investors who were not carrying their savings to the stock market.[18]

COUNTRY INVESTORS DESIRE REPRODUCTIVE INVESTMENTS

The discontinuance of British support to revolution and reaction had been sudden and complete. Not that there was a decline after 1825 in the demand of European monarchs for money. There was war in the Near East. In the West there was insurrection. There was no lack of pretext for expanding the public debts of Europe. Neither was there a dearth of capital in the London money market. From 1828 to 1832 at least, money stagnated in Lombard Street and was to be had of bill-brokers in discount of commercial paper for as little as 1½%.[19] Yet until 1830 not a foreign government was able to float a public loan in London. And when the business was resumed it was supported chiefly by stock-jobbers and by merchants who bought up foreign securities for remittance.[20] The investing public had had enough of political loans.

To a degree the investor's change of heart went along with the depression which from 1825 to the passage of the Reform Bill characterized British trade and industry in general. There had been disastrous speculations; there were crop failures and a terrifying amount of social unrest at home and thruout western Europe; pessimism was easy. But the investor was also forming a different appreciation of the functions of capital. It was observed that borrowed money could be spent for various objects, and it was reasoned that the purposes for which a loan was employed affected its security. Country bankers complained that the Stock Exchange was too fond of loans which were "a mere prop for military despotism." Such loans were wholly unproductive, reasoned Henry Burgess in his *Circular to Bankers;* their main security was the set of political conditions which they were contracted to preserve; and so far from being of advantage to Great Britain, they only gave help to her political enemies and supplied the means by which her foreign trade might be undermined.[21] There were many investors looking about for securities not open to these objections. Safety was of no small consideration. But they held in view consequences of more remote pecuniary importance to themselves. They had calculated the unearned increment of progress and were seeking its appropriation. It was not enough that the money they invested be spent in one way or another for the products of British workshops. That was but a single transaction and of no abiding consequence. The application of their capital should be reproductive. It should assume the form of what modern economists have called "producers' goods." The capital should be so used as to create the means for its repayment. It would thus constitute a stimulus to the permanent volume of the commerce of the British Empire and ensure, it was believed, the augmenting well-being of its members, at any rate of its governing classes.

It was the country investor who was looking about most earnestly for reproductive investments. And by the "country investor" is meant the totality of persons whose fortunes had been enhanced by the industrial changes of the preceding fifty years. These persons were by no means all engaged in manufacture and trade. Many had been so, but had purchased a country estate and were in a fair way to become swallowed up in the county families. Others, and those with large fortunes were of this sort, had been the fortunate proprietors of land upon which new factory towns sprang up or in which lucrative mining operations were carried on. High as their standards of consumption were, these magnates could not find use for the inflated rent-rolls with which the Industrial Revolution had dowered them.[22] It was from Lancashire, from Ireland, from the eastern and midland counties where the rent of land accumulated in sums which were not spent nor profitably reinvested locally that balances flowed constantly to the London bill-brokers. Unplowed parks and huddled tenements told of this migration of capital to London. But the preference of stable markets to political vanities spoke with promise of a closer cooperation of the rentier with the industrial life to which he owed his superfluous wealth. In another decade his bank-balances, supplemented by the savings of the middle classes, and energized by the wizardry of the deposit system, would pave the English highways with iron and complete the identification of the interests of the proprietors of land with those of the managers of steam. In the thirties foreign investments seemed more available, especially the securities of American states and municipalities issued in promotion of public works.

BRITISH CAPITAL IN AMERICAN EXPANSION

Doubtless without the advent of large quantities of British capital, American expansion would have taken place, albeit at a slower rate, and possibly a happier one. Already the political power of the West had been sufficient to plunge the nation into one imprudent war. By 1830, the population of the trans-Allegheny West was greater than that of the entire United States at the time of the first census. The rivers and lakes of the North, the rivers and bayous of the South, were the avenues along which the centers of population and political gravity were rapidly shifting westward. But the frontier was still only the frontier. It was the pale of civilization, not its stronghold. It was a speculation, not a going concern. To weld the log-cabins of the Ohio and Wabash valleys into political and economic cohesion and to create solidarity between them and the seaboard better transportation was needed and transportation required capital.

Capital was no unknown article in the United States. What American did not own his farm, his forge, his schooner? But the annual surplus arising from his farm and schooner and forge could almost without exception be fully employed in the further exploitation of those tools. Hence the promoter-politicians, who perceived the advantages, whether public or private, which could accrue from the building of highways, canals and railroads, turned to foreign capital, filtered thru the public treasuries for support.[23] Nor would this recourse have been effective had it not been for the sensational success of the first venture of its kind. State-owned and state-constructed the Erie Canal was financed by the issue of New York state bonds. Something over seven million dollars' worth were sold between 1817 and 1825, and they passed almost at once into the hands of Englishmen. But it is doubtful whether the revelation that states could borrow money in London was more encouraging to state enterprise in canal-building than the marvel that Erie paid its way. As not even its best friends imagined, the canal carried enough produce in the first year of operation to meet the interest upon its debt. Within ten years the profits accumulated from its business were sufficient to redeem the obligations entirely and at a premium before maturity.[24] Western New York and northern Ohio had been opened up to a tide of permanent settlement, and the bulk of the interior trade was taking its direction through New York City.

The jealousy and envy of rival seaports knew no bounds. Before the Erie Canal was open for traffic Philadelphia and Baltimore were clamoring for state enterprise and foreign capital to construct similar routes to the interior. Washington and Richmond were not far behind. Unable to choose between the claims of the Chesapeake & Ohio Canal and the Baltimore & Ohio Railroad, Maryland blessed them both, and gave a rich dowry of bonds and guarantees to the private companies which undertook to build them. The enthusiasm for trans-Allegheny trade routes spread rapidly to other lines of communication. In the Middle West state canal systems on a comprehensive scale, supported by federal land grants, were planned in Ohio, Indiana, Illinois, Michigan and Kentucky. Along the coast private enterprise perfected a financial technique which was able to take advantage of state and municipal generosity without injury to the surplus profits. A series of railways extending from New York Harbor (Amboy) to the Delaware river at Camden and from Philadelphia to Baltimore, Wilmington and Richmond, thus came quickly into existence in the hands of private corporations, guaranteed against loss by public bounty. Two canal companies which promised to bring a steady supply of Pennsylvania coal to New York City were rewarded with banking privileges. Only the Pennsylvania coal routes, the Schuylkill Coal & Navigation company, the Philadelphia & Reading Railroad, with some short railroads in New England and central New York, ventured to proceed with neither guarantee nor bonds from a paternal legislature. Before 1836 over ninety million dollars had been invested in canals and railways in the North, of which more than half was a charge upon public credit. The bulk of this capital had been procured from England.[25]

South of the Ohio River the forces of expansion were exerted in a different manner. Even more rapidly than the movement across the Alleghenies, the cotton-growing area was spreading through the Gulf states, transferring the primacy of the South from Charleston to New Orleans. Fewer settlers were required for this development. But there was a correspondingly heavier demand for capital. There were slaves to be purchased and supported. Moreover cotton was an export crop, as far as the South was concerned, and the services of middleman and banker were a necessity to the plantation. From the early twenties the branches of the Bank of the United States took an active part in rendering this service. But the terms of a "foreign" institution were thought too exacting by the planters, and a variety of locally controlled banks sprang up, some relying upon public, a few upon private funds. In 1824 Louisiana inaugurated a system of land banks under state patronage. The plan was for the stock in the banks to be subscribed by the planters, who would pay up their subscriptions by tendering mortgages upon their several estates to two-thirds of their market value. The state would then issue bonds, or guarantee those issued by the bank, and these would be sold in the East or in London to secure working capital. The subscribers were eligible to borrow from the fund thus created, pledging their growing crops as security.[26]   Several banks of this type were formed at New Orleans. To finance the Planters' Bank, Baring Brothers made a public issue of Louisiana securities in 1829.[27] In 1832 a Planters' Bank was founded in Mississippi; the next year there was a similar institution in Alabama; Tennessee followed them, and in each state there was more than one land bank. Several private banks were also opened at New Orleans; while Florida, Arkansas, Missouri, Illinois and Indiana came to boast of state-owned banks, all deeply concerned in the land business. And loans for most of these undertakings directly or indirectly were sought in London.

There was another expansion, too, which was gathering momentum in the eighteen-thirties; an expansion which was not geographical, but functional—the movement of industry under the business system to the forefront of economic life in the North and Middle Atlantic states. Whether there was ever an "Industrial Revolution" in the United States in the connotation of the term which attaches to the English transformations from 1783 to 1832 has not been determined with satisfactory clarity. It is certainly premature to apply the term to events before that era of economic growth in which the Civil War was an episode. Yet in the age of Nicholas Biddle industry bulked increasingly large in the consciousness of the North. The rapidity with which the pioneers advanced upon the West meant a degree of forced specialization. There was not time for their families to be as self-sufficing as formerly. And the profits from land furnished the means with which to make increased demands upon remote manufacturing establishments, as soon as cheap transportation was assured. This was the hey-day of water-driven textile mills in New England, and of the literary young lady spinners of Lowell who so impressed Charles Dickens. More specifically the rise of public works boomed the coal and iron industry; it hastened the application of anthracite to the smelting of ore; it concentrated production in Pennsylvania. In ten years plant was quadrupled and output (reckoned to the depressing year of 1840) was doubled.[28] By the end of the thirties the Norris Locomotive Works of Philadelphia were delivering engines to Gloucestershire, Prague and Moscow.[29]

With these industrial developments British capital had little directly to do. It is perhaps not surprising that merchant-bankers whose principal business was to export British manufactures to the United States should not display zeal to develop in that country industries which would be competitive. Nor is it surprising that the stocks of no American manufacturing concern were publicly on sale in London, for scarcely any British industries were financed in that manner, or indeed bore the aspect of joint-stock enterprise at all. Nevertheless the British capital which promoted transportation and westward expansion indirectly financed industry as well. American merchants and banks could draw credits for objects unspecified, and these were available in the United States for the expansion of industry. It is certainly to this relation that a contemporary newspaper refers in declaring that "millions of foreign capital are invested in manufactures in this country." [30] Public securities apart, a few railway undertakings in the East, private banks in New York and New Orleans, and a few mining enterprises were the objects of specific English investment.[31]

HOW THE BONDS WERE MARKETED

But it must be understood that for the average investor who thus financed American expansion, the details of these varied undertakings were irrelevant. America was so distant that so far as the ultimate British purchaser was concerned her securities could not well be differentiated. Her state loans did not usually come to London as those of the South American republics had done, one by one, in the custody of agents offering generous commissions to genial contractors. They were not publicly issued. There was no subscription, no allotment. They were slow to be listed upon the Stock Exchange, and few of them were traded in actively, at least until 1837–38. They were to be had of the merchant-bankers by favored country banks for distribution to favored clients.[32] Marketed originally in New York or Philadelphia or Baltimore, they came to London in blocks as cover for drawing credits. They were payable in the United States in dollars, but payment of dividends at fixed rates of exchange was commonly guaranteed to English holders by the American money-lender. All of these conditions tended to satisfy the desire for detailed information which an investor might have entertained. In particular they avoided that flood of apparent publicity which the issue of a prospectus and appeal for subscriptions throw upon more recent financial movements. So Englishmen did not invest in Baltimore & Ohio (Maryland guarantee) 5's or in Ohio 6% (Wabash & Erie mortgage) stock. They purchased American state securities, Bank stock, canal bonds, bonds recommended by Samuel Gurney, the great Quaker bill-broker, or by Joshua Bates, the shrewd Yankee who from 1825 to 1864 was the managing partner of Baring Brothers. The only particular discrimination that can be traced is the disinclination of many investors to buy securities of southern states, on the ground that it would be an encouragement to slavery.[33]

As a fact the securities differed widely in merit. They all bore the aspect of being issued for what might be broadly termed "productive purposes." They bade fair to pay for themselves. Most of them were for the building of canals, a form of enterprise that had been immensely profitable in England. But the purposes were not all being pursued so wisely nor was the accomplishment likely to be so remunerative as the Erie Canal. The canal and railway enterprises of Pennsylvania and Maryland presented special engineering difficulties; and precisely those states were most swayed by the pressure of local interests in the survey and organization of their respective systems. The consequence was that construction proceeded irregularly, and the building of branches and transshipment centers was preferred to the early completion of a lucrative main line. Few states followed the prudent example of New York in assigning definite funds to meet interest charges during the construction period; and as dividend payments became due it was found necessary to borrow new money to meet the interest upon the old. The investments, in a word, became less productive and more usurious the longer the movement continued.

Of the varying solvency of the undertakings his money fostered, the English investor was, however, wholly ignorant. It was difficult for even a trained investigator to ascertain anything about the finances of many of the states.[34] And of the fact that the debtor states claimed sovereign powers and were beyond the jurisdiction of any court of law, no Englishman would have claimed understanding had he enjoyed the knowledge. What the British investor did know made a broad appeal. The interest was high, five or six per cent for state loans, nine and ten upon the bonds of southern banks. And this advantage, with the promptness of dividend payments, the productive uses for which the capital was ostensibly employed, the evident prosperity of the country, the probable advantages to British trade, conspired with such imponderables as kinship, common language and the common law to elevate America above other regions as a field for investment.[35] The *Circular to Bankers,* the weekly publication of the association of country banks, conducted incessant propaganda to this effect, especially from 1832 to 1838. And it was among country gentlemen that American stocks were chiefly distributed. Social and political circles, however, took their share. Whigs and radicals traced a fancied resemblance between Jacksonian democracy and the Reform movement, and conceived of the purchase of American securities as a friendly gesture toward the rising hope of liberalism.[36] On the other hand many Tories, convinced that the passage of the Reform Bill would lead to a breakdown of the funding system, withdrew their savings from consols and purchased American bonds, determined to secure a pittance in some foreign country upon which they could live when the wreck took place.[37]

There were doubtless other considerations at least subconsciously present in the minds of the merchant-bankers who directed the movement of capital to the United States. The attitude of the typical British merchant toward the United States in the second quarter of the century was a compound of a fear, a desire, and an anticipation. The fear was of the competition of the New England merchant fleet in the carrying trade, a competition begun during the Napoleonic wars and not to be ended until the Civil War. The desire was for free access to American markets, unhampered by protective tariffs. The anticipation was of a populous Mississippi valley, exporting grain in sufficient surplus to supply the subsistence for a more industrialized Great Britain. The fulfilment of these aims depended upon one event—the development of the West—a West which would unite with the South in the rejection of high tariffs, a West which would divert the current of American capital and labor from the sea to domestic exploitation.[38]   This prospective development was a picture which became more alluring with each moment of contemplation.   However base the tokens by which it was represented, the future of the United States was of pure gold.   Thus between the immediate utility of converting floating credits and the ultimate utility of a commercial revolution, the intermediate object of solvency tended to be lost to view.   The West was expanded and the merchant-bankers were paid, while many a "reproductive" investment proved sterile.   The business activities to which the credit system we have described gave rise led directly to the crises of 1837 and 1839.

A MATTER OF ELATION

The lack of opportunity for investment at home has frequently been assigned as the cause for the export of capital. And this explanation was offered in its justification in the eighteen-thirties.   Some time before Rodbertus and Marx and Hobson, Edward Wakefield and his group of colonial reformers were arguing that wealth accumulated in the hands of British capitalists more rapidly than it could be expended. They reasoned that in consequence there were periodic overflows in tides of reckless speculation which stirred excitement for a time in business and industry, but that those tides in the end dissipated much wealth and plunged the population into increasing misery.   It was to relieve an overabundance of capital as well as of labor that Wakefield championed his policy of systematic colonization.[39]   He seems to have felt that both capital and labor needed encouragement to make them move.

However, the migration of capital in the early thirties did not mechanically relieve the capital market and establish equilibrium between the differences of opportunity at home and abroad. English business was depressed when the movement of capital to the United States first attracted much attention. But that movement attained its maximum volume upon the wave of business elation which, gathering momentum after the passage of the Reform Bill, reached its peak in 1836. The bulk of British investments in the United States were made precisely when the largest volume of capital was being absorbed at home.

Between the third quarter of 1832 and the second quarter of 1836 the prices of a selected group of commodities rose in the ratio of 93 to 116 according to Silberling's index. A thirty per cent increase in the capital invested in textile machinery alone took place during the three years 1835, 1836 and 1837.[40] A thousand new mills had been opened and sixty-eight thousand persons given employment. The success of the Liverpool & Manchester Railway was flooding the market with railway projects. In 1836 Parliament authorized the raising of £22,874,998 for railway purposes; in the following year £13,521,799. The fifteen millions authorized between 1830 and 1835 were permeating the industrial districts and binding London to Manchester and Birmingham by rail.[41] In the shipping industry, company after company was formed to operate steamship lines across the Atlantic and around the Cape. Stimulated by demand from these directions the coal and iron industries began to assume large proportions. Seventy-two joint-stock banks, a type of credit organization first made possible by Parliament in 1826, involving an unlimited number of shareholders in unlimited liability, responded to the call for augmented credit facilities. All England was prosperous, but the hand-loom weavers.

Altho most of the manufacturers with whom the Industrial Revolution had begun had been ruined during the fifteen years following Waterloo, this renewed economic energy came almost wholly from the provinces. It came from a new generation of manufacturers who, starting with post-war capital costs, selling their goods in England instead of on consignment to a foreign port, and utilizing to the full improvements in factory organization and technique, throve upon low prices, reduced wages and small profits. The railway system was launched independently of the Stock Exchange and down to 1836 did not secure a fourth of its capital in London. The shipping interests of London and Bristol, the old East and West India houses, passed the lead to the men of Manchester and to the banks and commission houses with whom they dealt. Neither the Bank of England nor Rothschild's stock market operations were factors in their reckoning.[42] But London responded to their initiative. In a few months in 1836 Poulett Thomson was able to compile a list of more than three hundred companies calling for a nominal capital of two hundred million pounds.[43] The London *Times* for 1835 carried prospectuses of 20 companies proposing to do business abroad, in 1836 of 38, in 1837 of 5, in 1838 of 46, in 1839 of 20. An important group of these companies, promoted by a group of Lancashire Catholics for whom John Wright was the London banker, undertook to engage in banking in various British colonies.[44] Others contemplated a monopoly of the world's output of copper.[45] A third group controlled the known deposits of asphalt and divided the world for its marketing for pavements. Revolutionary factions from Spain and Portugal again found welcome on the now animated Stock Exchange; and London speculators financed a fresh series of civil wars for the thrones of those unhappy countries.[46] While the great national object of placing the infant Kingdom of Belgium upon a firm economic base was pursued through loans to its government for the encouragement of industry and the initiation of a railway system.[47]

The American trade was one important cause of this elation and the trade was stimulated by it. The expenditure of British capital upon public works stirred the internal trade of the United States. It set up a demand for goods which could be satisfied only by importations. The increased activity of British mills enhanced the price of cotton, and this promoted the expansion of the cotton-growing area and the demand for loans for its financing and was a basis for banknote inflation. The net effect upon both North and South was to institute an enormous boom in land values, leading to speculation in public lands and building lots, which increased the apparent wealth of the Americans at a prodigious rate. And this augmented the demand for consumers' goods from Europe. Ostentatious consumption follows hard on the trail of the speculator. The increased sale of American cotton was more than matched by the purchases of British implements and cutlery, silks and cloths, and some railway iron. Between 1830 and 1836 the volume of Anglo-American trade doubled, and in the year ending September 30, 1836, the imports from Great Britain exceeded the exports to that country by more than twenty million dollars. On her entire trade the United States was debtor for the year to the extent of sixty million dollars. And she was debtor besides for interest upon previous borrowings. The export of British capital had created a relation which only still larger capital exports could sustain.[48]

CRISIS IN ANGLO-AMERICAN ECONOMY

Large as the American mercantile balances had become, the sales of securities in Great Britain were even larger. It had been the policy of the American government under Jackson to substitute a gold currency for the silver and paper currency to which the United States had been reduced. In 1834 a mint ratio which placed a premium upon the export of gold was replaced by one which stimulated its importation. At the same time Jackson was busy collecting indemnities from France and Naples which he insisted upon receiving in gold. As a result of these maneuvers, an average excess of $10,-000,000 a year in gold was imported into the United States from 1833 to 1836. This was partly balanced by the sale of securities abroad and the depleted earnings of the carrying trade. Moreover during these years the United States government was paying off the public debt, much of which was held abroad. This process too was aided by the sale of the new state and corporation securities. It will not be far wrong to estimate the total quantity of British capital invested in the United States during the thirties as approximately equal to the indebtedness incurred by the several states. By 1835 this amounted to $66,000,000. In the three following years, $108,000,000 were added to this amount.[49] In one trip to London in the late spring of 1836, Samuel Jaudon of the United States Bank is said to have carried twenty million dollars' worth of securities, besides bonds for a gold loan of two million pounds which Baring Brothers were to issue on behalf of the Bank.[50]

The progressive transmutation of export balances into securities was kept in motion by the increasing volume of mercantile credit which the "American houses" were able to extend. Their methods had undergone a striking development. For a number of years invoices and bills of lading had largely disappeared from exchange relations between the United States and Great Britain. Exchange was stabilized and resources economized by the practice of "open credits." [51] Thus shorn of their documentary encumbrances bills of exchange took on a new and wonderful life. To American speculators, the opportunity to draw at will was a providence which added dollars to the market value of New York lots and bubble corporations. They did not fail to take advantage of it. If trade increased in rapid ratio, the volume of bills increased at twice the pace. The complaisance of London merchant-bankers knew no bounds. Between January 1, 1834 and January 1, 1837, the acceptances of three houses (not the largest) rose from £2,354,000 to £5,573,000.[52] Toward the end of 1837 the outstanding mercantile debt of the United States exceeded twelve million pounds when it was thought to be lower than it had been in six years. It was estimated that it had been twenty million in the preceding year.[53] Thus speculation engendered speculation. The entire English-speaking world was knit by a definite set of credit relationships and animated by a common business elation.

Two acts of will and one of circumstance brought the system of Anglo-American credit into jeopardy. In July, 1836, the Jackson administration issued the famous Specie Circular, directing the payment for public land sales to be made in gold. At the same time that this action caused pressure for bullion along the Atlantic coast, the directors of the Bank of England became alarmed at the condition of their reserves. In four years these had fallen from eleven million pounds to seven. According to the theory of Bank policy which had been adopted in 1827, this drain indicated an unfavorable condition of the exchanges, and was to be checked by raising the discount rate.[54]   The Bank rate was raised by stages during July and August to 5%, and the Bank intimated that it would discount no more bills arising from the American trade.   The latter action had been taken once before, toward the end of 1834, without serious disturbance. And in this case, altho a great deal of excitement was created by the action and by the secrecy which shrouded it, the American houses seem to have felt strong enough to proceed with their discount and acceptance lines without the Bank's support.[55]   Consols and public securities responded at once to the altered Bank rate.   But commodity prices held fast and trade continued in undiminished volume for several months.   Indeed the last quarter of 1836 shows a slight rise in the prices of the imported articles indexed by Silberling. The merchant-bankers bade defiance to the Bank.   The fact that the break, when it came, occurred first in cotton, which was most closely related to the floating credits, and which was affected by an unusual crop, suggests that it might have ensued whatever the monetary policy of Andrew Jackson or the discount policy of the Bank of England.   In any event, those policies aggravated its force.   The fall of 25% in the price of cotton in February and March, 1837, heaped calamity upon the "American houses" and with them upon traders and speculators, planters and farmers throughout the United States.   Three of the merchant-banking houses were carried to the ground in the financial storm which broke on both sides of the Atlantic.   American banks generally suspended payment.   Hundreds of tradesmen of high and low degree were forced into insolvency.   Nine out of ten factories in the eastern states shut down.   Half the employees in seaboard commercial houses were on the streets.[56]

The crisis of 1837 in the United States and England was

essentially the outcome of a foreign credit mania and formed a partial interruption of it. Its American aspects can not be satisfactorily isolated. It was foreign credits which gave encouragement to public improvements, and gave substance to the note-issues of the western banks. Foreign credit emboldened Biddle to stand against Jackson and enabled him to carry on his discarded institution. It was the excessive development of the credit system which made it vulnerable. For the United States it was disaster. For the United Kingdom there was in 1837 only a crisis of finance in the American trade. It did not entail general commercial depression of any consequence in the United Kingdom. British trade with the Continent, Africa and the colonies was unaffected.[57] Home trade was not depressed. The agricultural laborer was reported to be in improved condition and the masses better able to consume manufactures and colonial wares. At its height the London money market supported loans to Holland and Portugal and subscribed nearly three million pounds to shipping and other joint-stock enterprises not domestic. New railways were being launched in the provinces. A real terminus of the cycle as far as England was concerned did not come until 1839. And for that reason a liquidation of the financial difficulties created by the crisis was not difficult. The resuscitation of the traffic in bills and securities proceeded in definite accordance with plans laid by Nicholas Biddle.

FINANCING A COTTON BOOM WITH BRITISH MONEY

In school histories Nicholas Biddle peers out of dark corners as a venomous ogre from whose wiles the American people were providentially preserved by the fortitude of

Andrew Jackson. The political struggle for the renewal of the charter of the Second Bank looms so large in popular estimation of the period as to throw into oblivion the services which Biddle sought to render to our nascent economy. Considerations of profitable management aside, his policy as president of the Bank was essentially to nationalize the credit and monetary systems of the United States. He did not surrender this purpose when on March 3, 1836, the federal charter of his bank expired and it was re-born as a Pennsylvania corporation. He did not surrender it, altho years of business activity had bred confusion of policy with profit. The opportunity for vindicating his claim to financial leadership came when the crisis of 1837 found the pettifogging Van Buren administration unprepared to take any measures to relieve the panic-stricken country.[58] The Bank of the United States, with other banks along the coast, was caught between the demand for gold in the interior and the rapidly maturing indebtedness to London. Ultimately it joined in the general suspension of specie payments. However this action could only defer liquidation which must be effected in commodities and securities whose prices were falling rapidly. It appeared to Biddle that the country could only be rescued, in the first place, by persuading the London money market to absorb more American securities in liquidation of the most pressing obligations, and secondly, by extending sufficient credit to American planters and cotton factors to enable them to hold their stocks for a rise in the price of raw cotton. As it developed the two policies were but aspects of a single grandiose operation.[59]

How was London to be captivated by new securities when she was paying heavily for possession of the old? Some short-term paper with something of the prestige of a Treasury note, which the Bank of England could not reasonably refuse to discount, seemed to be required. A conference of leading bankers of New York and Philadelphia took place in the former city on the evening of March 29, at which Biddle disclosed his plan and enlisted support. On the morrow he announced the readiness of the Bank of the United States to sell "post-notes"—interest-bearing bonds to bearer, maturing within ten to eighteen months—up to $5,000,000. The Manhattan Banking Co., the Bank of America, the Girard Bank, and the Morris Canal and Banking Company issued similar notes for smaller amounts.[60] In New York these six per cent notes commanded an immediate premium of 12½%, but even this was less than the premium demanded for gold. The correspondents of British firms bought them in with avidity for shipment to London in place of bullion or bills. The arrival of the "post-notes" on Lombard Street at the end of April created great excitement and surprise. Journalists became sensational as they considered the momentousness of the event. No one ventured to doubt their intrinsic security. Not even the Bank of England would decline to honor them. And it began to appear that that venerable institution was being outwitted by the clever Mr. Biddle.[61] Its policy during the crisis had turned upon manipulating the discount rate and circulation to recover gold from the United States. Instead of gold, its net was gathering more securities.

Biddle had gauged the psychology of the London money market correctly. Nor was he slow in taking advantage of the situation to form a permanent scheme for the exploitation of the British weakness for a high rate of interest. As they issued post-notes, the United States Bank and its fellows came into possession of domestic bills representing loans in anticipation of the cotton harvest or advances upon late shipments of the 1836 crops. It was necessary to protect these bills from the loss which a continued fall in the price of cotton would certainly entail. Cotton shipments, furthermore, constituted the regular mode of settling foreign balances and must be relied upon in the long run to retire the post-notes. The higher the price that could be secured for American cotton the more secure the position of all the eastern banks, and the more certain a quick recovery of domestic trade from the effects of the panic.[62]   The plan adopted under Biddle's inspiration was to make further advances to cotton factors and merchants to enable them to hold cotton as they purchased it for more favorable prices. To accomplish this effectively agencies were set up throuout the South under Biddle's control, with authority to draw upon Bevan & Humphries, merchants, of Philadelphia for notes of the Bank of the United States with which to buy up cotton. It was arranged that in due course the cotton should be consigned to a specified house in England, at first Baring Brothers. Later the firm of Humphries & Biddle of Liverpool was specially created in order that the matter might be entirely in the hands of agents over whom Nicholas Biddle had complete control. A son was partner in the Liverpool house. There remained the crowning touch to this business masterpiece. A ring of Bank officials headed by Biddle himself engineered the enterprise with funds of their own institution. And with such success that $800,000 were distributed as profits of the first eighteen months' operations, over and above commissions of agency and interest to the Bank.[63] Cotton recovered rapidly in value and a saving estimated at from ten to twenty-five million dollars was effected for American planters and merchants. By November, 1838, the old mercantile indebtedness had been paid in full.[64]

To further his operations Biddle found it advisable to have a London financial agent more completely under his control than Baring Brothers. Accordingly there appeared in London in October, 1837, Samuel Jaudon, who had been for several years cashier of the Bank of the United States. It was announced that the object of his agency would be to popularize American securities, provide an open market for their exchange, and to create a market for American bills.[65] There was nothing unsound about this. It was, however, an encroachment upon the field of business of the Bank of England and of the "American" houses. They are not to be blamed for manifesting some jealousy, which did not diminish when Jaudon advertised in the Stock Exchange his readiness to discount bills below the market-rate.[66] The new agency was quickly brought into the cotton speculation. As bills drawn on Humphries & Biddle for cotton shipments fell due, to avoid forced sales, they drew upon Jaudon. This was borrowing from the agent of the United States Bank to pay a creditor, the southern factor, who indirectly represented the Bank itself. It was simply a financial hocus-pocus, designed to cover up the fact that Biddle had a corner in cotton. Jaudon had resources, however. He had plenty of post-notes and he had a full vault of American stocks. To cover its acceptances his agency issued post-notes of the Bank of the United States, and found a market for fresh instalments of state securities to meet them as they fell due.[67]

One of two conditions was necessary to the system thus set in motion. The price of cotton must remain increasingly favorable, or the British appetite for American stocks must remain unappeased. Until the spring of 1839, with brief interruptions, both conditions remained operative. The continental demand for yarn was falling off, but the competitive character of the spinning business was slow to reflect this condition. If yarn did not advance in price with cotton, it was not difficult to maintain the margin of profit by reducing production costs. So the Manchester operatives paid for high cotton prices in low wages and unemployment, while the gentlemen of England financed their exploitation.

Meanwhile the apparent success of Biddle's undertakings was corrupting the financial mores of every American state. Following the example of the Bank of the United States, each commonwealth in turn sought to support the cotton market by chartering new banks and selling fresh issues of stock. Wild-cat banks sprang up thruout the South and West, issuing paper currency in unlimited quantities and accumulating millions of demand liabilities against trifling reserves.[68] Speculation in public land revived. What Biddle was attempting on a large scale, other speculators with more limited resources were also engaged in.[69] Public works set in motion to provide relief in the unemployment crisis of 1837 required funds for their completion.[70] The New York stock market teemed with companies and projects. The competition of railroad promoters revived. Massachusetts sought a sterling loan to complete her railway from Worcester toward Albany. New York not only enlarged the Erie Canal, but commenced a railway to Buffalo through the southern counties. The Reading Railroad challenged the monopoly of the Schulkill Canal. Richmond, Charleston and Savannah sought to renew the already fading prestige of the Old South with transportation lines to rival the northern routes. States which had borrowed money before issued new securities to continue their public improvements and to meet interest as it accrued upon their prior obligations. Arkansas, Missouri, Georgia now developed state banking systems and public debts.

The Bank of the United States was of course not the only channel thru which these stocks reached London, just as Biddle was not the only cotton speculator. Such intermediaries as the Morris Canal Bank and the North American Trust Company handled some of the more questionable stocks. Massachusetts dealt directly with Baring Brothers. The old East India house of which J. Horsley Palmer, a personage in the Bank of England parlors, was the head, floated sterling loans for South Carolina, Florida and other states, thus financing American imports of Chinese tea and silk. American agents began to appear directly in London to solicit funds. George Peabody founded in 1837 the banking house now known as Morgan, Grenfell & Co., and organized a market for Maryland securities. Generals, congressmen and canal commissioners roved from London to Paris, and from Paris to Amsterdam and Hamburg, leaving neat packages of engraved paper in their wake, and accepting handsome emoluments from grateful clients on their return. "This is the time for Virginia to make a loan for the purposes of internal improvements," wrote the American minister near the court of St. James's. "I can make any loan for the State, to the amount of five or ten millions, that she may want, irredeemable or not, for fifty years. Rely on it, she will never have so good a chance. It will not be necessary to send out an agent. Why not let me negotiate for them, before I return?" [71]

And what is to be said of the infatuation with which the London money market regarded this inundation of American stocks? Begun in shrewd calculation of the interest of the investor and of British economy, swollen to dangerous limits in support of the "open credit" system, the flow of British capital to the United States had created a vested interest in its prosperity which warped the judgment of the leading merchant-bankers. No other conclusion is possible. In distributing securities abroad Biddle had been quick to appraise the prestige which the Bank of the United States and his own personality enjoyed in consequence of their political prominence. The fact that he was a cultured gentleman and of Quaker birth did not diminish the regard in which he was held. "We found the most eminent Bankers of London," states Henry Burgess in apology for a decade of propaganda on behalf of American stocks, "many of the most cautious and successful Country Bankers, some of the most renowed statesmen . . . and a conspicuous bill-broker [Samuel Gurney] who virtually directs the course of investment for one-half of the surplus floating banking capital of the country, all inspired with the same confidence in Nicholas Biddle." [72] This confidence in the man procured an enormous following for the stocks and short-term securities of his institution. Merchants and bankers of the first rank sought them for their reserves and recommended them to their favored clients. It was purchasing preferred shares in the prosperity of the United States. By 1841, 197,551 shares in the United States Bank out of 350,000 were held in Europe.[73] This was by all odds the strongest element in the Biddle system. It created a large and powerful interest in Great Britain bound to support the credit of the Bank against hostile criticism, and as a corollary American credit in general, so long as it had a particle of substance.[74]

THE COLLAPSE OF BIDDLE'S SYSTEM

A succession of events, political and economic, united to bring the Biddle system to disaster in 1839, and to wreck the credit which it had been the medium of restoring for a time to American enterprise. The resources of the London money market were, in the first place, imperilled by the crop failure of 1838 which necessitated the expenditure in that year and the one succeeding of ten million pounds for foreign grain.[75] At the same time the new textile industries of Belgium, Prussia and Saxony reached a crisis in their development which curtailed their demand for English yarn. The consequent strain upon the resources of the Bank of England was only partly relieved by large gold borrowings from the Bank of France. The stoppage of the Bank of Belgium in December, 1838, was an early symptom of acute financial malaise throughout western Europe. The political news from all parts of the world was of the most unsettling nature. In the Near East a major European crisis was brewing over the pretensions of Mehemet Ali. In Asia the Afghan border seethed with intrigue and unrest. In China the dispute over the opium traffic was sundering a highly important link in the foreign trade system both of Great Britain and of the United States.[76] There was a French blockade at Buenos Ayres, destroying trade to protect the merchants. At home the Chartist movement was alarming to fundholders, while the periodic flare-ups over the Maine boundary were causing private investors to turn a deaf ear to the blandishments of American securities.[77]

Thus at the very moment when the slackening demand for cotton rendered it desirable for the speculators to be able to retain their stocks of cotton, the current of investment which alone could make this possible ceased to flow toward the United States. Strategic control of the cotton market now rested with the buyers in Great Britain. Early in the spring of 1839 the competitive cotton spinners agreed to terminate their competition for supplies of cotton, restricted their purchases and went on short-time.[78] To rescue the large American interests dependent upon the price of cotton, Biddle's cotton combination was revived. That strategist had retired from the presidency of his bank in March, 1839, possibly foreseeing disaster. However, he directed the dealings organized thru the agency of S. V. S. Wilder, the respected New York correspondent of *Hottinguer et cie* of Paris and Havre.[79] It was proposed to advance three-fourths in value upon every unsold bale of the 1838 crop computed at fourteen cents a pound, to enable it to be held for six months by Humphries & Biddle. At the same time southern politicians such as George McDuffie and James Hamilton bestirred themselves with ideas of "direct trade" and a credit scheme to stabilize cotton prices independently of the northern banks.[80]

The Wilder speculation began auspiciously. Cotton recovered in price for a few weeks, but then sank rapidly as the spinners held together and the rising discount rate of the Bank of England discouraged fresh enterprise. Jaudon was called upon to meet the Humphries & Biddle bills as they came due, and he circulated post-notes industriously. But the limit had been reached. England would buy neither cotton nor securities. With a million pounds of notes maturing in the autumn and its safe full of unsaleable stocks and bonds, Jaudon's agency found itself in an impossible position. It was enabled to go on for a month by drafts upon Hottinguers. But at the beginning of September Jaudon was compelled to announce defeat and the Biddle system collapsed. The interest of the European shareholders in the Bank of the United States brought them to the defense of its maturing notes. No less than £800,000 were raised among these friends upon a two-year loan for the Bank. Three months later the balance of the Bank's obligations abroad were covered by loans from the Paris Rothschilds and Hope & Co., secured by an apparently ample margin of bonds of Mississippi, Illinois, Indiana and Pennsylvania.[81] But the cotton at Liverpool had to be released for what it would bring.

The speculators calculated their losses at $900,000, much of which managed to fall upon the Bank of the United States.[82]

Not all the support of the merchant-bankers of Europe could, however, secure additional credit for the sponsors of so disastrous a speculation. Success could have been forgiven, even at the expense of spinners and operatives. Failure was ignominious. And without additional credit American finance could no longer sustain the artificial fabric of fraudulent prosperity. Values must be deflated; real as well as paper wealth destroyed; thousands turned bankrupt and rendered property-less; a few made richer or wiser; and an intolerable burden of debt and capitalization incurred at high money prices absorbed at lower levels before it was possible for the development of the United States to continue. Angered at the folly with which they had incurred indebtedness, American commonwealths sought to vent their rage upon the obliging creditors. And from the collapse of American trade and banking and from the succeeding epidemic of private bankruptcy and public repudiation there arose a debacle of American credit as complete as the confidence which it had formerly elicited had been unquestioning. The tide of revulsion flowed anew in England against the foreign borrower. Investors wrote down their hopes of gain from six to three per cent and dumped their reproductive American loans upon the speculative dust-heap with the mortgages upon Colombia and the dishonored bonds of Spain. The trade of three continents dwindled by a half. And England of the Reform age cried out from economic deformity.

CHAPTER IV

MIGRATION OF CAPITAL AT A STAND

"It is a divine thing to lend; to owe, an heroic virtue."
—Rabelais, III, ch. 4..

THOSE PERFIDIOUS UNITED STATES

It is useful to recall that eighty years before the British debt settlement of 1923 there were few regions in the world whose public treasuries and private enterprises had as little credit as those of the United States. There had been a decade during which American trade, transportation and banking flourished extravagantly as a function of the credit policy of British bankers and the investment taste of their clients. And then there was a decade during which there was no market in London for any American security, however valuable intrinsically. There were more promising investments, to be sure, in the railway business. And for once in a way Great Britain was turned from her perennial search for foreign markets to find her best customers at home. But what caused American stocks to join those of Portugal and Mexico and Greece in the ghettoes of finance was the failure of nine sovereign commonwealths to pay the interest upon their debts.

It is not easy to do justice to the many elements involved in the overthrow of American credit. Certainly a large share of the responsibility must be laid upon the politicians of the Jackson school. They had sought professedly to place the United States upon a "hard money" basis, to rid her of foreign and centralized banking control, to stabilize prices in the interest of farmers and laborers, and broadly to favor the South and West at the expense of the mercantile and manufacturing East. Actually their policy, with its low luxury tariff and the deposit of government funds in "pet banks," encouraged the worst excesses of the inflation period, and by supplementing the Specie Circular with the Independent Treasury bill, contributed to the violence of the reaction. While opposing federal efforts at internal improvements, they had by the distribution of the Treasury surplus definitely stimulated the undertaking of public works by the several states. Now that those improvements had involved the states heavily in debt, "locofocoism" threw doubt upon the validity of the bonds and displayed no ardor for their repayment.

The lead in discrediting state securities was taken by the Senate of the United States. On March 6, 1840, it adopted resolutions which expressly disclaimed the responsibility of the federal government for the debts. The committee report went out of its way to censure severely the states which had incurred them. Only with difficulty the more radical resolutions of Benton were suppressed.[1] But in the party press and state legislatures the "locofoco" element had full rein. These were the years of the anti-rent movement in New York, of the Dorr rebellion in Rhode Island. Leggett and Brisbane and Brownson were oracles of an egalitarian opinion which verged upon communism. In Pennsylvania, Maryland and other states the government fell entirely into the hands of the debtor classes and their political champions. The delay of Pennsylvania in paying her semi-annual dividends due in February, 1840, was an earnest of what was to follow over the country.

For more than a year after the closing of Jaudon's agency in London, the value of merchandise and securities gradually declined, while the Bank of the United States sought to put its affairs in shape to resume specie payment. It had led the van in supporting American credit in 1837. The brunt of the universal depression now fell upon it. Biddle's generous financiering had fallen upon stony soil. The Bank found in its coffers southern bills secured on crops whose value had been steadily declining. Its northern acceptances were on behalf of merchants who failed successively with the retailers to whom they had traded. In liquidating these accounts and the cotton speculation the Bank came into possession of quantities of stocks and bonds which were becoming progressively unmarketable at any price. Most of the banks which had sprung up under its protection, North as well as South, were failing with negligible assets. And they were heavily in debt to the Philadelphia institution. In the summer of 1840, for instance, the Morris Canal Bank, which had been a contractor for state bonds and a speculator in others, collapsed. Its liabilities included large sums still unpaid to Illinois and Michigan upon bond contracts, but the bonds were not among its assets. They had been assigned long since to innocent foreign possessors.

In February, 1841, after a brief attempt at resumption, the United States Bank suspended for the last time and presently went into the hands of an unsympathetic committee for liquidation.[2] And so its mad, greedy, glorious experiment in financial nationalism came to an end. Its management had been doubtless corrupt, certainly imprudent. But it had never set up narrow advantage in opposition to a conception of economic good which was nation-wide in scope. The Bank never profited a tithe as much in prosperity at the expense of interior farmers and merchants, as in its ruin the seaboard merchants, shipowners and noteshavers gained by forced sales of goods and real estate.[3] With its failure the last ground of faith in American credit was swept away, so far as Europe was concerned. And this not only because the notes and shares of the Bank were largely held abroad. In its fall it carried with it states which had depended upon it for loans to meet their interest payments. A wave of bankruptcy swept over the states of the Union, and involved most of them in one form or another of what was broadly termed "repudiation."

It is possible to find much sympathy for some of the states which suffered from the failure of the Bank and other agents. Politician-speculators had run them into debt for advantages which were often as much private as public. It was not easy for the politician-farmer who had enjoyed only a temporary advantage to shoulder the responsibility. Credit institutions swept away, markets disorganized, his slender hoard was needed entire to keep his farm going from year to year and to meet land office payments as they fell due. In many cases store and homestead were sold to meet the claims of eastern creditors. "Instead of $200,000,000 seeking the west on credit through the hands of merchants and dealers," wrote a sympathetic observer, "loading the canals and public works, and employing armies of laborers and speculators . . . the remains of these loans and credits are coming back in produce, at low money prices. Every $100 which was then borrowed at a value equal to 10 barrels of flour, is now being repaid, if at all, in a value equal to 20 barrels of flour."[4] The debts incurred had really been far beyond the means of pioneer states. In Louisiana, for instance, a three dollar tax upon every man, woman and child in the state would have been necessary to meet the annual interest, if taxation were to be resorted to.[5] And there were reasons why this was not feasible. Why should the pioneer farmer remain to be taxed? Land was cheap and unlimited beyond the Mississippi. His household had not forgotten how to be self-supporting. A very small tax in one place, Charles Francis Adams pointed out, would cause small owners to sell out for what they could get and leave the burden to fall upon less migratory capitalists.[6]

In the face of the unwillingness of all classes to be taxed to pay interest, there was in most states no recourse. The public works on which the borrowings had been spent were incomplete and therefore unproductive.[7] Of all the enterprises financed by guaranteed bonds the Baltimore & Ohio Railroad was the only one which had so far met its interest from its own revenues.[8] There was much of the money raised by bond sales which had never reached the state treasuries at all. Some states had pledged their credit to banks whose assets had been dissipated in cotton and realty speculations. And the reflection that such obligations could not be quite binding derived a gloss of patriotic sanctity from the consideration that much of the debt was owed abroad and to non-Christians.[9]

Under these circumstances nine states stopped payment of interest in the course of 1841 and 1842.[10] Two states, Michigan and Mississippi, repudiated them outright (Michigan only in part) on the twofold ground that they had been contracted *ultra vires*, i. e.—in an unconstitutional manner, and that the contracts had been broken by the unwarranted conduct of agents. Florida pleaded minority; she was only a territory, a ward of the federal government, when her debt was contracted and constitutionally unable to incur any obligation. Indiana, Illinois, Louisiana, Arkansas, Pennsylvania and Maryland merely professed their inability to pay without announcing formally that they did not intend to do so. Thus one hundred million dollars in deflated securities were piled upon the losses from banking, canal and mercantile investments which the British had already suffered in the United States. Three states had declared that they would never pay their debts. There was no certainty that others would not follow their example. And those Englishmen who were willing to purchase stocks cheaply of Englishmen more timorous said confidently that they would.

It was highly embarrassing for an American to be in London in the winter of 1842–43. The securities which had gone into default had been purchased at a premium by large numbers of the governing classes. And the resentment which they felt at their mistaken judgment spread without delay to all persons and things American. The United States were held collectively responsible for the shortcomings of their members. Business letters to merchants of impeccable standing contained impertinent allusions to American credit. English houses took pains to let their clients know that they owned no American stocks.[11] At least one American of irreproachable antecedents was barred admission to a London club, specifically because he belonged to a republic which did not fulfil its engagements.[12] And schoolboys were encouraged to render *"ad kalendas graccas"* as "the American dividends."[13] The caustic pen of Sydney Smith, a professional liberal who did not lose gracefully on the stock market, has preserved the sentiments of that winter in his "Humble Petition to the House of Congress at Washington."[14]

Your petitioner lent to the State of Pennsylvania a sum of money for the purpose of some public improvements. The amount, though small, is to him important, and is a saving from a life income, made with difficulty and privation. If their refusal to pay (from which a very large number of English families are suffering) had been the result of war, produced by the unjust aggression of powerful enemies; if it had arisen from civil discord; if it had proceeded from an improvident application of means in the first years of self-government; if it were the act of a poor State struggling·against the barrenness of nature, every friend of America would have been contented to wait for better times; but the fraud is committed in profound peace, by Pennsylvania, the richest State in the Union, after the wise investment of the borrowed money in roads and canals, of which the repudiators are every day reaping the advantage. It is an act of bad faith which (all its circumstances considered) has no parallel, and no excuse.

Nor is it only the loss of property which your petitioner laments; he laments still more that immense power which the bad faith of America has given to aristocratical opinions, and to the enemies of free institutions in the Old World. It is in vain any longer to appeal to history, and to point out the wrongs which the many have received from the few. The Americans who boast to have improved the institutions of the Old World have at least equalled its crimes. A great nation, after trampling under foot all earthly tyranny, has been guilty of a fraud as enormous as ever disgraced the worst king of the most degraded nation of Europe.

. . . Little did the friends of America expect it, and sad is the spectacle, to see you rejected by every State in Europe, as a nation with whom no contract will be made, because none will be kept; unstable in the very foundations of social life, deficient in the elements of good faith—men who prefer any load of infamy, however great, to any pressure of taxation, however light.

So saddening was the spectacle that possessors of American stocks lost no opportunity to contrive its removal. Scarcely was it plain that Biddle's experiment had broken down, when Baring Brothers began an agitation to persuade the federal government to assume the responsibility for the state debts. The idea first occurred to Samuel Jaudon;

and London merchants easily gathered the impression that Whigs of the Webster school were likely to carry out this policy. And so the Whig cause in the campaign of 1840 received generous support from England. American politics, however, are not easily manipulated. The most important contribution made by the victorious Whigs to relieve the economic situation was a national bankruptcy act which is said to have extinguished mercantile debts to foreign creditors running into millions of pounds.[15] Political propaganda was early abandoned by London in favor of financial boycott.

In the summer of 1842, agents of the United States Treasury appeared in London soliciting a loan to cover the shortage which the decline of the import trade was causing in the customs receipts. They met a cold reception. "The people of the United States may be fully persuaded," thundered the *Times*, "that there is a certain class of securities to which no abundance of money, however great, can give value; and that in this class their own securities stand pre-eminent."[16] Bankers echoed the refrain. "You may tell your government," said the Paris Rothschild to Duff Green, "that you have seen the man who is at the head of the finances of Europe, and that he has told you that they cannot borrow a dollar, not a dollar."[17] The difficulty, as Overend, Gurney & Co. explained to the commissioners, was that American credit stood too low. Nevertheless that credit could be enhanced. If the federal government assumed the debts of the defaulting states, or of all of the states, bankers would be appeased.[18]

The Congress was deaf to the reiterated suggestion. A report favorable to assumption was drawn up by a House committee and presented on the last day of Tyler's first congress too late to be acted upon. In the interminable squabbles of the sessions which succeeded it, the proposal became lost to view entirely.[19] And meanwhile reviving trade in the United States had made it possible for the Treasury to borrow money in New York.[20] The London boycott crumbled. New methods for causing dividends to flourish must be employed.

The scheme which now met with favor was to advance money to the bankrupts to enable them to put their public works upon a paying basis. Thru the perseverance of George Peabody the Baltimore and Ohio Railroad secured money with which to reach the Cumberland coal district, and dividends were soon resumed upon the entire Maryland debt.[21] Illinois bondholders advanced a million dollars to complete her canal works.[22] Indiana pawned the Wabash canal to her creditors for half the principal of their claims. Michigan turned over her public works for the portion of her debt which she acknowledged. In the cotton states another device was possible. There banks were compelled to accept state bonds in payment of notes and mortgages. So a steady stream of bonds started from England in payment for cotton, and were automatically retired when American planters used them to pay off their debts.[23]

Thus some Englishmen profited at the expense of other Englishmen while the commercial wheel performed its dilatory circuit in the channels of American trade. In due time reviving commerce swelled the revenues of American corporations and public bodies. Dividends were resumed by all but the three repudiating states. Some who had lost money won it back, while others were not able for many years to forget Sydney Smith, or to learn the unwisdom of buying at the top and selling at the bottom. With an important exception, the Illinois Central Railroad, it was fully a generation before the investor-at-large, as contrasted with the banker, merchant or jobber, ventured with confidence into the field of American securities.[24]

THE MISSING DIVIDENDS OF BACKWARD STATES

It is to be considered that it was not innate depravity which underlay the failure of the American states to pay their debts. They could not do so until their citizens had written down their hopes of sudden gain, and until the movements of trade gave value to the goods they were able to supply. It had been easy for England to export merchandise and defer payments by means of a credit transaction. What was difficult was to get the investment of capital to produce means of its repayment. What was difficult was to stir backward regions by its application to produce a surplus of goods for export. That the American South was doing. It was the result more of a highly concentrated market for its goods than of British investments during the twenties and thirties. The nascent economic nationalism of the United States collapsed with the Bank; its revival in more complicated form came slowly. It awaited an open British grain market, the completion of transportation systems into the Middle West, and the movements of population from Ireland and the Germanies.

Economic backwardness was likewise an important element in the bankruptcy of the Spanish-speaking world. Napoleon had thrown its political life into confusion. And the consequences of his action did not diminish in importance. For both New Spain and Old its influence upon economic relations was cumulative and distressing. The case of Mexico is representative of the financial problems which confronted the new republics.

As the Viceroyalty of New Spain, Mexico in 1803 furnished a revenue to its government of more than twenty million dollars. Its internal administration cost ten millions and a half, and the balance went to the upkeep of less productive colonies and was remitted to the Spanish Treasury.[25] A half century of liberalized trade had given a distinct capitalistic trend to her economic life. The produce of the mines had doubled; the haciendas produced wheat for export, as well as the cochineal indispensable for dyeing calico; while the development of manufactures under the domestic system supplied the bulk of the clothing of the Europeanized part of the population. There was thus a large volume of trade, internal as well as foreign, and a generation of enterprising Spanish merchants controlling it were rapidly coming to dominate the economic life of the entire colony.

It is not surprising, perhaps, that precisely this class suffered most from the break with Spain. Forced loans were levied upon them to support the wars for independence. Their markets were destroyed, trade interrupted, their connection with dependent miners and manufacturers and agriculturists disorganized. And long before their definitive expulsion in 1828, most of them had turned their property into cash and left the country. It is supposed that they carried with them one hundred million dollars in specie.[26] And there went with them the whole of the organized economic life of Mexico.

British and American traders were not slow to fill the place left vacant in the conduct of foreign trade. British capital, as we have seen, was encouraged to rehabilitate the ruined mines. But the social as well as the political and economic solidarity of the country had been shattered. Some men sought quiet in the self-sufficiency of their estates. Others sought wealth in the exploitation of political power, or in lower orders of society in vagrancy or banditry. Thus mines and internal trade which had been the basis of taxation under the viceroyalty, proved unavailing under the republic. The chief sources of revenue became duties on the import of manufactures and on the export of precious metals. And it was difficult enough to enforce the collection of them. No one estimates the smuggling trade at less than one-third of Mexico's commerce between 1825 and 1850. And in no year during that time was the Mexican treasury able to raise more than thirteen million dollars in taxes. At the same time it was more expensive to run a republic than a viceroyalty. Mexico had been created by her army; and successive revolutions imposed the prime necessity of keeping that army well provided for. The budget of expenditures ranged from fifteen to twenty million dollars a year.[27] Forced loans and delinquent salaries made up the deficit; and officials managed to make a living by devices which effectually prevented the revenue from increasing. There was plunder enough to be made out of control of the offices; at least immunity from spoliation by others. And the literate classes devoted the bulk of their activity to struggles for that control. "Between 1821 and 1857 the country had more than a half dozen forms of government, under imperial and republican regencies, empire and federal, central and dictatorial rules of varying shades, and over fifty different administrations, for which fully two hundred and fifty revolutions were undertaken." [28]

It is amazing that foreign bondholders got anything out of Mexico at all. Under terror at a possible Spanish invasion the new republic floated two usurious loans in London in 1824 and 1825 for a total nominal sum of £6,400,000. A little more than eleven million dollars was actually placed at the disposal of the Mexican treasury.[29] The original interest burden was about a million dollars and a half, and was met at first out of the proceeds of the loans. Both of the London firms which acted as agents failed in the course of 1826—Barclays' with a whole year's interest on hand; and dividends to October, 1827 were advanced by Baring Brothers. Then struggles between Yorkinos and Escosses distracted Mexico; there were alarms of invasion from Spain, and the dividends failed. It was 1830 before the conservative government of Bustamente sought an understanding with the bondholders. They agreed to fund the dividend arrears at twice the market price of Mexican stocks, and to defer the interest thereon. To secure payment for the future of interest upon the original debt, Mexico assigned one-sixth of the customs duties at Vera Cruz and Tampico, her two chief ports, to be collected by the vice-consuls of Great Britain. For their part bondholders brought pressure to bear upon the Foreign Office to give informal assurance that the encroachment of Spain or the United States would not be tolerated.[30] And dividends were paid for two years. Then a series of revolutions made the restless Santa Anna president, and the customs receipts were diverted to other purposes. Barings threw up the agency in disgust.

After the loss of Texas, Mexico made a fresh attempt in 1837 under the second Bustamente administration to adjust her finances. A conversion scheme was launched under the auspices of F. Lizardi & Co., merchants in the Gulf trade. The original loans and accumulated arrears were turned into one consolidated debt at 5% interest, one-half of which was to be called "active" and to pay interest immediately, while the remainder was not to bear interest for ten years. Dividend coupons were to be receivable, if unpaid on maturity, in payment of customs in Mexico at a fixed rate of exchange, while it was sought to give value to the deferred debt by a colonization scheme. The deferred bonds with interest were receivable for unappropriated lands in Texas, Chihuahua, Sonora, New Mexico and California at the rate of four acres to the pound sterling. A reversal of Mexico's immigration policy was involved. Nothing came of the arrangement but intrigues which enhanced American suspicion of English motives in Texas and California.[31]

Indeed no part of the conversion scheme brought dividends. There was a French blockade of Vera Cruz in 1838 and a campaign which Mexicans refer to as the "pastry war." This cut off trade, and revenues dependent on it. There were fresh revolutions. The first dividends came in 1842 with the triumph of Santa Anna. Mexican stock rose rapidly in value, but within a year dividends began to be dilatory. Controversy developed between bondholders' committees and the Mexican agents, which swelled into open scandal in 1844 when Lizardis connived at the seizure of the assigned portion of the customs from the hands of the vice-consuls. About the same time the Stock Exchange discovered that it was dealing in securities which bore higher numbers than were supposed to be in existence; and it came out that on the rising market Lizardi & Co. had secretly floated more than a million and a half pounds of wholly new Mexican bonds, the proceeds of which had gone in large part to pay their 7½% commission upon the face value of the entire converted debt.[32] Thus the nominal total of Mexico's debt had been raised to £11,000,000, upon an original advance of as many dollars.

The war precipitated by President Polk chastened the spirit of Mexican politicians. It persuaded bondholders to write down their interest expectations from five to three per cent. And it brought Mexico an indemnity for her territorial losses which London was able to get hold of to redeem the unpaid

coupons which accumulated during the war. A fresh as-
signment of customs was made, and Mexico was guaranteed
from further loss at the hands of imprudent or rascally
London banks by an agreement to turn over the money to
an agent of the bondholders stationed in the country. There
was constant friction over the assigned revenues, but interest
was paid with fair regularity until 1857 when that series
of revolutions began which culminated in the French intervention. This brought an era of frenzied financiering
which opened another chapter in the history of Mexican
economy. Down to this time bondholders had been paid
nearly thirty million dollars upon their loans.[33]   And the
Mexican debt had doubled.

Mexico and her finances did not constitute a horrible example. Between 1826 and 1850 the dividends paid upon
the securities of Spanish-speaking countries were negligible,
and the prospect of ultimate redemption grew more hopeless
with each of the incessant conversion schemes which gave
constant employment to many London financiers. For whatever the economic potentialities of the population, their
energies were exhausted in political turmoil. Factions and
particularism were rampant in South America. Colombia
and Guatemala had broken up into half a dozen quarrelling
republics, and the division of their common liabilities to
foreign creditors was an opportunity for dissension which
they did not neglect. Only such military dictators as Rosas
in Buenos Ayres and Francia in Paraguay maintained a
semblance of political authority, and their régimes subsisted
in part by abetting suspicion of European relations. Fear
of Spain as an engine of government was succeeded by enmity
of neighboring republics; and intermittent war went on
between adjacent states when revolution did not occupy them
internally. In the mother kingdoms of Spain and Portugal

affairs were no better. Carlists and Miguelists harassed
successive governments with their escapades; loyal generals
intrigued for the favors of Maria and Isabella. The empire
of Brazil was the one example of stability amid these political phantasmogoria. Everywhere else government was a
struggle between public spoliation and private immunity,
and foreign creditors received short shrift.

None of the Spanish states effectively disowned its debts.
Each had an abiding sense that it might wish to borrow
more money, indeed sought to do so. From time to time
agents appeared in London to arrange a compromise with
the bondholders, to resume payment of dividends, and perhaps to be so fortunate as to secure an advance of more money
to go on with. And scarcely a year went by without its
compromise with one of the delinquent states. Their terms
differed in detail rather than in conception. Essentially they
involved the funding of dividend arrears into new stock,
and the deferment of interest thereon for several years, while
payments were resumed upon the old. But the terms might
differ widely. At what rate should the arrears be funded,
and what interest should the newly created stock bear? The
original bonds were selling in the market at the nominal
prices of 15 or 20. If the arrears were funded at par, the
bondholders would sacrifice four-fifths of their dividend
claims. On the other hand, if they were funded at 20, an
intolerable burden would be added to the debt, with an enormous bounty to the bondholders if the country did get onto a
paying basis. A debt of five millions would be created for
every million of arrears. Here was a matter for compromise
if not for sharp bargaining. As between the republics and
the bondholders the London issuing agents continually pressed
the advantages of reissuing old bonds and arrears in new
common stock, thus tending to veil the interest which bond-

holders were sacrificing, giving an opportunity for market operations to improve the price of the bonds, and incidentally bringing a good commission to the agents. Under these conversions, which were frequent, the principal of the debt of most of the Latin American countries mounted rapidly. Some of the unpaid dividends were usually sacrificed in one way or another, but as a rule no sum once recognized as principal. As security for continued patience bondholders were given some sort of mortgage on the customs of the various countries, which formed their most reliable source of revenue, and which brought important advantages to the British merchants residing abroad to whose care this control was intrusted. Nourished by these agreements and by occasional advances, dividends frequently began to flow, only to fail when a new war or revolution transpired.[84]

INVESTORS AND THE FOREIGN OFFICE

What is astonishing in this record of finance in Old Spain and New is not that the governments found it difficult to pay usurious debts, but that their political status was not impaired in consequence. Fifty million pounds in foreign government stocks were in default at one time in the early forties, with unpaid dividends from five to twenty years overdue. Yet the Foreign Office did not land marines or take over the Treasury of a single country. It is customary for modern states, like the United States under Roosevelt or Great Britain under Salisbury or Grey, to do something in such cases on behalf of bondholders, something dramatic, and not necessarily inexpensive. Customs control, financial advisors, armed intervention, political sterilization—modern diplomacy provides a bag of tricks that will astonish the unwary issuer of doubtful bonds. Solvency is the prime requisite of sovereignty; recognition, freedom of action, even independence depend upon placating the foreign creditors. Not so in early Victorian diplomacy. Downing Street stirred not to collect a penny advanced by loanmongers and cotton merchants to economically backward countries. It told distinguished bankers to their faces that they had loaned their money on their own responsibility, had exacted high interest in compensation for the risk which they ran, and must depend upon their own exertions to recover their principal and interest.

To Castlereagh, who was Foreign Secretary from 1812 to 1822 when the foreign loan business began, the matter was highly embarrassing. He was engaged in extricating his government from a situation in which it had been financing half of the governments of Europe by means of subsidies and guaranteed loans which were only subsidies in disguise. And when loan-agents sought to entice him into declarations which would encourage the market for their offerings, they were sharply rebuffed. Castlereagh feared that in some way his government might be involved in financial responsibility, and that at best its diplomacy might be involved in matters of irrelevant concern. For the profitable investment of money abroad was not regarded as an interest of the United Kingdom. And protection of investment, it was felt, would be required only if in some specific way the government stood sponsor for a loan. British diplomats were not tender-minded on the matter of intervention. The restored regime in Europe, of which Castlereagh was a chief architect, rested upon a general policy of intervention. But the interests for which the British were ready to intervene were mainly political. The balance of power, the independence of the Low Countries and of the Spanish peninsula, the freedom

of the seas, and the defense of English trade, had been traditional objects of British foreign policy. The suppression
of the slave trade and the championship of liberalism were
added to them as corollaries; and it was also a corollary that
Castlereagh did not find it a British interest to intervene
with the Confederation of Europe on behalf of absolutism
in Naples and in Spain. Nor were foreign loans an interest
to be promoted and conserved. True there is no better source
of information for post-Waterloo finance than the dispatches
of British ambassadors from the various European capitals.
But Castlereagh's interest in the fiscal arrangements of the
great powers was political and military rather than economic.
International disagreements were already being settled less
by *coups de canon* than by *coups d'emprunt.* And loans
bulked relatively large in the finances of any state. It was
imperative to know all about them.

But the problem of unpaid dividends did not confront
Castlereagh. It first arose in 1823 when South American
merchants besieged the Foreign Office for relief, particularly
with reference to the Colombian loan of 1822 which was
already in default. Canning was invited to make acknowl-
edgment of such obligations a condition of recognition of the
Latin republics. He flatly refused.[85] And he "distinctly
apprized" the contractors for the loan that "His Majesty's
Government would in no case feel themselves at liberty to
make the Colombian Loan the subject of National Interference. Such an interference if adopted in respect to the
Colombian Loan would be expected equally by the Contractors
and Holders of other Loans negotiated with other unacknowl-
edged States of South America. The Colombian Loan like
all those other transactions having been entered into by the
Parties with a perfect knowledge that their Government
was in no degree implicated in their proceedings."[86]   A

diplomatic agent to Mexico who promised the political influence of Great Britain to secure repayment of a loan was summarily recalled and his action disavowed.[37]   Nor was Canning more zealous on behalf of unpaid mercantile claims. "Assistance would in no case extend to the claiming as from Government to Government, the discharge of a debt due by a Foreign Government to an individual British subject." [38] And when after the burst of enthusiasm for South American loans in 1824 and 1825 the bottom fell out of the market as they fell into default, the attitude of the Foreign Office remained unchanged.   It would receive memorials from disappointed merchants and investors and forward them thru diplomatic agents to the governments at fault.   It would not move officially in the matter.

Certainly Canning did not achieve his popularity with commercial men in his own time and since by the closeness with which he timed his foreign policy to the movements of the markets.   Few British statesmen have held more rigorously aloof from speculative contacts.   He curbed the mercantile activities of British consular agents.   And he censored those of foreign representatives in London.   He refused to negotiate thru agents who were in a position to profit from diplomatic confidences.   His foreign policies tended to promote British trade.   But it was the trade which meant political prestige and was measured in the statistical summaries, not shipments of Manchester goods to Callao, which engaged his attention.   The development of his South American policy is to be accounted for chiefly in terms of political relations with Europe and the United States.   But Canning was not all-powerful in his government, nor were all of his colleagues so scrupulous.   Some of them were investors in South American mining companies.   And when the time came for Canning's diplomacy to culminate in the recognition of South American independence, he pressed as one reason for its approval by the cabinet the large financial interests of many British subjects in South America.[39]

Under Aberdeen and Palmerston, who were responsible for most of the characteristics of British foreign policy from 1828 to 1866, the rigor of Canning's administration was gradually relaxed. Consuls were allowed once more to trade upon their own account. And Palmerston at least had no compunction about using the prestige and navy of Great Britain for the economic advantage of individuals. The Opium wars in China and the Don Pacifico intervention in Greece are too well-known to require elaboration. The persons and property of British merchants abroad became sacrosanct and gunboats swarmed the sea for their protection. But disappointed bondholders were still put off with promises that "friendly offices" would be used on their behalf. And the great moral heroism of paying debts joined the subjects upon which British ministers abroad periodically lectured foreign governments, along with the iniquity of the slave trade, the beauties of liberal government, and the advantages of low tariffs.

"Friendly offices" were permitted to go farther. Consuls were permitted to become agents for the bondholders abroad, to hold funds for their account, and by the management of monopolies and customs to participate in their collection. This was all on a plane below that of diplomatic action. The consuls acted in these respects on their own account, not as British officials. Nevertheless it may be believed that it was difficult for politicians in unenlightened countries to perceive the chasm which separated the official from the unofficial activity of these agents. British prestige abroad found fruitful occupation, while Downing Street escaped responsibility. So consuls bestirred themselves in negotiating concessions which would bring dividends to the bondholders and commissions to themselves. A great deal of the Central American debt was turned into tobacco monopolies in the respective states.[40] In Chile one active consul-general procured the confiscation and sale of church lands, but was unable to obtain the proceeds for his clients.[41] In Mexico and elsewhere the consulate adjoined the customs-house; all invoices were made out in duplicate, and importers paid a percentage of their duty direct to the British consul as agent for the bondholders. Only one of these many undertakings brought financial relief to the government and punctual dividends to the bondholders. This was the Peruvian guano contract, a monopoly of the export of guano from the Lobos and Chincha Islands which was secured in 1842 by Antony Gibbs & Sons.[42] What assistance British diplomacy rendered in arranging this matter, if any, is not known.

But Palmerston performed none of his celebrated interventions on behalf of bondholders, or for investors of any kind who were not personally on the ground. He successfully blocked efforts of the Greek national assembly in 1833 to make provision for the loans the Philhellenes had floated.[43] And so far from being influenced by foreign investors in his eastern policy, Palmerston signed the four-power pact against Mehemet Ali in 1840 expressly against the protests of the City.[43a]

It must be allowed that British public opinion as a whole did not deprecate this unreadiness of the Foreign Office to champion foreign investments as an object of paramount national interest. In 1843 small holders of the defaulted stocks of North American states drew up memorials of protest which were conveyed to the United States government under diplomatic seal. But the opinion was candidly expressed that where Barings and Rothschilds had failed For-

eign Office representations would be of little avail.[44]   The
Times declared on another occasion that the government
would "depart from every profession which it has made . . .
if it hazarded an hour of national peace, or wasted a shilling
of public money, to secure the fulfilment of contracts which
it neither invited nor guaranteed." [45]

But precisely such action was demanded by the holders
of bonds of many of the Hispanic nations, and the more insistently as those securities came to be concentrated in the
hands of a few wealthy individuals prominent upon the
Stock Exchange.[46]   Committees were formed to represent
the interests of aggrieved investors, mainly composed of
stockbrokers and merchants.   There was a "Spanish Bondholders' Committee" as early as 1827, and most of the other
delinquent goverments gave name to similar bodies by 1829.
A "Colombian Bondholders' Committee" contained so representative a group of men that it developed into a "Central
& South American Bondholders' " organization.   A second
group looked after the important case of Mexico.   These
committees held meetings of their clientele occasionally.
They carried on continuous negotiations with the agents of
foreign governments, sent endless memorials to the Foreign
Office, and consumed much time and office stationery in
endeavors which did not fail to receive full publicity.   When
conversions and other fresh financing were afoot the committees formed a convenient means of forming the opinion
of those most likely to be interested.   But the principal result of their gestures was a continual movement of the bonds
in question upon the Stock Exchange,' which must have
afforded frequent opportunities for profit to the committee-
men.   It cannot be too strongly emphasized that all of the
securities upon which dividends were in arrears had a market value in London and were traded in actively.   And at

any one time there were probably as many people interested in having these stocks fall as there were in ensuring their rise by collecting dividends.

Moreover the interests of British subjects were in other respects conflicting. This is well illustrated by the intervention of France and Great Britain in the Rio Plate, in 1845.[47] Uruguay was a country brought into existence in 1828 largely thru the efforts of Lord Ponsonby to ensure peace between Brazil and the Argentine Confederation and thus to stabilize trade in the Plate. It developed rapidly, encouraging immigration from Italy and France at a time when Buenos Ayres under Rosas was suspicious of foreigners. And especially when French blockades from 1837 to 1840 injured business at that port. And Rosas determined upon the recovery of his lost province under guise of offering support to a revolutionary faction. France and Great Britain came to the support of the Banda Oriental, urged thereto by Brazil, as well as by the foreign residents of Montevideo who had profited heavily from the blockade of Buenos Ayres and welcomed its reinstatement. Gore Ousely, the British minister, went so far as to guarantee loans which were raised from the British and French merchants in anticipation of customs duties. But there were British interests at Buenos Ayres as well which now began to be heard from. Liverpool merchants had agents there; and Baring Brothers had concluded an arrangement in 1842 with Rosas by which dividends had been resumed upon the Argentine debt, which were interrupted by the blockade. A storm of controversy broke in the press of London and Paris and Liverpool. And when Palmerston succeeded Aberdeen as foreign minister in 1846, Gore Ousely was recalled in half disgrace, and new agents were sent out free from commitment to the Montevidean interests. England withdrew from the blockade in 1848, and it was ultimately left to Brazil to stir a revolution in the Confederation which put an end to Rosas and restored peace in the Plate. But it cannot be summarily stated that Aberdeen in these matters listened to Rothschilds and the merchants of Montevideo, while Palmerston acted upon the advice of Barings and Buenos Ayres concerns. England's relations with France were involved, and were of the first consideration; and Palmerston's withdrawal from the blockade could be fully explained as a part of his revenge for the Spanish marriages. It seemed to him much more a matter of national concern that Queen Isabella had married a man reputed to be impotent, with the wife of a French prince as next heir, than that Isabella was not paying interest upon her bonds to British investors.[48] And it was chiefly pique at the diplomatic defeat over the marriages that brought him to utter threats about the bonds.

For it need not be supposed for a moment that disregard of bondholders arose from any fine sensitiveness about using the resources of the nation to forward the interest of a few subjects. It simply had not been conceived as a national interest to help bondholders. There was no precedent for intervention to collect a debt or enforce dividend payments. Moreover Great Britain was now posing, with some success, as champion of the doctrine of "non-intervention" in protection of Belgium and Greece, and the South American republics themselves. Talleyrand is said to have defined non-intervention as "a political and metaphysical term which means almost the same thing as intervention." But it was a convenient label by which to distinguish the interest of Great Britain in those countries which was antagonistic to that of other European powers. And it also meant that singlehanded intervention by Great Britain in the affairs of most of the defaulting states would have contravened a major policy of either France or the United States.   It might have involved Great Britain in a first-class war forthwith.   And to intervene in any case which did not obviously have these disadvantages seemed likely to afford a precedent which would be embarrassing in cases which did.

The Spanish marriages, however, made it possible to look at bondholders in a different light.   They spelled opportunity to Palmerston, in search of tangible grievances with which to confound Isabella and her ministers.   And there was urgency to take advantage of the matter, for bondholders, seeing French diplomacy victorious, had been pressing Guizot to intervene in their behalf.[49]   Accordingly a full-dress debate in the House of Commons was arranged in the summer of 1847 as an adjunct to diplomacy.[50]   In the midst of an interminable discussion with which indignant radicals were seeking to embarrass the government's policy in India, Lord George Bentinck, the Tory leader, moved a formal address to the Crown to take steps to secure redress for the distressed bondholders.   He directed his attack particularly at the corruptness which was believed to cause the dissipation of the revenues of Spain.   And in reply Palmerston was at pains to agree with all that he had said along this line. But he wanted to make it clear that the government had seen no reason to encourage foreign loans, and indeed had viewed them with concern.   There was a distinction between the dealings of British subjects with foreign citizens, where it was the duty of the government to see that justice was done, and dealings with foreign governments.   "If the principle were established in practice that the claims of British subjects would be enforced by the arms of England, it would subject the government to the liability of being involved in serious disputes with foreign powers, on matters with regard to which the government of the day might have had no opportunity of being consulted." Nevertheless, it was shameful that the generous feelings of men who had loaned money should be requited with dishonor. Governments had squandered the funds which they had received; they maintained systems of commercial restriction (and at this allusion to free trade the Commons majority cheered the telling stroke at the Tories), tariffs, evaded constantly, which prevented their finances from being adjusted; and a foreign power (one looked across the Channel) had placed obstacles in the way of liberalizing the commerce of Spain. And if the British government had seen no warrant for taking positive action on behalf of its defrauded subjects it was not that it did not claim full right to do so, should it see fit. The question of intervention or non-intervention was wholly a matter at the government's discretion.

That it was a stirring speech, all were agreed; bondholders felt with some justice that it was nearly as impressive as an actual gun-boat. And at the beginning of 1848, the diplomatic mail-bags carried a circular letter which brought definitely to the attention of the governments concerned the stand which the Foreign Office had assumed.[51] It considered foreign loans undesirable, and had thought that the losses of the imprudent would prove a salutary warning to others. But the loss might become so great "that it would be too high a price for the nation to pay for such a warning as to the future, and in such a state of things it might become the duty of the British Government to make these matters the subject of diplomatic negotiations." What had been an embarrassment to Castlereagh, a subject to be virtuously shunned for Canning, was appearing to Palmerston as an opportunity and as a right to be employed with discretion, and was foreshadowed as a possible national duty.

CHAPTER V

THE RAILWAY REVOLUTION

"All seemed to come from the provinces, and from unknown people in the provinces."
— Disraeli, *Endymion.*

"Tout peuple reveillé se forge une autre loi;
Autre est le crime, autre est l'orgueil, autre est l'exploit."
— Verhaeren, *Aujourd'hui.*

REVIVAL OF HOME INVESTMENTS

Meanwhile the depression of 1837–42 with its political squalls in Egypt, Afghanistan, Canton and Maine and its gathering storm of Chartism at home had given place to two remarkable economic transformations. The first, the railway mania, brought to completion the main lines of the present British railway system and literally revolutionized the conditions of domestic trade. The second, the repeal of the Corn Laws, necessitated in no small degree by the drain of capital and labor from field to roadway, symbolized the abandonment of the last remnants of the mercantilist system. This process, which took place between the years 1841–49, brought about a revolution as complete in the conditions of the foreign trade of Great Britain.

Upon the trend of investments, these two changes had similar effects. The railway boom provided a domestic outlet for the energy of promoters and the savings of the well-to-do. In absorbing most of the sixty million pounds which were believed to constitute the annual British surplus seeking investment, it tended to deter the movement of British capital abroad.[1] But it also brought into existence promoting and constructing organizations whose energy could not be restrained by political accidents and which were loath to cease activity when domestic opportunities became more restricted when competition reduced the profits. Free trade, some of its advocates contended, would also check the export of British capital. By enabling England to take foodstuffs and raw materials in payment for exported manufactures it would remove the necessity of financing exports with loans. Employment would be found for increasing amounts of capital at home; money would be cheaper for farmer and trader. In the long run, however, free trade was also to have the opposite effect. As England found herself increasingly dependent upon imported supplies, her capitalists found increasing profits in the business of procuring these supplies, and invested money accordingly. Thus a transformation of market relations as complete as the changes in production of the preceding generations, and more rapid, distracted the England of "the young Queen and the old Constitution."

It is true that conditions abroad were not alluring to a prospective British investor in the early forties. The "six hostile tariffs" of Russia, France, Belgium, Portugal, the United States, and the Zollverein had given momentum to the cyclical decline of Britain's export trade.[2] With a year's surplus income expended fruitlessly in the Americas there could be no early revival of the capital routes which had given passage to much merchandise and culminated in such chagrin. Nor was frustration in the New World compensated by any grounds for optimism with respect to the Old. British workmen and machines had scattered the industrial virus here and there over western Europe; but the fevers they inflamed had not grown epidemic. Absolutely and relatively the volume of British commerce with north Europe was declining. Dividends from continental securities were being brought home instead of reinvested in Dutch rentes or Russian bonds. And in London bank deposits stood idle. In 1843 it was stated that there were from twenty to twenty-five million pounds of inactive capital in the City east of Temple Bar. Commercial discount rates sank in 1842 to 2½% and remained there until March, 1845. Bar iron which had brought over £5 a ton in 1830 was to be had at £2.10.0.[3] The most complete industrial depression of the century roused menacing gestures among the populace and gave Disraeli's melodramatic *Sybil* something of the weight of a sociological treatise.

What stirred new life in the capital markets and relieved the social pressure was the discovery that despite the depression some of the undertakings of the enthusiastic thirties had brought success. That the railway lines built without great stir by provincial capitalists were not only meeting expenses but declaring dividends was an event which challenged emulation. With mills closed down, commodity markets dull, discounts dragging, the *London & Birmingham,* the *Liverpool & Manchester,* the *Grand Junction,* the *York & North Midland* companies steadily paid dividends of ten per cent and more. A dozen other railways were earning six and seven per cent in 1842.[4] There was an increment in land values along these railway lines which overbore the prejudice originally entertained by country gentry. Towns which were brought into rail communication throve to the envy of potential rivals. And these circumstances, with the complaisance of a Parliament largely composed of probable beneficiaries, furnished ingredients for a boom which between

1844 and 1847 assumed colossal dimensions. Prior to 1842 Parliament had authorized companies with limited liability to raise about fifty-five million pounds for the construction of railways. In that year five million more were authorized, in 1843 three million. In succeeding years the acceleration of railway construction may be indicated by the following table: [5]

Year	Acts of Parl. for ry. construction	Capital authorized (000,000's)	Total Actual Capitalization (000,000's)	Miles in operation
1844	48	£ 17.8	£ 72.3	2148
1845	120	60.8	88.4	2441
1846	270	136.0	126.1	3036
1847	190	40.3	166.8	3945
1848	85	4.6	200.4	5127
1849	34	3.1	230.0	6031

The consequences of this rapid extension of transportation facilities were manifold. By quickening and cheapening transport, in the first place, the railways added enormously to the productive powers of the country; and this altho passenger traffic formed the larger portion of the business. The time element in transactions was reduced. Smaller stocks were possible in the domestic trade and they could be turned over more quickly. The territorial division of labor was facilitated. More capital was made available for remote investment by its economical employment in the reorganization of trade and transportation. The very building of railways, moreover, gave stimulus to all branches of industrial life and thus augmented production. Metals were in demand for rails, for tools, for rolling stock, for bridges and tresses. Their ores must be mined and coal dug for their smelting. This meant employment for men who were out of work; and there was a new occupation, which turned agricultural labor-

ers by the thousand into "navvies" for railway construction.[6]
Tooke considers that five hundred thousand men were employed at one time in 1846 in building railways.[7] The operation of lines already opened furnished work for 56,000 persons by 1849.[8] And the increased power of consumption of
the working classes found expression in an increased demand
for the products of textile mills and for groceries of tropical
origin. To handle them warehouses and docks must be extended. It is small wonder that the Chartist movement
dwindled through the forties and shrank by their close into
a minor propagandist organization.[9]

THE TRANSFORMED MONEY MARKET

A transformation of the investment market was not the
least important aspect of the railway revolution. "What is
remarkable in this vast movement," comments Disraeli in his
Endymion, "is, that the great leaders of the financial world
took no part in it. The mighty loanmongers, on whose fiat
the fate of kings and empires sometimes depended, seemed
like men who, witnessing some eccentricity of nature, watch it
with mixed feelings of curiosity and alarm. Even Lombard
Street, which never was more wanted, was inactive, and it was
only by the irresistible pressure of circumstances that a banking firm, [Glyn, Halifax, Mills & Co.] which had an extensive
country connection was ultimately forced to take the leading
part that was required. All seemed to come from the provinces, and from unknown people in the provinces." [10] The
names of Rothschild, Baring and Ricardo loom large in the
annals of financial London. But they will not be remembered
as having inspired or encouraged the domestic railway movement. Nor did the leading bankers, Lord Overstone of

Jones, Loyd & Co., J. W. Gilbart of the London & Westminister Bank, or Barclay, Bevan & Tritton, the leading firm
in point of clearings, have anything to do with railways.[11]
Bankers who owed their greatness to the railway business
performed the financing as it became needed, and commanded
respect in an altered money market. Glyns, Masterman, Mildred & Peters and Denison, Heywood & Kennard grew as railway bankers at London, J. Barned & Co. at Manchester and
John Moss & Co. at Liverpool, and numbers of joint-stock
banks. And with them brokers and jobbers specializing in
railway securities·crowded from the Stock Exchange men
habituated to dealings in the funds. The interest of the stock
market was definitely deflected from the debts of home and
foreign governments to the securities of private companies.[12]
Finance found fresh field for its play, credit a fresh basis for
its expansion, in the railway business. And altho the impulse to the change came from without London, in the end
there resulted a more complete concentration of the capital
resources of the country, as well as their expansion. The
early years of the railway boom produced numerous provincial money markets, such as Leeds which for a few months
outclassed London as a center for transactions in railway
securities. But as railway building progressed, as small lines
became consolidated into large systems with London termini,
financing migrated to a common center. The British capital
market achieved unity and national scope. The gulf between
industry and finance was spanned. And after a generation
of sturdy independence the provinces, Lancashire at their
head, bowed to London.

With the new leadership and orientation and its expanded
scope came democratization to the money market. The bulk
of the middle classes were now embraced in its clientele. For
the railway system was made by an outpouring of mass invest-

ment.[13] "In every street of every town," says Thomas Tooke, "persons were to be found who were holders of Railway Shares. Elderly men and women of small realised fortunes, tradesmen of every order, pensioners, public functionaries, professional men, merchants, country gentlemen— the mania had affected all." [14] Thus there came into existence a numerous investing public, habitually interested in new things, acting not severally upon the advice of a trusted banker, but approachable *en masse* through a central market and a common technique of advertising. All the resources of mass suggestion were opened to the promoter. The swallowing up of provincial bourses and the old funds market in a Stock Exchange with a new orientation simply aided his endeavors. And investment proceeded in consequence of direct appeals to a unified public, acting largely upon information supplied in the financial press.[15] The Stock Exchange joined the House of Commons as an institution upon which the common hopes and fears of the enfranchised classes centered. Thus an interest in the results of the revolutions in marketing and technique was widely diffused. A generation before, joint participation in the funds had bound merchants and aristocracy together in defense of the continuity of the constitution. Now the railway dividends bridged still wider chasms and drew aristocrat and petit bourgeois into a common pilgrimage along the gleaming track of a more industrial civilization. The Prime Minister, the Royal Dukes, the heads of the great Whig family clans, swarmed to the levees of George Hudson, the linen draper turned "Railway King", and listened anxiously to the whispers.

But the widening of participation in the profits of business did not mean its democratic control. In theory the joint-stock companies commissioned to build railways echoed the democratic constitution of their Jacobean precursors. To each man or each share (the franchise differed in detail) there was one vote; there was a body of directors, elected by the shareholders and reporting to them once or twice a year at a public meeting; some of the directors at least vacated their office annually. But the prerequisite for this sort of representative government is a common enterprise. And it is precisely the virtue of stock-and-bond capitalism that it makes it possible for enterprise to be vicarious. Scattered over the British Isles, engaged in all sorts of other activities, individual proprietors of the new companies were unable to have any real knowledge of or to exercise any important control over the affairs of the enterprise which they owned. They gave proxies readily to those who were willing to pay stamp duties for their use. And while several hundred shareholders customarily attended the periodic meetings at Cannon's Hotel, while criticism was free and the heated debates were reported in great detail by the daily press and financial weeklies, it was rare for shareholders' meetings to exercise any other effective control over the policies of their companies than was involved in the demand for dividends and the frequent issue of new stock at par. There came a divorce of proprietorship from control. Not even boards of directors were adequate to the latter function. To manage both business and its nominal organs of control there developed in shadowy form financial and promoting groups, centering now about an indispensable banker such as George Carr Glyn, now about a flashy organizer such as George Hudson, and again about the personality of a great contractor and railway builder. The interests of such groups in many instances dominated policy. Railways came to be built because contracting organizations needed work, ironmasters orders, bankers and business organizers a project to work upon. And railway building became a service which Great Britain could dump abroad when her financial and constructing plant could not be kept employed at home.

THE RAILWAY CONTRACTOR

The railway did not invent the contractor. It set him problems which made infinite demands upon his powers and made him significant. Contractors had been employed in canal construction or in building turnpikes and maintaining them. William Mackenzie had been a builder of roads and bridges, the right-hand man of Telford.[16] One of the most prominent contractors, Morton Peto, succeeded his father in the building trade and had won national reputation as builder of the Houses of Parliament before the railway offered larger inducements.[17] And there was already a disciplined hierarchy in a small way in construction work. Mackintosh, earliest of contractors to achieve a fortune, started as a gang-foreman.

But there were personalities drawn into the business of contractor by the railway. Charles Fox, builder of the Crystal Palace, was a medical student of twenty when the *Liverpool & Manchester* railway was completed. He deserted his books for engineering and by the end of the thirties was partner in an organization which undertook both engineering and construction work.[18] Thomas Brassey, for his part, was a road-surveyor and estate agent, who managed a quarry from which stone was required by George Stephenson for the *Grand Junction Railway*. And he was persuaded by that influential engineer to take some small construction contracts.[19]

It was in a large number of such small contracts that the first railways were built. The company's engineer, a man like one of the Stephensons, Joseph Locke, Isambart Brunel,

Charles Vignoles, supervised the work, which was parcelled out among many petty contractors.   But competent engineers were scarce; and as railway projects multiplied the demands upon the attention of each became so overwhelming that personal superintendence of railway building by the technical agent of the company was out of the question.   Yet concentrated responsibility seemed advisable.   Moreover there were economies promised from letting the work in large contracts. Thus engineers came to rely increasingly upon one or two contractors whose responsibility and efficiency they had proved.   Entire divisions were let out to one man or to a partnership, to be sublet in smaller units.   Thus the mobilizing of labor and material for railway building passed from the hands of the companies and became a specialized craft.

As master of a craft, the assembly of factors of production upon a scale not hitherto known in modern times, the contractor acquired a dignity and prestige independent of the companies that employed him.   Even to undertake his responsibility he needed connections with important dealers in railway materials, contact with sources of labor supply, his own credit arrangements with bankers.   And such relations once established became a permanent part of his stock-in-trade.   They enhanced his reliability and his usefulness. They also compelled him to continuous activity if they were to be retained.   And the investment of fixed capital required to carry on even a single contract operated to the same end. "Hundreds of earth-waggons and horses, scores of miles of rails and sleepers for 'temporary way,' several locomotive and several stationary engines, tools of countless numbers and endless variety—these, in addition to enormous accumulations of timbers, brick, stone, rails and a host of other materials, all vociferously call for more employment.   And although mere 'hands'—the Titanic 'navvies'—can be gradually diminished as works approach completion . . . the contractor must have a very large staff of scientific, commercial and skilled employees, whom he must keep in permanent employ or pay, else the whole work of superior organization and drill would have to be re-undertaken when every new enterprise was inaugurated." [20]

Under pressure of competition for their services the permanent organizations of the contractors expanded in scope. That of Thomas Brassey was perhaps the most elaborate. A simple man, of kindly dignity, direct, incessantly active, but unhurried, Brassey was raised conspicuously above his fellows by his tact and his perception of the advantages of high wages and low profits. In his character traits of prowess and achievement fused without avarice with the spirit of calculation. Unlike many contractors he did not retire early to consume a fortune in emulation of the county families. Nor did he squander his gains in reckless coups of finance. It was his passion to see his business grow and to keep his associates employed. By 1845 his reputation was established both in England and in France, and contracts beset him. To ensure the material with which to carry out his undertakings he built iron works and rolling-mills. He had a locomotive and carriage works at Rouen, France, in the name of Buddicom, his partner. With William Jackson he built another at Birkenhead. He financed more than one banking house as a means to secure emergency credit. Eighty thousand men were at one time in his employ. English schools, priests, chapels and physicians followed their migration from one contract to the next. To keep such an organization employed agents and partners roved the commercialized world seeking opportunities and concessions. At one time Brassey had railways and docks under construction in five continents. Every country in Europe possesses a specimen of his craft, with the possible exception of Greece, Albania and Finland. In his thirty-five years of business life he was engaged upon one hundred and seventy different contracts, involving nearly eight thousand miles of railway.*

The enterprises of Sir Morton Peto, sometimes Brassey's partner, often his rival, were regarded in his own time as having the character of an experiment in society-forming. Even in the forties he had fourteen thousand "navvies" continuously in his employ; later he had thirty thousand. He provided them with books, teachers, benefit societies, savings banks. Bishops visited the scene of his labors and reported that the grog shops were deserted and the schools were full. "If not physically, he was morally ubiquitous." There were Englishmen to be made great by the railway as well as England. Moreover, as William Jackson succinctly pointed out, it was much more profitable to look after the men.[21] And the more they were looked after, the more necessary that they be steadily employed.

Thus there was a tendency, which reached its full proportions between 1852 and 1866, for the original relations between railway companies and their contractors to be reversed. Instead of people desirous of building a railway employing men to build it, contractors built railways and organized companies to sell what they had made. To his burden of technical responsibility for the railway plant, to the task of assembling the elementary factors of production, the contractor added the hazard of its business success. Thru him bonds were negotiated, bankers' accommodation secured. Upon his prestige depended in no small degree the graciousness with which public authorities conceded the building privilege, the eagerness of the investing public to purchase

* See Appendix A for a list of Brassey's foreign contracts.

shares. Every detail of railway enterprise, financial, legal, technical, was managed by his organization. In some cases contractors even undertook to operate the lines on behalf of the nominal proprietors. The organizations which undertook these things had none of the impersonal form of incipient trusts. The relations of contractor with banker and iron manufacturer were personal, represented by contracts and partnerships and borrowed money. And this very lack of structural cohesion added to the power and celerity with which scattered resources could be concentrated upon one contract or released to engage in alien functions. It made the personality of the contractor all-important in the conduct of his business aggregate, and vested his career with a romance that fired the imagination at the peak of the century.

It was under the auspices of Brassey and Peto and Wheelwright that the full effects of the industrial transformation of Great Britain were transported abroad. And in the middle of the nineteenth century they were the active agents in the migration of much British capital upon the Continent and elsewhere. In the forties the expansive energies of the contractors were already carrying British enterprise to France and Belgium.

THE BEGINNINGS OF CONCESSION-HUNTING

If the Continent was more backward than England in the development of railways it was not that it was even more reluctant than London to admit productive enterprise to the aristocracy of high finance. Where the new industry flourished in Europe it was that bankers had rivalled kings in its patronage. True, French investors preferred rentes, whose payment was regular and certain, to the chances of greater profit in undertakings that required attention and hazarded default. And speculators were habituated to a technique of play in the fluctuations of public funds, which followed political events more closely than commercial trends. The French bourgeois improved his house and garden and the peasant-proprietor his field. And unlike England there was in France no provincial manufacturing community of wealth or solidarity or enterprise enough to launch railway building upon its own account.[22] As in the case with the public credit of France after Waterloo, the vogue of railway finance needed to be imported from across the Channel. It required a demonstration of Englishmen, vigorously spading the earth, riveting tresses, pocketing public subsidies, declaring dividends and coining profits out of the sale of shares at large premiums, to rouse the latent but ample capacities of Frenchmen for doing the same things. Until then the readiness of Paris bankers under the July Monarchy to organize railway companies was of little consequence. Baron James de Rothschild, Disraeli's "Sidonia," more far-sighted than his London kinsmen, might aid Emile and Isaac Pereire to build the line from Paris to St. Germain, the first railway in France to use steam locomotives.[23] But one short stretch of rails does not make a transport revolution. Nor do money markets rush headlong after Rothschilds. Paris brokers would not trouble at first to quote the shares. A portion of the capital had to be secured from London. The governments and Chambers of Louis Philippe hesitated over the very desirability of railway transportation. Guizot and Thiers were sceptical. And in the early forties, when railways ran four ways from London to the sea, only a few, short, scattered local lines had been constructed in France.[24]

Belgium was the first European country to engage vigorously in railway building.[25] Her independence from Holland disturbed the navigation of the Meuse upon which the industrial development of the Liegeois depended, and made necessary a new means of transport from manufacturing areas to the sea, if her industries were to support an active export trade. One of the first concerns of King Leopold upon his arrival from England in 1831 was to direct an inquiry into the feasibility of railways; and one of the earliest measures laid before the Belgian parliament called for a line from Liege to Antwerp, a connection analogous to that from Manchester to Liverpool.[26] Moreover there was a serious state of unemployment calling for relief.[27] In 1834 a systematic network of railways radiating from Brussels and Malines was authorized by the Chambers, in accordance with plans drawn by George Stephenson. The government itself undertook the enterprise, which involved the expenditure of more than one hundred and fifty million francs. A considerable portion of the capital, however, was procured in London by loans issued in 1836, 1837 and 1840 through the agency of Rothschilds. Thus a system of 336 kilometers of railway was in operation in Belgium before France had so much as made up her mind that she wanted railways. And the Anglo-Belgian ironmaster, John Cockerill, was planning a railway invasion of France from the north, which was interrupted only by the crisis of 1838–39 and Cockerill's sudden death. State and private enterprise in the Germanies had not been idle, and by the forties there was already talk of rail routes from the Atlantic to central Europe and the East, which might conveniently pass elsewhere than thru France. And railway development on the upper Rhine threatened to complicate the defense of the Lorraine frontier.[28]

Railway construction received its first impetus in France as the direct result of English competition in the routes of travel between London and Paris. As early as 1836 the directors of the *London & Southeastern Railway* were promoting a company, which embraced any number of eminent Whigs, proposing to build a railway from Boulogne to Paris, to connect with boats from Folkestone.[29] But it was not possible to obtain approval from the Chamber of Deputies so long as the more important seaports of Havre and Rouen were still unconnected with Paris by rail. Hence the first Paris connection was developed by the *London & Southampton* company, which was interested in the route by way of Havre. The initiative seems to have been taken by Edward Blount, a young Irishman who after a season in the diplomatic service had set up a banking business in Paris in 1831, warmly supported by numerous members of the British aristocracy residing upon the Continent. Despite the threatening state of Anglo-French relations he procured a concession in his own name in 1840 on behalf of the *London & Southampton* directors to build a railway from Paris to Rouen. And this grant was completed two years later by the fresh award of a concession to build from Rouen to Havre.[30]

Thus to British initiative and capital France owed her first important railway, the connection of Paris to the leading seaport of the country. All in the way of business, of course, for the Englishmen in question induced the French government to provide the right-of-way and to lend them money at low rates, amounting in all to nearly half the capital cost.[31] A company was organized under French law with a quota of French directors and with Charles Lafitte, Blount's partner, as chairman. The English directors included William Chaplin, who had sold out the largest coaching business in England in 1838 in anticipation of the triumph of the railway; Sir John Easthope, stockbroker, member of Parliament, part-

owner of the London *Chronicle,* the leading Whig newspaper; and two bankers from Liverpool, John Moss and
Charles Lawrence, who were prominent figures in the board
of the *London & Birmingham Railway.* It was the English
directors who named the engineer, Joseph Locke; and Locke
named the contractors, William Mackenzie and Thomas
Brassey. British "navvies" crossed the Channel to do the
work. Iron and railway materials came from British shops
or from shops in France manned by British operatives. English methods of construction were employed. And to the
astonishment of the French government construction went
ahead with such energy and resourcefulness that the road to
Rouen was opened to traffic in the spring of 1843, and continued to Havre, despite the collapse of a brick trestle, within
the contract period into the fall of 1846.

The *Paris-Rouen* railway was the first conspicuous effort of
British construction enterprise abroad. It made the reputations of the contractors and the engineer. It also opened
a period of Anglo-French cooperation in railway building
which continued, with interruptions, for nearly twenty years.
And its success encouraged the French government to formulate plans for a national railway system, consisting of lines
radiating from Paris to the several frontiers, for which it announced in 1842 its readiness to grant concessions. The same
success no less than the generous terms of the concessions
attracted other British capitalists to enter competition for the
privileged routes. It seemed possible to build railways in
France for one-half the cost of English roads to the shareholders, and with little less certainty of a large traffic. Moreover there was the chance of disposing of the railways when
built to French investors at a profit. Not more than three or
four hundred thousand pounds had been employed at any
one time in building the *Paris-Rouen* railway, and it was

believed that the promoters had realized a profit of two millions.[32]

Naturally the directors of the *London & Southeastern* recognized without delay the necessity of matching the Rouen railway with one to Boulogne or Calais if their continental passenger traffic was to be retained. Robert Stephenson was commissioned to make an elaborate study of the problem, with the view to combining the Channel connection with the authorized route to Lille on the Belgian frontier.[33] They too secured Lafitte as their French sponsor, an arrangement which led to inevitable suspicion and resentment; and they commenced a railway from Amiens to Boulogne. They sought the concession also of the *Nord,* as the railway to the northern frontier came to be called.[34]

The publication of Stephenson's report upon French traffic and revenue possibilities synchronized with the opening of the line from Paris to Rouen and drew numerous promoters to France to look over the ground. Most active of these was J. D. Barry, formerly a mine agent and stockbroker at Manchester, who was sent over by a group of capitalists to open offices in Paris, inspect routes, and establish local connections. A concession was secured through his efforts in 1843 of a line from Orleans to Tours, which was extended in the following year to Bordeaux.[35] Mackenzie fresh from his triumphs at Rouen brought the organisation and good-will that he had acquired to cooperate in the project. A financial group developed which included representatives of Denison, Heywood, Kennard & Co., bankers with important subsidiaries at Liverpool and Birmingham; a partner of J. Barned & Co. of Manchester; William Gladstone and Thomas Weguelin of the firm of Thomson, Bonar & Co., merchant bankers in the Baltic trade and one of the Bank of England houses; and Alderman William Thompson, member of Parliament and a leading member of the iron trade. Edward Blount united his enthusiasm and connections to the combination. Line after line was constructed in the western part of France by this group, including the principal component parts of the systems known until recently as the *Orléans* and *l'Ouest*. Brassey and Peto cooperated with the group in partnership after the death of Mackenzie. The association found means to build two small railways in Belgium, besides developing the *Northern & Eastern Railway* in Great Britain.[36]

Meanwhile the capitalists who were building the *Paris-Rouen-Havre* railway procured London banking support which gave them new leaders. Their promoting group by 1843 included John Masterman, Jr. of Masterman, Mildred & Peters, and Matthew Uzielli of Charles Devaux & Co., a firm of foreign exchange bankers. Masterman's leadership was ubiquitous. He formed companies to seek concessions for the *Nord,* the *Paris-Lyons* and the *Orléans-Vierzon* routes. And while maneuvering for the ear of French deputies and bureau chiefs the same capitalists organized the *Dutch-Rhenish* railway company which controlled for several years the only considerable line in Holland.

These groups, two of them brought together originally by their concern for traffic extension, the third as an organization of merchants and financiers interested in the iron trade about the activities of a famous contractor, do not exhaust the British capitalists who participated as directors or shareholders in French railway projects between 1844 and 1847. As the railway mania drew to its height in Great Britain, the number of Englishmen multiplied who saw less competition and a chance for larger profits in French railway development. Gentlemen who had made something upon a quick turn of shares in railways running through their counties were ready to join provisional boards of directors. Occasionally an eminent capitalist, a Goldsmid, a Morrison, a Ricardo, a Salomons, was snared. The promoters were brokers, solicitors, contractors' scouts, men who were being made by railways. The fever for projects spread upon both sides of the Channel. The Paris Rothschild was won back to a market in which he was embarrassed to choose between willing allies. Old Swiss Protestant banks—*la haute banque* as distinguished from *la banque juive*—stirred from routine and planned syndicates. Hottinguers, now managed by a Labouchère, struck an alliance with Barings.

The number of lines which France proposed to build was limited. But rival companies flourished, jostling one another for concessions, all encouraged by the Ministry of Public works. For such favored routes as those to Strasbourg, Lyons and Lille, as many as eight to twelve companies were afloat, fluttering French notables from the head of their prospectuses, manned by family bankers under the lash of emulation. Each sought subscriptions impartially in France and England and flourished dual boards of directors. They found little difficulty in securing tentative lists of shareholders. In March, 1845 one company seeking the *Nord* concession had applications in London alone for 400,000 shares, with 150,000 to sell.[37] Out of 1750 original subscribers to the shares in the Amiens-Boulogne company, more than one-half were English and from all parts of the island. The deposit was small upon subscriptions, being ten per cent of the capital. Under French law which prevented the directors from spending money before they had a concession, the deposit was secure. And each company issued share certificates, pending the award, which could be traded with in London and Paris in an active market, and whose transfer in London was free of the stamp tax imposed upon all sales of domestic securities.

They bore interest from the start, and coupons attached made its collection easy.   A lucrative business in arbitrage sprang up for bankers with intimate cross-Channel connections, and gave further motive to the formation of companies.   It has been possible to trace no less than fifty companies organized in 1845 alone to build railways in France, for which at least eighty million pounds of capital were promised by the London market.[38]

The participation of British capital in French railway building did not escape criticism in Great Britain.   Prompted partly by the notion that British resources were being used to strengthen a rival nation, partly by an exaggerated notion of the strain upon British capital which was involved, partly by a whole-souled suspicion of things continental, there were numerous attacks in the daily and weekly press.   At the time when Stephenson's report first attracted public attention to them, the *Morning Post* (Conservative) vigorously denounced French railway schemes in general.   They would prove a delusion and a snare.   The French government would subject capital to impossible conditions.   There would be police at every turn.   Only third- or fourth-rate speculators would have anything to do with them.[39]   "So long as there is a bog to drain, a fertile mountain side to cultivate, a shoal of fish to gather at home, and colonies to people abroad, the Government of England ought not to suffer a pound of British capital to be lent to foreign states for want of a market in London," urged the *Circular to Bankers*.[40]   The replies were overwhelming.   To criticisms of security it was enough to point out that "the Rothschilds were in it," although no one knew just where, or for how much, or upon what terms. Upon consideration of wider values it was argued that the extension of railways would be the best guarantee of a durable peace between England and France.   It would promote intercourse and cement their commercial interdependence. The special dependence of the French capital market upon British support would, it was believed, act as a powerful deterrent to untimely hostility on the part of France.[41] Indeed Anglo-French relations did warm perceptibly between 1842 and 1846. And the intimacy of the money markets may have strengthened this phase of the diplomatic cycle. At least the British government placed no obstacles in its way; Lord Normanby, the ambassador to Paris, "was of the utmost service"; [42] and relatives of the prime minister, Sir Robert Peel, served as directors upon French railway boards.[43]

The French government, for its part, seems to have taken a reciprocal view of the matter. Not that there was no resentment over the activity of foreigners in the country. The Chamber of Peers evinced a healthy distrust of *agiotage*, and debated measures which British spokesmen declared would bar them from participating further in French railways.[44] In March, 1845, a worried delegation from London journeyed to Paris in protest and appeal. Guizot's Chambers have their reputation. It is not unjust to suppose that legislators in upholding virtue found that they enhanced its market price. Certainly the administration of Louis Philippe showed no unfriendliness to British promoters. It regarded them as probable defenders in case of disagreement with the Foreign Office. The Duc d'Orléans became silent partner in *Lafitte, Blount et cie*. Nevertheless political considerations of a local character delayed from year to year and month to month the promulgation of details of the concessions and their final award after the bids were in.

If this delay did not kindle affection, it at least assured the construction of main radial lines as rapidly as the scruples of politicians could be adjusted. One company might have failed to get its capital actually paid up; but hardly eight, each of which had deposited a tenth of the necessary capital in a bureau of the French Treasury. As the government delayed, the competing companies became numerous. It was to ensure the benefit of this situation that a suggestion of Enfantin was put into effect when the Ministry of Public Works finally began to call for bids.[45] "Fusions" were arranged. Competing companies were persuaded to amalgamate in proportion to their strength; weak subscribers were able to escape with a profit upon their hazard; and rival bankers found places upon a joint directorate. Thus the French minister found himself confronted by a single bidder instead of rivals, and was obliged to take the offered terms or withhold the award. When the *Nord* was conceded, September 20, 1845, to a fused company headed by the Rothschilds, the cry that Louis Philippe had abdicated to the Jews was raised only by the unimportant people whom Baron James had not drawn into his combination.[46] And these did not include Englishmen. About a third of the shares were allotted to a handful of them for their disposal. Every group secured a part. There were eight English directors besides the London Rothschilds, and two of them were named Baring.[47]

It is not possible to trace statistically the fluctuations of English interest in the French railway companies which were finally constituted and procured concessions.[48] The completion of the railway itself between London and Paris and the telegraph which accompanied it made the two cities virtually a single market so far as the securities were concerned in which both Englishmen and Frenchmen were interested. There is no reason to doubt, however, that about one-half of the privately furnished capital for the French railways begun before 1847 came from Englishmen.[49] This would be about twenty-five million pounds, and by the latter date possibly a half of this sum had been called up from the shareholders. About three million pounds in bonds had also been floated by the *Paris-Rouen* and *Rouen-Havre* companies. These sums cannot, however, be regarded wholly as permanent investments of fresh British capital in France. The large shareholders were active men, with widely distributed commitments, depending upon quick turnovers of their capital to enable them to meet their varied obligations and to make large profits. Their object was very much that of the subscribers of the Baring loans in 1817 and 1818. A contemporary railway journal described their activity as follows:[50]

These railway operations, properly speaking, are only directive organizations for employing the labour of a country in the construction of railways. The amount of capital really sent out from this country is very small; for when once the enterprise is set going, the means are derived from the scene of operation, money being raised from local capitalists on loan, and shares being disposed of to foreigners at enhanced prices. Other countries are paying for our skill in finance, our enterprise, and our foresight in business.

Nevertheless it seems certain that a great deal of foreign capital entered France during the early forties. From 1828 to 1839 inclusive her exports exceeded her imports on an average of twenty-five million francs a year. From 1840 to 1847 there was a surplus of imports which totalled 790,000,-000 francs.[51] The only adequate explanation of this remarkable shift in the trade balance is that during those years France was absorbing on the average four million pounds a year in foreign capital. Not all of this was represented by railway stocks, however. Nor did it coincide in point of time with the maximum activity in railway speculation. French rentes sold steadily in foreign markets, and many

Frenchmen who bought railway shares sold rentes in order to do so. And there were others than British with money to invest that found France desirable.[52] Above all it must be considered that the investments made by Englishmen were almost all in securities which had an international market, and which could be disposed of readily to meet financial emergency at home. They did not figure largely in British foreign trade at the time that they were being made. And we have no means of knowing to what extent they consisted in bills on London which circulated as money from portfolio to portfolio between Paris banks.

ANGLO-BELGIAN RAILWAY ENTERPRISE

It was zeal for the profits of promotion that led to the activities of the railway-makers in France. And the same fine emotion brought into the London money market in 1845 and 1846 companies designed to construct railways in every part of western Europe and the British Empire. Most of them had no serious consequence beyond the traffic in premiums, and the fees of solicitors, prospectus-makers, financial editors and purveyors of office furniture. One railway was brought to successful completion in Jamaica at this time by persons connected with the sugar trade. It seems to have been the first colonial railway (or public utility company of any kind in the colonies) to be financed through the London stock market. There was a short railway in Tuscany, from Florence to Pistoja, built by William Jackson as contractor-concessionaire. One large London house is said to have put up the money outright for a small line from Duesseldorf to Cologne.[53] And English engineers were everywhere in consultation over plans, in Sardinia, in Austria, in Switzerland.

Englishmen interested in the possibilities of Spanish mines sought concessions at Madrid. But serious enterprise in Europe by the British was confined almost wholly in the forties to the Low Countries.

The government of Belgium, having built the main traffic lines itself, abandoned the policy of state construction and to secure branch-line development, distributed concessions with a lavish hand. Eight companies were formed in 1845 to exploit such grants with capital subscribed almost wholly in England amounting to £6,290,000.[54] These companies, although formed under Belgium law, had their headquarters in London. They were organized only after the concessions had been secured; and their shares were held closely by directors and their friends. The *Namur & Liege* railway, for instance, seems to have been almost entirely by directors and clients of the Union Bank of London. And it was planned for a time to go ahead on a partnership basis without organizing a company at all.[55] So advantageous were the selected routes believed to be that no guarantees or subsidies were required of the Belgian government.

There was thus at the outset little of the premium-chasing and sensational publicity which attended the exploits of the Anglo-French companies. Neither did the prospects of iron contracts form the kernel of Anglo-Belgian undertakings. "The iron necessary for the road," stated the Namur-Liege concession, "shall be had from the foundries of the country provided it could be had at not more than ten per cent above the price of foreign iron delivered at Antwerp."[56] And Cockerills were making locomotives at Seraing as cheaply as Stephensons in England.[57] In the Tournay, Jurbise, Landen & Hasselt and the Anglo-Belgian companies the construction contracts of Mackenzie, Barry & Co. were crucial. And the Sambre & Meuse and West Flanders companies were built about the contracts of W. P. Richards & Co., Richards himself being both chairman of the board and contractor. But the real lure of all of them was the traffic of closely populated industrial districts, the steady dividends which on such lines as the West Flanders were expected to be nine per cent at the very least. And remittance was no problem. It could be made by selling in Brussels the rentes in buying which British investors had earlier financed the state railway system of Belgium. For Belgian investors did not share the British enthusiasm for the bargains they were getting in railway grants.[57a]

THE RAILWAY CYCLE COMPLETES ITSELF

Thus while Great Britain turned £150,000,000 or more into railway plant at home, she found means to employ her engineers and contractors and laborers in Belgium and in France in building at least a sixth as much railway in length and capital cost. Thru their assistance the railway had become a financial and engineering reality in these countries. French capitalists at least had been stirred to emulation. French workmen had learned construction work at the side of British "navvies," had learned to eat meat and to work harder and to demand higher pay. Skilled personnelle had been trained to handle traffic. Coal mining was stimulated, and business life was adjusting to a situation in which celerity of transportation was a possibility.

This relation of British capital and enterprise to the Continent depended upon a belief in England of the larger profit margins to be secured by concessionaires without greater risk. It also depended upon steady exchanges, easy trade conditions, and the convertibility of English holdings of rentes, by sale or pledge, into the means of paying for railway shares. The growing critical condition of the London money market, the strain imposed by the corn and potato famines, and the tangled skein of credit disorders which culminated in the panic of 1847, caused the movement of British capital to flag perceptibly in 1846, to stop altogether in the following year, and in sequel to the revolution which broke in France at the beginning of 1848, to be entirely reversed.

That this crisis and reversal was in any sense caused by the adventures of British business men across the Channel can not be urged. From one point of view, however, it followed the rapidity with which circulating capital was being tied up in the fixed and inelastic form of railway plant both at home and abroad.[58] Retrenchment was a consequence, at the expense of some departments of business life. For so extraordinary a demonstration of economic power as the railway revolution had not been financed out of accumulated wealth. It was a characteristic of the railway mania that the people who made up the subscription lists invested beyond their means.[59] They carried consols to the bank, to secure loans to make initial payments upon railway shares, and pledged those shares anew to start the purchase of more. And it was a characteristic of the railway banker and broker to pyramid loans in this fashion. Indeed it was during this era that documentary wealth of every description was made the regular basis for credit extension by firms who would have feared a loss of credit had they earlier sought advances on their dock warrants or bills of lading, or on bills drawn against unharvested crops. When calls came due upon shares thus acquired, investors sold some to secure funds with which to make good their investment in the rest. Or they clamored for extensions, and the issue of new shares with which to build them, at par to the original subscribers. They hoped to sell such shares at a premium; and indeed, while the speculative fervor spread to an ever-widening clientele, they were largely successful. Thus the original subscribers to a large degree became proprietors of the railway painlessly.[60] Many were of the type caricatured in *Punch* as "Jeames of Barkley Square," the cockney butler turned millionaire.

But as calls multiplied and shares crowded the market for realization, prices came to a stand, then sagged. The springs of circulating capital ran less freely. To enable railways to be built and provide for the construction of bridges, warehouses, new mills and factory town sites which accompanied them, some parts of British economic activity must be curtailed. Capital and labor deserted agriculture, especially in Ireland. And at this juncture the procession of economic events encountered a series of meteorological phenomena; the shift of productive power from agriculture coincided with a potato famine in 1845 and a corn shortage in the following year. Gold was drained out of the country to procure supplies from the United States, from Russia to relieve the food shortage. As it moved, discount rates advanced, margins were contracted, paper profits dwindled. Brighton £50 shares which sold at £70 at the beginning of 1846 could be had at £60 at its close and fell to £40 during the following year. *London & Northwestern* stock, most substantial of all, sold at 220, 195 and 110 at corresponding periods.[61] Newmarch computed the fall in values of several leading railway securities between 1846 and 1849 at from 1175 to 444.[62] Investors found themselves unable to dispose of their stock yet bound in law to pay their assessments. The only relief was in economy. A drastic curtailment of expenditure took place thruout the middle classes. It showed itself in the reduced employment of domestic servants. As early as 1846, small shopkeepers were finding difficulty in collecting bills.[63] The grocery trades especially felt the effects of diminished consumption, and the markets for their produce collapsed. Compelled to seek assistance from the Bank, colonial merchants found that institution extended to the limit in maintaining the exchanges. When century-old houses began to fail in the autumn of 1847, including five Bank of England firms, with those of the Governor-elect and of the Lord Mayor of London, panic swept the business community. And upon the first occasion of its testing the Bank Act of 1844 proved its inadequacy. It was necessary for the government to authorize the Bank of England to exceed the legal limit of its note-issue to save the money market from dissolution.[64]

It is not possible to correlate step by step the phases of this critical period in England with the changes in activity of her capital and enterprise abroad. But it can be stated broadly that as financial strain tightened at home, most British capitalists reduced their foreign commitments. And they did so for a number of reasons. Economists from the time of Adam Smith have observed a natural preference in capitalists for investments near at hand, the domestic as opposed to the foreign.[65] This is reflected in differences in the interest rate; and it had taken the prospect of higher profits to draw British capital into Russian rentes and French railway shares. But the increasing need for circulating capital in London, occasioned by the sinking of so much in fixed railway plant and reflected in the rise of the market rates of discount, reduced the margin of advantage to be obtained from granting credit abroad. It was the condition of the exchanges that made it desirable to recall capital already invested. The heavy importations of foodstuffs required in 1846 and 1847 disturbed

the equilibrium of trade and shook the exchanges. Great
Britain required grain at a moment when the United States
was at war with Mexico and when France had a short crop,
and it was not possible to pay for a great proportion of the
needs of the country in augmented exports of merchandise.
Large shipments of gold were made in the first instance,
which placed the English credit system in its precarious condition. But as securities payable in francs and rubles and
dollars came into the market for sale it was more advantageous to ship them for sale to the country from which they
originated than to ship gold.[66] This situation rendered virtually impossible the remittance of fresh capital for investment in Europe.[67] And if these considerations were especially true of foreign government securities, such as those of
France, Russia, Holland, and the newly solvent American
states, which could be sold without serious loss, they effectively ended British enthusiasm for continental railway projects for a time.

But that the conditions unfavorable to a continuance of
Anglo-French railway association had their root in fundamental economic disorders was not always clearly perceived
at the time. The retreat of British capital was frequently
rationalized in terms of nationalistic feeling. The difficulties of British investors in carrying stocks on a falling market
found expression in friction between French and English directors on the joint boards and in meetings of shareholders.
The French railway companies were organized under French
law, held their meetings in France, and conducted their proceedings naturally in French. But very few of the Englishmen interested in foreign enterprise troubled to speak
a foreign tongue. Not even Mr. Brassey with his extensive
operations could understand anything but the English language. Hence there were stormy sessions of the *Amiens-*

Boulogne company, with shareholders irate because they were not privileged to debate in English, and with the clever Charles Lafitte unable to clear himself of the suspicion that haunted the companies he controlled.[68] The Salomons-Morrison group broke with their French associates in the *Bordeaux-Cette* railway and demanded that their deposits be returned. The Belgian companies, unable to get their shareholders to pay calls or to borrow at the banks, found themselves isolated in a foreign land, with no local interest economic or political to make a movement for their help.[69] Their meetings resounded with the recriminations of the few anxious shareholders who remained steadfast. They could neither go on with nor get out of their undertaking. And they cursed the Belgians. The revolution of 1848 in France only heightened national feeling. The government took over the construction work upon some of the railways, with French engineers and workmen. And there was excited talk about confiscating railway property for the benefit of the masses. Lord Normanby was obliged to speak sternly to Lamartine about the matter.[70] And it was a disturbing circumstance that strikes against the employment of Englishmen in railway operation were a feature of the summer's rioting.[71]

Thus nationalistic feeling accompanied the temporary cessation of British activity in continental railway enterprise. But these episodes were really the fever-pains of a business community whose monetary and financial technique had not kept pace with its industry, and whose dependence upon an ample supply of precious metals exposed it to peril at every crop failure and turned its most boastful achievements, free trade and the railway, into burdens.

CHAPTER VI

COSMOPOLITAN ENTERPRISE

*"The strength which is derived from the confidence of capitalists
. . . flies, by the law of its nature, from barbarism and fraud, from
tyranny and anarchy, to follow civilization and virtue, liberty and
order."*

—Macaulay, *History of England*, c. 19.

THE DISCOVERIES OF GOLD

How closely financial England steered to the cataract in
1847 and 1848, her economists and public men never fully
realized. They were impressed by the fact that a Bank Act,
the sum of available financial wisdom, had to be suspended
within three years of its enactment. They were uneasy that
government must borrow ten million pounds, when railway
kings spoke still grandiosely, for the relief of starving Ireland. And they suspected dimly that railways were being
constructed extravagantly and beyond proportion. But the
successive removal of duties on corn, raw cotton, raw wool
and timber, and the final repeal of the Navigation Acts in
1849 had roused their enthusiasm, and made them confident
that England's economic future was assured. Only in the
United States has a vivid impression of that crisis survived,
in the memory of Irish immigrants whose earliest recollection
is of an eviction. In Great Britain free trade became a
fetish, to whose potency the burst of business prosperity after
1850 was ascribed; a political abracadabra, whose frequent
repetition shut off the past in soothing oblivion.

It was to its good fortune, however, rather than to its unaided merit that free trade owed its sanctified repute. England had become a manufacturing community unable in emergency to suppply her population with foodstuffs, and able to procure them only by menacing the foundations of her business life. She could supply manufactures for export in abundance. But in an emergency gold credits could not be procured by their sale. Gold was to be had only in Latin America and in Russia, which could not suddenly augment their supplies, nor increase their purchases in recompense. Grain too was to be had largely from eastern Europe, and the village communities from which it came had no desire for the products of Lancashire. And the tastes of their lords were for the fineries of France and Italy and the Orient. There was a market for English goods in these regions. But to buy corn in Dantzig and pay for it with piece goods in Leghorn meant exchange transactions too complicated to be carried on extensively in 1847 without the use of specie. Only her gold reserves, upon which were pyramided by bank credit the economic relations of the entire business community tributary to London, and her foreign investments which commanded an international market, could procure her food upon short notice. Industrial England had outrun the world. Her plant—the railways not least, which had drawn labor from the soil while improving its capital value—and her population, had outgrown the means of subsistence and the markets for their produce. England faced a crisis of more moment than a money panic, whose conditions were altered but whose gravity was not lessened by the suspension of the Corn Laws in 1846, and their final repeal. And the root of the evil was a dearth of money affecting chiefly her relations with the commercially backward countries.

France and the United States brought relief in the early

stages of the crisis of 1847 by repurchasing some of their securities. The United States after the Walker tariff of 1846 was a good market for a judicious amount of "dumping." But England was not alone in feeling the dearth of bullion. France was more than any other commercial country dependent upon specie for internal trade. In coming to the relief of the West with gold from his reserves, the Czar of Russia in 1847 purchased rentes as well as consols. And the stringency in France was one element in the general discontent which burst into revolution in February, 1848. As that upheaval spread in concentric circles over the Continent, it sent successive waves of emigrés scurrying to London with their savings and mobile property. The accumulations of the thrifty Orleanists and their followers preceded the salvage of liberals from France and the Germanies fleeing the subsequent reaction. And once again England profited from the shelter which her political stability afforded.

Hence her rapid escape from the ruin which the crisis of 1847 foreshadowed was not wholly providential. But permanent relief of the strain upon the international exchange mechanism depended upon contingencies almost wholly accidental—the sudden inflation of the world's supply of precious metals. Gold might have been found in California in 1840 or earlier. Its discovery conceivably could have waited a couple of decades. For the prestige of San Francisco over the better known Oregon arose from the discovery. There was a West large enough for indefinite expansion to the north and west of the Sacramento Valley. And the discoveries of gold in Victoria in 1851 were largely the result of deliberate search inspired by the rush to California. Thus it was almost wholly fortuitous that in 1848 a Swiss guardsman thrown out of work by the July Revolution in France, who had been carried by the movement of westward migration to engage in sheep-raising in Mexican California, found gold in his mill-sluice.[1]

Between 1811 and 1840, it has been computed, the total production of gold and silver in the world was worth about one billion dollars. All of this and more was drained off immediately to the Far East or to the more remote agricultural areas of Europe and withdrawn from commercial circulation. The opening of mines in the Ural Mountains increased the stock of gold between 1837 and 1848 by about four or five per cent. The average annual production of gold during the forties has been estimated at $36,393,000. But in the five years after 1850 the average output soared to $132,513,000. The stock of money in circulation began to increase at nearly the rate per year which had formerly required twelve. In the two decades from 1850 to 1870 more gold was brought into the markets of the commercial world than the mines of New Spain combined had furnished since the days of Cortez and Pizarro.[2] And for the economic and business history of those decades the augmenting gold supply forms the basic fact. Without it free trade would at that time probably have encountered grave difficulties.

Europe did not get the gold of California and Victoria as income from capital invested directly in its exploitation. A swarm of gold-mining companies buzzed about the Stock Exchange in 1852 and 1853 and extracted about five and a half million pounds for investment, particularly in quartz-rock mines. But their activity was of no great consequence either for the gold output or for immediate dividends.[3] It is not possible to exploit labor where every man can get land and hopes for fortune from his own unaided efforts. But it is the misfortune of a gold rush to occupy areas which are lacking in everything but gold. The men from England and New York who brought what the gold-diggers wished to buy, got several prices for their goods, and thus the gold, which they carried to older commercial centers as profits of their venture.

Even in anticipation of its coming, the mercantile opportunities of the gold fields gave life to business. And as the reserves of banks in shipping centers mounted, the secular trend of prices which had been downward since Waterloo reversed itself.[4] There was a world-wide rise of prices and a consequent stimulus of enterprise in which the railway and free trade became for Great Britain leading assets instead of liabilities.[5] The business of international trade and remittance, freed from the terrors of a general shortage of the circulating medium, entered upon an indefinite expansion, extending the use of commercial credit into the hinterland of every port which had enterprise to make use of it, and to some which did not. And there opened a period in the history of Europe in which labor and technique, capital and enterprise, business and fashion moved in an ever-widening cosmopolitan field of activity. France embraced industrialism with a new zest. Germany welcomed the machine and exposed her mines. Austria, Italy, Spain, each European country in turn opened its gates to the railway, the telegraph, municipal works. A spirit of enterprise pervaded the western world, which drew new vigor from every community its activities disturbed.

British enterprise and skill and credit were principal agencies for the diffusion of this movement. The outward migration of British capital reached its maximum of the century during the twenty-five year period which followed the discovery of gold at Sutter's Creek. The cosmopolitan activities of the contractors and their friends were the foremost of the modes in which it was manifested. But there were also Britons who without much capital promoted more directly the industrial and mining development of the Continent. Moreover the endless accommodation of bill-brokers and lesser firms in London, energized with credit currency regions and endeavors in which the enterprisers did not themselves engage. And when we have said something of these labors upon the European frontier, inquiry must yet be made of work of the finance companies and cosmopolitan bankers in harnessing the money market to the plow of progress.

"L'EMPIRE C'EST LA PAIX"

After the gold discoveries, the important fact in the business outlook in 1850 was the wave of revolutions which had swept Europe in 1848. These revolutions proved to be trifling in their direct political effects. But the governments which survived or were established by them depended for their place and for freedom from attack, upon the business classes. And for the pleasure and distraction of this powerful element in the community politicians turned with one accord to the exploitation of the freshening streams of purchasing power and of technical achievement.[6] They would surrender to the social and industrial revolution with the hope of retaining more surely the perquisites of political power.

"L'empire c'est la paix," declared Louis Napoleon to the Bordeaux merchants whose doubtful adhesion he was endeavoring to ensure.[7] "We have immense uncultivated regions to fructify, roads to open, ports to dredge, rivers to render navigable, canals to finish, our railway system to complete." And indeed the most characteristic performances of Napoleon in the years immediately following the coup d'état of December 2, 1851, dealt with the internal development of his country, and meant wealth to the capitalists he commissioned to do the work. Almost the first decree of Napoleon after his coup d'état granted a concession for the long-disputed, still uncompleted *Paris-Lyons* railway.[8] The concession went to a consortium which combined the names of Rothschild, Baring, Brassey, Masterman and Pereire. And it had been one of the last acts of the railway commissioner of the Second Republic to reject the application of the English capitalists for this concession.[9] There need be no mystery over the heartiness with which some sections of British opinion greeted the coup d'état. Three more railway grants followed within a month to Anglo-French promoters.[10] And by the time Napoleon III proclaimed himself Emperor as many miles of new railway were under construction as had been in operation at the end of the Second Republic.

To perform his undertakings Napoleon and his engineers relied largely upon the surplus energy of British enterprise. There were the savings of many emigré Frenchmen to be tapped by way of London. There were great contracting organizations, with experience, reputation and technical resources to be depended upon. Moreover it was quite as important for an adventurer like Louis Napoleon to conciliate foreign opinion as it was to manage the politicians and bourgeoisie at home. And no element of foreign opinion in the early fifties was so articulate and influential as the merchants and capitalists of Great Britain. Nor was there any nation whose friendship it was more essential to Louis Napoleon to maintain. That friendship jeopardized, as it came to be in the fruitless quest of glory, security at home or abroad was inconceivable. But in 1852 Napoleon III was *"un bon européen"*—the instrument of progress—the arbiter of humanity—the spokesman of engineering and technique.

There revived thus under most promising auspices the Anglo-French railway cooperation which had flourished in the forties until interrupted by crisis and revolution. New personalities figured with the older groups in competing for the perquisites of Napoleonic concessions. The Masterman combination was now really a stockbrokers' syndicate. Of the original 32,000 shares in the *Blêsme et St. Didier à Gray* railway, which it controlled, all but 1390 were allotted to Englishmen, and brokers, headed by James Hutchinson, president of the Stock Exchange, largely made up the list.[11]   With John Masterman, Jr., who was shortly to run afoul the Belgian commercial code, were associated John Sadleir of the London & Counties Bank, whose record furnished suggestions for *Dombey & Son,* and Samuel Laing, a young university man, whose varied career as public servant was interwoven with notable activities in private finance. Several contractors received their support, but they usually were found backing the undertakings of George Wythes. Sir Charles Fox, Henderson & Co. rivalled the undertakings of the Brassey and Peto contracting groups; and the *West of France Railway Company,* constituted January 27, 1852, united all three in an enterprise where the contractors owned all the shares, and the directors were their nominees.[12]   In the early fifties the shares of twenty working French railway companies were publicly quoted in London, and at least one English director was on the board of nineteen of them.[13]

The number of directors, however, gives no clue to the extent of interest held by English investors. Its distribution at all events was not extensive. The meetings of the French companies received but scant notices in the British railway press. There were no more journeys of irate Lancashiremen to Boulogne. French railway stock was proving a most desirable investment to first purchasers. The *Nord* paid dividends even during the Revolution; and in the fifties when English railways averaged a 3% return, French rails paid seven and nine.[14] So the original subscribers were in no haste to sell. But an increasing proportion of the actual capital cost of her railways was being supplied by residents of France. The French government provided much by one of several devices, which helped the dividends to be so encouraging. And it was being recognized how much it enhanced the shareholders' profits to secure considerable capital upon bonds bearing a limited and low rate of interest.[15] Such bonds were very much to the taste of the French investing public. They were heard of in London, too. But it was shares and contracts and the reserved profits of promotion that English capitalists were interested in. And their gains secured in these directions, the more permanent concerns of control, of strategic development, of coupon clipping, did not greatly attract them. Beyond finance and construction, English connections with the railways did not go. That French traffic follows the English rather than the continental rule of the road, is nearly the only trait of the promoters left upon railway operation.[16] Methods of administration and management from the first were French. The very designs conformed to French conceptions.[17] Where the lines of their railways ran English promoters did not miss opportunities to purchase mining property and building sites for development or re-sale. But over all projects of development the concession system prevailed. And Napoleon's deliberate policy was to prevent such a grouping of interests as might menace his position.

Thus there was no trace of imperialism or of trust-building in the activity of British contractors and capitalists in France. It was the emperor who threatened the concessions of branch or parallel lines to rival groups, and compelled companies in being to undertake extensions. Initiative, leadership, decision were in French hands, and in the hands of the government in France. And because Napoleon thus possessed favors which could be bestowed upon the constituents of worthy politicians, and shares to gratify themselves, and because those shares rose daily in a market made buoyant by steadily rising price levels, the natural organs of political activity showed a wonderful deference to his dictation.[18]

CONCESSIONS EVERYWHERE

Elsewhere in Europe the same fruitful accord prevailed between men who had offices and dignities to keep and the men who could be interested in making money.

In Piedmont it was the natural concomitant of a liberal constitution that whole cadres of restrictions upon commodity movements should be relaxed, that limitations upon the association of capital, upon the undertaking of agricultural and industrial improvements should disappear. The passing of feudalism in Hungary worked social revolution without the aid of quasi-liberal politics. For Austria, having suppressed a Hungarian revolt by abolishing feudal privilege and enfranchising the serf, found it necessary to attach all classes to the new regime by associating with it an immediate measure of prosperity for all. She pinned her hopes upon the railway and the development of the accumulating estates of the crown.[19] Did nationalities resist, did peoples raise themselves against oppression, the railway would efface nationality, and the vanquished minorities would forget defeat in well-being. The king of Prussia might be chary with constitutions and paper freedoms. But gild restrictions had gone, and in 1851 he relinquished to private owners the privilege of disposing of mineral resources beneath the surface of their land.

France and Belgium were no longer the only countries with a welcome for British contractors. Their enterprise was simultaneously engaged in Piedmont and in Switzerland. Austria, Spain, and after the Crimean War, Russia and Turkey displayed concessions for the bids of foreign capitalists.[20] By the end of the fifties the railway epidemic was spreading to the outskirts of the European world. Brassey's fellows were building lines in Asia Minor, Algiers, Portugal and Brazil. In Denmark and her Scandinavian neighbors, Sir Morton Peto had something of a monopoly of railway construction. He carried thru successive projects which had a bearing upon the supply of Swedish iron and Danish butter to the English market. And his *Schleswig Railway* was no doubt one of the aspects of the Schleswig-Holstein question which it is said only Prince Albert, Lord Palmerston and one other ever thoroughly understood.[21] Thru British contractors and without their intervention in some cases the London money market had acquired a heavy stake in the railways of the United States, Canada, British India and Australia.

The political implications of railways became more visible with every rail that was laid. There were "national" objects everywhere to be accomplished by building lines whose immediate commercial possibilities were doubtful. Unaided capital showed a delicate reluctance to build such railways; and it was not difficult to persuade governments in the fifties that only the great resources of international enterprisers would meet the case, and that only the most generous treatment should reward their adventure in the service of a foreign country. Sometimes there were subsidies of land, of capital, of preferred treatment for the fortunate concessionaires. More often there was a kilometric or mileage guarantee of income upon the capital invested. Rarely was there demur to the great principle that private enterprise should be rewarded with the profits; and rarely was that enterprise suffered to sustain the loss, if government had anything to do with the matter. Hence there was a curious tendency for railways which had lofty national purposes in view to be constructed with great rapidity, while important commercial transportation lines might linger.

Certainly the perception of the identity of railways with politics did not need to be imported from Europe into the North American world. The United States provided its own enterprise, its own contractors, its own happy coincidences of private profit with objects of public concern. It even exported them to some extent to Canada. But railway iron and working capital America could not provide as rapidly as its development required. And Frankfurt and London thus made the acquaintance of a wide selection of bonds, without having much of anything to do with railway management and promotion in the United States. The bulk of the shares as well as the bonds were owned by Englishmen in the *New York & Erie,* the *Illinois Central,* the *Philadelphia & Reading,* and the lines from Marietta to St. Louis that later were merged into the *Baltimore & Ohio.* The pick of the mortgage bonds of the railways in Ohio were purchased by Germans in the Rhineland. Only the *Atlantic & Great Western,* absorbed after much travail in the *Erie,* required the talents of a British contracting organization. And that is in itself a story.

Public encouragement went chiefly to railways. But they brought with them other opportunities. Speculative activity in land, in shipping, in company shares spread from country to country with the movement of enterprise and money capital. The development of Mediterranean areas—and the failure of some of them to develop—and of the chief lines of communication to the East, reflected the interest of British capitalists in their great oriental possession. And all of this activity of British capital was performed by a handful of men, with comparatively little publicity. Indian securities were well distributed, and so were some of the American railway bonds. But in the risks and profits of carrying the railway revolution to Europe and its environs, the ordinary investor had at this time an infinitesimal share.

BRITISH CAPITAL AND ITALIAN UNITY

France under the Second Empire called the tune to which politics and economy in Europe danced for two decades. But for the little kingdom of Sardinia-Piedmont, the example of Napoleon and of Leopold of the Belgians was not needed. A native nobleman who had travelled widely and considered deeply, was already by 1850 organizing banks and railway companies, importing guano and agricultural implements, stirring the enterprise of his countrymen, when the revolutions of 1848 gave his nation the leadership of the liberal movement in Italy. And when Count Cavour entered the ministry in 1851, it was to turn the energy of the Sardinian government to the promotion of the objects which had concerned him in private life. His published correspondence reveals him fresh from conferences with concession-hunter and financier, fascinated with their personalities, enthusiastic for their views.[24]   Now he is drawing Brassey or the Pickering Brothers into construction work, now arranging for contracts and credits for shipments of iron from Wales, now endorsing plans to rebuild the port of Genoa to fan the reluctant embers of that individualistic city's patriotism. For not war nor commercial profit was the final object of Cavour's economic policy. All converged to the great aim of Italian independence and unification. It was to railways that he looked especially to arouse a lively sense of nationalism and to promote emancipation from Austria and the Hapsburgs.[25] Englishmen were quite as enthusiastic as Cavour over some features of this policy. Entirely apart from the desirability of a strong state in the Mediterranean, free alike from French or Austrian control, the commercial value of progress and of liberalism upon the Continent was perceived even by the diplomats. British representatives displayed tactful zeal for the development of Genoa. They pressed frankly the importance of a railway across the Alps at the Lukmanier pass, to establish communications with Switzerland and the upper Rhine.[26] It seemed to them quite as important as to Cavour that Genoa become the port for the Levant trade with central Europe. A route for commerce and mail from the Channel to the Mediterranean, not subject to the control of either France or Austria, inspired the hope of business men and diplomats. And they were as active at Luzerne and Berne, the new capital of the Swiss Bund, as at Turin.[27] But there were financiers interested in the port development of Trieste, and the Austrian government as well. It is said that the intervention of Rothschilds interrupted plans for the passage of the Alps by the Lukmanier.[28] It cannot be claimed that the interest of the British government in these transactions was committed to the support of particular investments, although Lord Palmerston was believed to be an investor in Swiss railway companies.[29] For only part of the railway development inland from Genoa was secured by English contractors. Part of a loan floated in London in 1851 by C. S. Hambro & Co., symbolizing Piedmont's financial independence of Rothschilds, was devoted to building a railway toward Turin.[30] But there was no complaint when portions of the line were conceded for private construction to a French company in which British capital had only a one-third interest.

The union of Italy and Switzerland was eventually accomplished by way of the Mont Cenis passage of the Alps into Savoy and Geneva. And British capital took a large share in the Victor Emmanuel company organized by Charles Lafitte, to accomplish this and at the same time to join the Sardinian and Swiss systems to the French.[31] Three governments assisted in the financial arrangements, and so important did they regard this undertaking that when the company found difficulty in securing capital during the Crimean War, it was relieved of its obligation to construct some branch lines and shareholders were guaranteed the right to exchange their shares for rentes within six months of completion.[32] This estimate of the importance of the Savoy railways was not exaggerated. Their existence affording rapid transportation from Paris to Piedmont was one of the deciding factors in the Austro-Sardinian war of 1859.[33]

Austria, for her part, did not block building as such in the Italian peninsula after the revolutions in 1848, and she indeed built considerable stretches as a governmental undertaking.[34] In 1856, to help Austria finance her expensive neutrality in the Crimean War, these lines together with some English-built roads in central Italy, were consolidated into one private system running from Trieste and Venice thru Milan toward the Sardinian frontier and branching to Florence, Parma, Modena and Rome. The *Lombardo-Venetian Railway Company* was a Rothschild affair, with headquarters in Paris. Sir Anthony Rothschild, Samuel Laing, Matthew Uzzieli and Edward Blount were the Englishmen who were among the concessionaires. Toward the end of 1858 this company bought from the Austrian government the South Austrian railway, partly built from Vienna to Trieste. The funds about to be received in payment added to the lightheartedness with which Austria went to war in 1859. But the railway, incomplete as it was, was still further incapacitated for service by the fact that it was administered by Frenchmen and consequently fell into chaos when Napoleon entered the war. The bearing of this upon the Peace of Villafranca deserves inquiry. But as Cavour foresaw, the fact of railway connections between the different Italian states worked strongly for Italian unity, whatever the interests of the railway proprietors. Pio Nono, who had yielded to the persistence of French and English promoters, united the north to the south of Italy by rail and thus helped to overthrow his temporal power.[35] But the Savoyard railway, completed from the side of France and broken at the Mont Cenis passage, nourished commercial relations which were an important factor in the overwhelming preference of Savoy to be united to France in 1860.

Thus British enterprise stamped its prowess across the map of Europe, and the map was changed; but the imprint was not British. Industrialism bestrode political frontiers, yet bowed to national idiosyncrasy. The empire which was peace gave its energies to war; and railways dismembered as many states as they united. And in the stir cosmopolitan enterprise flourished upon national pride.

THE EXPORT OF CAPITAL AND CAPITAL GOODS

One feature of the activity of British contractors in Europe and elsewhere was the marked increase of the export from

Great Britain of producer's or capital goods. The countries which were the most busy in the development of their transportation especially increased their purchases of items which would come under this head. The exports of iron and steel from the United Kingdom doubled in value and nearly doubled in volume between 1850 and 1853. They continued to increase steadily, and in the early seventies averaged five times their value in 1850. "Railway iron" of the declared value of thirty-five million pounds was shipped from British ports between 1856 and 1865. In the succeeding ten-year period this item exceeded £83,000,000. Machinery, including steam engines, which had been exported to the annual average value of one million pounds from 1846–50, averaged 1.7 millions, 3.5 millions, and 4.5 millions, in successive five-year periods. An average of eight and one-half million pounds' worth of machinery was exported each year from 1871 to 1875.* Such increases as these were cut of proportion both to the rise in general price levels, and to the increase of population. They implied a decided increase in the proportion of British exports which were made up of iron, copper and tin products. In 1849 these had constituted 16.3% of the total exports; in 1857 the proportion had risen to 21.5%. During the thirty years from 1848 to 1877 inclusive capital goods to the value of more than eight hundred million pounds were exported from the British Isles.

A good deal of this movement no doubt was associated with an investment of British capital. It was caused by the enterprise of the contractors, or, at a later period, accompanied the generous loans of cosmopolitan financiers to foreign governments. Nevertheless this correlation must not be too

---

*For the data upon which these statements rest, see Appendix, for Table showing Values of Principal Items of Capital Goods, Produce of the United Kingdom, exported from 1846 to 1877.

closely drawn. It was most exact perhaps in the case of India, for whose railways all of the iron material was imported from England. Approximately one-third of the capital cost of her railways may be accounted for by these purchases. American railways in the fifties, and again after the Civil War, required a good deal of railway iron and issued bonds in payment. But the bulk of the investment which ultimately found its way into American railway securities was not directly related to such transactions. Moreover no relation can be traced between the destination of exported capital goods and the apparent field of activity of British investment. In the fifties, for example, Spain was the leading European country in its absorption of machinery and railway iron, but it was not conspicuous as an investment field. Speaking more generally, the export of producer's goods of all kinds from Great Britain tended to be in excess of the net export of surplus capital; while the movement of railway iron was a great deal less than the usual amount of the capital surplus.*

Creative power of another sort was also exported. The building of railways in Europe implied the migration of not only railway iron and financial credit from Great Britain. There travelled British "navvies" and skilled operatives and engineers, directed by elaborate contracting organizations. The demand for these was more buoyant and elastic than the willingness of European countries to employ foreign iron, even when cheaper, in their building projects. Proportionately more of enterprise and less of iron went to Europe than went to India and the United States where great railway works were also being aided in the fifties by British capital.

Indeed, however much the contractors who secured con-

* See note 5, chapter X, for detailed discussion of the capital surplus from 1854 to 1880.

tinental concessions were inclined to cooperate with British bankers, British manufacturers and British labor, there was no decided preference for bringing these factors of production together upon British soil.   One of the first steps taken by Thomas Brassey toward the construction of the Paris-Rouen railway was to establish the Buddicom locomotive works at Rouen.   A decade later these works consisted of eight separate factories.   Waring Brothers, in building a railway from Manage to Wavre in Belgium, organized under Belgian law a constructing and supply company which had works at Nivelles.[36]   Pickering Brothers had a plant in Piedmont.   In many cases hostile tariffs were thus circumvented.

There was no attempt either to give a national character to the work which British enterprise performed.   In the formation of syndicates there was if anything a preference for international combinations.   Considerations of policy had brought about Anglo-French promoting cooperation in France.   And this cooperation led to permanent alliances of financial groups for concession-seeking all over Europe. Capital sailed under whatever color was convenient.   The *Crédit Mobilier,* most dazzling of the financial institutions born of the Second Empire, enjoyed British participation from the outset.[37]   Brassey and Buddicom were silent partners in the private bank which Edward Blount conducted at Paris.[38]   Thomson, Bonar & Co., joined with Bischoffsheim & Goldschmidt of Brussels, Paris and Frankfurt to form a bank of industrial and commercial credit at Paris in 1859.[39]   And continental capital in turn sought the opportunities of the English money market.   London was the continual resort of financiers the exact nationality of whose resources it is out of the question to determine.

This cosmopolitanism pervaded every phase of continental

railway construction. Brassey undertook contracts now with English rivals or dependents, and as often with such Franco-Belgian contractors as *Parent, Schaken et cie* and *J. F. Cail et cie*.[40] The Spaniard Don José de Salamanca joined a syndicate with Brassey, Blount, Parent, Talabot and others to build the Neopolitan railways.[41] A network of railways in the Papal States was conceded in 1857 to a Paris banker, Mires, who sold the stock chiefly in clerical circles in France and Italy. But his materials came from everywhere. The rails and joints were brought from Newcastle, the locomotives from Paris, the wheels from Belgium, while the carriages were manufactured for the contractor in Italy.[42] For the Lombard railways under construction in 1858, the Rothschilds bought rails in England and Belgium, and set up a French branch factory at Verona to turn out rolling-stock.[43] Two Englishmen who secured a concession of a railway from Poti to Tiflis in the Caucasus, formed their company in France, sold debentures in Amsterdam and Frankfurt, and purchased their supplies principally from Belgian manufacturers. The locomotives and carriages, however, were ordered in England.[44] For the *Rutschuk-Varna* railway in Roumania, Messrs. Peto, Betts and Crampton, the contractors, bought materials in Belgium, paying for them with obligations which were sold to the Belgium public through a Bischoffsheim syndicate.[45] The directors of the company were English, although most of the shares had to be sold by the promoters upon the Continent, in liquidating their losses in the panic of 1866. At the end of 1868 the *East Hungarian Railway* was awarded to a syndicate comprising Charles Waring and the Austrian Baron Hirsch, backed, there is reason to suppose, by the Belgian Bischoffsheim. The Anglo-Austrian Bank organized the company with a glittering board of Hungarian notables. Eighteen thousand tons

of rails were ordered in England, twelve locomotives in Bavaria, thirty-five passenger coaches in Switzerland, thirty-
five in Hungary, and five hundred freight cars in Austria.[46]

So far as possible the undertakings of the contractors were
thus not national but cosmopolitan. Instead of being the
activities of strongly nationalized groups operating beyond
clearly envisaged national frontiers, they were operations of
cosmopolitan groups, acting in a cosmopolitan field. It is
only in terms of national balance sheets that the "export of
capital" is of importance in these transactions. The sale of
railway materials did usually mean a purchase of railway
securities.[47]   That was a prevalent feature of railway finance.
And the terms of the concessions frequently stipulated that
contractors might import their materials duty-free. But their
work may be more properly thought of as a migration of
enterprise *and* labor *and* capital from one part to another of
a commercial area conceived as an expanding economic whole.
And the income derived by British nationals from their endeavors consisted even more in the profits of enterprise than
in interest, large as the French dividends were.

BRITISH CAPITAL IN CONTINENTAL INDUSTRY

Equally unrelated to an "export of capital" and equally
cosmopolitan was a great deal of the direct impetus given by
Englishmen to industry upon the continent. It is impossible to make any sort of a quantitative statement of the
volume of British capital which at various times engaged
directly in the development of manufactures upon the Continent. The scattering instances which can be assembled
do not exhaust its scope, we may be sure. It is preeminently the joint-stock form of enterprise which secures

publicity. And the joint-stock principle was invoked in very small degree in the beginnings of the Industrial Revolution in France as well as in Great Britain. Yet there had been migrations of British capital, British enterprise, skill and inventiveness, of which the stock and share lists knew very little, since early in the nineteenth century. And in some respects these movements had been of importance in domesticating the Industrial Revolution upon the Continent.

Survivals of mercantilist legislation were to a great extent responsible for the establishment of English factories in Belgium, France, the Germanies and Russia. On the one hand there were tariffs imposed by these countries against British goods, often with the intention of promoting domestic industry. On the other a British embargo on the export of machinery, in the vain attempt to limit the knowledge of technical improvements to the Isles, compelled British manufacturers of engines and machines to procure patents and erect factories abroad to forestall pirating of their products.[48] For there was no effective way of preventing the smuggling of designs and of machines in parts. And those Englishmen or others who were willing to connive at violations of the law smuggled both machinery and workmen out of the country during the stormy decade after Waterloo. By 1824 the movement had become so noticeable as to call for parliamentary inquiry; and voluminous reports detail the nature of the migration and the speculations of witnesses as to its consequences.[49] The lace trade of St. Pierre-les-Calais furnishes an illustration.[50]

After the Treaty of Paris in 1815 a smuggling trade sprang up between Dover and Calais, spirits being brought to England in return for textiles. Of these, machine-made lace was seizable wherever found in France as obviously smuggled over a prohibitive tariff; so a few machines were carried over and put to work at Calais to cover the smuggled imports. The manufacture was found to be profitable, and the number of machines increased so much that they had to be set up in the near-by hamlet of St. Pierre, which came to be in some respects the Nottingham of France. Lace manufacture at Lille and St. Quentin and also the linen and other textile trades of those towns, and of Dunkirk, Armentières and Amiens, similarly originated with English machines, English workmen and English capital. The development of the district created a demand for machine-shops, and Englishmen established these, too. The first French factory for linen manufacture, promoted in 1838 by the North country banker, John Maberly, engaged a British engineer to build its machinery for it at Amiens.[51] Reports from British consuls in 1842 indicate that there were four lace factories, a flax factory and a large foundry in English hands near Calais; there were five factories at Caen, and four foundries at Rouen besides the plant of Buddicom & Co., builders of locomotives.[52] And there seems to have been no enterprising journalist to feature this "English conquest of Normandy."

It was, however, in the manufacture of machines themselves rather than thru their exploitation in spinning and weaving that Britain contributed to the rise of French industry. There were three important machine-shops in France in 1824, all run by Englishmen.[53] Of these the most important was that owned by the firm of Manby, Wilson & Co., at Charenton.[54] Young Charles Manby, born to the Staffordshire iron business, set up in the twenties a remarkable record of achievement. At the age of sixteen in 1820 he had designed and built the first iron steamship to make a sea voyage, and sailing his own vessel as chief had carried a cargo direct from London to Paris. There he erected a gas-works to supply Paris with street-lights, became manager of the iron works at Charenton, put iron steamboats upon every navigable river in France, remodelled the rolling-mills at Creusot (which have since become the leading center of French steel manufacture), undertook to manufacture tobacco for the government, and returned to England at the age of twenty-five, to continue there in the iron business and engineering. The Creusot enterprise was in financial difficulties in 1834 and the Manbys later disposed of their property to the creditors. But there were other British machinists to develop other iron works, usually in connection with specific construction projects. In the fifties there were the Taylors building iron steamboats at Marseilles;[55] John Masterman and his contractor George Wythes had a coal and iron company at Aubin in south central France;[56] a Devaux group was developing the Carmeaux district in the Dordogne.[57] But the French machine industry at large was now being carried on by domestic enterprise and capital. The English cooperation in docks and warehouses and land and building companies, while profitable to the investors, mainly Englishmen concerned in railways, was no longer important to France.

Belgium preceded France in her modern industrial development, at least relatively, and its outstanding feature before 1840 was the work of William Cockerill and his son, John.[58] In their achievement no British capital was involved, only British skill and initiative. The elder Cockerill came to Verviers in 1798, after failing of success in several occupations and countries, to build a linen spinning machine on contract for a Hamburg firm. The machine was a success, and within a few years Cockerill besides beginning the Belgian linen industry had founded the first European machine-shops at Liege, and was inundating Europe 'with machine-made machinery. Under each changing regime in the Liegeois the

Cockerills flourished. The King of the Netherlands went into partnership with John in 1817 and granted him the château of the Prince-Bishop of Liege at Seraing, as a seat for his machine-works. Cockerill expanded his activities to control every process from the securing of raw materials to the exploitation of his own machines. The Belgian revolution of 1830 gave him entire proprietorship of his concern. And by the late thirties he had developed Seraing to the largest establishment of its kind in the world, employing 2500 men and turning out machines with 1800 horsepower a year. At Liege his machine-works engaged 800 more. He had cotton, woolen and linen factories, a paper mill, zinc mines at Stolberg, spinning mills in Saxony and Silesia and at Berlin, forges in Languedoc, a clothing mill in Poland, a sugar plant in Surinam, a cotton mill at Barcelona, and was interested in four coal-mines, a gun-factory and several rolling-mills. He was the leading spirit in the industrial movement which stirred Belgium from 1834 to 1838, and his name survives in the corporate designation of outstanding Belgian enterprises of the present day.[59]

To the early development of Russian industry British capital as well as enterprise and skill was important. For Russia had machine industry long before it became large enough to affect her political and social destiny.[60] But before the reforms of Alexander II domestic commerce was relatively small. The landed estates were mainly self-sufficing, and even sought to assimilate the machine to the village organization, until the emancipation of the serfs and the cotton famine from 1861–65 ruined the baronial factories. Thus the development of cotton manufacture for a general market, and the very manufacture of linen by machinery were originally foreign undertakings. They flourished under high tariff protection and special privileges from the government. And they sought as much to find a market in the overland trade to Asia as in the limited demand of the city-dwellers.

Around St. Petersburg this textile manufacture was carried on directly by British factories, with British machines and British supervising staff, founded in large part by surviving firms of the old Russia Company.[61] Wilson, Hubbard, Thornton, Wright and Shaw were leading names among their number. Their spinning-mills developed in the late thirties and early forties, especially after the suspension of the embargo on machinery permitted the direct purchase of the best English models. In 1852 Egerton, Hubbard & Co., with the Petrovsky mills and in 1866 Thornton & Co., secured incorporation under Russian law, but there was no appeal to the English investing public. There was no object in publishing knowledge of possibly generous profits to a community full of potential rivals. One mill which earned profits below the average, paid 270% in dividends upon an original capital of a million silver rubles between 1836 and 1860, besides expanding its plant sixteen times out of undivided profits. Even mills which were not nominally English, depended upon English management and upon English merchants for credit.

It was at Moscow, however, rather than at St. Petersburg that the Russian cotton industry really developed. It grew under the domination of half-anglicised German importers, who controlled the supply first of English yarn and later, when they had encouraged spinning-mills, of American cotton. "The importers financed the Russian spinner," says Schulze-Gaevernitz, "provided him with English foremen, even with English managers, and thus secured in him a steady customer for cotton."[62] In time this process came to revolve entirely about the personality of Ludwig Knoop, a native of

Bremen, who spent a few months in John Bright's calico mill at Rochdale, and came to Moscow in 1839 at the age of eighteen as clerk with a Manchester yarn-exporting firm. Knoop's convivial temper commended him to the Russians and his enterprise to British merchants and manufacturers. Even before the embargo on machinery was lifted, Knoop managed to bring the first English spinning-machines to Moscow, with Lancashire operatives whom he turned into foremen; and thus he began a lifelong traffic, which resulted in the founding of 122 spinning-mills in Russia. If a Russian cotton-weaver desired to spin, Knoop arranged everything. He had a monopoly on the trade in machines, and in turn contracted with English houses for his supply. All the machinery set up around Moscow was purchased of Platt Brothers of Oldham; the steam engines, until the eighties, came only from Hargreaves. Knoop built the mills and installed the machinery, which was accompanied by a special consignment of workmen from England, and he followed the process with constant advice and technical direction to the owner. He came to monopolize the market for raw cotton also, absorbing the firm of Jersey & Co. at Manchester, with which he had begun the business. He was banker for his clients, lending on their stocks and giving credit endlessly upon their purchases. Moreover he came to dominate the Russian yarn market through the output of his factory at Kraenholm on the Narva, which he operated under the most favorable conditions with the most up-to-date machinery from 1860. At his death in 1894 his factory was reputed to be the largest spinning-mill under one roof in the world, and Knoop was undoubtedly the largest industrialist in Russia. As middleman in the migration of British capital and skill and technique and mercantile credit he is a memorable figure.

The British contribution to the early development of the Russian iron industry was also considerable. In 1843 the Messrs. Evans at Warsaw were reported to be the largest manufacturers of agricultural implements in Europe, outside of Seraing.[63] But the real pioneer in metallurgy was John Hughes, who was in large measure responsible for the development of the resources of the Donetz basin after 1860, and whose New Russia company, organized with £300,000 capital, began the manufacture of railway iron for the Russian government about 1870, importing skilled workmen from England.[64]

But the number of British industrial establishments on the Continent as a whole did not increase more rapidly between 1850 and 1875 than earlier. For continental industry was increasingly able to develop from its own impulsion. And the rise of business cosmopolitanism as exemplified in the activities of Knoop was altering the conditions which had encouraged Englishmen to set up branch factories abroad. Tariffs ceased at least to be prohibitive against British-made goods. The series of "free-trade" agreements initiated by Richard Cobden and Michel Chevalier in 1860 brought nearly all of western and central Europe to a competitive basis. Manufacturing was an activity from which British capital could no longer secure special advantages abroad.

PUBLIC UTILITIES AND MINES

It was works of public utility and mines promising to yield lead, copper, zinc and iron that filled the prospectuses of the fifties and sixties. About 1850 there were English gas companies supplying Amsterdam, Rotterdam, Ghent, Cologne, Carlsruhe, Rome, Constantinople, Christiania, Tours and

Renes.[65] The Imperial Continental Gas Association organized in 1825 had thirteen establishments by 1866, including gas-works at Berlin, Frankfurt-on-the-Main, Hanover, Aix-la-Chappelle and Magdeburg, and it had a subsidiary company operating in Austria.[66] The Union Gas Company, with headquarters in Paris and English management, supplied Strasbourg, Toulouse, Nimes, Cette, Roanne, Vienne, Beaucaire, Tarascon, Rueil, Alby, Génes, Parma, Modena and Alexandria.[67] In 1852 Sir Charles Fox promoted a company for the Berlin water-works, for which he had the contract.[68] English capital built a water system at Amsterdam in the preceding year.[69] And one-half of the capital and directors of the *Compagnie des Eaux* of Paris, launched in 1853 by the *Crédit Mobilier,* with George Wythes as contractor, were supplied by John Masterman, Jr., Samuel Laing and their associates.[70]

In the mineral industry British capital was not a dominating factor upon the Continent except in Spain, where modern mine development began only with the reform of the mining code in 1867.[71] Belgian iron and zinc resources interested British capitalists in the forties and encouraged the efforts of some of them at railway building.[72] The famous Gellivara iron mine in Sweden and the Alten copper mines came under British control in the same decade. One enterprise of which it would be interesting to know more was the "La Cava" copper mine in the valley of the Arno in Tuscany, taken up by a Mr. Sloane about 1837 after a long history under other management. There was a smelter at Briglia in the fifties, and contemporaries pointed out how the introduction of the mining peasantry to schools, savings-clubs, and to a miner's band, with music written especially for its use by the proprietor's friend Rossini, exemplified the "moral and social aspects" of "the ever-increasing spread of English industry and English capital." [73]   It seems more certainly to illustrate the un-national love for things Italian which many Englishmen possessed.

Most of the companies formed in England to exploit foreign mines were inclined to look for large dividends, and at once. In the early fifties the demand for copper, lead and zinc, the world markets for which were in England, encouraged the formation of a large number of companies, operating especially in the Linares district in Spain, in northern Italy and along the lower Rhine in Prussia and Nassau. Most of them disposed of their concessions in a short time to local interests. For the management of the companies tended to be centralized in England and to adhere too closely to the English system. Moreover mining companies were taken up in small lots by a large number of investors without means to extend operations after the initial capital was exhausted. It was so necessary to the shareholders that they pay dividends that very few were able to do so. Only a few of the mines along the Rhine tapped the great coal and iron resources which were shortly to form the basis of the economic transformation of Germany.[74]   And of these only the "Hibernia" and "Shamrock" mines near Duesseldorf remained long out of German hands.[75] These mines were opened by W. T. Mulvany, one time government engineer in Ireland, backed by Dublin capitalists and aided by British technicians, and they flourished under his management. Mulvany, however, became himself naturalized in time, as the Cockerills had done in Belgium, and he took a leading part in the development of the metallurgy of the Rhine and in the organization of industrialists for political purposes.[76]

Thus Great Britain stood in much the same relation to most of the regions of Europe around 1850 that Europe and the United States bore to the Orient and South America a half century later. Her enterprise and skill and capital in varying combinations and under varying conditions contributed to the rise of industrial life upon the Continent. The Continent would certainly have become industrialized in any case. The British contributions meant a quicker process, and in several directions a more intelligent one, reaping the advantage of experiments in England. The capital involved was by no means proportionate to the skill which Great Britain placed at the disposal of her neighbors, after 1841 without restriction. The romance of fortune was not infrequent in the relationship. But the great impulse to British industry on foreign soil came from nationalistic commercial policies. And in the face of lowering tariffs and expanding markets it was more advantageous to set up in industry or expand the plant at home.

"BILLS ON LONDON"

Probably the sporadic industrial undertakings of British technicians and capitalists were after 1850 of less importance for the transformation of European society than the services of the mercantile credit mechanism of London. It was from its activities that arose the first serious set-back to the elation which the gold discoveries and the transport revolution were encouraging.

Wherever commerce was dominated by British shipping and mercantile connections, generous credits excited business activity in the fifties. And British connections were ubiquitous in the Old World. A list of foreign bankers published in 1846 shows an English private banking firm in every Mediterranean port, forty in all, from Gibraltar to Jerusalem.[77] In the Baltic there were houses with English names at Riga, St. Petersburg, Dantzig, Memel and Stockholm. In the fifties the number multiplied. Book credits, acceptances, short-term accommodations of many sorts were at the command of customers of London, for whatever purpose required. "Open credits" were to be had at as low a rate as one-fourth of one per cent, with one and one-half as a highly exceptional maximum.[78] At Hamburg, Luebeck, Copenhagen and Dantzig as well as at New York and Constantinople, there arose swarms of commission houses operating entirely upon short credits continually renewed in London. Their funds were available in the first instance for commodity speculation; but they released others for promoting banks, building projects, municipal works.

The Germanies outside the Rhine provinces were especially stirred by the stimulus of London credit. There was considerable vigor and independence in the economic relations that were developing around Frankfurt-on-the-Main, Mannheim and Cologne. Industrially self-sufficient, the Rhinelands were already exporting capital. But their relations were more intimate with Brussels and Cincinnati than with London and New York. The bulk of German commerce still moved by way of the Hanse towns rather than the Rhine, and it moved with the support of English connections. Along historic lines of communication capitalistic activity of a curiously artificial sort developed in the fifties, sustained by bills on London.[79] Every little German state must have its bank of issue, its investment bank, its mortgage institution. The Bank of the Principality of Schwarzburg-Sonderhausen, for instance, a state with a population of 60,000 inhabiting an area of 17½ German square miles, had a capital of three million rixthalers, about $2,500,000. The Duchy of Saxe-Coburg-Gotha, with 150,000 inhabitants, boasted a bank with a twelve million dollar capitalization.[80] All issued paper

money which was worthless at the frontier. Floated into
existence by funds procurable indirectly from London, such
organizations were the means of drawing idle capital hoards
from the non-productive members of the community into the
possible service of production. The means were frequently
unscrupulous. That was business. In sequel Germany discovered that she could stand financially upon her own feet.
And that was empire.

Similar credit accommodations even more than direct investments were the means by which London in the fifties
helped New York and Boston merchants to bind the Atlantic
seaboard by railroad to the Mississippi.

And it was this chain of pseudo-mercantile credit ranging
from New York to Dantzig which developed weakness when
the panic of 1857 brought the first serious revulsion in the
money market in a decade. There was a bear raid upon
railway stocks in New York which sent banks first, then
brokers and companies financially to the wall. There was a
collapse in the sugar market, and Hamburg merchants were
caught. There was a sudden drain of money to the Far
East to meet the terrifying contingencies presented by the
Mutiny of the Sepoy regiments. And as the Bank rate
soared in London and discount rates were curtailed, a clear
majority of the merchants of the Hanse towns went into
liquidation, along with the bulk of the local banks they had
set in motion through the Germanies. The outstanding acceptances of Hamburg merchants alone amounted at this
time to four hundred million marks banco ($153,000,000).[81]
And for this in turn they looked chiefly to London, to merchants there of standing and brokers of optimism and nerve.
And London felt the effects of the failure. Thirty-one firms
in London who failed in consequence detailed their affairs to
a select Parliamentary committee.[82] Only two of them had

required a capital of more than one hundred thousand pounds with which to do business. But all of them together had managed to fail with total unsecured liabilities of thirteen million pounds and seven millions in assets good and bad. The volume of capital activity suggested by these figures was not necessarily a net export of capital. It cannot be definitely traced in any balance of trade payments. The essence of the transaction from the point of view of the exchanges appears to have been that British bills of apparently good standing entered into circulation between merchants and banks in foreign countries. There was a demand for sterling paper entirely apart from the demand to use it to pay for British goods. It was required as circulating capital to support speculation in produce markets. There was no saving at London necessarily involved; hardly any metallic reserve employed as its basis; no shipment of goods. The bills on London became to a degree currency in German market centers, stimulating enterprise and, at several removes, production.

Thus in another way the cycle of Anglo-American finance was repeated in Germany, and to a certain extent it terminated in a similar revulsion. A gloom settled down over most of the Germanies which increased rather than diminished as the political struggles of the sixties developed. But it freed that country from the excessive drafts upon the future that were to be a handicap to the rest of Europe at the moment when the German Empire was ready to commence its triumphant industrial career.

For the panic of 1857 brought no general financial housecleaning in England. Many of the accounts which it should have liquidated were still pending when the collapse of 1866 dragged a mass of business rottenness into public view. The panic scarcely interrupted the migration of capital abroad.

But it signalized at least one important shift in its direction. It quickened the movement of investment to India. And it gave an opportunity to French and Belgian iron manufacturers and associated groups, which were scarcely affected by the crisis at all, to enter the foreign field in sharper competition with British ironmasters.[83] In 1859 a Belgian syndicate wrested an important rail contract in Spain from the British, with the aid of generous financing from the *Société Générale de Belgique*. In subsequent years Switzerland and Holland fell under the dominance of Belgian ironmasters. And Russia sought her locomotives in Belgium and at Berlin. And while the Belgian output was entirely inadequate to be a formidable contestant in many quarters at once, and while, financially, concession-hunting continued to be carried on by international groups, it was startling for Great Britain to be unable to command any market open to foreign competition which she chose to supply.

The unsettled credit involvements of 1857 and the beginnings of concession competition on the part of foreign centers, independent of London, with their own capital supply, provoked efforts toward a more elaborate organization of British enterprise. They also turned the movement of British capital away from western Europe and into more remote areas, notably into the British possessions in India.

CHAPTER VII

THE STAKES OF EMPIRE

"Who shall doubt the secret hid
Under Cheops' pyramid
Was that the contractor did
Cheops out of several millions?"
    —Kipling, *Departmental Ditties.*

"India is at our mercy; we can charge her what we wish."
    —Sir Charles Trevelyan (1873).

A PERIOD OF PAINLESS INCOME

Nearly every part of the world borrowed of England's capital surplus before she made notable use of it in her empire overseas. The spoil of India and the sugar colonies had indeed laid the foundation upon which her imposing financial edifice was built. The business aristocracy of London, at least before the railway era, consisted of the great East and West India families which drew their steady income from the dependencies. But it was income without commensurate investment. The profits of the eighteenth century empire were painless. Important as British possessions were to British trade and to the financial structures which depended upon its growth, their extensive development by the export of saved capital or thru the magnanimity of the London bill-broking mechanism had not been seriously undertaken before 1850. Neither the economic development of dependencies nor the political control of areas of commercial interest had become axioms of policy in Lombard Street and Whitehall.

It was wholly agreeable to the laissez-faire philosophy which was winning its most daring triumphs in the thirties and forties that investor and empire should be so distant. But too much must not be made to hang upon devotion to doctrine. With British fleets riding unchallenged every sea, the supreme commercial importance of areas under the British flag did not seem so axiomatic as it has to a later generation of business men. British traders dominated the economics of Africa from 1800 to 1875 far more completely than they have done in the age of imperialism. And Great Britain then possessed but a few trading posts and victualling stations on the way about the Cape to India. Commercial men who stirred with excitement over impediments to trade in the alien Caribbean and the China Sea, were frankly bored by Britain's possessions in Australasia and the Canadas. There was a small group of "colonial reformers" headed by Edward Wakefield, which set various colonizing activities on foot between 1830 and 1850. They preached the doctrine of an oversupply of capital and labor in the British Isles, and urged its employment under the British flag in the development of British domain.[1] But the sporadic undertakings which ensued relieved England of little of her capital and did not develop her domain or earn her dividends until Australia became a synonym for gold.[2] The empire stirred men not. And for speculations that merely were remote, without other romantic appeal, the British investor in the first three-quarters of the century had no particular fancy.

In fact British capital was not allured by distant undertakings which involved the element of continuous control, if commerce with its turnover annually or more often be excepted. British enterprise built railways in western Europe in the early fifties to sell them at a profit. The builders did not remain in control. The investments which they retained did not need their oversight. Capital accounts upon the Continent were manipulated at the expense of the state, not at that of the security holders. The continuous administration of any sort of a foreign enterprise from London was a rarity. Such instances of it as the Belgian branch railways were not particularly happy. The industrial and mining undertakings on the Continent which made a permanent success in British hands involved the migration of the capitalist, and in some cases the transfer of his national allegiance.

But toward the end of the fifties British capital began to move in volume into countries which had neither the means nor the administrative capacity to redeem and carry on with ease the public works which they desired. Hence the companies formed to build railways in Russia, Scandinavia, South America, Canada and India made their headquarters with some permanence in London and operated their properties from there. Thus opened a period of enterprise administered abroad from London. Not that the British investor gave preference to these investments because they involved that sort of control. London control seemed necessary for the undertakings which British capital desired to promote.

There was, on the one hand, a half-conscious attempt at an economic distribution of capital. The progress of the railway and of industrialism in western Europe meant the rapid extension of plant without corresponding improvement in the production of raw materials. The tendency of the machine was to outstrip the land. It was only by putting steam to the task of persuading farm produce to seek a market, that equilibrium could be maintained and, with equilibrium, profits.

The effects of the Industrial Revolution were thus communicated to countries in which railways needed to be operated as well as built by aliens. For not all agricultural areas were so free from traditional mores as the United States then were, or as adept at using borrowed money to suit themselves.

Thus the economic situation favored a redirection of the current of capital and enterprise at the very time when railway contractors and their associates were finding the profits of their activity in western Europe curtailed by the rising competition of French and Belgian and German entrepeneurs. In the decade from 1860 to 1870 there were more miles of railway built in France and Italy than in the one before. But British contractors did not build so many of them. Most of the capital was arranged for by the bankers of Paris and Frankfurt and Brussels. The center of activity of Brassey and Peto, of the Warings and the Pickerings moved to the fertile plains of eastern Europe, to India, to the fringes of commercial civilization. Thus a change of direction in the migration of British capital formed part of a movement for the development of new areas of production.

The elements of the situation can not be disconnected. There were new sources of raw materials to be made available. An expensive engineering and constructing plant must continue to produce an income. And in sequel there came the initial stages of the expansion of British industry as a working whole beyond the borders of the British Isles. We can discern the first manifestations of that spirit which may be properly denominated "economic imperialism." *   At the

* A great many areas of the world had been in a vital economic dependence upon Great Britain before the fifties for markets and for supplies. They had been dependent for capital in the quantity immediately desired, and they were in turn in-

same time we can witness the first widespread concern for the employment of British capital in the development of British possessions. The migration of British capital did not suddenly cease in 1857 to be cosmopolitan and become at once imperialistic. A considerable part of British investments abroad never took on imperialistic traits, never involved the direct control from England by economic or political means

volved in the correlative obligations of debtor. The American "cotton kingdom" was such an area. In this case the dependence was mutual between Lancashire and the South.

There was nothing of imperialism in this. My conception of "economic imperialism" involves more than *vital dependence.* It means *control* from without. It means conscious direction, however blundering, however ignorant of its own social significance. Moreover it means control of any directive kind, whether economic or political, whether thru the pressure of a navy or thru the purposive employment of a discount or exchange rate, whether thru a restriction upon loans or as exerted upon isolated units of a country's economic life thru the decisions of alien companies operating within its frontiers. Where these companies control an essential industry, either as to market, output, or production, where they dominate the social life of a community, economic imperialism certainly exists whether it bears a sinister connotation, threatening a disturbance of the world's peace, or not.

The real question in control is not the matter of dependence for markets or sources of supply. It is the center of enterprise. In this sense there is no Egyptian, Argentinian, almost no Indian or South African, certainly no Cuban or Peruvian economic system. The economic activities of these regions are all functions of a spirit of enterprise manifested either in the British Isles or at New York. They form organic portions of a British or of an American economic system. It is this expansive power of enterprise which gives rise to economic imperialism, as the term is here employed.

of economic life outside the British Isles. There have always been some which did. It was not until the fifties, however, that they became momentous for the countries concerned. For Canada and India the importation of British capital at that time implied a persistent measure of business control from London. And it gave rise to memorable episodes in which arts of political manipulation gave aid to the craft of enterprise.

THE GRAND TRUNK OF CANADA AND OTHER CONTRACTS

Canada, at least, had not been unmoved by the clamor of railway building in the mother country and across her southern boundary.[3] There were plans for railway systems as early as 1836, and they may have had some remote connection with contemporary troubles with the United States. The company stage was reached in the early forties. With the encouragement of various land companies a number of projects were launched during the mania of 1845 and enabled to fly the colors of a London board of directors. Only one line was actually begun, however. This was the first international railway in the world, the Atlantic and St. Lawrence, running from Montreal to Portland, Maine. Construction was slow. But the urgency of an American promoter, John Poor, the interest of the British-American Land Company, thru whose territories the railway ran, and the fitful support of the London money market brought the Atlantic and St. Lawrence under Canadian management safely through the crisis of 1847. And in the early fifties it was looking for more capital to complete its line.

By this time Canadians had discovered that there were important connections between railways and politics. It was not necessary to import this folkway from Europe. "Railways are my politics," is the slogan under which Sir Allan

McNab, Conservative leader, is said to have contested elections. Canada, like the monarchies of Europe, sought refuge from her domestic broils in visions of profitable contracts and increments in town-site values.

For several years following 1845 the politician-contractors in Montreal and Toronto and the land company proprietors in London bent their efforts to procure a British government guarantee for the railways they wished to build. If they had capital they certainly did not wish to risk it except upon terms which would insure them against loss. They pinned their hopes upon Earl Grey at the Colonial Office, who was member of a political clan which had been thoroly infected with Wakefield's ideas of colonial reform.[4] Canada had earlier been given guarantees upon some canal loans, and there were some short lines of railway in the Crown Colonies which were receiving imperial assistance. Moreover one of Grey's kinsmen, Edward Ellice, had large estates in Canada likely to benefit by railway development. The Canadian promoters were pursuing a railway and reciprocity program which, while uniting the Canadas politically, would intercept a portion of the American grain trade and carry it to the sea at Quebec or Halifax or Portland. But these advantages seemed to Victorian statesmen only commercial, and there appeared to be no special reason for a guarantee for such a line if the advantages were real. The Colonial Office would hear to nothing but an all-British route, primarily strategical and shunning the American border. For their part Canadians did not care for the line surveyed by government engineers which ran so far from the American border that it passed thru no towns at all.

So railways lagged behind proposals. The provinces talked of building at their own expense, borrowing upon their own credit in London. But they were assured by their financial agents, Barings and Glyns, that their credit was not good enough to warrant government construction on a large scale. There seemed to be nothing to do but to wait upon private enterprise in the provinces. In the early fifties it appeared that the railways which local capital would build would be, like the Great Western between Buffalo and Detroit, chiefly of interest to American cities and calculated to render the provinces permanently tributary to New York.

Canada was so far fortunate, however, that a group of the largest contractors in England became convinced of the possibilities of the intercepted grain trade, or at least of the possibilities of a railway company which proposed to intercept it. In the slack period which lasted for construction work to the end of 1851, contractors began work to secure a favorable contract. Agents of Messrs. Peto, Brassey, Betts & Jackson toured the Provinces in 1851 and dabbled in the elections in Nova Scotia, opposing candidates who were pledged to state construction. When the Hon. Francis Hincks, Inspector-General of Finances, was sent to London in the following year to negotiate a guarantee with the Colonial Office, the flattering attentions of William Jackson enabled him to forget his instructions entirely. Instead of procuring a British guarantee for Canadian promoters, Hincks pledged a Canadian guarantee to British. And Jackson, following later in the year to lend expert assistance in handling the legislature, spoke so spaciously of the vast resources of his associates that from sheer self-respect the provincial assemblies were constrained to deal as casually as the contractors in millions. They bargained for generous payment for earlier contracts and concessions in which their members were largely interested, and pledged the credit of Canada for three million pounds in guarantee of the projected company's debentures. The government's financial advisers in London assured it that while British capital might purchase Canadian bonds with reluctance, it could not resist the attraction of a railway planned by Robert Stephenson and constructed by Peto, Brassey, Betts & Jackson. And upon the advice of the same great business thinkers it was resolved to make this railway as comprehensive as possible, a grand trunk line from the Atlantic through the length of the province to the West.

Thus in the spring of 1853 the Grand Trunk Railway of Canada was presented to the British public. The auspices were impressive in the extreme. Thomas Baring and George Carr Glyn headed the board of directors, and with their names were coupled those of Alderman William Thompson, Kirkman D. Hodgson, Robert McCalmont, H. Wollaston Blake, and the entire cabinet of Upper Canada, dressed out in their official designations. "Commencing at the debouchére of the three longest lakes in the world," ran the prospectus of the railway, "it pours the accumulating traffic in one unbroken line throughout the entire length of Canada into the St. Lawrence at Montreal and Quebec, on which it rests on the north, while on the south it reaches the magnificent harbors of Portland and St. John on the ocean." Dividends of 11½% upon the shares were promised. And a very few of them were offered to the public to subscribe. The bulk of the nine million pounds it was believed the railway would cost, were to be raised by debentures. More than two million pounds of the shares and bonds were used from the start to buy out the interest of existing companies and contractors especially in the Montreal to Portland railway. And securities were also put down to the credit of Canadian statesmen, naturally very much against their will, and to the subsequent embarrassment of some.[5] The bulk of the debentures, including those guaranteed by the Provinces, were reserved for the contractors, to be sold for their account as construction progressed. It seems to have been believed that the shares would really be as remunerative as the prospectus promised, for they were held closely by the financial agents, until the flying rumors made it disadvantageous to sell.

Meanwhile the great technical organization which was to show Canada how to build railways brought its resources into play. At Birkenhead a complete engineering plant, the Canada Works, embodying the latest American morticing and planing devices, was erected expressly to supply structural iron and rolling stock as rapidly as was demanded. Special agents roved Lower Canada and Ireland in search of husky workmen, on whose wages they earned a generous percentage. And labor, employed at the high wages imperative in America, was used in as reckless profusion as on the Continent, where it was cheaper, and with equipment, the left-overs of other undertakings, which impressed American contractors as hopelessly out-of-date.

While the expenditure of money for the works continued, there was very little in the power of a Canadian legislature to grant, which the contractors were not able to procure. And they needed a good deal to avoid eventual loss. In 1855 the Grand Trunk encountered financial difficulties; its funds were so exhausted that it could no longer pay interest on its debentures out of capital. Its securities were already a by-word. A shareholders' committee headed by the Governor of the Bank of England, considered the situation and decided that Canada should give a five per cent guarantee for ninety-nine years upon the entire capital, as Belgium had done and India. A mission which included Brassey and Betts themselves journeyed to Canada to press the demand. One ministry refused outright. The Provinces resounded with controversy. Ministers resigned, and a new government taking the advice of the governor-general, Lord Elgin, arranged a compromise. "For a decade after 1855,'" says a recent Canadian historian, "scarcely a year passed without a bill to amend the terms of the Grank Trunk agreement. One year it was an additional guarantee, another a temporary loan, again a postponement of the government's lien." [6] And by 1859, when the dedication of the expensive Victoria bridge at Montreal brought the railway to completion, the finances of the Canadian government were hopelessly compromised, together with those of the company. On its operations from January 1, 1858 to June 30, 1860, the railway did not even make expenses. By 1861 it had a deficit of thirteen million dollars, carried largely upon bankers' loans; it was delinquent in interest upon its unguaranteed debentures; and its road-bed and rolling-stock were already in such deplorable condition that heavy renewals had to begin at once. Instead of a railway built upon the best English models, contractors had built as cheaply as possible and turned over a line that had to be rebuilt thruout twice over before twenty years had elapsed. Some unprofitable sections had been built for patriotic reasons. The line managed to avoid many towns which might have developed local traffic. The thru traffic was slow in developing. The advantages of rail routes over lake-and-canal were not at once important. The Grand Trunk had no permanent connections to Chicago. It had difficulty in developing return freights to balance the movement of grain and agricultural products from the West. Capital accounts had been hopelessly demoralized by management from London. And the insistence of London upon English railway managers burdened the operating costs with officials who toured the land in vice-regal splendor and won for their road an animosity which grew.

A timely conversion of Canada's scattered obligations in

1860 brought solvency to the government. But successive attempts at reorganization extending over sixty years did not enable the Grand Trunk to pay·a cent of interest either upon its common stock or upon the preferred shares into which the original debentures were in 1862 converted. Something of the prestige of its inaugural always clung to the ill-starred railway. However badly managed by its London directors, however abused in the Dominion, it seldom failed to command a support on the Stock Exchange quite out of relation to its circumstances. For the sake of the control of its financing and of Dominion remittances, which its ownership maintained, the large shareholders never permitted their unremunerative stock to be written off. And until the coming of the Canadian Pacific more than a generation later, the Grand Trunk remained the one great investment link between Great Britain and her oldest dominion.

Not even the British promoters, however, found the profits all that had been hoped. It is believed that the firm of Gzowski & Co., of which A. T. Galt was the leading spirit, did proportionately better out of the Grand Trunk than the more celebrated British group. But the "vast resources" of Peto, Brassey, Betts and Jackson were never really hazarded for the railway in Canada at all. A complaisant legislature and a winning governor-general helped them over every difficulty. It was for the glamor of a distant syndicate and the ineptitude of absentee administration that the Canadian taxpayer was saddled with the bill of costs.

The investment of British capital was reckoned in the books of the Grand Trunk in the early sixties at twelve million pounds. And the net debt of the Canadian provinces, including twenty million dollars borrowed for canal purposes in the forties and guarantees upon such smaller railways as the Great Western, amounted to more than seventy million dollars.

It was not the fault of the English company which controlled the Great Western of Canada that its story was not in every respect the same as that of the larger system in which it was ultimately absorbed. The Great Western was really an American railroad at first, a link between Buffalo and Detroit over foreign soil. Its original contractor was Samuel Zimmerman, a lusty Pennsylvanian, who became virtually political boss in Ontario for a time. And its early stages were financed by merchants in Detroit and by some of the Yankee capitalists who in the fifties put together the New York Central. It was in reality a westward extension of the latter. But in 1852 the need for railway iron brought the road to London. And the capitalists associated with Samuel Laing, John Masterman, Jr., and the contractor George Wythes took command. They too secured a guarantee from Canada as price of acquiescence in the Grand Trunk scheme. But they did not look to dividends for their reward. Some of the directors are said to have financed the contractor and to have shared his profits. They did finance extensions, even into the United States. Among them was the Detroit, Grand Haven & Milwaukee, also built by Wythes, which they later sold to their company at cost when it proved unprofitable. They sold about six million pounds of securities in Great Britain for their undertakings. And by 1860, a stockholders' committee reported, they had wasted the company's resources, at least in part to their own profit, to the extent of one million pounds.[7]

Lesser railway projects, mines, land and mortgage companies, banks and municipal loans absorbed about five million pounds more of absentee British capital in the fifties and sixties prior to the formation of the Dominion in 1867.

London was also called upon for capital in the fifties for railways and docks and municipal works in the Australian colonies, at the Cape and in the West Indies. In 1858, Victoria, new-born of the gold discoveries, commenced an eight million pound construction program. Morton Peto and Thomas Brassey undertook railway contracts at the antipodes. The Australian colonies did not encourage the amphibious finance in which Canada became involved. They had been equally ready to negotiate an imperial guarantee to help them float their own bonds, and some of the crown colonies received it for small loans. But after 1857 they found that they could borrow money on their unaided credit for the purpose as rapidly as they wished to build their own public utilities. There was opportunity for fortune and achievement in Australia for those who wished to make their homes there. But it was not thither that most enterprising business men about 1857 were directing their hopes.

CARRYING CIVILIZATION TO INDIA

For the British Empire was not wrought of the regions which have become equal partners in the post-war Commonwealth. It is India which has made the empire. And the rebellion of 1857, miscalled the Mutiny, marks the turning-point in imperial history. Its stirring episodes focussed the attention of both business men and statesmen upon the dependency which had been born of British trade and left so long to a trading company to rear. The winning of India for a second time gave that possession fresh value to the race whose hearts were wrung with stories of men who fought to save themselves from death and of women who had been exposed to hidden perils in a rebellious land. Here was not merely a continent of land, but people, with an established economic life and a civilization—which the Victorians referred to as "superstitious practices." It would not only mean profit, it was a duty to carry the torch of civilization and progress to a land from which the light had been so long withheld. The nonconformist conscience of England, prophet of radicalism and laissez-faire, would remake India in England's image. It demanded the East India Company, last relic of the mercantilism it had overthrown, in propitiatory sacrifice.[8] In meeting-house and chapel, upon the hustings and in the provincial press was voiced the spirit which animated less explicitly the policy of the government and the behavior of the money market. From 1857 to 1865 the major movement of British capital was toward India, to transform the land with public works. The government passed at the same time from Company to Crown, augmenting its activity and expense. And the effort that was made brought home with the dividends a spirit ripe for imperialism and impatient of laissez-faire.

The original investment of British capital in India was very small. The trade of the East India Company in the eighteenth century was carried on principally with Dutch capital, borrowed readily at a low rate and securing excellent profits to the shareholders. The subjugation of successive portions of the decrepit Mogul empire to the Company's authority paid for itself.[9] Subsequent wars and annexations were financed by rupee loans, floated in Calcutta, in which the civil and military servants of the Company invested for safe-keeping their accumulations, which included not a little booty.[10] And as independent mercantile establishments grew up to carry on the trade and to engage in exchange banking, they too were financed from the savings and plunder of the

Company's servants.[11]   So in the middle of the nineteenth century, residents of England were in possession of plantation mortgages, shares in the mercantile and banking establishments, and rupee loans, which had been brought there from time to time as Indian officials returned to educate their children or to enjoy a quiet old age. These interests represented simply portions of the Indian spoil and revenue reinvested in India. They did not constitute an export of British capital. Only the income from them entered into the commercial balances. There it went to swell the annual economic drain upon India—the surplus export of tea, indigo and cotton to England, of textiles to the Continent, and of opium to China, to provide for the home expenses of the Indian administration,—the salaries of the London bureaucracy, pensions and dividends to East India shareholders. By such revenues and profits the British nation had been deriving an average annual income of three or four million pounds from its Indian estate for seventy years, with neither expense nor trouble to itself.[12]

It is easier to understand, however, that Great Britain made money out of her occupation of India, than to realize that she was not in 1850 developing the country so as to make as much money as possible. The stimulating effects of canals and railways in Europe were well known to members of the East India Court. Some of them had been making excellent dividends upon their railway investments in France and England, and upon the consequent appreciation of other property in which they were interested. But to 1848, according to the evidence of one of these directors, the Company had spent only £1,434,000 in public works since the reforms of 1834 out of a revenue of twenty million pounds a year.[13] To the government of their great dependency Englishmen had so far contributed only a certain efficiency. The methods and ideals of its administration they had borrowed from their predecessors, not necessarily without wisdom. The Company treated its domain as an oriental despot his estate, to be exploited not improved, an important economic difference being that the European landlord was an absentee. The chief economic results of the first century of British rule in India had been the ruin of the cotton manufacture in the face of Manchester competition, a diversion of labor from raising grain to the raising of opium, sugar, indigo and to a slight extent of tea, and a compulsion upon the ryot to market a larger proportion of his yearly crop in order to procure silver to pay his tribute to the government.[14]

The negative character of Company rule did not prevail merely because it was oriental, however. Nor was it simply because to its dual government in London, as to successive generations of high-minded Britons, India was "somewhere east of Suez." It was part and parcel of the governmental pessimism which guided British statesmanship in varying degrees from 1825 to 1874. There being no economic process which government would not mar by its intervention, policy consisted in doing as little as decency would permit. If true at home, this doctrine was of special validity with reference to a great dependency such as India, of whose ultimate future no one would dare to think hard. So for many years road-building and railways, river-steamers and the cultivation of tea and cotton existed chiefly as subjects for interminable minutes which continued to increase in bulk. No one formulated objections to these things in principle; no one stirred to bring them into practical realization. Capitalists hesitated to invest because they were uncertain of the political situation, of land tenures, of the adaptability to oriental culture of western technique.[15] They desired encouragement from the Company, a privileged status, penal process for the enforcement of contracts. And the Company, which had been taught commercial liberalism by the reforms which in 1813 and 1834 destroyed its own privileges, demurred at interference with the natural laws of trade. It required the strong interest of influential people to set the Company to promoting progress in India.

The mania of 1845 produced nearly a dozen companies in London which proposed to build railways in India. They were apparently as much interested in premiums upon their shares as in transportation.[16]   And only two of them survived the panic. There was the *East Indian Railway Company,* promoted by Macdonald Stephenson, relative of the more famous engineers, who seems to have been the earliest person to plan railways for India. Stephenson was backed by Cockerill & Co., Fletcher, Alexander & Co., Crawford, Colvin & Co., Palmer, Mackillop & Dent, and several others of the great East India houses, and by the shipping interests, the new Peninsular & Oriental, desirous not only to expand the volume of Indian trade, but also to procure access to the Burdwan coal mines. As early as 1846 the governor-general, Lord Hardinge, recommended that the *East Indian* company be given land and a guarantee upon its capital for a railway to run from Calcutta up the Ganges.[17]   Five lacs of rupees a year could be saved on the army if it could make the transit of India by rail. But there was a Board of Control in London, headed by British politicians, to satisfy as well as the Company and its agents. And another railway project was competing for the favor of the London authorities. The *Great Indian Peninsular* contemplated a line from Bombay to tap the great cotton-producing districts of Nagpoor. Its support came from Bombay and Liverpool, and the Lancashire mill-owners made its cause their own thru their lobbyists at London. The cotton famine of 1846, no less than the diplomacy of President Polk, had reminded Lancashire of its dependence for cotton supply upon the United States and the Southern slave-system.[18] And during the session of 1847–48 a parliamentary committee headed by John Bright investigated the growth of cotton in India and agreed that deficient transportation was a leading difficulty.[19] The East India Company had been incredibly remiss in its attention to public works. And the need was great enough to justify some departure from the high ground of economic principle. The company should assist railways to overcome the initial friction of adventure in the Orient. But if it was going to give guarantees to any railway, preference should be given to one which would help cotton. After months of recrimination from all concerned it was decided to give land and interest guarantees to "experimental" lines along each of the competing routes. Neither experiment was completed until 1853.

For guarantees did not build railways, much less encourage capital to rush recklessly into projects which did not bear them. Enthusiasm as expressed in stuffy banquets and weighty memorials was great, but the faith that moves money markets was lacking. Successive governors-general and Anglo-Indian publicists represented the incalculable advantages to be realized from the development of a railway system embracing all India. And the political benefits were not unmentioned. It remained, however, for Lord Dalhousie—an empire-builder of the power of Warren Hastings and the prestige in London of Cecil Rhodes—to formulate these considerations with the voice of final authority.

"Great tracts are teeming with produce they cannot dispose of," wrote Dalhousie in a minute dated April 20, 1853, which is in a sense the fundamental charter of Indian railways.[20] "England is calling aloud for the cotton which India does already produce in some degree, and would produce sufficient in quality, and plentiful in quantity, if only there were provided the fitting means of conveyance for it." Moreover a few railway lines radiating from the three Presidency capitals, Calcutta, Bombay and Madras, would have "immeasurable political advantages." They would "enable the government to bring the main bulk of its military strength to bear upon any given point, in as many days as it would now require months." In consequence it would be possible to reduce materially the number and expense of soldiery in India. With such a saving in prospect not even the most censorious of financial radicals could demur at the policy Dalhousie proposed to pursue in securing railways. During the railway mania in England Dalhousie had stood almost alone among public men in advocating more strict regulations by the government, the control of capital expenditure, the prevention of competitive waste, the adjustment of rates with a maximum of passenger traffic in view. In India it seemed even more important to prevent the multiplication of English enterprises over which the English rulers could not exercise strict control. There was political dynamite in the railway and it needed close handling to make sure that its explosion did not menace the British Raj.

On the other hand, Dalhousie was impressed, as many other observers, with the tendency of English rule to paralyze initiative in India, to make the prompting of central authority indispensable to the least undertaking, either of Indians or their conquerors. Hence Dalhousie did not wish the government to undertake to build the railways itself. He wanted to bring capital and enterprise direct from England, hoping that in the process there might be revealed something of the alchemy with which the British contractors had wrought in

France, that India herself might be stirred to enterprise
under the sage guidance of a benevolent despotism.

As formula for the accomplishment of his aims, Dalhousie
recommended a comprehensive railway system, to be developed by companies under plans approved by government
engineers, with contracts which freed them from danger of
competition. The government should acquire the land necessary for right-of-way, lease it to the companies free of rent
or taxes for ninety-nine years, and guarantee five per cent
interest on the capital expended under the supervision of
public engineers. The risk was insignificant, he considered.
The railways would pay their charges as soon as they were
completed, for they could be built easily for eight thousand
pounds a mile. But the government would secure the railways that it wanted in the way it wanted them, and at the
end of the concession period would automatically become proprietor of the system.

Dalhousie carried everything before him. By 1853 the
virtues of the French railway policy which paid ten per cent
to investors in comparison to the English three were the
commonplace of the City; Napoleon was the hero of the railway interest. India should have guaranteed railways and
plenty of them. The experimental lines were granted extensions, the *East Indian* company a thousand miles up the
Ganges to Delhi, and plans for three more large railway
systems were speedily approved. Partly, no doubt, for its
zeal, the East India Company received indefinite extension
for its charter of government. In execution of these railways, three hundred miles of track had been completed for
traffic by the summer of 1857, and fourteen million pounds
had been raised from British investors for railway construction in India.

THE CROWN ENCOURAGES PRIVATE ENTERPRISE

The events of 1857 demonstrated the soundness of Dalhousie's political argument with dramatic conclusiveness. The railway proved to be one effective step that statesman had taken to enable his successor to cope with the rebellion his annexation policy had inspired. The railway lines already available shortened by days the movement of troops to upper India; while the telegraph which accompanied, and in a degree preceded, the railway, gave cohesion to the scattered British commands.[21]

Thus one of the first consequences of the Indian revolt was a focussing of money market zeal upon transportation in India. There was a decline in the guaranteed stocks on the first news of the rebellion. But the decline was only for a few months, and it was not as great as that caused to many other securities by the concurrent panic. The shares of the East Indian and Great Indian Peninsular scarcely fell below par, and they had completely recovered by Christmas, 1857. It was clear that Great Britain was determined to keep her empire, and few claims upon it seemed so promising as "guaranteed" railways. Guaranteed by whom or to what extent many investors did not inquire. The savings of the middle classes which had borne the burden of home railway construction and had found little enough share in the cosmopolitan adventures of the contractors, warmed to the call of empire and the "guaranteed" five per cent. Commoners demanded clamorously that railways under construction be carried rapidly to completion. A parliamentary inquiry was held to ascertain why their building was so slow. Under the pressure of public opinion especially in the manufacturing districts the Company and the dual government were replaced by a new régime for India which promised to be more directly responsive to the wants and interests of the people of the British Isles. The Queen herself thru a principal secretary of state assumed charge of the great dependency. And her government was generous with its support to those who had blessings of progress to carry to the East.

"It is our earnest desire to stimulate the peaceful industry of India," ran the proclamation in which the Queen announced the new order of things to her puzzled wards in the East; "to promote works of public utility and improvement, and to administer its government for the benefit of all our subjects resident therein. In their prosperity will be our strength, in their contentment our security, and in their gratitude our best reward." [22]

Other recompense would, however, not be spurned. When Lord Stanley assumed the seals of the new India Office in 1858 the hopes of his Lancashire neighbors were great. "It was expected," testifies a jovial bureaucrat, "that great encouragement would be given to what was called private enterprise in India, which meant, of course, that private individuals should go there, Government undertaking to guarantee the parties against all loss, and leaving them all the profits." [23] And it was not difficult to perceive that the projects already begun were not enough. The cotton of the Gujerat must be brought to port at Bombay. Bombay must be joined to Calcutta by way of Juppulpore, and to Madras. Calcutta must have a new port, named for the Queen's first viceroy, Lord Canning, with a railway to intervene. There must also be a railway from Calcutta into eastern Bengal. And to give solidity to the strategical fabric of India, the entire Indus valley, acquired from Afghanistan by war, must undergo intensive development. So there appeared a *Scinde* railway to carry where the Indus was not navigable, an Indus Steam Navigation Company to carry where it was, a *Punjaub* railway to join the valley to Amritsar and Lahore, and a *Delhi* railway to complete the circuit of upper India. There were numerous port development companies, also with public guarantee, to take advantage of the contemplated importance of Kurachi. Many of these projects had substantial merit. There was also a Madras Canal and Irrigation Company, which after an expenditure of £1,600,000 of guaranteed capital, completed a canal thirteen years later which could not be filled with water, and which there was no assured water supply to fill.

It was the Indian taxpayer who had to pay for this progress. He had no voice in the matter. The Indian government was responsible to the taxpayers of Great Britain. And British opinion was anxious to show that the Crown could do more for India than the Company. A few Englishmen were beginning to suspect with Dilke and Arnold that the railways would make India for the first time a nation. But no one in a position of responsibility doubted that it was desirable to transform India more closely into likeness with the West, and to do it as speedily as possible. The *Economist* admitted, for instance, that under the conditions "fewer and cheaper railways, and more numerous roads and canals" would have been better investments.[24] The importance of the railway lay in its "civilising influence," its tendency to promote the "principles of secular government which, without any touch of intentional proselytism, have struck so effectually at the rapidly decomposing structure of native superstition." It must be said that in India older members of the services, including many of those most tinged with religiosity, struggled valiantly against the tide of extravagance and the pressure for increased tax levies to meet the costs of progress. Sir John Lawrence, the most vigorous personal-

ity in India during the decade following the Mutiny, and possibly the most Christian, frowned steadily upon promoters.

But there were quarters in India where men who sought
fortune and career found a warmer official welcome. Sir
Bartle Frere, Commissioner of Sind in the fifties, later of the
Viceroy's Council at Calcutta and finally Governor of Bombay, was an Anglo-Indian almost as notable as Lawrence and
with conflicting ideas of policy.[25] His geniality gave heart
to promoters, and his Rooseveltian indifference to red-tape
made the strategical official positions in which he was placed
a source of frequent extra-legal aid to British enterprise.
Mackinnon, a young Scotchman running coasting steamers
to Rangoon, obtained an introduction to Frere at Calcutta,
and tendered a proposal to extend his business around India
to Kurachi, with government assistance. "You are the man
I have been looking for for years," exclaimed Frere. He
hastened Mackinnon's project through the necessary formal-
ities at Calcutta, and his first act at Bombay was to accord the
sanction of that presidency which was essential to some of the
provisions. And there thus originated the British India
Steam Navigation Company which in the ensuing generation,
through Mackinnon's activity, was to be a great instrument
in empire-building from the Persian Gulf to Zanzibar, cul-
minating in the British East Africa Company and the present
Kenya Colony.

Bombay under Frere's presidency entered upon an Augus-
tan age. The blockade of the American South gave sudden
impetus to the cotton exports from that port. A land boom
accompanied this access of commercial prosperity. Frere
seized the opportunity to level the ramparts of the city, to
sell the liberated land for building lots, and to embark on the
construction of public buildings, with widened streets and
modern sanitation. Too late, he sought to check the course

of the speculative mania which developed at Bombay. Parsees and Englishmen became as one in the traffic of a hundred bubble companies. There was no restraint possible for the recklessness of English bank managers and bill-mongers. But there was no distinction of race in the ruin that followed the close of the American Civil War, the break in the cotton market, and the collapse of the Bombay boom.[26] It was not Frere's fault that the Bombay Presidency itself did not become a large shareholder in the Bank of Bombay, which took the lead in the speculative banking which abetted the mania and disaster.

But for any favors showed by British officials to enterprise in India, they could plead the generous approval of the Home Government. "For some time past," Sir Charles Wood assured the House of Commons in 1863, "there has been no check whatsoever as far as money goes."[27] It was generally believed in England that "there would be room with the growing prosperity of the country, to increase indefinitely if need were, the resources of the Government."[28] And the chief criticism in Parliament of the Indian régime was that in addition to its railway policy, it did not create a special status for Englishmen who proposed to take up waste land in India, exempting them from local authority, enabling them to commute the land tax and obtain freehold tenure in perpetuity, and providing them with compulsory penal process to enforce contracts with tenants and workmen.[29] The Port Canning boom was one project forced upon India by pressure from home. The English political community was uncritically on the side of the projectors.

Nor was the money market any hindrance to the steady movement of British capital to India in as large quantities as the government would guarantee a return upon or subsidize with privileges. For a few years after 1857 no investment field appeared so promising. Competition was reducing the return from Continental enterprise. American investments were rendered uncertain by the domestic crisis which broke into Civil War in 1861. In 1858 Thomas Brassey indicated his readiness to handle an Indian contract. Other large English contractors followed him into the new field of activity, and contributed to the celerity with which railway building went on after 1857 as compared with previous years when building had largely been done by the companies themselves.[30] Thus the prestige of the great contractor was added to the charm which perfect security at a minimum rate of 5% offered to the investor. There were many who believed that in buying Indian guaranteed securities the guarantee that they had was that of Great Britain. Many who were better informed felt that Indian securities were as safe as English because if India was ruined, England would be ruined also. And Lord Stanley, the accommodating Indian Secretary of State, had expressed official doubt whether England could ever permit a default in the Indian debt.[31]

So great was the outflow of British capital to India that in the early sixties the cry was raised by railway and agricultural interests at home that it was causing a serious rise in the interest rate. The amount of capital expended upon Indian railways alone from 1858 to 1869 inclusive is summarized in the following table:

Year	Amount	Year	Amount
1858	£5,500,000	1864	£3,800,000
1859	7,150,000	1865	5,400,000
1860	7,580,000	1866	7,700,000
1861	6,500,000	1867	7,000,000
1862	5,800,000	1868	4,500,000
1863	4,780,000	1869	4,400,000

These amounts represented the savings of an exceedingly wide class of investors. On January 1, 1868 there were 49,-690 share and debenture holders, practically all of whom were residents of Great Britain, who held an average of about £1,500 of Indian Guaranteed railway securities. The market was a quiet one; its fluctuations were not great; and there was little publicity involved. It was not necessary to advertise new issues with elaborate prospectuses in the financial press. And when the railway credit was low, that of the Indian government could be depended upon. The India Office was the real fiscal agent for the railway companies, and actually advanced sums to cover their capital needs when the market was temporarily tight.

This was one of the few economies involved in the capitalization of the Indian railways. There were no costs of promotion and flotation to meet. In all other respects the guarantee system was extremely expensive, to the guarantors. Dalhousie's idea had been to limit guarantees strictly to original estimates and to provide penalties for breach of contract. He intended further to limit the obligation of the government to the stipulated per cent upon the capital, irrespective of whether the railway earned its operating expenses or not. On the face of the contract dividends were not to be guaranteed. India was not to be taxed to make up deficits. But these safeguards of economy in construction and operation were tampered with when the contracts were arranged in London. And to the criticisms of the government in India, Lord Stanley returned the answer that the money market demanded guarantees that were virtually absolute. A subsequent Public Works Secretary at the India Office has characterized the resulting situation as follows: [32]

How in one clause of these remarkable indentures it is pro-

vided that at the end of ninety-nine years' lease the railway
treated of shall by mere fluxion of time pass absolutely and
gratuitously into the Government's possession, and how by
the very next clause the proprietary Company, if preferring to
be paid for the line and its appurtenances instead of parting
with them for nothing is empowered to exact from the Government, their full cost price; how in one place the contracts reserve to Government the right of disallowing any expenditure
incurred without its sanction while in another the governmental
guarantee of interest is virtually extended to all expenditure,
whether sanctioned or not; how the Government has pledged
itself, in the event of its desiring to purchase a prosperous
railway before the expiration of the lease, to pay the full market value, yet has equally pledged itself, however loath to purchase, to pay, on demand, for a line that cannot earn even its
working expenses, every penny that may have been wasted on so
utter a failure; how in short, it has bound itself by formal
deed to accept every possible loss, and to forego any possiblity
of gain—is not all this and more of the same sort written in
the Blue Books of the Parliamentary Committee on Indian
Finance?

If these contracts were the result of the dealings of American railway corporations of the period with American legislative bodies, it would not be difficult to give the transactions
an appropriate character.   It is one of the peculiarities of
the British public service, however, that the integrity of its
members has since the Reform Act of 1832 scarcely ever
been publicly assailed.   And British prestige in India has
rested squarely on the presumption of the honesty of the
administration.

Nevertheless under such contracts no one concerned with
the building of the railways had any interest in economy.
"All the money came from the English capitalist," testified
an Indian Finance Minister, "and so long as he was guar-

anteed 5 per cent. on the revenues of India, it was immaterial to him whether the funds that he lent were thrown into the Hooghly or converted into brick and mortar." [33] Government engineers supervised every detail of expenditure, at the cost of the railway, with no real power to do anything but obstruct. And the company's agents thought only of doing a thoroly good engineering job, irrespective of cost or appropriateness. The original estimates, especially upon lines built under contract, were doubled and trebled. It was notorious, testified Lord Lawrence in 1873, that "if the work had to be done over again, it could be done for two-thirds the money." [34] Instead of the £8,000 per mile for which Dalhousie planned to cover India with railways, those in operation by 1868 had averaged £18,000, without reckoning dividends advanced upon the guarantee, which were charges upon the future possible earnings of the roads. Down to 1881, more than twenty-eight million pounds had been paid out by the government under the guarantees in dividends beyond what the railways could earn.[35]

Under the guarantee system, however, railways were built in India, and built rapidly and well. It would have certainly been much cheaper for the Indian taxpayer for the government to have undertaken them directly, as after 1868 it decided to do under the policy associated with the Duke of Argyll in London and the brothers Strachey, Sir Richard and Sir John, in India. But there would probably have been interruptions of building work whenever a political crisis imposed extraordinary financial burdens upon the government. And it can hardly be doubted that it was in the immediate interest of British rule in India for a railway network to be completed as rapidly as possible. In consequence investors were able to claim a higher interest than they would have exacted for loans upon the direct credit of the Indian government, altho the difference in security was chiefly metaphysical. The political interests of Government by the Queen coincided happily with the pecuniary interests of a considerable body of her British subjects.

THE COST OF GOVERNMENT BY THE QUEEN

The precipitation of British capital into India for railway purposes was thus sudden, and its application was expensive. Immediate return upon the investment could be provided only by augmenting the burdens of the taxpaying ryot. But it promised progress as well as public order.

Crown government also meant calls upon the British investor which made no pretence of progress. After the Mutiny had been suppressed by a handful of British troops it was resolved to augment materially the number of British soldiers to be maintained in India. In the early sixties a military establishment was developed there which cost more than that of any European monarchy, more than the entire army of the British Empire outside of India. And this despite the fact that the introduction of railways was expected to enable one regiment to do the work of ten. So competent a critic as Charles Dilke declared that the principal value of the arrangement was that it "allows us to maintain at Indian cost 70,000 British soldiers, who in time of danger would be available for our defence at home." [36] Ten million pounds were expended upon new barracks to house the troops.

The burdens that it was found convenient to charge to India seem preposterous.[37] The costs of the Mutiny, the price of the transfer of the Company's rights to the Crown, the expenses of simultaneous wars in China and Abyssinia, every governmental item in London that remotely related to India down to the fees of the charwomen in the India Office and the expenses of ships that sailed but did not participate in hostilities and the cost of Indian regiments for six months' training at home before they sailed,—all were charged to the account of the unrepresented ryot. The sultan of Turkey visited London in 1868 in state, and his official ball was arranged for at the India Office and the bill charged to India. A lunatic asylum in Ealing, gifts to members of a Zanzibar mission, the consular and diplomatic establishments of Great Britain in China and in Persia, part of the permanent expenses of the Mediterranean fleet and the entire cost of a line of telegraph from England to India had been charged before 1870 to the Indian Treasury. It is small wonder that the Indian revenues swelled from £33 millions to £52 millions a year during the first thirteen years of Crown administration, and that deficits accumulated from 1866 to 1870 amounting to £11½ millions. A Home Debt of £30,000,000 was brought into existence between 1857 and 1860 and steadily added to, while British statesmen achieved reputations for economy and financial skill through the judicious manipulation of the Indian accounts.

India must allow peace, order, and justice to the credit of her account with her conqueror. And these things are not to be measured in lacs of rupees. Many Indian economists have, however, been disposed to contend that these services cost a good deal too much in the overhead charge at Westminster. At least they could be met in the sixties and seventies only by frequent borrowing. Down to 1878 there was a loan for India in London every year except during the cotton boom from 1862 to 1865.

THE "ECONOMIC DRAIN"

The most important characteristic of an investment is that it contemplates a profit. The outstanding feature of a foreign investment is the income it is expected to bring home. English politicians had promised English business men an income on behalf of the Indian ryot. And drawing hope largely from the promise something like one hundred and fifty million pounds of British capital were invested in India between 1854 and 1869. Capital continued to move to India at the rate of about five million pounds a year during the seventies. But its climax in volume was reached immediately after the Mutiny. About seventy-five millions went into railways by 1870, at least fifty-five million pounds of the Indian debt had come into British hands in addition to the stock which had been previously held. An estimated amount of twenty millions had been ventured upon private account in tea plantations, jute mills, banks (both by means of shares and deposits) and shipping and mercantile establishments. In return upon these investments and in payment for administration from London the average export balance of merchandise from India had swelled during the same period from four million pounds to between fifteen and twenty. And to this extent there grew in volume the payment which is known in the literature of Indian economics as the "economic drain." [88]

There can be here no attempt at a comprehensive estimate of British rule in India during the last three-quarters of a century. And into a company where controversy glows in inverse ratio to the zeal with which data are collated, the historian enters at his peril. But conflict of opinion is itself of the story of events which give rise to it. No investments before 1875 had social consequences admittedly as great, or whose nature has been so disputed.

It will cause neither pain nor astonishment to say that Englishmen who invested in India intended to profit by the act, and to profit more largely than they could have done under the same conditions at home. But it is fair to point out that they had no idea of impoverishing India in doing so. That one nation could profit in trade at the expense of any other was regarded in the middle of the nineteenth century as a degraded superstition, altho it was known that individuals could do so. And it was believed that the influx of railway capital and enterprise into India would operate as it had done in France and in remote localities in the British Isles. Local contractors and workmen and tradesmen dealing with them would accumulate profits. The purchase of stone, lime, bricks, timber and materials would release other local funds for activity; while merchants and retailers would profit upon the increased exports of English manufactures which would form the means of remitting the capital. These funds would seek investment, find it in the railways, and enable Englishmen to sell at a profit. "The real operation, after all," stated Hyde Clarke with penetrating candor, "is to make the Hindoos form the railways, and enable us to reap a large portion of the profits." But this would only mean that India would herself profit later. "In a subsequent stage of railway proceedings, when larger operations are carried on . . . the development of railway traffic will in India, as here, have effected a large economy of production, and will have stimulated an increase of production so as to supply new resources . . . the sphere of enterprise will be enlarged, the reward of exertions will be increased, and with the addition to the working power of the country of the vast engine of railway traction, it cannot be doubted that its wealth and capabilities will be enormously above the present standard." [39]

It is difficult to demonstrate that the introduction of the railways did have effects so decisive. Certainly the capital for them was not drawn from the natives. Not even in Great Britain had railway development been carried on so rapidly, and the railways which France absorbed were built at a slower rate. In these countries an intensive development of roads and canals had accompanied the growth of local trade and bound local markets to metropolitan centers. Moreover as Bagehot pointed out India was a land of "customary" commerce. And a railway system dominated by the political desirability of connecting the Presidency capitals with each other and with the northwest frontier was calculated more to disturb than to transform existing economic institutions.

Again the remittance of capital for railways in India did not take the form of consumers' goods. It did not follow upon a manifested rising standard of living. And it did not call to life in India a vigorous industry to provide structural materials. For the case of the railway in India is that of the machine in all lands where it is imported from without. It destroys occupations in economizing labor. And the compensating demand for workmen to mine coal and to make machines which characterized the coming of industrialism in Great Britain, Germany and the United States, was not manifested. India had coal and she had iron. But enterprise and empire could not wait upon their development. These things had to be provided from England. More than one-third of the capital invested in Indian railways down to the early eighties was spent in England for railway iron and the cost of its transportation to the East. [40] The importation of coal from England and the building and operation of railways with staffs which were English from foremen up and who had to be paid according to English standards, diminished further the benefits which could accrue to Indians from the railways.

The remaining two-thirds of the railway capital, as the bulk of the public loans not spent upon Home Charges in London, were remitted to India in bullion, mainly silver. Their effects merged with that of the even larger quantities of specie sent eastward in partial payment for the increasing exports from India. For during the fifteen years 1854–69, more than two hundred million pounds in precious metals were imported into India in excess of her bullion exports. Among the consequences of this remarkable movement there were a fall in the value of money and an increase in prices which was serious enough to call for an investigation in the Bombay Presidency in 1863. It was ascertained that in a comparatively short time grain prices had trebled, prices in general had doubled, wages had risen fifty per cent. There had been a consequent stimulus to industry and commerce in the immediate vicinity of Bombay, at least. And the prosperity of all classes had been increased except those with fixed incomes, persons without produce or labor to dispose of, and petty manufacturers deprived by dearness of material of the means of working.

This prosperity was a highly precarious one. It was highly disruptive of traditional arrangements. "All our commerce and our enterprise, our great works and improved systems," stated the Commissioners who investigated the Orissa famine of 1865, "create or increase the class of labourers depending on regular wages; and all increase of private wealth, enabling the richer to entertain labourers who are no longer slaves or serfs, adds to this class." But persons depending upon regular wages, and bound to no one in any other economic relation were exposed as never before to the hazards of extraordinary scarcity. Frequent famine was a painful corollary of the transformation of India by British capital. It is a phenomenon that at the best apologists for British rule must take considerable space to explain away.

Dr. Lillian Knowles regards with some justice the coming of the railway as the turning-point in Indian political and economic history.[41] She credits it with helping to maintain law and order, with attracting capital, creating new employment, abolishing slavery and serfdom, creating wider markets, stimulating population movements, providing safety of travel, and facilitating famine relief. It increased moreover the volume of trade, the growth of specialized crops, and the equalization of prices in India in conformity with world prices. These things in the course of fifty years were certainly true of the economic movement which the railway typified. And some of them no doubt augmented the tax-paying ability of the Indian people.

The point at issue, which can not be resolved, is whether the sudden investment of British capital in large quantities in India in the fifties and sixties imposed a burden upon the country. The railways and canals were not self-supporting. Deficits were made up from increased taxation. And the complaint of some Indian economists has been well stated by Romesh Dutt: [42]

When taxes are raised and spent in a country, the money circulates among the people, fructifies trades, industries, and agriculture, and in one shape or another reaches the mass of the people. But when the taxes raised in a country are remitted out of it, the money is lost to the country for ever, it does not stimulate her trade or industries, or reach the people in any form.

British investment continued in India after 1870.   It did
not begin to amount to the volume of annual interest remittances, however.   Great Britain drew income from India in
the last quarter of the nineteenth century to expend in developing other areas of the world within her empire and
without.

AN INCOME OF IMPONDERABLES

The migration of capital to India returned also to Great
Britain an income of imponderables.   Improved communication was to help the British rule India, as well as to give employment to British contractors and mills and safe investment
to retired army colonels.   It also assisted Indians to know
each other.   "India is being made," wrote Dilke in 1869.   "A
country is being created under that name where none has
yet existed." [43]   It was the railway among other things that
was doing the work.   Out of the economic activity it was
expected to nurture there rose a native merchant class comparable to that which had in the fifteenth century assisted
at the birth of nations in the West.   Indian nationalism rose
from the changes that were desired to make empire secure.

. On the British side too the basis was laid for a widening
gulf between rulers and their subjects.   Improved communication within India and without made the journey home
more rapid, and holidays more feasible.[44]   Increasingly Englishmen came to view India as a career to be exploited, as the
source of riches to be enjoyed elsewhere.

Of more immediate importance was the effect of the Indian experience upon the thinking of British public men.   It
was about 1870 that the trend of opinion which for more than

half a century had been strongly *laissez-faire,* swung sharply
in the direction of increased government activity.   Strains
of Continental thought made familiar to Great Britain by
John Stuart Mill, Frederic Harrison and Lord Acton assisted
in the intellectual readjustment involved.   But it may be
urged that on the practical side, it was the business activity
of the Indian government which gave strongest impetus to
collectivism.   The decision of the Duke of Argyll in 1869
that public works in India would be built thereafter by the
government, broke definitely with Palmerston's dictum that
"the business of government is to leave things alone."

And with collectivism, Englishmen drew from their new
intimacy with India a renewed imperialism.   They mounted
to a view of Empire upon their accumulating investments in
their possessions overseas.   British rule, as Goldwin Smith
pointed out, did not give British capital advantages which
other investors could not theoretically enjoy.[45]   But it was
too closely associated with established levels of security values for those who held Indian and colonial debts to be zealous
anti-imperialists.

India was not the only part of the empire with which investment ties grew more firm after 1857.   Fifty million
pounds were loaned between 1860 and 1876 to the governments of the rapidly growing colonies in Australasia, chiefly
for railways and other public works.   And in the same
period various private enterprises in India and other colonies
issued securities in London for thirty million pounds.
Twenty-five millions more were loaned to the governments
of Canada and smaller colonies.   Thus the stake of the middle classes grew in investments made under the protection of
British rule.   They aided in the formation of a state of mind

which was ready to think of foreign policy in terms of Empire rather than of England. These interests were at hand to justify decisions so extraordinary as to make the Northwest Frontier of India appear at times the pivotal point in the defense of the British Isles.

CHAPTER VIII

FROM BILL-BROKER TO FINANCE COMPANY

"If you succeed, your profits are stupendous—
And if you fail, pop goes your eightcenpence."
—Gilbert, W. S., *Utopia, Limited.*

STOCK-AND-BOND CAPITALISM

The change of organization in man's financial behavior
seems often to be strangely missing from the chronicles of the
historian. The very omnipresence of the corporate form in
business dulls the curiosity as to its antecedents, and per-
plexes effort to distinguish its characteristics. Yet it can
not be doubted that the corporation, the "joint-stock company," the *"société anonyme,"* the *"Aktien-Gesellschaft,"* is
at least one of the most important institutions in the great
society which in the past fifty years the world has been becoming. And it may be urged that its influence upon
economic life has been manifest in the tendency to deper-
sonalize business, to make of it a thing of by-laws not of
men.

The fundamental feature of modern commercial technique,
is the bookkeeping concept of "capital," the notion of it as a
debt owed by a business concern to its proprietors. In the
view of Sombart and Max Weber no idea has done more to
rationalize the economic struggle, to cast out ritual and personal qualities, to turn endeavor for a livelihood into quest

of the largest return for capital.[1]   It is the very heart of our much-decried "capitalism." And with its invention was born the concept of a business concern as an entity apart from the individuals engaged in carrying it on. Next to this notion the coming of transferable shares in the owner-ship of concerns shaped business life most significantly. It enhanced the independence of business from the man who at any time happened to own it. But it left him exposed to loss as unlimited as the advantages he might hope to gain. The final step to stock-and-bond capitalism was taken when the liability of shareholders for the conduct of their company was made purely pecuniary and limited to the amount of their investment.[2]   The number of proprietors of a concern might now expand indefinitely. The number of concerns in which one proprietor might safely engage received indefinite ex-tension. Capital was organized into Company, engaging in economic activity with not so much as a sign of the Capitalist to be seen. And in the midst of a world of such impersonal commercial entities, philosophers and busy men continued to prate of individualism.

The modern state has been loath to recognize the very existence of these business organizations. For many years it denied them status in its courts, except at the price of a special charter from the Crown or legislature.[3] Limited liability was a privilege more rare. It is to Ireland that credit belongs for the first general procedure by which com-mercial societies could free their members of full responsibil-ity for everything the companies did. The Irish Parliament legalized in 1782 a type of business organization which was developing in France and which received first legal recogni-tion there in Napoleon's *Code de Commerce*.[4] New York State was not far behind. On the eve of the War of 1812 it enacted a general incorporation law to encourage capital to engage in certain manufacturing industries. The principle made rapid progress through the American codes. And by 1850, incorporation by special legislative act had almost disappeared from the American commonwealths and in many of them had become unconstitutional. The scarcity of capital, the uncertainty of standards of honor among people who engaged in business and sought capital from others, and the whole-souled ardor with which the American people from their beginnings assimilated the spirit of capitalism, combined to make the United States the great field for the growth of corporate activity in business and in industry.[5]

But in Great Britain a business organism of great vigor and solidity had developed out of one-man concerns and partnerships. They had stood in one generation for competition and economic freedom, as it seemed, against the privileged companies with which mercantilist statesmen had developed England's foreign trade. And in another they stood for the ascendancy in business of men of measured worth and proven character, the rating of credit by personal attributes rather than by liquid assets. Many companies had been formed with limited liability by act of Parliament to build turnpikes, bridges, canals, railways, docks, waterworks and other public utilities which required the sanction of Parliament in any case. And there were numerous "companies" without legal status whose shares were traded on the Stock Exchange.[6] But special legislation was expensive, and always opposed by possible competitors. And without it companies were the most extravagant sort of speculative risks. There was no general incorporation law in Great Britain until 1855.

Twenty years of repeated parliamentary inquiry had been necessary to modify the law of mercantile organization. There was a Select Committee which held hearings in 1836 and 1837. Another sat from 1841 to 1843. There was a Royal Commission from 1852 to 1854. And the difference of opinion developed among people invited to express their views was great.[7] Lord Overstone, Thomas Tooke, J. Horsley Palmer, George Carr Glyn—elder statesmen of finance —resolutely opposed it. J. R. McCulloch—most heartlessly classical of economists—would have none of limited liability. It was on a par with public repudiation. And its practice was to be borrowed from the United States, which were supposed to be ever ready to draw the line between group and individual responsibility. The very idea of conducting business enterprise by means of companies was criticised by John Stuart Mill, among others, on the precise grounds which in other generations have been alleged against government ownership.[8] Responsibility was diffused; individual initiative was wanting. There were many, moreover, who were sure that a general incorporation law would encourage speculation, which was morally bad *per se,* and a great fomenter of crises. But there was the investor to consider, a brood greedy for security at ten per cent and embracing well-nigh the entire electorate. There had been campaign talk of opening opportunities for the middle and lower classes to employ small savings and to get on. And by 1855 the pressure of public opinion, made hopeful by a period of unusual prosperity, could not be resisted.[9] It is stated that but one newspaper in Great Britain, the Leeds *Mercury,* would at that time publish articles in opposition to limited liability. In the midst of the Crimean War, the Commons outvoted the government and instructed it to bring in a bill amending the law of partnership. Manchesterdom was more powerful than the economists. As Lord Palmerston saw it, by denying business associations the right to do as they pleased, government was thwarting the progress of freedom. So sacrificing individualism to laissez-faire, the sovereign delegated its prerogative to the registry office. In the name of freedom, England welcomed the business corporation.

This ceremony was accomplished by degrees. Companies were empowered to appear in court thru a recognized officer in 1837. They were given legal personality upon registering details of their constitution under terms of an act of 1844.[10] The law of 1855 privileged registered companies with twenty-five proprietors and a proportion of their capital paid-up to limit their liability to creditors.[11] Banking and assurance companies were excluded. What was treated as a privilege in 1855, was made in the following year a matter of right and to some extent a duty.[12] All partnerships with seven members might and all with twenty must register as limited liability companies. And in place of legislative regulation of capital accounts, the beginning was made of that elaborate system of publicity with which Great Britain has sought to protect investors. Banking companies were still excluded from the benefits of the act until 1858.[13] And limited liability was not then conceded to note-issuing banks with respect to their note-issues. But as most banks were already substituting deposit accounts for note-issues as a means of expanding loans, this was not a serious restriction.

Under these acts the organization of new enterprises by means of companies proceeded rapidly. Between two and three hundred concerns were registered every year. But the statutory provisions were confused and conflicting. They called for repeated amending acts and clauses indemnifying everyone for various unavoidable infractions of the law. And companies flourished under half a dozen distinct codes, to the distraction of shareholders, to their solicitors' delight, and to the considerable repugnance of established concerns to reorganization upon a joint-stock basis. Hence the emphasis of Gilbert's mocking lines in greeting to the

> " . . . Invention new—
> The Joint Stock Companies' Act—
> The Act of Sixty-two"

echoes the enthusiasm of the business community for the consolidation of company law for concerns of every description into one comprehensive code.[14] It was an invitation to the trade and industry of the United Kingdom to cast more widely for their capital and to investors to view business companies as safer risks. Banks found securities of wider variety a suitable basis for their loans. And an era of company formation began which may be most quickly described by the following table: [15]

Year	Number of Companies	Nominal Capital	Capital Issued	Capital Called Up
		(£ millions)		
1856	227	14	There are no official returns	
1857	392	20	for these items; and no	
1858	301	29	adequate compilations before	
1859	326	13	1865. The figures include all	
1860	409	17	company flotations in Lon-	
1861	479	24	don, whether registered in	
1862	502	68	England or not.	
1863	760	137		
1864	975	235		
1865	1014	203	122	59
1866	754	74	32	38
1867	469	28	29	17
1868	448	33	23	16

Thus the early sixties found the capital market at London filled with the excitement of the transformation of a considerable part of British trade and industry into the form of companies with limited liability.[16] And this favorable market situation developed at just the time when organizers of British enterprises abroad found it important to arrange a wider and more permanent support at home for their undertakings. So long as they had depended upon foreign rather than British capitalists to buy up the concerns which they developed, contractors and promoters had organized them under continental codes. But as they advanced into regions where resident investors were not likely to buy them out, it was necessary to secure a status which would be popular in London. Securities must run in pounds sterling; headquarters must be located in the British Isles; the promoters' wares must be adapted to the tastes of an insular market. And this was facilitated, so far as railway enterprise was concerned, by the fact that the policy of government subventions upon the Continent was being generally replaced by that of kilometric guarantees, which while limiting the possible profits of the founders, promised greater security from risk to the permanent proprietors.

But there was need too, as well as for a market for continental securities, for channels thru which they could be worked off with great rapidity. For competition was growing in the concession-hunting field. And the pressure for quickly mobilizable capital increased as commitments were extended. If the British money market was to hold its own in the cosmopolitan struggle, there was need to develop financial institutions more elastic in function than the English commercial bank, with resources to encounter greater risks than any of the merchant-bankers but Rothschilds and Barings were ready to incur.

There was in consequence introduced to Throgmorton Street a type of financial agency which had been developed in France and which was largely responsible for the rapidity with which the capital resources of the Continent had been brought to bear upon industry during the fifties. The joint-stock principle, still almost suspect as regards trade and manufacture, was applied to investment banking. "Finance companies" on the model of the *Crédit Mobilier* flourished in London, promising investors the profits of promotion and underwriting, and gaining an investment clientele from the publicity which the magnitude of their exploits commanded and the generosity with which they opened deposit accounts for the purchase of securities. And under their patronage business concerns multiplied whose owners were themselves impersonal entities, owned by other limited liability companies, in infinite series. A whole society of creatures of stocks and bonds was interposed between capitalists and production.

THE CRÉDIT-MOBILIER IDEA

It had been no coincidence that the same month, November, 1852, witnessed the birth of the Second Empire and of the *Société Générale du Crédit Mobilier*.[17] For to Napoleon the empire meant not only peace and advancement of transport and the beautification of Paris. It meant as well the the organization of credit—the mobilizing within a decade of private resources that Colbert and Turgot, the elder Napoleon and the bankers of the July Monarchy had been unable to make abundantly available for social purposes. And Napoleon, or his ministers, desired this not only because it seemed good in itself but because they were anxious to build up a financial power in Paris which would render the government independent of the Rothschilds who had been very intimate with the Orléans family. No agents seemed more promising for the purpose than the brothers Pereire, Isaac and Emile.

Born in Bordeaux of Portuguese Jewish extraction, the Pereires had come to Paris toward the close of the Restoration period to engage in the brokerage business. The Saint-Simonian school under Bazard and Rodrigues was then at the height of its popularity. And the Pereires, who were related to Rodrigues, fell under its sway and gave publicity to its doctrines in various journals. It was from it that they learned that industrialists, that the engineers, were the true rulers of society, and that the banker commanded the engineer to serve him; that it was from the banker, in a word, that should come the initiative and the direction of the industrial energies of society.[18] Unmoved by the mystical development of the Saint-Simonian cult about the personality of Enfantin, the Pereires sought an early opportunity to interpret their social gospel in terms of business. Their articles attracted the attention of Baron James de Rothschild. And in consequence there began an association with him in the railway business which continued until the revolution of 1848. They were the active managers for Rothschild of the *Nord,* the *Paris-Lyons* and other railways which he sponsored. The events of 1848 aligned the Pereires politically with the republicans, threw the railway business into chaos, and cast discredit upon private banking. And it brought into power a Saint-Simonian sympathizer who was willing to let Rothschilds' agents set up as his rivals.

The idea of the *Crédit Mobilier,* explained the administrators in their first report to the shareholders, is born of the insufficient credit available for the organization of business on a large scale in this country, of the isolation in which the forces of finance are placed, of the lack of a center strong enough to draw them together.

It is born of the need to bring upon the market the regular support of new capital designed to aid in the development of public and industrial credit.

It is born of the exorbitant conditions under which loans are made upon the public funds and the difficulties which arise therefrom for the definitive placement of even the best securities.

It is born moreover of the need to centralize the financial and administrative activities of the great companies, especially railway companies, and so to utilize for the greatest advantage of all, the capital which each in turn has on hand . . .

It is born finally of the necessity of introducing into circulation of a new agent, a new fiduciary currency, carrying with it its daily interest, and enabling the humblest savings to fructify as well as ample fortunes.

The *Crédit Mobilier* intended, in a word, to infuse life and organization into an industrial and business society which was anarchical and moribund. It proposed to assemble resources for the purpose by the extensive sale of its shares and obligations to small investors. The Pereires thought of it as socializing the Rothschild business. They did not intend to enter commercial banking. Theirs was to be no agency of commercial discount, although it deserves credit for introducing the check-and-deposit system into France in a small way. Nor was it to be merely a holding company, although it retained share control of some of the more important companies it promoted. But its resources were to be used chiefly as basis for generous advances and "reports" upon securities, which would give great encouragement to speculative investors and incite others to promote public utility undertakings. In this way the Pereires

hoped to make their bank the major instrument in the
great task of making France prosperous by means of public
works—nay, of more than France. Humanity was not
bounded by the Pyrenees, nor was progress to be checked at
the bridge-heads of the Rhine.

The banking ideas which thus first achieved institutional
form have been of outstanding significance in financial history.[19] German bankers trace the origin of their highly
organized system to the *Crédit Mobilier*. The recent development of "department-store" banking in the United States
and of bank concentration in England find here their pre-
cursor. In the multiplicity of single transactions and the
translation of venture and accomplishment into ledger en-
tries the aim of social utility for which the security-issuing
bank was founded has frequently been lost to view. But
the social and political consequences of its management have
been far-reaching, however indifferent its managers to all
but an immediate goal.

Indeed the *Crédit Mobilier* of France did not fulfil the
more sanguine hopes of its projectors. It did not succeed
in dominating the market for the issue of new securities,
industrial and governmental. During the years when it was
at the height of its power and esteem it handled about thirty
per cent of the new security business arising in Paris. It
organized the financial support for the transformation of
Paris and Marseilles. It founded and conducted for many
years the *Compagnie Générale Transatlantique*. It engaged
in railway undertakings in the Midi and the Dauphiné. But
it was abroad that its enterprises were impressive. It controlled a huge system of Austrian railways which had been
constructed by the state. It purchased another from the
Russian government. It competed everywhere with the
Rothschilds for the business of dealing with European gov-

ernments. And it set up daughter societies in Spain and Holland, with mines, gas-works, shipping companies and railway undertakings which they financed upon their own responsibility. From the beginning its clientele was highly cosmopolitan. As much as one-third of its shares were at times in English hands. And in its international loan business it was supported quietly but powerfully for many years by Baring Brothers. In 1864, for instance, this alliance was responsible in part for the fact that English investors owned some two-fifths of the shares of the *Great Russian Railway* which it managed.[20]

But the initial popularity and prestige of the *Crédit Mobilier* raised up rivals both at home and abroad. In building up a clientele in France, it paid enormous dividends at the outset, partly out of capital. And Napoleon III was indisposed to allow the institution he had patronized to become a financial monopoly. The plan of the Pereires to circulate an enormous quantity of obligations in small denominations, enabling small savings to be drawn into their enterprises, and enabling risks to be covered by a wide diversity of commitments, met with obstacles from the government. The Pereires found themselves increasingly unable to carry on their business and reap both social utility and profit. And the entire good-will of their concern demanded profits. It took on less and less the character of a security bank and more that of a speculative pool. Despite this, dividends fell off, and the credit of the company and its enterprises steadily sank. And in 1867 the Pereires were driven from the management of their bank as a condition of help from the Bank of France which was necessary to its survival. In reorganization the center of its activity was shifted to its deposit banking features. And other institutions in France, the *Société Générale pour favoriser l'Industrie et la Com-*

merce, the *Crédit Foncier,* the *Comptoir d'Escompte,* and after 1873, the *Banque de Paris et des Pays-Bas,* took the lead as security-issuing banks.[21] Thus the idea of the bank as the directive spirit in the movement of industrial capital continued to dominate in continental money markets, realizing its fullest development in Germany.

THE BANKING TRADITION AT LONDON

The Crédit Mobilier idea did not spread so quickly to Great Britain as to other countries in Europe. The need for it was less apparent. There was a fully developed banking organization already in existence, based upon a quite different set of ideas, which made of the banker the passive not the active agent in the movement of capital. But the distribution of property was such that great credit expansion was possible along the lines of orthodox commercial banking. The investing classes were in large part commercial people who could readily procure credit by discounting their bills and acceptances, and rentiers, whose consols were ready security for bank advances. And commercial credit flourished in forms more various and more extensive than in 1800.

The check-and-deposit system had had a remarkable development, displacing entirely after 1844 the issuance of notes by private banks.[22] Bank deposits which in 1830 had been only £30,000,000, had grown to £200,000,000 in 1856 and to £350,000,000 in 1866.[23] And this reflected in part an expansion of credit by means of deposits and partly a real augmentation of the savings of the country entrusted to the banks. Ninety-five per cent of all transactions in London were by 1860 being made by the use of checks, whereas the Continent scarcely knew the device.[24]

Moreover the commercial bill mechanism, which was world-wide in its scope, had continued to grow in England with the expansion of trade and to be connected with more stages in the processes of exchange. In 1840 the leading London private bankers alone paid bills of exchange amounting to more than one billion pounds.[25] Dock-warrants and warehouse receipts were by the forties made the basis of bill-drawing in the ordinary course of business.[26] The volume of domestic bills continuously in circulation between 1856 and 1871 varied, according to Palgrave, between 150 and 200 million pounds. The total foreign bills drawn during each year increased from £349,300,000 in 1859–60 to £587,100,-000 in 1870–71.[27] Neither Rothschilds nor Barings, neither the private banks nor their joint-stock competitors, were the representative institutions of this stage of London's credit evolution. None were so powerful as the bill-brokers, who bought bills from those who needed ready money, and sold them on their guarantee to bankers, still chiefly from the great agricultural districts of East Anglia and Devon, who had more funds than they could otherwise invest. In this business Overend, Gurney & Co. had no peers. Their average of discounted bills outstanding about 1860 was £64,-000,000. Between 1859 and July 1865, their total business turnover amounted to £115,000,000.[28]

We owe the portrait of this great financial house to Stefanos Xenos, one of the many Greeks who in the fifties and sixties engaged in daring operations between London and the Levant.[29] Its founder, Thomas Richardson, was long since dead. Samuel Gurney, who had made its reputation, died in the early fifties. David Barclay Chapman withdrew his millions from the business about the same time. A generation of men who had inherited their wealth occupied in 1860 the shabby "Corner House" at Lombard Street and Birchin

Lane. There was Henry Edmund Gurney, chief acting partner, pompous but benevolent and of high moral tone, ambitious of commanding the commercial world and especially the fleets which carried England's commerce. There was David Ward Chapman, something of a grand seigneur, handsome and correct in manner, lavish in hospitality, surrounded by a train of ingratiating gentry whose business suggestions were of weight to him and profit to themselves. There was Arthur George Chapman, a sanguine and somewhat cavalier youth, ready to endorse anything. And there was Robert Birkbeck, talented and prudent, absorbed in the details of bill-broking. A staff of assiduous clerks mounted on stools at high desks crowded the counting-room and screened the partners in a room beyond from the importunities of ordinary clients and hopeful hangers-on. Xenos invests the dingy scene with something of the awe and grandeur and atmosphere of sinister intrigue of a court of the *ancien régime*. He envisages the firm as already a usurer upon a grand scale. For industry had to be financed, and in performing the function by means of ninety-day bills the firm was becoming involved in business operations out of harmony with English banking traditions. Nevertheless it was those traditions upon which the prestige of Overend, Gurney & Co. rested. And it was as a commercial bankers' bank that it held its unique place in London and increased the mobility of the loanable funds of the British Isles.

So between the prosperity of its trade and industry and the credit capacity of the banking organization which it already had, Great Britain had not been greatly in need of new contrivances to increase the efficiency of its capital market. the ideas of organization of investment and of centralized initiative which seemed so congenial to the Continent conflicted with the spirit of English business life which was already traditional. Englishmen enjoyed the profits which the Crédit Mobilier idea earned upon the Continent. Merchant-bankers allied themselves with companies that knew how to obtain concessions. Partners in private banks and directors of joint-stock banks did the same. Some of them even sought to introduce commercial banking methods upon the Continent. But most London bankers held aloof from active undertakings. The great private banking firms of Smiths, of Barclays, of Jones, Loyd, would have nothing to do with company promotion even at home.[30]   And the London & Westminster Bank, under James Gilbart, was equally rigorous in its policy. The connections which existed between other bankers and enterprise were largely personal and contractual. The banker, as promoter, did not usually represent his bank, nor did he draw an extensive investment clientele into his enterprise. He did not seek to astound the capital market with his coups.

THE FINANCE COMPANIES

The Crédit Mobilier idea reached the British Isles for the first time in 1863, soon after the codification of company law in the Companies' Act. It took the form of a series of "finance" companies.

The International Financial Society, Ltd., made its debut in London in May, 1863.[31]   It stated that its purpose was "to assist and take part in financial and industrial undertakings, especially foreign loans and enterprises possessing Government guarantee." Its board of directors was made up of partners in a number of merchant-banking houses which were just beginning to gain prominence in the City. There was Junius S. Morgan of George Peabody & Co., soon to take over the business of that firm under his own name and to found an international banking house of fame in other generations. There was Herman Stern of Stern Brothers, already a power in Portuguese finance. There were representatives of Heath, Huth, Frühling & Goschen and Dobree, all of which firms were "Bank of England" houses, with partners on its board. R. A. Heath, who had long been consul-general in Great Britain for Italian states, was chairman of the International. It boasted the close alliance of the original *Crédit Mobilier*. They were to collaborate in important issues, and each company held a third interest in the shares of the other.

The General Credit and Finance Company of London, Ltd., announced in the following week that its objects were:

to negotiate loans and concessions; assist industrial enterprises, public works, and railway undertakings; negotiate Foreign, Indian and Colonial Bonds; conduct mercantile transactions; and establish agencies for large commission business; in a word, to undertake all such operations as an intelligent and experienced capitalist might effect on his own account with a capital of millions.[32]

With an eye to the reputation just acquired by the promoter, Samuel Laing, as Financial Secretary in India, and to the unbounded confidence which prevailed with reference to Indian enterprise, the prospectus declared that the company would "ally the demand of India for capital at ten or twelve per cent. with the English demand for investment at four or five per cent." It was a promoters' company. Thomas Brassey, Charles Devaux, and W. P. Andrew, the leading figure in the Indus and Euphrates Valley projects, were among the directors with Laing. And it too had a French ally, the *Société Générale pour favoriser l'Industrie et la*

Commerce, constituted for the very purpose later in the year.[33]

A horde of similar companies with pretensions as great followed in London within a year, most of them, however, without continental alliances.[34]   Some were formed by joint-stock banks to handle types of security loans which could not be reconciled with commercial banking. Some were formed by contractors and promoters, as a device for limiting their risks, rendering liquid their commitments. And the markets for public security issues were soon crowded with their offerings.

During the first few months of 1864, for instance, the International floated a loan for the Danubian principalities to enable Brassey to build one railway, shares for the Lemberg-Czernowitz railway (another Brassey affair), an Anglo-Italian Bank (headed by the late British minister and an Italian foreign secretary), an Italian Land Company with a capital of a million and a half, a land company in Mauritius; and it cooperated with the *Crédit Mobilier* and Glyn, Mills, Currie in converting the entire Mexican debt. A reorganization of the Hudson's Bay Company, stock taken at 300 and issued to the public at 400, was of its most ambitious undertakings.[35]   The flotations of Brassey's own company, the General Credit and Finance, showed a similar range.

One of the most amazing of the finance companies was the International Land Company, usually called the Crédit Foncier of London, which was itself almost immediately parent to a Crédit Mobilier, with which it entered into incestuous nuptials almost as soon as it gave it birth.[36]   The Crédit Foncier grew out of the plans by which a Belgian promoter, Count Langrand-Dumonceau, was seeking to exploit the sentiment and savings of ardent Catholics, especially those accumulating in the ecclesiastical foundations. He proposed to "Christianize" capital and had a special rescript from the Pope. His original scheme had been to buy up Hungarian land which was being placed on the market in the process of overthrowing the feudal system in that country, and to dispose of the estates in small farms, taking mortgages in payment which were to be gradually amortized. But one idea set another in train. Building speculations in Marseilles, Brussels, Milan and other growing cities promised larger interest upon mortgages and premiums upon shares. The shady promoters of half a dozen countries and of no country at all were drawn into the network of companies which flourished. And bad management brought about the collapse of the whole system to the dismay of many prelates and noblemen. Political life in more than one country heard echoes of the failure. The London company, got up by Edward Watkins Edwards and "Baron" Albert "Grant," became holding company for the entire affair. So artificial was its financial basis that it is difficult to say how much British capital its eight million pound capitalization actually represented. Nevertheless it was the means of drawing many of the High Church aristocracy into the stock market. Notable among them was Lord Cranborne, soon to become Marquis of Salisbury, who was chairman of the board for a portion of its career.

But the real business of the finance companies did not consist in company obstetrics. Their flotations astonished the world with their financial prowess. They attracted clients, depositors, investors, patients in need of pecuniary treatment. They afforded excellent opportunities for the directors to engage in speculative pools. And they gave shareholders the impression that their company was dividing in dividends the fabulous profits of promotion. But as

Samuel Laing explained with clarity and candor to the first shareholders' meeting of his company, the real object of the concern was to lend money upon securities of less certain risk and at longer dates than commercial banks had been willing to do.[37] The real activity was to consist in the development of a deposit and acceptance business upon the security of stocks and bonds. It was to develop industrial banking suited to railway needs. And the readiness with which railway contractors had lent the prestige of their names to the directorates of the finance companies was not accidental.

Railway finance was encountering increasing difficulties, as competition increased in railway building and as the construction plant grew which needed to be kept in employment. Railway companies were creatures of the contractors. The latter kept the shares and sought capital for construction by the sale of bonds, mortgaging the roads before they were built.[38] And they undertook new concessions as rapidly as they could get them and borrow money to commence. Between 1860 and 1869 the European railway system, United Kingdom included, increased from 51,496 to 94,901 kilometers. Even in the mad forties England had not built railways so rapidly as from 1860 to 1865. Elsewhere construction was just reaching its peak. And the capital cost was terrific.[39] For during the same period the national finances of the great powers were being strained by costs of military preparation which grew tremendously after 1859 in fear and emulation of France. India was absorbing fifteen million pounds of capital a year; the Lancashire cotton industry was alternating chills with fever in consequence of the American blockade; and the shipping industry was facing a transition from wood and sail to iron and steam as the normal ocean-going unit.[40] Loanable funds all over

Europe grew scarce. From Nov. 15, 1860 to April 11, 1861; in February, 1863; from November 2, 1863 to March 2, 1865; and finally from October 5, 1865 to September 27, 1866, the Bank of England rate was five per cent or more. It was higher than that thruout 1864. In such a market bonds sold at a heavy discount, and companies quickly exhausted their borrowing powers without filling their capital requirements. But it was necessary to continue construction; so they issued notes, frequently renewed, circulating on the security of their own shares, which contractors pledged with banks for more advances. At any stage before the final disposal of his railway to investors or to the Stock Exchange, the contractor's debtor and creditor relations with the company were hopelessly entangled. And the finance companies contributed another knot to the involvements. They discounted their own acceptances at the bill-brokers and banks and lent their funds to the contractors in amounts that had to be incessantly renewed and expanded to give value to the securities they took as cover. But in a sense they limited the risks both of contractor and banker. They became pools for providing the capital needs of the railway and other projects under construction. And at the same time they were agents for shifting the burden of this financing into more permanent investment channels.

The organization of railway finance advanced another stage in complication when company solicitors turned their attention to the business of contracting. Few men could be as ubiquitous as Brassey or Morton Peto. And to secure the advantage of their organization without the impulse of their personality and with reduced risk, contracting firms in existence became companies, and others were formed to take up specific concessions. The public were invited to participate in the adventitious profits of the contractor.

Thus the incorporated population of England grew and enabled enterprise to engage abroad upon a smaller margin of capital reserve.

All of these companies sought shareholders and competed with old businesses which were raising new capital or relieving proprietors of burden by registering under the Companies' Act. And a new financial journalism grew to promote and profit from the publicity which these endeavors entailed. The *Money Market Review* began to appear weekly at the end of 1859. A decade later its proprietors were publishing a daily edition, the *Financier*, five times a week; and soon after there appeared the *Bondholders' Register* under the same management, specializing in monthly announcements of new issues, coupons and drawings. A rival weekly was the *Bullionist* which was first published in 1866. The staid *Economist* caught the enthusiasm and began to issue the *Investors' Monthly Manual* in 1863, with a comprehensive tabulation of all officially quoted companies. The money articles in the daily press swelled to tremendous size. The *Daily News,* reaching widely the class of readers which dabbled in the market, carried nearly a page of quotations and comment.

It was of prime importance in the new issue business which the finance companies were introducing to London to secure comment from financial editors who had a following. And their favorable estimate could frequently be arranged for.[41] If a company did not advertise its prospectus it could depend upon being severely panned. But the policy of such journals as the *Money Market Review* seems to have followed closely the nature of their material and of their public. Appealing to speculative readers who were interested in companies and loans which needed the support of heavy advertising, it would have been unnatural for the *Review* to recommend safe in-

vestments in well-established securities. That was not what
its readers wanted. They wished to be warned off the things
which a Rothschild would recommend. And it was a feature of the case that the things a Rothschild had to recommend did not need advertising. A small notice in the *Times*
was enough. Doubtless the fact that advertising in the
Times was expensive kept all but the largest companies from
publishing prospectuses there. And it is a fact that the
Times money articles were highly critical of the prevalent
"productive" investments in small concerns and correspondingly enthusiastic with regard to large foreign loans, sponsored by great private banking firms. It was currently
believed that the *Times* city article was a sort of Rothschild
daily letter.[42] It was the other organs of financial publicity
that praised and incited the finance companies and their flotations.

Some of the railway financiers had their own organs of
publicity. There was the *Railway News,* backed by James
McHenry, and edited by the father of his private secretary.[43]
And this was not the only journal that spoke hysterically of
the prospects of the railway McHenry was building in the
United States.

JAMES McHENRY'S RAILWAY

Something of it must be told. Without McHenry and
his road, the story of the finance companies and their crisis
would be Hamlet without the King of Denmark. The transactions of this booming, optimistic, assiduous projector precipitated financial drama upon two continents.[44] We shall
remain in the British theatre, however. That other "chapter
of Erie" must be dramatized upon another occasion.

The *Atlantic & Great Western Railway,* which began several hundred miles from the Atlantic and ran with vagueness into the Great West through the states of New York, Pennsylvania and Ohio, had been little more than a series of local lines on paper until 1858. In that year its promotion fell into the hands of James McHenry. McHenry was a sanguine Orange-American, who had come to Liverpool in 1853 to develop the American produce trade, and who had thriven on failure. He conceived the audacious idea that if the railway was built, it could be sold to the *New York & Erie,* which was on the verge of bankruptcy. And with that in view he set to work. His technique is instructive.

It was discovered that the Queen of Spain owned some land in Pennsylvania, which had been among the assets of the defunct Bank of the United States and which had come to her in settlement of an interest she had held in that institution. The railway was to run near her estate, and would give value to it. And for representing matters properly at Madrid, Don José de Salamanca, who was a personage in Spanish politics and finance, was persuaded to accept the initial contract for building part of the railway. There is a junction point upon the *Erie* which bears his name. It is not recorded that he ever visited the United States or hired a laborer. Nor do the capital commitments which he persuaded the far from virgin queen to accept, appear to have been heavy. The purpose of the Spanish negotiations was to give credit to the project in Liverpool which neither the railway nor McHenry then possessed. Instead of McHenry paper, Salamanca paper could be circulated among the banks, until a portion of the line was built and there was something to mortgage.

Briefly, McHenry was about to build the line and to own it without putting a cent of capital into it. The stock, which was never paid up, was issued largely to himself. And he undertook the active burdens of contractor. Some of the stock he pledged with London banks as security for his ninety-day bills as his credit improved. In September, 1859, the first bond issue could be announced, £200,000 bearing 7% interest, issued at 80. And McHenry's credit had come along so well that the Bank of London guaranteed payment upon the first four coupons of these bonds. Other bonds were issued to Crawshay Bailey and to the Ebbw Vale Company for iron rails, 55,000 tons of them, paid for at $40 a ton with bonds reckoned at 50. Barneds of Liverpool and Kennards of London were the bankers chiefly helpful in turning Salamanca paper into cash.

It was announced that the railway would run from Salamanca, New York to Dayton, Ohio, linking the *Erie* to the *Ohio & Mississippi Railroad* (in which a good deal of British capital was also invested) into a continuous six-foot gauge system from New York to St. Louis, which was at that time the commercial metropolis of the West. Construction began at once, and went forward rapidly under the direction of McHenry and British engineers. The Civil War proved scarcely an obstacle to the building. Fifteen thousand laborers were imported, five thousand from England, and the work went on.[45] Dayton was reached in 1864. And in the autumn of the same year the first through train travelled from the Hudson river over McHenry's road to the Mississippi.

This rapid construction under trying conditions in both labor and capital markets had taken place at an enormous capital expense. McHenry's money cost him fifty per cent in London; his debts compounded at ten per cent a year. Moreover he had seen to it that his interests as principal stockholder did not compromise his earnings on his con-

tracts. By 1865 there was a property capitalized for three
times its actual cost, unable to control traffic conditions at
either end of its line, and dependent, except for the developing oil business, entirely upon through traffic for its revenue.
Seventeen London banks and finance companies had accepted
McHenry paper which was piling up rediscount charges and
compounding interest arrears. And McHenry had managed to secure the partnership of no less a person than Sir
Morton Peto for the concluding portion of his contract. All
financial London seemed to believe in McHenry and his
road. And all financial London was involved in their ultimate fortunes.

But London was not the ultimate investor. The English public would not be persuaded that a railway beginning
and ending in towns of which they had never heard and
touching no great body of water, could have any earning
power commensurate with its sixty million dollar capitalization. Successive bond issues brought into the market with
the utmost éclat in 1864 and 1865, when the railway was
actually in operation, resulted only in a classification of
creditors. The banks and finance companies still owned
them or held them as security for discounted bills. "The
shrewd observer," commented the *Economist,* "knows a peculiar glow which now and then comes over commercial literature. It is the breath of the great capitalist."[46]   And the
British public suspected that the great capitalist had drunk
more deeply than was wise.

Late in 1865 there was a great junket of British capitalists
to the United States, headed by Sir Morton Peto himself.
The party toured generously upon an expense account
charged to the promotion of the *Atlantic & Great Western.*
They talked largely of routes to Chicago and St. Louis.
They threatened *Erie* with a separate route to New York.

They took counsel with Garrett of the *Baltimore & Ohio* and fed his hopes. But the Yankee directors of the British-owned *Erie* had their own ideas. They did not involve the purchase of the road McHenry had built to sell to them.

The Peto party returned to London, so stirred by the resources and prospects of the United States that Sir Morton lent his name as author to a book upon the subject.[47] And he addressed an anxious throng of creditors at the London Tavern upon the fundamental soundness of their property.[48] The entire net earnings of the *Atlantic & Great Western,* he assured them, would be remitted direct to London. But there were no remittances; no net earnings; and the banks continued as heretofore to advance the interest upon the coupons of the railway's mortgage bonds. McHenry and his railway were insolvent. But they had so involved London in their fortunes that they must be sustained, lest all succumb to a common catastrophe.

THE FAILURE OF OVEREND, GURNEY & CO.

For McHenry's was but one of many railways, within the British Isles and without, that contractors had built upon the credit of their smiles, and whose bills encumbered the vaults of London financial institutions. The market was simply congested with securities. And the finance companies, seeking to justify their existence by large profits, were impelled to a progressive aggravation of the difficulty. In the summer of 1865 the private banks which had been most active in company promotion, Mastermans, Kennards, Barneds, sought the protection of the limited liability law and appealed to the public for the support of fresh capital.[49] And with them, the partners in Overend, Gurney & Co., facing a deficit of £4,000,000, drew up articles of incorporation and sold their business to the public. We have the word of a British jury that the successors of the vigorous old Quaker, Samuel Gurney, were not evil in their intentions. They were not held accountable in the end to the people to whom they sold shares. But they ruined their shareholders with the certainty and dispatch of a bucket-shop.[50]

The multiplicity of company names scarcely concealed the feat of self-levitation which railway finance was attempting to perform. Barneds' Banking Company bought shares of the Joint Stock Discount Company. The Joint Stock Discount owned the Contract Corporation, a concession-hunting concern. The Contract Corporation owned Smith, Knight & Co., an incorporate contractor. Each of these organizations was involved with the contractors Watson and Overend in Irish railways and with McHenry in his road. And Overend, Gurney & Co., Ltd., in turn had advanced money to all of them, and to many more—shipping and shipbuilding companies insolvent for years, fly-by-night speculators, bubble companies. It had become, in fact, a super-finance company.

In this same year 1865, the Civil War in America, which had created a profitable business for certain elements of the cotton trade, was ended. With it crumbled the short-lived prosperity of Bombay, of Egypt, of numberless speculators unable to hedge their commitments. There was a panic at Bombay in the fall, which involved numerous "exchange" banks which had done a business in remittance and arbitrage between India and England. There were enforced alterations in the channels of trade which brought strain to the money market, although British foreign trade swelled in volume from the sudden American demand. Then too came to an end with the Civil War, Maximilian's brief dream of empire in Mexico. And Smith, Knight & Co., which had undertaken to build a railway for him, found themselves unable to meet their bills.

Early in the spring of 1866, Smith, Knight & Co., the Contract Corporation, the Joint Stock Discount Company and Barneds' Banking Company successively failed. Railway financiers began to look anxiously for cover. The share capital of one of Peto's railways was suddenly issued upon the market at 25, to reduce his banking commitments. Mc-Henry securities which the failing institutions had held were taken over by Overends and others. Brassey and Jackson put their surplus constructing plant at auction. Ninety-day bills, secured upon violently fluctuating stocks and bonds, began to come to maturity. Overends and other finance companies found their falling shares a source of alarm to depositors. And on Monday, May 4, 1866, a British court held that one of the favorite forms of railway paper which banks had been discounting,—"Lloyds' bonds," mere promissory notes in the name of the companies—were illegal and uncollectable from British railway companies.

Four days later all business England was startled by the news that Overend, Gurney & Co. had closed its doors. The British Foreign Secretary took the unprecedented course of sending circular telegrams to the embassies that the national finances were in no danger.[51] With the fall of the institution which next to the Bank of England was the mainstay of British credit, the whole brood of finance and contracting companies were swept into the court of chancery.[52] Only the most heroic cooperation saved the majority of commercial banks from following them. Peto and Masterman, Kennard and Gurney went the way of the Bundelcund Bank and Dombey and Son. The liquidation of doubtful assets which the catastrophe made the main business of the surviving banks and brokers and accountants for several years, stirred concentric waves from Hong Kong to Buffalo. It was 1893 before final settlement of the affairs of Overend, Gurney, & Co. could be completed.

Thomas Brassey and the institutions most closely associated with his enterprises survived the storm. We read that he had never brought himelf to countenance the new fashion in railway finance. He did not undertake what he could not perform. Nor did he sell his property before he had made it. Success unparalleled crowned his efforts. Perhaps to a man so modest, a man who had the courage in the days of Cobden to prove well-paid labor to be cheap, success was not an unearned increment. Brassey's organization was busy when he died in 1870, finishing railways in Transylvania and Poland, building a great dock at Callao in Peru, laying the Delhi Railway in India.

In Germany, the American West and in South America "contractors' roads" flourished undismayed. Of the blowing of bubbles there is no end, least of all in England. But the panic of 1866 put an end to the ascendancy of the Contractor, of Railway Finance, of Cosmopolitan Enterprise, in the London money market. British banking turned disdainfully from the technique that Overends had abused. The unterrified investor turned with new confidence to the promises of foreign governments. And after the finance company, the cosmopolitan banker enjoyed his day of power.

CHAPTER IX

THE GOVERNMENT LOAN BUSINESS

"A prince!" exclaimed Fakredeen. "Princes go for nothing now without a loan. Get me a loan, and then you turn the prince into a government."

—Disraeli, *Tancred.*

PROGRESS BY BORROWING

The story is told of old Mayer Anselm Rothschild—and for the authenticity of Rothschild stories no one vouches— that when a petty German prince or commune applied to him for a loan, he would pay no attention to the rehearsal of present necessities and future revenues. He took to his carriage and drove out to see the land, the people, the fields, and based his decision upon the evidences of a sound economy there visible. The story, if apocryphal, is good to tell; it has nothing whatever to do with the transactions to be treated of in this chapter.

Governments borrow money immoderately because they are torn between zeal for progress and the desire to propitiate the taxpayer. The generation of enterprise which crowned Louis Napoleon was no exception. Europe was busily obliterating the traces of old inquisitive and obstructive fiscal systems. It had little time to devote to new. Sufficient for Gladstone's financial reputation that he reduced the taxes. A financier like Lord Randolph Churchill need not understand decimals; but it was indispensable that he know how excise schedules may be reduced.

Progress was even more obligatory. After the revolutions of 1848 governments rested themselves frankly upon the opportunities they held out for material achievement. They commended themselves to the busy men whose support they craved by becoming tools for the building of fortunes. It was their concern that capitalists be kept by fruitful employment from a fresh debauch of political intrigue. And how more certainly than by engaging them in public contracts? Louis Napoleon showed the way. And most European states, like the governors of India, turned to Paris for fashions in warships and arsenals, boulevards and cities beautiful. Brussels vied with Rome and Cairo in seeking to rival Haussmann's Paris. Dingy capitals sprouted public buildings in uninspired but expensive classic adaptations. Medieval walls became boulevards. Cleanliness, late among the virtues to become an object of public concern, presided over a great establishment of water and drainage systems. There was endless preparation for war. And there was war itself—an expensive pastime—inspired by the general excitation and apologized for by the fashion of nationality. All of these things were progress. They all meant profit for the fortunate contractors. They meant money for which the taxpayer must not be burdened. They meant continuous appeals to the money market. Between the universal desire for progress and the equally universal desire for lower taxes there was a discongruity which could be bridged only by public borrowing.

Theory trimmed quickly to meet the changing wind of practice. Classical economists had frowned upon public debts.[1] They were a drain upon the resources of a country, a burden upon its enterprise. At their best a necessary evil, they should be reduced as rapidly as circumstances allowed. But there were new masters in Germany to proclaim an altered gospel. It was discovered that loans were a positive good, that the stronger a state would be, the more money it should borrow. Dietzel enunciated the proposition that all productive works and all works likely to benefit future generations should be paid for by borrowing.[2] "The subscription of a public loan," he declared, "is identical with the formation of new capital through increased productivity. . . . A people is so much the richer, its economic life so much more prosperous and progressive, the greater the part of its entire public expenditure which is made up of interest on public loans." This doctrine was elaborated less naïvely in Lorenz Stein's classic *Textbook of Finance*.[3] The use of credit facilities was as natural and necessary to a government as to the conduct of any private enterprise, reasoned Stein. If a fiscal system did not resort to credit, the best that could be said of it was that it was undeveloped. The greatest debts were those of the greatest world powers, and were incurred where world relations were most extensive. Thus a generation of civil servants grew up devoted to the pious superstition that progress may be made without cost, that the issue of public securities is a sort of conjurer's trick, causing wealth to appear which has not heretofore existed, and which will automatically provide for its own replenishment. And like most superstitions this one frequently held true.

To most countries which fashioned policy in awe or emulation of the Second Empire, it was as inconvenient to borrow at home as to levy taxes. Even France at the time of the Crimean war and again in 1870 and 1871 depended upon London to enable her largest loans to be filled. Austria and Russia habitually met emergencies by issues of inconvertible paper currency, and in 1848 and 1854 respectively had permanently suspended specie payments. Spain and Italy pursued the same tactics. In those countries as in Turkey and China and in France under the *ancien régime* the most available road to private fortune was in the collection and expenditure of public revenues. Native enterprise and industry were inadequate to provide even the materials for progress at as rapid a rate as was desired by nations who wished to enhance their political prestige by an impressive exhibition of material culture. And native productivity was equally insufficient in many cases to provide a *quid pro quo* in the way of raw materials demanded by manufacturing regions. In western and central Europe, to be sure, and in the regions populated by their cultural elements, the coming of foreign capital did awaken a vigorous and independent response. It stirred local resources and capabilities. It released thwarted initiative. As rapidly as it was introduced industrial capitalism domesticated itself in Germany, Belgium, France and Switzerland. Where it encountered handicaps on the part of existing political institutions it contrived their removal. But a generation is too short for the leap from feudalism to industrialism. Over large areas of eastern and southern Europe the western type of economic life is still in the twentieth century a veneer, an alien system, often a parasite, without roots in the behavior of the folk. Its very existence has depended upon the initial patronage of the state; and that patronage was originally accorded thru a wish to ape the superstructure of the west without remodelling the foundations of non-western society. Enterprise and technique as well as plan and materials were importations. And successive applications of the fertilizing capital ripened no seeds to ensure a perennial bloom.

Even in regions which were rapidly becoming industrialized by 1870, progress demanded foreign loans; and foreign loans depended directly or indirectly upon London. It was not that London was still the only center in which money could be raised upon large issues of foreign securities. In 1870 Paris fully equalled that city in the range of her long-term undertakings. Frankfurt was a mecca to which capital and capitalists moved from all the Germanies. And Amsterdam, Brussels and Vienna, each satellite to a more refulgent sun, were centers of independent financial activity. But none of these money markets challenged the position of London as the supreme market for commercial bills and for accommodation paper. It will probably never be possible to tell how much investment of fixed capital, nominally Continental in origin, meant the employment of British capital engaged at second hand through renewed commercial credit operations.[3a] Whoever the capitalists engaged in the government loan business and from whatever source their initial capital was derived, they did not long delay in establishing financial residence in London.

THE COSMOPOLITAN FAMILY BANKING FIRM

Indeed most of the houses which rose to prominence in British finance after the crisis of 1866 were of foreign origin. They came from all parts of Europe, even from the United States. Only a few of them assumed English nationality. There was the firm of Frühling & Goschen which had come from Leipsic in the book trade and in the second generation was inoculating London with Egyptian finance and was supplying a minister of state. C. J. Hambro & Son after a century of distinction in banking at Copenhagen opened a London house after the revolutions of 1848 and became Anglicised. This firm was in 1870 the leading one in the Scandinavian trade and was at different times preeminent in Italian relations. J. S. Morgan & Co., succeeding to the business of George Peabody during the Civil War, was a firm so English in character that it headed the London syndicate which offered the only serious competition to the Rothschilds for handling the French indemnity loan in 1871. Of the numerous American houses opened in London after the Civil War to market "Five-Twenties." Morton, Rose & Co. alone became acclimated.*

The other firms which enjoyed prestige as loan contractors and heads of underwriting syndicates were equally foreign, but they remained cosmopolitan in spirit. Many of them were swept away when the public loan business collapsed in the later seventies. That business was carried on in the main by a number of Jewish firms, many of which sprang from Frankfurt. To these astute dealers in progress and poverty one center of operations had proved too circumscribed. And they had established branches at Paris, London and elsewhere which became the principal centers of their business. Of the firms which followed the Rothschilds over Europe the Bischoffsheims, the Sterns, the Erlangers, and the Raphaels were the most ubiquitous. The Oppenheims came from Cologne; the Bambergers from Mainz. The Frankfurt connections they enjoyed were important in the early history of the Speyers and the Seligmans.

Without doubt these families were emulous of the Roth-

* Speyer Brothers had opened a London house in 1862, and Seligmans had under various organizations a banking business with California. Their importance in the issue business at London arose in a later generation, altho Speyers were issuing Baltimore & Ohio bonds in 1872.

schild fame and wealth. The circumstances which worked in favor of the more noted house aided the younger rivals. Their business was primarily that of international remittance and secondly that of speculation in the media of remittance. They dealt in credit beyond the adequate jurisdiction of national tribunals and before financial interdependence had achieved the complexity which makes today for order and self-government in business. And they possessed an economic motive which "Christian" bankers could not always rely upon for the fulfilment of engagements. Their branches were linked by family loyalty, pride in the possession of a common name, and in some cases by community in profits.

The ramifications of any one of these family firms suggest the potency of the family tie.[4] The Bischoffsheims, coming from Frankfurt, settled at Brussels in the early years of Belgian independence. One member of the family became a personage in the *Société Générale de Belgique*, prospered as a railway magnate and became part owner of the *Société John Cockerill* and other metallurgical enterprises in Belgium. His son-in-law was the famous Baron Hirsch, who procured the concession for the *Orientbahn* from Vienna to Constantinople in 1868. He was reputed to hold Count Beust, the Austrian prime minister, in his hand. And his interests were a factor in Balkan diplomacy for two decades.

Another Bischoffsheim established the *Banque des depôts de Pays-Bas* at Amsterdam in 1820, which came to have branches in Antwerp, Brussels and Geneva. The same Bischoffsheim had private banking houses in Paris, London and Frankfurt as early as 1850 under the name of *Bischoff-sheim & Goldschmidt*. He engaged actively in railway finance, especially in Italy. And he was a leading promoter of the *Société Générale pour favoriser l'Industrie et la Commerce de France* which was the ally of the *General Credit & Discount Company.* His son, Henri L. Bischoffsheim, was the London partner of Bischoffsheim & Goldschmidt. Except for the few years immediately following 1866 this firm was not prominent in London. But within that period it threw Jay Gould out of *Erie* and plunged that railway into one of its numerous bankruptcies; it reorganized the *Atlantic & Great Western* for McHenry; it marketed a worthless loan to Costa Rica; it was implicated in the scandals of Honduran finance; and it compounded interest upon millions of pounds of Egyptian securities. The continental Bischoffsheims were high in Egyptian stockjobbing. They owned the *Banque Franco-Égyptienne* and they had a bank at Constantinople. But their affairs achieved widest scope through collateral branches of the family. The Bambergers of Mainz were their nephews. One of the latter became a leader of the National Liberals in the German Reichstag; a second was a personage in the *Deutsche Bank* founded at Berlin in 1870; the third, Henri Bamberger, came to Paris and in 1871 united the *Banque de Paris* and the family *Banque des Pays-Bas* into the *Banque de Paris et des Pays-Bas,* which was to become the most powerful of the French investment banks. The Sterns, with whom this amalgamation brought the Bischoffsheims and Bambergers into close relations, were interested in a number of mortgage companies on the Continent which were reaping the fruits of city development. They managed the tobacco monopolies in Spain and Italy. In London, where they inherited the prestige of the Goldsmids, they had largely taken the place of Richard Thornton in control of Portuguese finance. And the first venture of the *Banque de Paris et des Pays-Bas* was into the morasses of

Spanish credit, dimly connected with the restoration of the Bourbons. Thus the links of business association, wrought more firm by kinship, drew in endless chain financial involvements that reached around the world.

The consequences of the panic of 1866 helped to bring these family firms to greater eminence in money markets than they had enjoyed before. The fall of the Pereires had placed the Crédit Mobilier group under a cloud. In England, the entire City was involved in the fall of Overend, Gurney & Co., and obliged to curtail operations until the tangled skein of railway finance could be partially unravelled. The Rothschilds had not entirely escaped the disasters of railway finance; in Italy and Spain they suffered reverses which called for careful liquidation. Beside the cosmopolitan financiers there remained unembarrassed only a few houses in each money market of conservative policy and unquestioned eminence. And these bankers were under no pressure to seek new business in order to keep government funds flowing thru their hands. The interest and amortization payments upon loans contracted long since gave them a supply of current business which rendered them relatively indifferent to the hazardous lure of new loan offerings. So Baring Brothers, engrossed in competition with Rothschilds for the honor of lending money to the Czar, and in the marketing of American bonds, allowed Argentine financing to slip into the hands of rival bankers. Chile turned to J. S. Morgan & Co., to supply her needs. J. Henry Schroeder, who was closely affiliated with Erlangers, became banker for Peru instead of Thomson, Bonar & Co. And the Raphaels replaced Rothschilds for a time in Hungarian finance. The new houses needed business, and the bulk of the new loan issues fell into their hands.

NEGOTIATING LOANS IN LONDON

The personalities of the most active firms had changed; and the market for their operations had become international. But the technique of the loan-issuing business was not unlike that of 1825. Its profitable opportunities were more systematically developed. We know more intimately some of its more sordid details, thanks to the parliamentary investigation of 1875.[5] The evidence brought before the Commons committee with respect to the disastrous loans to Honduras, Costa Rica, Santo Domingo and Paraguay makes it possible to describe with some confidence the procedure followed in transactions which did not become matter of public scandal. And we may recognize two distinct problems of salesmanship in the business; that of persuading governments that they needed a loan, and that of persuading people with money to lend it.

The first task was not an heroic one, except from the point of view of the new firm just becoming established in the issuing business. Such a house needed agents and *souteneurs* to rove the commercial world and to establish preferential connections with governments that were contemplating war or public improvement. And older houses had their hangers-on, who sometimes brought in some business, and could always be repudiated. But there was a tendency for the affairs of countries that came often to the loan market to fall into the hands of a single firm or group of bankers. There was competition in the loan business. But it was competition to secure monopoly position. Not a single loan, but the foreign remittance accounts of the government in question, its short-time borrowing needs, the permanent management of interest and amortization balances, and the consequent dominant position with reference to the exchange of that particular country, were all at stake.

The competition did not enhance the credit of the borrowing governments or give them money at better rates of interest. For competition simply augmented the risks of marketing the loan in the face of efforts of the unsuccessful banker to cry it down. And the terms of loan contracts did not fail to make provision, secret provision, against these risks. What the competition did encourage, however, was the pressing of more money upon the frequently bewildered borrowers. So governments quite unacquainted with the mysteries of finance, like Morocco in 1860, learned from roving agents how easy it was to arrange loans in London or in Paris. Politicians desirous of looting their country's treasury decently and without ostentation discovered how readily the matter could be arranged by way of a floating debt. And manipulation of short-term indebtedness became a favored means by which bankers obtained a commanding position with reference to the finances of a country.

In a word, the loan business was monopolescent.[6] Great Britain, and, at times, France and the United States, were the only countries that sold their securities by public subscription to the highest bidders. It was enough to blast the credit of any ordinary government for it to be known that it had shopped around London with its bonds in search of better prices. By control of maturing coupons or short-term notes, by favorable position for making remittances, by some sort of preferential intimacy with persons authorized to borrow money for their government, one firm or group of bankers usually had the inside track in any loan negotiation. And if they were busy or disobliging, a government dealt elsewhere at even greater disadvantage.

Some aspects of the typical loan negotiation of the seventies can not be suggested more vividly than has been done by Sir Henry Drummond Wolff, one of the most assiduous personalities on the frontier of diplomacy and finance, in his *Rambling Recollections.*[7]

A loan . . . is required by a foreign Government, supposes Drummond Wolff, and one financier hears of it through his agent, or he is informed of it by one of the smaller intermediaries who troop about offices near the Bank. The foreign Government, perhaps, has sent an agent to England, or a friend of the Finance Minister is known to be lodging at Morley's Hotel, and to have left Baring's office the day before with a heavy countenance. The financier, of course, knows everything concerning the country. The duty on cinnamon is still unmortgaged, or the revenues of two provinces are paid direct into the Treasury. A tax on land is about to pass the Chambers. The traffic returns on the Government railway have paid a pound a mile a week additional.

"If," says the intermediary, "you only carry out this loan, you will have the whole country at your feet."

The financier cares little for the future.

"I think it can be done at 52," he soliloquizes, and sends for two confidential brokers.

"Can't be done," says one. "It was offered Baring's at 53, and they refused."

"Yes, but they volunteered to take it firm at 49," rejoins the other.

"That was last year," breaks in the first.

"And they have paid off the old cinnamon loan since," continues No. 2.

"I think it can be done at 52," again soliloquizes the financier, and putting on his hat he makes for Morley's Hotel.

The contract once signed, the financier proceeds to bring out the loan. A prospectus is drawn up, announcing that he himself, or some firm charged by him, will receive subscriptions. In this prospectus, a solictor must naturally intervene as well as a professional manufacturer of prospectuses with a command of epithets, the attractive traits of which do not exceed the strict limits of legal veracity.

Before the issue of the loan, a dinner is often given in the name of the financier, but at the cost of the Syndicate. It fairly comes within the item "market expenses." Here our financier presides, the diplomatic representative of the country on his right, a relative of the Finance Minister upon his left. Near them are some retired Indian and Colonial officials be-ribboned, a few Admirals, a Member of a late Government—all anxious to become Directors of Companies, all counting upon selling the new loan at a premium. Near them are capitalists, leading stockbrokers, some newspaper-writers, a politician who has perhaps made a hobby in Parliament of the country in question, and a clergyman whose face is well known to most of the guests as a dabbler in Turks and Lombards, and as an eager though silent attendant at meetings of discontented bondholders. Dinner over, and the speculative divine having said grace, speeches are made by the M.P. and the financier, who look forward to this loan as a new pledge of alliance between the two countries. The prospectus-maker airs the adjectives cut out of his prospectus by the solicitor. The diplomatic representative makes speeches in a language utterly unknown to his fellow-guests. The financier, not the better for his dinner, confides in English equally unintelligible to the Finance Minister's relative that the loan, if successful, will be entirely owing to his— the financier's—abilities; that if unsuccessful failure will only be attributable to the rotten and bankrupt state of the borrowing country. The relative and the diplomatic representative retire home perfectly satisfied with their relations with British finance, and calculating how many loans the Finance Minister can bring out before the unhallowed cabals of his opponents have forced His Excellency into resignation or exile.

MARKETING THE LOAN

With the arrangement of terms and the announcement of the loan, the work of the financier had, however, just begun. It was necessary to sell the bonds to a public which could not be presumed to be eager to buy those particular securities. And in this respect there was perhaps the greatest difference from the technique which sufficed in 1825. Then a contractor was able to make up a list of subscribers from his clients and friends before issuing the loan. He bought the bonds outright and distributed them among his "underwriters" who continued to hold the bulk of them for investment. But in 1870 loans had to be brought out in a market already congested with securities. They had to be distributed among investors who were widely scattered, but who were interested in following the stock market. Thus technique was determined with reference to the market. The banker took the loan on a commission basis, and made arrangements for a market-rigging operation to guarantee the sale. The procedure, which had been developed in connection with railway finance, was approximately as follows.

On the publication of the prospectus, and before allotment, the banker and his syndicate of friends entered the market and bought heavily of the new loan upon time bargains, forcing the price of the bonds to a premium before they were even issued, and often buying up in the open market nearly all of the loan in so doing. The premium was bait to subscribers. It was supposed to demonstrate the enormous eagerness of the public to acquire the loan; and it brought in real subscribers, as well as speculative ones. It did not always do so. The loan sometimes failed. But there were usually more applicants than there were bonds, and allotment took place at the discretion of the banker. It was the practice to give preference to people who were likely to retain their bonds, and to close friends of the syndicate. And in most cases this meant that when allotment was completed the syndicate had control of all the shares that were for sale. Thereupon a certificate was made out to the Stock Exchange that the issue had been fully subscribed. And there followed formal listing upon the Stock Exchange, which was necessary to make a public market for the loan.

If the bonds actually had been allotted to secure investors, the work which the syndicate was called upon for was simple. It had to buy up any bonds which came into the market, and protect their price from falling below par until the purchasers had paid up their instalments. But usually the syndicate still had its hands full of bonds to sell. And it was necessary to arrange for the price to move temptingly up and down, simulating an activity which would encourage hesitant investors. It might cost a good deal of money to do this, especially if the operations had to be carried on for any length of time. But the syndicate had a portion, at least, of the proceeds of the loan with which to work. Frequently it was arranged in the loan contract that a variable amount of bonds might be bought up by the syndicate at a price far enough below the price to the public to give its members generous profits in addition to the commission. And there were instances, as in the case of the loan to Paraguay in 1871, where by secret contract the syndicate were enabled to buy in as much of the allotted stock as they wished and dispensed from accounting for it unless they sold it within twelve months.

It must be evident that great wealth was not essential to the successful flotation of loans under these conditions. Ability to make a market rather than financial prestige was the crucial qualification for a successful dealer in government loans. And this technique aided small firms to come rapidly forward to prominence. A banker needed enough capital to ensure favorable publicity for his loan, and to cover margins upon the quantity of bonds which he would have to buy and sell to himself on the Stock Exchange during the first few days. Thereafter, with ordinary luck, he might continue his operations out of the proceeds of the loan itself. So important was the market-rigging aspect that such stock-broking houses as Mullens & Marshall, P. Cazenove, and Capel & Co., were among those who brought out loans for governments or railways upon commission. Even the issues of strong governments, such as France, were nursed into the market with the aid of artificial stimulants. And nearly every cosmopolitan banker engaged in it. Only the spokesman for Baring Brothers assured the Investigating Committee of 1875 that his firm had nothing to do with market-rigging.[8]

THE INTERNATIONAL LOAN MARKET

A striking feature of the loans negotiated by European governments in the sixties and seventies was the importance which statesmen attached to bringing them out in several markets at once. Turkey offered her bonds simultaneously in London, Paris, Amsterdam, Brussels, Frankfurt, Vienna and Constantinople. Russian stocks made their bow in Berlin, Hamburg and St. Petersburg at the same time as in Paris, Amsterdam, Frankfurt and London. The reasons for this procedure from the standpoint of the borrowers were largely political. It certainly did not assist the borrowing state to secure the best price for its bonds. For when a security running in terms of several currencies is issued in several markets at once, the price must be low enough to float the loan in the market where capital is most dear. This was of course the investor's gain. It guaranteed him the best of several markets for his stock if he wished to sell. The advantages to the borrowing governments seem to have been these. It kept the credit of their nations from being bound inextricably to the cycle of a single money market, and from being at the mercy of any rival power which might control that market. Moreover, it was believed that political ties could be cemented by the investment relation, and it was well that these be numerous.

But the great impulse to the creation of the international security market and loan issues running in interchangeable currencies, was arbitrage.[9] It was nothing new around 1870 to play the exchanges. Speculation in foreign bills was practiced in Antwerp in the sixteenth century. And arbitrage on a small scale had been conducted for a number of years in the limited number of securities known in more than one European market. But the simultaneous issue of securities redeemable interchangeably in several currencies multiplied the available combinations, and created a business whose participants had every motive to swell the volume of the objects in which they dealt. The more abundant the supply of international paper the greater became the resources under the control of the cosmopolitan bankers specializing in arbitrage, and the more formidable their ability to handle international loans. For in the absence of an international circulating medium other than gold, international securities became the constant means of making remittances. They were even the means of making many a public loan against the actual balance of payments. Austria, raising money by a foreign loan in preparation for war with Prussia, found bonds' of earlier issues together with bills on

Vienna flung in such volume upon her money market that a contemporary economist was able to show that Austria indirectly subscribed the loan herself and paid the cosmopolitan bankers handsomely for the privilege.[10]

IN QUANTITATIVE TERMS

Between 1860 and 1879, more than £320,000,000 was raised in the London money market upon foreign government loan issues.* In the same period half as much again was raised upon the credit of the governments of India and of other parts of the British Empire. £232,000,000 was paid up in the same years on the shares and debentures of private companies engaged in railway-building or other enterprises outside the British Isles. And these figures do not measure the extent of the financial activity of London, nor of the increment of British investment abroad. The United States did not market her securities publicly in London, except by way of converting those already sold at lower rates of interest. Yet by 1875 the bulk of her foreign-owned debt, amounting to one billion dollars, had accumulated in British hands. The bonds were bought entirely thru private channels, pushed indeed by numerous brokerage houses, but without the formality of a contractor's introduction. "Five-Twenties," the favorite category of American bonds, were not the only government securities to be bought by Englishmen in this way. Probably as large a quantity was purchased privately as was bought from contractors. And Seyd's estimate cannot be far wrong, that in 1875 there was an international public debt due British bondholders amounting to

* See Appendix D for summary of foreign security issues made in London, 1860–76. A table of foreign government loan issues is given in Appendix C.

£800,000,000, a sum approximately the volume of the National Debt.

European governments increased their public debts, 1848 to 1872, according to Van Oss, from £1,730,000,000 to £4,-605,000,000.[11] During the last ten years of that period they borrowed at the rate of £240,000,000 a year. Of the total sum, Seyd estimates that at least two billions consisted in internationally held debts, with a market value in 1875 of about £1,700,000,000.[12] Germany and France were each creditors for £400,000,000. The smaller investing regions, Switzerland, Belgium and Holland, were believed to have invested £100,000,000 in international indebtedness.

The distribution of securities between these countries fluctuated sharply. Between 1870 and 1875, there was something of a game of "general post" in the location of the debts of several countries of Europe as well as of the American bonds. This was a sequel to the Franco-Prussian war and the indemnity of five billion francs which France was called upon to pay to the new German Empire.[13] Berlin became the leading market for Russian loans, and absorbed a good deal of the Italian and Austrian debt as well in the adjustment of the French indemnity payments. England lost interest in Austria and Italy as eventually in Russia, and she bought up nearly all of the American bonds that could be found in Germany at prices which represented not far from fifty per cent profit to the original German purchasers. At the same time the absorption of continental money markets in the remittance of the French indemnity made London the chief source of supply for loans to Turkey and Egypt, and checked a growing disposition of South American republics to interest Paris in their finances. These investment shifts involved tremendous sums of capital; but they can not be quantitatively traced.[14]

There can be no doubt that the point of highest intensity in foreign government financing was reached between 1870 and 1873. Turkey and Egypt were compounding their debts at terrific rates. Austria, Hungary and Russia were embarked upon programs of railway building, in which the device of government guarantees which had been so profitable to British contractors in France and India was given further employment. All eastern and central Europe was stirred by a *"Gruender"* movement—a promotion mania. And the unprecedented demand for capital goods and the prospects of opening new grain areas to easy access to market roused Englishmen to hopeful enthusiasm. Many of the Latin American states, and, most ambitiously, Peru, were yielding to the persuasions of plausible engineers. Any government which claimed sovereignty over a bit of the earth's surface and a fraction of its inhabitants could find a financial agent in London and purchasers for her bonds. Remittance was no longer a problem for any loan of only a few million pounds or so. The commercial relations of most countries had become so complex as to distribute the strain. Moreover, hope was current at a premium in all the markets of the world. There is nothing like it as a means of payment. And then there were such cases as that of the Colombian Loan of 1866, one million pounds and a half to be remitted to a country with a diminutive volume of trade. There was a floating debt to be scratched off, a road company to be financed, some warships to encourage the Colombian sense of statehood. And when deduction had been made for a year's interest and commissions and expenses Colombia found herself in receipt of some $560,000 cash each year until 1873 in remittance of the loan proceeds, and owing the contractors in return in interest and amortization, $800,000 a year for twenty years.[15]

FOREIGN LOANS AND PUBLIC POLICY

Of the desirability of investing British capital abroad, or in such quantity, there was no public questioning. One heretical civil servant, James Geddes, told a Commons committee on Indian Finance in 1871 that the £150,000,000 of capital invested by the British in India largely since 1857, in railways, government bonds, tea plantations and jute mills, had not benefited that country and might have been applied to the greater advantage of the British workingman at home.[16] The committee became so interested that it continued to take testimony about Indian railways for three years. And then there was a general election; a new Parliament; Disraeli instead of Gladstone at the helm. The Committee on Indian Finance never made a report.

There was no public policy about foreign loans. They were made to such persons as contractors pleased and on such terms as they might arrange; and they were marketed in Great Britain under such restrictions alone as were imposed by the by-laws and mores of the Stock Exchange. There was no discernible interference of the British Government with any projected loan, in these days, even to countries whose policies were hostile. In Paris and in Berlin, the respective governments exerted strict control over the foreign loan-issuing business. Congruence to their immediate foreign policy was a prerequisite to a loan. And while negotiations proceeded, diplomats did not miss the opportunity to impress important political considerations upon the attention of the prospective borrower. France and Germany had no intention of allowing the public, official money markets, at any rate, to lend money for purposes subversive of what they thought their interests were.

But London, like Amsterdam and Brussels and Frankfurt, was a free capital market. The Stock Exchange was entirely independent of the government. It was even devoid of status in the courts; it exercised control over the activities of its members only thru its by-laws and economic sanctions. And one of its rules was the chief element of control upon foreign borrowing. About 1825 it established the precedent of refusing quotation to securities of governments which failed to fulfil their obligations or come to terms with their creditors. It ignored this rule in 1833 when it admitted to quotation an international guaranteed loan to Greece, when two outstanding issues were in default. In this case it conformed to the diplomatic policy of the Government. But it was really not the credit of Greece which was involved, but that of the guarantors, Great Britain, France and Russia, which was indisputable. At other times, the Stock Exchange went so far as to exclude even the industrial issues of countries whose governments were in default.[17]

But it could not altogether prevent trading in London. The market for many kinds of American securities was outside the Stock Exchange. To stockjobbers who specialized in certain stocks, such as defaulted loans, it might very well be an advantage for them to be excluded from the public markets. And what was a Stock Exchange rule to cosmopolitan bankers who could bring out loans in any of several markets, and handle trading orders from half a dozen countries in securities which had official quotation in but one?

It may be possible to detect a control of a vaguer kind in London, which caused the main currents of British foreign investments to flow in the general direction of the interests of British foreign policy. For, interest percentages apart, the movement of capital and of foreign policy came from the springs of action, and was largely in the hands of men who were of a common social group. Institutional relations were irrelevant when there was such an interpenetration of personalities between politics and banking. A. H. Layard, Samuel Laing, George J. Goschen, Henry Drummond Wolff and Stephen Cave were a few of the men who alternated between important undersecretaryships of state and undertakings in finance. Banking houses had partners sitting in the House of Commons with greater regularity than in the directorate of the Bank of England. There need be no suggestion of scandal about these relations. The conduct of these gentlemen must have impressed their fellows as being such as was becoming in politicians and men of affairs. But we may be sure that this interpenetration enabled governments to have full regard to the interests of London bankers abroad. We may be equally certain that the more substantial issue-houses could manage their efforts with intimate knowledge of the diplomatic considerations involved.

To be sure this comfortable accord was by no means unvarying. At an earlier period there had been events in the City which amaze the twentieth century student of war finance. There was the curious case of the loan floated for Russia in London in the midst of the Crimean War.[18] True there was an embargo upon shipments to Russia; and the objects of the loan would be fulfilled by the payment of interest upon the Russian debt already held by Englishmen and Dutch. Those investors would be so much the better off. But so would Russian credit. Barings cheerfully marketed the loan, and were not hanged for treasonable intercourse with the enemy.

There had been earlier instances of successful loan negotiations in the face of a considerable body of hostile opinion in the City, and in some degree in negation of British policy. The Baring loan to Russia in 1849 and the Rothschild loan to Austria in the following year, in reality furnished the means for carrying on the war to suppress the Hungarian revolutionaries, whom Palmerston at the Foreign Office was doing a great deal to cheer along. The Peace Societies, then at the height of their enthusiasm and activity, held great meetings in London and elsewhere, denouncing the lending of money to bolster up the military monarchies.[19] Samuel Gurney joined Richard Cobden in exerting every effort to frustrate the loans, and David Urquhart, successful organizer of a large body of Russophobic opinion, was for once in a common cause with the pacifists. But money was cheap; the interest was attractive; there was a disheartened lull in railway financing. In short, business considerations prevailed over everything else.

So too it was doubtless business considerations which caused French and American securities to fluctuate violently when diplomatic relations with those countries grew tense. And those fluctuations in turn acted as a steadying influence upon diplomacy.

Railways, steamers, telegraphs, and free trade, [declared Samuel Laing in the midst of one Anglo-American crisis], are fast creating a diplomacy which will supersede notes and protocols. The ablest note of Lord Clarendon speaks with feeble force compared with a Stock Exchange List or Price Current, which tells people of a civilized country by breakfast time next morning that their property is depreciated 10% because their Government has committed a folly over night.[20]

But as for formal relations between government and the loan business, they were usually exceedingly chilly. There was not the least disposition on the part of the Foreign Office to do anything but make "stern representations" when debtor governments failed, as they frequently did, to make good on their promises. The British Government was not above making claims on behalf of its subjects. Indeed after Palmerston's eloquent speech in behalf of Don Pacifico, Englishmen the world around appealed with success to the doctrine "Civis Romanus sum." England joined with France and Spain in intervention in Mexico in 1861 upon that ground. Mexico owed money to British merchants. And it seemed simpler to conduct the affair upon that basis than to take up the quarrels of the long-suffering bondholders.

The affairs of Venezuela, which reached a crisis in 1867, illustrate the attitude assumed in the face of concerted pressure from the leading merchant-bankers. In 1862 Venezuela had arranged a loan through Baring Brothers, one million pounds at 63, to pay off bank loans, retire a depreciated currency and consolidate public order. The proceeds were not enough to become extravagant upon; and an agent was sent out from Barings to Caracas to act with the British consul general, Orme, in the collection of 55% of the customs duties pledged to pay interest on the loan. Collection was direct; the 55% should never see the treasury. In November, 1864, Venezuela took possession of all the customs receipts and stopped paying interest on the loan. Three successive foreign ministers made "representations." And in the fall of 1867 the money market was moved to prepare a public memorial to Lord Stanley, then Foreign Secretary, declaring that "the time has now arrived when it behooves the British government to take active and energetic measures in the matter." The signatures to the memorial form a directory of the loan-issuing houses of London in the late sixties. Thomas Baring, M.P., headed a deputation that waited in person upon Lord Stanley to receive his reply. And the noble lord, who had consulted the cabinet, declined firmly to declare that the customs duties were British property, and that the government was bound to protect Barings' customers in its possession. "Her Majesty's government," he proceeded, "do not feel justified in seeking the sanction of Parliament to adopt coercive measures which might involve this country in a war with the Republic of Venezuela." [21]   Was it war with Venezuela from which Lord Stanley shrank? Or did he think of France, which had set out to champion bondholders in Mexico, and had withdrawn in some confusion when the close of the American Civil War put meaning into Seward's allusions to the Monroe Doctrine? Whatever the thought, the City was well content. "If the monied classes will lend to people over whom no law exercises control," said the *Bullionist,* "they must be satisfied if the large risks are covered by large profits." [22]

ORGANIZING THE BONDHOLDERS

It was largely in frank acceptance of this official policy of laissez-faire, that there was formed in 1868 the nucleus of what has come to bear the name of the *Corporation of Foreign Bondholders.*

The original plan seems to have been to form an international organization, headed by the leading loan-houses and brokers, under the presidency of Baron Lionel Rothschild (the London Rothschild of the day).[23] It might be spoken of not unfairly as the "conscience of the loanmongers." It was prompted by a sense of obligation on the part of bankers toward people to whom they sold bonds. And perhaps, too, there was the reflection that it was bad business to sell bonds which proved unprofitable. It was hoped that an international organization would quickly bring to time any government that should be so inconsiderate as to fail to pay interest on its borrowings. It could close the markets of the world to further appeals from that government for financial aid; it could solicit such government aid as was appropriate; and with the entire mass of foreign bondholders at its command, it would possess great bargaining power in negotiating arrangements on their behalf with governments which had been at fault and were disposed to make amends.

However, when the time came to effect the organization a Rothschild could not be put at its head; for Italy and Austria were menacing their bondholders with a heavy tax upon their interest coupons, and the securities of those countries had largely been issued thru Rothschilds. Moreover, the inclusion of continental money markets proved impracticable. The bourses of Paris and Berlin were controlled by the governments in such a way that cooperation with them could not be untrammelled. Thus the only bondholders to be organized were the English.

That is to say, it was the English stockbrokers and bankers interested in foreign government securities who organized. The most active promoter was Isidore Gerstenberg, a prominent stockbroker who had been identified with several of the special bondholders' committees which had dealt in the affairs of defaulting Latin American republics. The original council included a Scotch viscount, two generals, an admiral, an alderman, and a few private gentlemen. But the majority of its members were members of private or merchant banking firms, or of brokerage houses. Doubtless most of them were large proprietors of foreign bonds. They were certainly interested in maintaining a market for some kinds of them. So far as the interests of private bondholders lay in the same direction, they were probably the best representation they could have had.

The Corporation of Foreign Bondholders was at least a

great improvement over the isolated committees for which it acted at first as a clearing-house, and which it later superseded altogether. The appointment of Hyde Clarke as secretary, and the commencement of a library of financial information and documents, provided services for the members which had not been so amply available to them. Not a profit-seeking organization in itself, nor tied to the fortunes of any one syndicate, it found a specialized function to perform in the investment market. Thru its agents in most of the leading countries it had a diplomatic apparatus at its command to negotiate about difficult foreign situations, with the ban of the Stock Exchange rather than British gun-boats for a sanction.

At an early stage in the organization of bondholders, the suggestion was made that it make its object to "insist that the Government of the day should take measures with reference to the claims" of outraged investors in foreign government securities. The suggestion came from an eloquent member of Parliament, Mr. H. B. Sheridan; and it was repelled at once by George J. Goschen, once of Frühling & Goschen, and at the time a cabinet minister, who presided over the meeting.

We should be damaged by the result of the meeting, said Goschen, if it went forth that the meeting have endorsed the view that it is the duty of the English Government to compel foreign Governments to pay the debts incurred to English subjects. If the Government were to go to war for such a purpose with Venezuela, they would involve themselves in this position—that if larger Powers should act in the same way, they should also go to war with them. I think it is dangerous to have the idea go forth that when an Englishman lends his money to a foreign Government he is creating a national obligation, guaranteed by the full weight of the English government. The Englishman lends his money to a foreign Government, and gets high interest, because he incurs a risk. I believe the duties of the Council will be most important . . . by exercising a moral power over the foreign Governments contracting loans; and also by exercising a moral power over our own Government by inducing them to interfere, if by their good offices they can do anything.[24]

THE HARVEST OF INSOLVENCY

The work of the organized bondholders was cut out for them. Before their incorporation was completed in 1873 events had taken place which were beginning to stay the recklessness of British investors to buy any security bearing the the name of a foreign government.[25] In 1872 a large Honduras Ship Railway loan, thru the opposition of the new bondholders' organization failed wholly to find a market; and a short time afterward bankers announced that previous loans to that government were in default. Costa Rica, Santo Domingo and Paraguay defaulted in the same year, amid whispers as to the legitimacy of their loans and as to the disposition of the proceeds. To relieve a desperate financial situation in Spain and keep King Amadeus on the throne, bondholders consented to a funding of the portion of the interest then due. There was in consequence a heavy fall in Spanish stock, a collapse of credit, the abdication of King Amadeus, civil war, and complete default in June, 1873.

By this time foreign government securities were tumbling madly downward in price. Some of the new areas in which enterprise and speculation had been stimulated in part by British loans suffered crisis and recession. In May, the *"Gruender"* movement in central Europe culminated in a panic which spread from Vienna to the other German money

markets.   In the consequent failure of banking and railway
enterprises London was agitated.   Governments like Turkey and Egypt which depended upon new borrowings to enable them to meet interest upon their existing debts found
a market for their loans only after prodigious efforts on the
part of banking syndicates.   Crisis followed in the fall in
the United States, where panic in New York and Philadelphia threw half the railways of the country into the hands
of receivers.   In November, 1873, the Bank rate in London was at a minimum of 9%, and the recession in stock
prices began slowly to spread into industry and commerce.
In the following year all South America became depressed,
as the currents of capital which had moved to that region
ceased to flow.   There was a fitful revival of enthusiasm for
Russia and Turkey and Egypt.   A sixteen-million pound
loan for the sultan (approximately the amount of his annual
debt and interest obligations) was oversubscribed four times.
And then the suspension of interest payment by Bolivia,
Guatemala, Liberia and Uruguay, the continued whisper-
ings with respect to the integrity of loan transactions, brought
about an agitation which culminated in the Foreign Loan
Investigation of 1875.

The report of the Commons committee issued in July,
1875, brought the foreign loan mania definitely to an end.
Its revelations concerning market-rigging, concerning loan-
issues made solely for the purpose of earning fat commissions, concerning interest kept up solely out of the interest
on the loans threw serious distrust upon several firms of cosmopolitan bankers.   This was cast especially upon Bischoffsheim & Goldschmidt, for whose proceedings the committee
considered that "a remedy . . . ought to be found in the tribunals of the country." [26]   It demonstrated, as Giffen says,
that "as there had been bogus companies in the days of the

company mania, so now there were bogus loans." [27] The distrust it spread was one factor in the insolvency which ensued of Turkey, of Egypt and Peru. And thus it helped to mark an epoch in the exploitation of new countries by the capital of the old. For the bankruptcies of Turkey and Egypt at least were tangled in diplomatic relations which called for the direct interposition of the British and other governments. No account of the foreign loan business could be adequate which failed to tell the story of how the cosmopolitan bankers ruined the finances of those countries and involved the British government in some of that complex of activities which, in the slang of the publicists and historians, has come to be called "imperialism."

CHAPTER X

THE BANKRUPTCY OF THE NEAR EAST

"Your feelings cannot be what they were before all this happened; when you thought only of a divine cause, of stars, of angels, and of our peculiar and gifted land. No, no; now it is all mixed up with intrigue, and management, and baffled schemes, and cunning arts of men. You may be, you are, free from all this, but your faith is not the same. . . . You no longer believe in Arabia."
—Disraeli, *Tancred*.

THE REFORMATION OF TURKEY

There is a closed closet in the cabinets of most European chancelleries, which bears the legend "The Near East." Here hang as in Bluebeard's story, the mangled corpses of their successive pledges to constancy and virtue. We are not assessors to weigh the temptations to which the Powers have in turn succumbed or to measure the forces which have brought the eastern Mediterranean to its present pass. The Near East is a cockpit of historical motivation. Today it is oil which gives wakeful nights to statesmen and financiers from western capitals. But yesterday it was the Bagdad Railway. The rights of Christian minorities, the Keys to the Holy Places, the prestige of all of the great powers and the route of one of them to India have directed political action in the Near East in the none too distant past. And there are the slower-moving tides of culture and decay which have lined the shores of the eastern Mediterranean with the driftwood of past cities, mocking at our national prides and international consortiums. It is with no confidence that one may speak of motives or achievement in this presence. And what the fates intended which poured European capital into Turkey and Egypt for a score of years, reduced their governments to bankruptcy and the peoples to desperation, brought the one under financial tutelage of the Powers and the other under British administration, and finally covered those lands with warring nationalities and contending capitalisms, we are not seers to declare.

The Near Eastern question has been defined as the disturbance of Europe caused by the break-up of the Turkish Empire. Some powers have been eager to assist this process, to add to their own possessions or to place more pliable politicians in control of affairs in various districts. Other governments, and not always the same ones at successive periods, have sought to check the dissolution of Turkey. In the first quarter of the nineteenth century it appeared already too late to prevent this. Russia had annexed the northern and eastern shores of the Black Sea; France was setting up a protectorate in Algiers; there was an independent kingdom in Greece; and the viceroy of Egypt was precipitating repeated international situations by attempting to conquer Syria from his overlord. "The Turkish Empire is evidently hastening to its dissolution," wrote Stratford Canning to Palmerston in 1832, "and an approach to the civilization of Christendom affords the only chance of keeping it together for any length of time."[1]

Among the powers, Great Britain displayed about 1840 the greatest eagerness to preserve the integrity of Turkey. She had a trade of long standing to the Levant, which was increasing as the machine-made products of Sheffield and Manchester drove those of Smyrna and Damascus from the market. With India too there was an interchange of products, the subject of centuries of tradition. It was no British interest to see this market pass under the control of a government such as Russia, with a hostile fiscal system and which was little more advanced commercially than Turkey. Moreover routes to India were beginning to be talked of. They were a hobby with William IV.[2] And the Afghan wars called attention to the strategic position of Russia with reference to India. Asia is a large continent, and its interior far from hospitable to a modern army of invasion. But prestige can do much which would not be possible to military columns. And few things could be more harmful to the relative position of Great Britain in the world than the occupation of the Bosphorus by any one of the great continental powers.[3]

All of these considerations called for the maintenance of a strong Turkey highly under British control. And in 1842 Stratford Canning was installed at Constantinople as British ambassador, with a broad commission to work for the reform of Turkey.[4] From the Turkish point of view, reform consisted essentially in the secularizing of a law which had been purely theocratic, and the modernizing of a scheme of civil and military organization which had been characteristically feudal. Canning's instructions went beyond discipline, however, to prosperity. They specifically mentioned the promotion of roads and steam communications. But not much was done either with reforms or with opportunities for deserving investors until after the Crimean War. The Turks—or more properly, the Armenian bankers who enjoyed a monopoly of credit facilities at rates ranging from twenty to forty per cent—were highly distrustful of western innovations. Not even the mania year of 1845 produced a prospectus from a company promoter in London to build a railway in Turkey. And tho talk of concessions was more frequent in the early fifties, no one ventured to submit his scheme for subscription to the British public.[5] British interests in European Turkey continued to be represented by the Greek merchants who had succeeded the Levant Company—the Rodoconachis, the Rallis, the Zarafis, the Baltazzis —and the Ionian and Maltese shopkeepers and grogsellers, who claimed British protection.

The Crimean war set loose new forces around the Bosphorus.[6] Constantinople swarmed with industrious westerners ready to point the Turkish government the way to reform and its leading men the way to wealth. Nothing seemed more vital to these "flowers of progress" than public works—docks, wharves, warehouses, railways, telegraphs, water- and gas-works and canals. And as the war drew to its close western money markets were electrified by the news that Turkey had published a Charter of Reform and was calling for applications to build a railway system. Contractors, jobbers, shipping-agents, engineers who had come to Constantinople with organization, materials and capital during the war, remained to win the peace.

The precise relation between public works and the notion of "reform" in Turkey it would be difficult to determine. What was intended by reform was a well-organized modern state, exercising full sovereignty, and dealing even-handed justice to all classes of subjects. But public works entailed the multiplication upon Turkish soil of foreign organizations, not in fact amenable to Turkish law, intent upon the propagation of an alien culture. They meant increased opportunities for intervention by foreign diplomats, the most serious obstacle to the "reform" they affected to esteem.

Influential Englishmen upon the ground were very frank in discussing their hopes. Let the clause of the Hatt-i-Humayoon of 1856 (the charter of reforms) be enforced which grants Europeans the right to buy land.   The entire coast of Asia Minor could be bought up for a shilling or two an acre.   It would eventually become the great outlet for English and German colonization, and without loss of nationality.   "The first and most important step," said James Whittall in avowing his aims to Nassau Senior, "is to make railways.   They will be constructed, and owned, and worked by Englishmen.   They will be enormously profitable; and they will render productive provinces now uncultivated. . . . The railway companies, and the European colonies will become little republics.   They will say to the Turks, 'We will pay your tithes and taxes, which will be twenty times more than you ever got before, but we will manage our own affairs.' " [7]   These hopes, however, were not realized, for the sultan's Hatt did not introduce European notions of land tenure into Turkey.   What Europeans wanted was not to hold land upon the same terms as.the Turks, which they had never been denied, but to procure such rights of mortgage and testament and tenure as were accorded by the common law and the Code Napoleon, and to make them enforceable in consular courts.   This privileged status was not acquired.   Feudal and communal and precarious tenures barred the way to the advance of capitalism in Mohammedan Turkey.[8]

But to Lord Stratford de Redcliffe railways seemed to involve reform in another sense.   They could hardly be built at all without improving the Turkish administration, he declared at the laying of the corner-stone of the Smyrna railway station in 1858.[9]   They must imply "a progressive diminution of abuses, prejudices, and national animosities." The property created by the railways "would call for securities in matters of police, of finance, and of administrative justice."   And such reforms must be made.   "Western civilisation is knocking hard at the gates of the Levant, and if it be not allowed to win its way into regions where it has hitherto been admitted so partially, it is but capable of forcing the passage and asserting its pretensions with little regard for anything but their satisfaction."

The great difficulty about railways, however, arose not from the sultan, but from western civilization. The groups which crowded Galata in their search for concessions were seldom narrowly national. But no group could be made so inclusive as to satisfy the claims of all the Englishmen and Frenchmen who thought to profit by participation. And those who failed to win the ear of Lord Stratford or Thouvenel were not slow under new national colors to find a friend from Austria at court. To an ambassador jealous of his influence no project could be good which did not arise from his intercession.[10] So diplomacy interposed its jealous rivalry in the way of most transportation projects, blocking not least of all those concerned with the way to India.

The concessions which were ratified and carried into execution before 1870 were confined to some provincial lines which the English thought would be of great value in promoting the grain and cotton output of Turkey. Two lines were run from Smyrna into the interior of Asia Minor, to Aidin and to Cassaba. Two others were built to bring the Danubian grain trade to Black Sea ports, Kustendje and Varna, across unsettled and unfertile areas. The companies which built these railways had a stormy history. The Aidin company, for example, began work in 1856 with a 6% guarantee from the sultan upon a capital of £1,200,000, which was enough in all conscience to build an eighty-mile line in an undeveloped country. One contractor failed; another revised the plans after attempting to build thru an impassable defile; and dividends were paid so generously out of

capital that in 1862 when fifty miles had been completed and
the guarantee was payable, the sultan was besought to add
£40,000 a year more to his pledge in order to secure more
capital with which to finish the road.   It was June, 1866 before the work was completed.[11]   Twenty years later dividends began to be paid out of earnings, and this was the most
successful of the railways undertaken.   Quite hopeless from
a diplomatic standpoint were railway projects which planned
to strengthen Turkey politically by improving communications from the capital to outlying parts.

THE HIGH ROAD TO INDIA

But the chief objects of concern to enterprising men and
diplomats in the Near East bore neither upon reforming the
Ottoman Empire nor upon enhancing its strength.   They
dealt with the high roads that led through the sultan's domains to empire and trade opportunities in the Farther East.

The revival of the Mediterranean route to India dates from
the coming of the steamship, the re-opening of the port of
Alexandria, and the pacification of Egypt by Mehemet Ali.
Its inspiration it owes to that vision of eastern glory which
Napoleon inherited from Vergennes.   And the British government wavered long between the advantages of quick communication with India, and a disinclination to share them
with the French.

It was slow to establish the overland mail route by way
of Alexandria and Suez.   There was official correspondence
about the matter as early as 1823.[12]   In 1829, Lieutenant
Thomas Waghorn demonstrated the feasibility of routing
mail thru Egypt.   But the pasha of Egypt was something of
a protégé of the French; and his Syrian ambitions brought

France and England nearly to war several times during the thirties. A regular passenger and mail service was established, with caravan stations thru the desert, before diplomacy or government aid was enlisted whole-heartedly in the matter. Galloway Bey, a British engineer in Mehemet Ali's service, even persuaded that chief to buy thirty-three miles of iron rails from Galloway senior, an iron founder, with the purpose of laying a railway through the desert. And the rails became sand heaps while diplomacy at Cairo and Constantinople found difficulties.[13]

In 1840 the British government granted a subvention to the Peninsular & Oriental Steamship Company to provide a regular mail service from London to Alexandria.[14] And the company obtained permission from Mehemet Ali to run ships on the Nile for a number of years, connecting Alexandria and Cairo. In 1843 Lord Aberdeen gave formal support to the Galloway railway proposal. France raised outcry, and urged Mehemet to think of the possibility of building a glorious canal. A procession of agents, diplomatic and commercial, commenced, with proposals which culminated in a drawn battle in November, 1844.[15] But two years later, the Foreign Office was out of touch with the situation when Mehemet installed a Nile monopoly under the auspices of a French company, and seized the British caravan route. The P. & O. had sold out its river boats before Palmerston discovered that their retention in English hands was an important interest of the British Empire.[16]

The same fitfulness characterized British policy with reference to the Suez Canal. In the early thirties, when the Saint Simonians began to agitate the matter, the East India Company considered it impracticable, but "foresaw none but desirable consequences from the accomplishment of such a work."[17] The chairman of the P. & O., Arthur Anderson, urged Palmerston in 1841 to endorse the project of a canal to be built by a private company, *under a political guarantee of the great Powers.*[18] The concession was to be obtained from the sultan; the canal was to be the boundary between Syria and Egypt; and the tolls were to be shared equally between company and sultan. The reply of Palmerston, if any, is not in the public records. But several years later, on his return to the Foreign Office, he instructed the Consul-General at Cairo that "any new arrangement which could facilitate commerce in general and which would shorten communication and cheapen transport, would necessarily be advantageous to England, the greatest commercial country of the world." He considered that France overrated the political advantages a canal might have for her, in view of England's superiority at sea. "On the whole, therefore, Her Majesty's Government do not wish to oppose the canal absolutely, but would greatly prefer the Railway." [19]

Nothing happened, however, until 1851 when the Francophil Abbas had been succeeded by Said Pasha, who was more amenable to British suggestions. The pasha undertook to build the railway himself, with the aid of British engineers and capital and supplies. Thereupon diplomats worked furiously at Constantinople. The sultan was prevailed upon to forbid the work. And Palmerston made it emphatically clear that in the judgment of the British government, the pasha could use his funds that way if he so desired. The sultan, having listened to other diplomats, urged that he must examine the accounts, to ensure that his revenue from Egypt be not endangered. And the City suggested that the fleet be sent to reason with the sultan. The railway was built. The Peninsular & Oriental Steamship Company arranged the loan of £285,000, partly out of its own funds, and the rest from its directors and friends.[20]

The railway accomplished, it was not easy for the pasha to repudiate a canal. And Ferdinand de Lesseps was his personal friend. In 1854 a concession was granted for the Suez Canal, and the search for capital began. De Lesseps hoped to raise a large portion of it in Great Britain. And when the settlement of the Crimean War had made money markets easy, he commenced a tour thru the English provinces. Tremendous ovations greeted him; the Foreign Policy Committees, of which David Urquhart was the mainspring, worked zealously in his behalf. And their efforts provoked a public declaration of British policy.[21]

"Her Majesty's Government certainly cannot undertake to use their influence with the Sultan to induce him to give permission for the construction of this canal," stated Palmerston, "because for the last fifteen years Her Majesty's Government have used all the influence they possess at Constantinople and in Egypt to prevent that scheme from being carried into execution. . . . The scheme is founded in hostility to the interests of this country—opposed to the standing policy of England in regard to the connection of Egypt with Turkey. . . . The obvious political tendency of the undertaking is to render more easy the separation of Egypt from Turkey. It is founded, also, on remote speculations with regard to easier access to our Indian possessions, which I need not more distinctly shadow forth."[22] In a word, Palmerston could see no reason to favor a highway which would bring Marseilles materially closer than Liverpool to Bombay, and whose development would make it increasingly difficult to keep up the myth that Egypt was part of an unbroken Turkish empire. Moreover, had not the great engineer Robert Stephenson examined the isthmus and proven the construction of a sea level canal at that place to be an engineering impossibility?

The attitude of the British Government ended de Lesseps' tour, and the sale of canal shares in England. It proved their best recommendation to his thrifty countrymen. France subscribed half of the capital with enthusiasm; the pasha of Egypt took the rest; the sultan's signature was obtained; and the first ground for the canal was broken in 1859.

It must be said that public opinion in the City was less inclined to jealous subtleties than was the Foreign Office. It frankly regarded the shortening of communication with India as greatly to be desired. It followed with the greatest enthusiasm the projects of the energetic Waghorn for perfecting mail and express services across Europe which would bring mails from Bombay and Calcutta hours earlier than steamships around the Peninsula.[23] And many promoters of railways upon the Continent featured in their prospectuses the time and mileage their line would save upon the route to India.[24]

Beyond the Mediterranean rival routes by rail to the Persian Gulf were being surveyed from the early thirties. Opinion inclined most strongly to the design of a railway from Seleucia thru Aleppo to the Euphrates, where a steamship line would navigate the river to the Gulf. A crowd of Anglo-Indians interested in the development of the Indus Valley took up the project in the fifties, and pressed the government for support. With the assistance of Lord Stratford de Redcliffe, they secured a guarantee of 6% upon their capital from the sultan in 1856. But this was not enough. Nothing but a vested interest and a pretext for intervention would satisfy the projectors. And only the entanglement of the British government directly in the affairs of the railway by means of financial support would answer this purpose.[25]   They wanted a guarantee from Great

Britain, too, before they would place the concern upon the stock market.

Fortunately British governments in those days had no mind for a Mesopotamian empire. Moreover Napoleon III decided to oppose the Euphrates railway as heartily as Palmerston was opposing the Canal. Although it was frequently resuscitated, and is thought to have played its rôle in British policy as late as the Congress of Berlin, this harbinger of the Bagdad railway never reached maturity.[26] A telegraph line down the Euphrates, completed in 1865, and the Lynch steamboat company's monopoly along its lower reaches, were the only fruits of half a century of effort to use the railway to pioneer the flag.

THE RISE OF THE OTTOMAN DEBT

Turkey had two reasons for existence, Nassau Senior was advised in 1857. First, to keep Christian powers from occupying the country. "And secondly, for the benefit of some fifty or sixty bankers and usurers, and some thirty or forty pashas, who make fortunes out of its spoils." [27] If reform was to be brought about in Turkey, it had to be made attractive to the spoilsmen. And very few steps had been taken when it became clear that it was going to cost a great deal more to run a reformed régime at the Golden Horn than the most extravagant sultans of an unenlightened period had been able to afford.[28]

The earliest deficits were supplied without difficulty by the local bankers and tax-farmers, who lent to the treasury at lower rates than those exacted of the peasantry, and who discounted the unpaid vouchers of various departments at generous rates.[29] As their own resources became heavily engaged in the paper which issued from the treasury, they began to draw upon London, and carried the current debts of the sultan by means of acceptances and bills of exchange, which they renewed quarterly as they fell due. The credit of the Galata bankers in London was good. Their methods were skillful. And the difference between the commercial market rate in London and the discount on Turkish bills left them a margin of profit which widened as interest payments were periodically compounded. At an average rate of twelve per cent, the sultan's floating debt doubled every six years and trebled every ten without augmenting his purchasing power and without straining the exchanges.

The invasion of the Crimea brought burdens too heavy for this commercial mechanism, and portions of the sultan's debt began to pass from banks to British investors in the form of sterling loans. Palmer, Mackillop, Dent & Co. handled the first of these issues which appeared late in 1854, secured upon the Egyptian tribute. In the following year, the Allied powers, Great Britain and France, jointly guaranteed a Rothschild loan which brought money to the sultan at a cheaper rate. Meanwhile the floating debt rose steadily, and, including paper money, acceptances for supplies and treasury notes, was estimated in 1857 at fifteen million pounds.[30] Paper money meant a new problem—deranged exchanges—which were a matter of concern to British exporters. So there was a third loan in 1858 expressly to retire the paper currency. The Stock Exchange, dominated upon this occasion by Greek and Hebrew elements, was hostile to the affair. It seemed likely to put an end to a profitable arbitrage business in a highly unstable medium of exchange. But the loan was taken up in the provinces where the market for British manufactures seemed more important.[31]

There remained the Galata debt, swollen to eighteen million pounds by 1860, despite the loan.[32] And the outbreak of Syrian massacres in that year rendered the most adventurous capitalists cold. Turkey approached England with a proposal to get her guarantee for another loan. Sir Henry Bulwer, as ambassador, replied with a list of six conditions of which the most important would have virtually turned over the public lands, forests and mines of Turkey to an international commission for the benefit of concession seekers.[33] This was a high price for Turkey, and would have curtailed the opportunities of her high officials. The sultan's advisers turned to the Paris market. Rothschild and the Pereires were as distant as London. The best Turkey could do was to arrange a loan with a popular speculator named Mires, who was arrested for misuse of funds soon after he failed completely to market his bonds. A panic broke out in Paris which spread rapidly to all which had anything to do with the Levant. Constantinople resorted to the printing-press to meet its obligations. And the piastre which stood at 129 to the pound in January sank to 200 by May.[34] London banks refused to renew many Galata bills as they came due. Many eminent houses failed outright. And the early financial demise of Turkey seemed certain. Two high English functionaries, Mr. M. H. Forster and Lord Hobart, sailed for Turkey to perform the inquest.

They returned with a report which gave fifteen years' lease of life to optimism respecting Turkey.[35] Her resources were abundant, Lord Hobart pointed out; the means of increasing her revenue ample. The problem was simply one of collection. Head by head the twenty-five items of revenue were passed in review, with conclusions which rang the same refrain. If the Porte would but lay aside jealousy of private enterprise and throw its forests, its fisheries, its mines, its estates open to the unrestricted competition of foreign capital, and collect taxes directly in money instead of through tax-farmers in kind, both treasury and people would abound in prosperity. Consequently, altho the actual deficit in sight for the year was between two and three million pounds, Lord Hobart did not urge curtailment of expenditure. "With an army scarcely sufficient to ensure the defence of the frontier from marauding tribes, and powerless in face of a fanatical outbreak; with a police which, in many parts of the Empire, casts not even the shadow of restraint upon the thriving trade of brigandage, with production and commerce paralyzed from want of roads . . . a mere reduction of expenditure would be costly in the extreme to this country." The proper policy was to procure more revenue.

Thus nineteenth century Europe approaches the administrative problems of the Middle Ages.

The Turk is not to be censured for regarding the advice as admirable, nor for pursuing such of it as seemed most complimentary. On the optimism which it engendered he floated another loan, "to retire the new currency and stabilize the piastre." Earl Russell, then Foreign Secretary, commended its support in the House of Lords as a great national object.[36] And between the patriotism of investors and the prospects of a speculative rise, London subscribed the loan many times over. Enthusiasm soared to new levels the following year when a fiscal agency for regenerate Turkey made its bow—the Imperial Ottoman Bank, sponsored by the *Crédit Mobilier* and some of its British friends, and with Lord Hobart as a managing director.[37] The new bank paid for its concession by issuing another loan. In 1865 there were two. Revenues were rising fast. Receipts which figured in the estimates for 1859–60 at nine million Turkish pounds, in 1872–73 were reckoned at eighteen million. And expenditures rose faster. Abdul-Aziz loved his little extravagances. Ambassadors agreed that he should augment the equipment of his army and navy. So shipyards and gunworks rose by the side of the Bosphorus. Turkey vied with western Europe in recognizing the inventive genius of munitions makers, in providing a market for Krupp and Armstrong.[38] And to cover the ensuing deficits, fresh loans were constantly required.

In 1869 Abdul-Aziz made a European tour and on his return entertained lavishly for western royalty in connection with the opening of the Suez Canal. The festivities preluded a new season of projects and concessions. Western banking groups crowded Galata with financial companies formed to make advances to the sultan and to speculate in his funds. The Oriental railway line, joining Constantinople to European railway systems, was at last conceded to the Bischoffsheim son-in-law, Baron Hirsch, who passed for an Austrian. In Paris, Brussels and London the bourses were filled with various denominations of Turkish paper, which sold at widely differing prices, with activity unceasing. The proportion of interest burden to revenue soon grew greater and the necessity for loans increased as the difficulty of finding plausible revenues to mortgage for their support became more difficult. In 1869 there was a loan for twenty-two million pounds, in 1871 one secured upon the augmented tribute of Egypt for £5,700,000, in 1872 a loan for eleven millions, in 1873 a loan for nearly twenty-eight millions, in 1874 a loan for £15,900,000 at 5% which was offered to subscribers at 43½!

During these years the devotion of London to the cause of Turkish credit was by no means constant. There were other offerings of Ottoman securities which did not come

to London at all; and it was the business of the cosmopolitan
financiers who competed for the loans to distribute them
widely among the money markets of Europe. Paris held
sway for a season, and when her energies were absorbed by
the war with Prussia, Vienna sponsored many financial combinations. But London continued to be a source of strength
to Galata bankers with their accommodation bills. And
when disaster overtook Vienna in 1873 it was the English
market upon which Turkey had chiefly to rely. There were
annual interest and amortization payments to be met in the
West amounting to more than eight million pounds, not including numerous usurious short-loan arrangements which
had been made at Paris and Brussels. If Turkey met them
from her mortgaged revenues she would be unable to maintain her government. The powers could not have both Turkey and dividends without supplying the money themselves.
And so long as Turkish credit enjoyed an adventitious esteem
which came from the conviction that a great British interest
was at stake there were always fresh investors to enable the
old to earn their interest.

But the decline in most foreign government stocks in
1873 and 1874 derived special momentum in the case of
Turkey from the fact that British opinion was groping its
way toward a fundamental change in its eastern policy.
The grounds for the change lay partly in the disappointed
hopes of Turkish regeneration. The door to legitimate
private enterprise had not been opened in Turkey. Formal
changes in administration had not altered its spirit. And
the accumulation of the material elements of military and
naval strength had not made of Turkey the power for which
Lord Stratford had labored. They lay also in the fact that
the recovery of the United States from her civil war was
relieving British industrialists from the concern for cotton

and for grain which had quickened their interest in the Danube valley and Asia Minor. And they lay even more in the change in commercial routes which from 1870 worked economic and political revolution in the eastern Mediterranean.

Palmerston's anticipations were correct. The building of the Suez Canal definitely severed Egypt from Turkey. In 1871 her viceroy won the title of khedive, a royal title, which was made hereditary in his family. The canal diverted valuable transit trades which had formerly enriched Alexandria and Smyrna. It constituted a challenge to British prestige in the Near East which could be met only by new tactics. And it placed in the hands of a rival nation a route to India which, once achieved, it was of the greatest importance to Englishmen to control. To British politicians and business men the integrity and development of Turkey became tremendously less important than the more direct control of Egypt. During the ministry of Gladstone from 1868 to 1874 Constantinople slipped more and more out of the hands of the British ambassador and into the hands of Russia, while British activity at Cairo took on new vigor. And Egypt too had her financial problems with which the Stock Exchange was familiar and at least one of Gladstone's ministers, Goschen.

THE RISE OF THE EGYPTIAN DEBT

Egypt's financial difficulties originated with the building of the Suez Canal and the blockade of the Confederate ports in America. Two-thirds of the cost of the canal, which could not possibly be of benefit to the country, fell upon the Egyptian treasury. Debt after debt had to be incurred to meet payments as they came due, and to find interest and amortization for the debts. The blockade of the American South, creating a cotton scarcity, gave promise of indefinitely expanding markets, and encouraged the viceroys of Egypt to enter upon enormous speculations in land, cotton, sugar and agricultural machinery, which met with disaster as prices receded. In consequence, viceroy, government and people fell into the hands of cosmopolitan bankers—Jews and Greeks with a clientele at Paris and London. The process is worth examining in some detail.[39]

To the stock of de Lesseps' canal company, the viceroy, Said Pasha, subscribed not only his original allotment of 96,517 shares but also 85,506 shares which it had been planned to sell in Great Britain, the United States, Russia. and Austria-Hungary, and which had failed to find purchasers. This gave the viceroy more than a half interest in promoting an enterprise which would not be of advantage to other Egyptian revenues. It would divert a valuable transit trade from the state railway which had been built in the early fifties by British engineers. But to a partly sovereign prince, anxious to enlarge his prestige and escape dependence, there seemed to be political advantages of consequence. There might also be profits some day. And altho Said had already begun to live beyond his means at the rate of five hundred thousand pounds a year, by means of treasury bonds and acceptances, it was not difficult to persuade Paris banks to discount the notes which he gave de Lesseps as initial payment upon the shares.

How long this banking accommodation might have been continued it is impossible to say. A more permanent arrangement seemed necessary when in the winter of 1861–62, Said began to consider a European tour for the benefit of his health. There was no lack of offers from international

financiers, at a price. But the contract fell to an eminent
Israelite, who in his capacity as Prussian consul industriously
supported his pretensions as partner in *H. Oppenheim,
Neveu et cie* of Alexandria.[40] Oppenheim agreed to provide funds to pay off the Paris debt, amounting to £1,600,000,
in return for an annuity of £170,000 a year for thirty years.
Bonds to the nominal value of £2,195,000 were pledged by
the viceroy with the sultan's approbation, secured upon the
land revenues of the Delta. The Bank of Saxe-Meiningen
appeared as contractor on the face of the agreement; and
Messrs. Frühling & Goschen, merchant bankers of eminent
respectability, were employed to market the bonds in London.

Thus at the first week-end in April, 1862, the British investing public was invited to consider the merits of a loan
to a country which had neither paper money, nor funded
debt, in whose political condition Great Britain was profoundly interested, and the rapid development of whose cotton culture was a matter of national anxiety. In the face
of opposition from disappointed bankers the loan was oversubscribed four times at 82½, a price which left nearly 12%
of the money raised to be divided between the contractors.[41]
A second issue of the loan, to pay the expenses of the viceroy's trip, was made at a better rate, the benefit of which
was generously conceded to Said.

Meanwhile the Suez Canal was building, in a zone over
which de Lesseps was as sovereign as the viceroy in Egypt,
by the labor of 20,000 fellaheen conscripted from the upper
Nile for the purpose. If it was the most momentous engineering feat of the century, it was as plainly working revolution in the relation of western Europe to the Near East.
And not a difficulty was left untried which British agents
could throw in the path of that revolution. When Ismaïl
Pasha succeeded his uncle at the beginning of 1863 it was not

hard to convince him that if he renewed the concession to de Lesseps, the company's political power should be curtailed and the system of forced labor abolished. Cotton was rising every day in price. The 20,000 laborers could be employed to the greater benefit of Egypt (not to say Lancashire) in the cultivation of that plant. It was a severe crisis for the canal. De Lesseps demanded compensation and succeeded in getting his claims referred to Napoleon III for arbitration. Napoleon submitted the case to referees, who considered the matter so diligently that Ismaïl found himself saddled with a new debt of four million pounds before he had fairly tasted the sweets of power.

It is not necessary to describe in detail the other embarrassments into which the new viceroy was led by the desire to exploit the cotton boom. This was one consideration, apart from dynastic reasons, which led to his purchase of the estates of his uncles, Mustapha and Halim, as a result of which Ismaïl became proprietor of one-fifth of the cultivable land in Egypt. It prompted extravagant attempts to introduce agricultural machinery. It led him to make large advances to the fellaheen when their stock was ravaged by epizoötic in 1864, and to issue "village bonds" to free the peasants from the hands of money-lenders when cotton fell in 1865–66. Each operation required money and meant an addition to the floating or funded debt. And revenue increased but slowly in comparison with the operations. For it was not only cotton that attracted this strange mixture of enterprise and autocrat, this eastern prince who had been educated in the Paris of the Second Empire. There was a navigation company to exploit the pilgrim trade to Mecca, an "Agricole" to lend money to the fellaheen which turned into a speculation in building lots, and a succession of banks in Alexandria to lend money at twelve per cent to the government. In these concessions to foreign capitalists Ismaïl himself was a principal partner, as were some of his leading ministers. Profits went to his expense account. Losses managed to fall upon the public treasury.

As early as 1866 bankers began to find it difficult to transfer their advances to the European public in the form of loans. In that year the viceroy concluded a loan upon his private estates with the Anglo-Egyptian Bank, Ltd., a concern organized and controlled by Jules Pastre, a Greek from Marseilles.[42] Offered to the public at 92, the loan was to realize only 4½% to the contractor, and only £280,000 were placed out of the three millions placed on the market. The Anglobank did not have to bear its losses, however. The Daïra (private treasury of the viceroy) was persuaded to take up the unsubscribed bonds, and they were disposed of in the course of 1867 thru the Crédit Foncier of France at 72, less 2½% commission.[43]

Meanwhile Ismaïl was bending his energies to the development of his private domains. Sugar was thought to be a profitable crop, now that the close of the Civil War had broken the cotton market. And sugar refineries were set up on a vast scale, with singular inattentiveness to the distribution of the cane. A system of light railways intersected the Delta, to facilitate the marketing of the crop, and there were irrigation canals and a Nile barrage to promote its growth. Moreover Cairo must be made over in the image of Haussmann's Paris, with boulevards, government palaces, vistas and suburbs. The Suez Canal triumphing over difficulties must be opened with celebrations of fitting extravagance. And in the new opera house, before Ismaïl's princely guests, must be presented an opera commanded for the occasion, Aïda, the climax of Verdi's art.

Thus during the first twelve years of Ismaïl Pasha the

funded debt of Egypt grew from four to twenty-eight million pounds, while the volume of treasury bills, recognizances of various departments, personal notes of the khedive, amounted in the summer of 1873 to thirty-five millions. Out of a maximum revenue of ten millions (not completely realized) the Egyptian government must pay an annual amount of six millions, for interest, and there were payments to make for sinking fund and redemptions.[44]   In connection with such amounts it would be grotesque to speak of secure investments.   The floating debts, discounted at from ten to fifteen per cent with banks and merchants in Alexandria, were carried on rediscount or report with financial groups in London and Paris which were seeking to gain control of Egyptian finance.

One attempt was made to check the rake's progress.   In 1868 the khedive, after vain attempts to conclude a suitable loan with other houses, was forced to accept the terms offered by Oppenheim for the redemption of the floating debt then due.   The loan was for a nominal sum of more than eleven million pounds, of which the Egyptian treasury was credited with about seven.   And it involved the condition, imposed by the sultan in reassertion of authority over his vassal, that no further loan should be issued by the Malieh (public treasury) for five years.   English diplomacy which had procured this arrangement at Constantinople took pride in its work.   But it appeared that "loan" did not refer to the discounting of treasury bills; and the limitation of the Malieh in no way applied to the Daïra Sanieh, the private estates of the khedive.   In 1870 there was a huge loan for the khedive to build railways, buy warships and sugar machinery. In subsequent years operations multiplied in character and expensiveness.   A weekly paper of Alexandria published at the end of 1872 a list of twenty-seven distinct operations concluded on behalf of the Malieh or Daïra since September, 1871.[45] More than four hundred million francs of new indebtedness were involved, easily a year's revenue, bearing an average discount of 13%. There were deals in sugar and cotton futures with Greek merchants, borrowings to ease the paths of diplomacy at Constantinople, issues of bills of all dates from two months to eighteen. Oppenheim, Dervieu, the Anglo-Egyptian Banking Company, Ltd., the *Franco-Égyptienne,* the Bank of Alexandria, Ltd. (Greeks under English protection), and other houses in most of which Ismaïl was a partner, were ready for all emergencies with an abundant supply of bills on London. Borrowing at from three to six per cent in Paris and London, they kept the rates at Alexandria well over ten, and found additional profit when they could employ discounted treasury notes, far from maturity, at par in making payments upon formal loans. In fact the high strategy of the gentry engaged in this business consisted in manipulating the short-time bonds with a view to compel their funding or renewal upon terms most favorable to themselves.

From this point of view it was competition for the grand loan which everybody regarded as inevitable when the five-year embargo was raised in 1873, which led to the scramble to lend Ismaïl as much money as possible upon short-time paper which would come due in that year and the one following. From this competition there emerged successful the powerful French financial group associated with the Bischoffsheim family—the *Société Générale,* the *Comptoir d'Escompte* and the *Banque de Paris et des Pays-Bas.* The contract for the 1873 loan was drawn in spacious terms. The syndicate "took firm" £16,000,000 at 75, and procured an option upon as much more at the same price. The option was to be good for two years, during which time the khedive should issue no loans of any kind. And for assurance that he would keep his word the loan was secured by all that seemed to be left of his unmortgaged revenues. The various branches of Egyptian revenues had been pretty well appropriated to earlier loans. The khedive had even had to forfeit his Suez dividends for twenty-one years to pay de Lesseps for some worthless properties and enable the canal to be perfected. But by scratching about among the financial accounts the Bischoffsheims found some unassigned revenues and others were invented which presented a showing good enough to fill up the prospectus. At the end of July, 1873, the loan was announced with a great flourish in Brussels, Paris and London, at the price of 84½! It must be said that the public reception was cool. Even including the generous subscriptions of hopeful members of the syndicate, only £12,500,000 were applied for. It was plain that it was going to be a task to shift this much into the hands of the public at a profit, not to speak of the optional bonds.

There is a theory in political economy which associates variations in the interest rate with the risk assumed by the lender. Risk need scarcely have entered into the calculations of the Bischoffsheim syndicate. For the credit of Egypt was bound up with the syndicate's success. Ismail was ready to take the unsold £3,500,000 off its hands at 82½ (*sic*) and to reduce the price at which he had sold the remainder to 71. In return for these favors, which amounted to a cash rebate of £762,500, the syndicate agreed to lend the khedive four million pounds for a year at 12%.[46] But it was not necessary to pay either this loan or instalments upon the 1873 loan in cash. Practically the entire amount could be paid the khedive in treasury notes, which were reckoned at 93 without regard to maturity, altho they could be picked up in the market at as low a price as 65. For it was in large part to fund these very notes that the loan was being issued. This procedure, comments Stephen Cave, the treasury official whom Disraeli sent a few years later to investigate Egypt, "added materially to the profits of the operation." [47] When the Bischoffsheim syndicate was dissolved in January, 1874, it was stated that it divided £1,600,-000 between its participants. And this result had been achieved despite the fact that by that time the loan had fallen to 67.

But there remained the optional bonds. The Crédit Foncier of France and the Anglo-Egyptian Banking Co., which had been passive participants in the earlier syndicate, now took the lead. Thanks to their capable management, the loan mounted steadily in the fall of 1874. From below 60 it rose to 77½ in September and was held at that point until the end of the year while the syndicate disposed of their bonds in the speculative market. [48] In the spring of 1875 the loan stood at 81, and in gratitude to the able management of the Crédit Foncier, Ismaïl honored it, the second financial institution of France, with a large share of his short-loan issues. All was not well with Egyptian finance. But Ismaïl had found a spring of vast resources in the deposit accounts of the Crédit Foncier. And while this was unexhausted, Ismaïl continued to pay nine and ten per cent plus two and three per cent amortization upon the money he had received.

It must be clear that Egypt was insolvent before 1873; that more than two-thirds of her revenue were required for the service of her debts; and it must be confessed that in face of these facts, the expenditure of Ismaïl upon administration and public works did not diminish. English engineers now overran the country full of plans for the extension of progress and civilization. In the Soudan, Sir Samuel Baker, Charles George Gordon, and Sir John Fowler, in their several ways, were engaged in enterprises which filled Ismaïl with pride and constituted a severe drain upon his purse.[49] At Alexandria a firm of English contractors were constructing port works for £2,500,000, which cost them about £1,400,000 to build.

It was not in Egypt but in Turkey that the event occurred which plunged the Near East into bankruptcy.

On October 7, 1875, the Turkish ministry, confronted with an indebtedness of two hundred million pounds incurred in only twenty years, beset by rebellion in Bulgaria, insurrections in Bosnia and Herzegovina, disorders in Crete, menaced with external war and palace revolution, listened to the disinterested advice of the Russian ambassador. It announced that for the next five years interest coupons would be paid half in specie and half in five per cent bonds.

DISRAELI BUYS THE CANAL SHARES

It was only in form that this was an initial act of insolvency. In fact it was only an attempt to accomplish by direct means what had been done indirectly through the expensive mediation of loan syndicates. And formally there was no relation between the Turkish bankruptcy and the Egyptian question. Yet both had run the same financial course. Both had been exploited by Levantine bankers by aid of unlimited open credits in Paris and London. Both had piled up huge debts which were held to a large extent in the stock market by active speculators. The panic in Turkish stocks which greeted that country's very sensible moratorium was paralleled by a fall in Egyptians which was if anything more catastrophic. And in western Europe this aroused even more immediate concern.

As the 1873 loan fell below 60 on the Stock Exchange and the discount rate of treasury bills advanced to twenty per cent, the first impulse of the Egyptian ministry was to bow before the inevitable, and to follow the example of Turkey. And bankers who visited Ismaïl toward the end of October, 1875, reported with dismay the fatalism with which that monarch contemplated the collapse of his credit. To the holders of maturing bills as well as to engineers whose will to achievement had been stirred by the works of the Pharaohs, it was of supreme interest to prevent an act of insolvency at this time. Moreover, there were banks like the Crédit Foncier of France, which, on a paid-up capital of 45,000,000 francs, had invested 170,000,000 francs in Egyptian securities, and which saw its entire capital vanish on the twenty-point fall in October.

Accordingly a campaign of optimism was begun in the London press and at Cairo. It was suggested to Ismaïl that he invite a financial expert to Egypt to investigate and report upon the condition of the treasury. And the Crédit Foncier group began to devise a scheme to cause securities to rise and to enable it to liquidate its Egyptian account. There was to be a loan, similar to many which had preceded, funding the outstanding notes, pledging this to be positively the last loan, and the whole secured upon the proceeds of a capital levy upon land, the port works of Alexandria, and the khedive's shares in the Suez Canal. Now these shares were the only elements of substance in the proposed guarantee. They had been divested of dividends and voting rights until 1891, for the benefit of de Lesseps; but they had a speculative value. And Ismaïl was persuaded that it was more im-

portant to him to raise money upon them to pay off the
notes maturing in December, than to enter upon a more
grandiose scheme which would cause the 1873 loan to rise in
the market.   So he authorized an attempt to sell the shares
outright through a second-rate banker, Edouard Dervieu, in
whose Alexandria business the khedive had formerly been
partner.[50]

Dervieu strove for some days to find support in Paris
for a project which might unintentionally have ruined the
Crédit Foncier.   De Lesseps helped in the search, and urged
the French government to buy.   The khedive offered to
guarantee as high as 11% upon one hundred million francs,
if anyone would give so much for the shares.   But everyone
seems to have been more interested in the painful predicament
of the Crédit Foncier than in Dervieu's hopeful idea for
earning a commission.

The negotiations went on, under extended options, in close
secrecy.   But news of them reached the ears of the former
Prussian consul to Alexandria, Mr. Henry Oppenheim, who
had been until 1873 perhaps the most generous of the khedive's moneylenders and who was now residing in London.
And on November 14, Oppenheim held a conversation with
Mr. Frederick Greenwood of the *Pall Mall Gazette,* who was,
like himself, an habitual guest at the daily Rothschild lun-
cheons in the City.   Greenwood suggested that it would be
a good idea for the British government to buy the shares.
There would be nothing like it, we may suppose he urged,
to send up Egyptian stock.   And while Oppenheim agreed
to keep Dervieu and his negotiations in train with counter-
proposals in Paris, Greenwood hurried off to Lord Derby
at the Foreign Office.

It must not be supposed that this was the first time
Derby or the British government had heard of the Canal

or of its shares.[51] For four years Great Britain had been at war with de Lesseps and his company (which was discreetly backed by France) over the basis for levying tonnage duties for the passage of the Canal. Under the concession from the khedive, the company was permitted to charge ten francs per ton for passage. The British government interpreted this as "net ton"; while de Lesseps sought to read it "gross ton." The Egyptian courts sustained Great Britain. But she had carried her point over the stubborn old engineer only by employing an Egyptian fleet and marching an army of ten thousand men, headed by an American military mission, to Port Said. This was but a foretaste, it was believed, of the difficulties which the hostile administration of the Canal would involve. And so alive was Disraeli's ministry to the situation that in 1874 it investigated the price at which de Lesseps' interests could be secured. The Rothschilds reported that his demands were ridiculous. The old man's life was wrapped up in the Canal; it was more to him than a method of spoiling the Egyptians. And the British government had chosen to pursue its aims thru the other partner in the enterprise. So long as the khedive continued to own one-half of the stock, some internal check could be imposed thru him upon inimical administration of the company's affairs. But with the control of the Canal about to pass entirely into French hands by means of an outright sale of the shares, no counteraction could be too prompt, no interference too decisive. If there must be consequences, they could be no more grave than those implied in the fact of a great maritime highway, controlled by a nation other than that whose ships made principal use of it.

It took exactly eleven days for the cabinet to overcome Derby's scruples, form its policy and carry it into execution. The British consul-general at Cairo was advised by cable that Great Britain would buy the shares if the khedive would sell. An offer was made and accepted by both sides. And Disraeli arranged, without consent of Parliament, for the London Rothschilds to advance the money 'to complete the purchase before December.[52]   Thus the world was startled on the afternoon of November 26, 1875, with the news that Disraeli had purchased 176,000 shares in the Suez Canal Company for four million pounds; and that Ismaïl had agreed to pay five per cent a year upon that sum until the dividend rights were restored in 1891.   The Egyptian loan of 1873 advanced six points the same afternoon, and continued upwards.[53]   Bankers recouped their paper losses. Ismaïl paid off his December notes as they matured, in cash. And the British government became, so to speak, the largest Egyptian bondholder.

As an investment, the purchase of the shares may be regarded as one of the most fortunate that Englishmen ever made.   Those shares which, *bien entendu*, cost the Egyptian people a debt of one hundred million pounds, and which Ismaïl sold Disraeli for four million, would have brought forty million pounds on the Stock Exchange before the World War and the decline of the franc.   And whereas Disraeli borrowed money of Rothschilds at three per cent to pay for them, Egypt paid five per cent with regularity into the British Treasury, whatever the state of her fellaheen or her treatment of other creditors.   Since 1891 the dividends have ranged from ten to twenty-five per cent.

Moreover, Great Britain acquired a half interest in the control of the Canal and the canal zone.   It is absurd to talk of strategical advantages in this connection.   Without Egypt, the Canal is of course useless from this standpoint. The advantages were commercial.   As a leading shareholder, despite the suspension of voting privileges, England demanded from the first a seat upon the directing board. And she has been able to influence decisively the policy of the canal company, especially in the direction of moderation of charges and the improvement of the channel.[54]

However to Disraeli's time his dramatic coup was regarded as chiefly political. It was symbolic of a change in British policy toward the Eastern Question. And that change in policy was in no small degree precipitated by the financial debacle of Turkey. The theory of Palmerston and Stratford Canning that it was possible to modernize Turkey sufficiently to enable her to oppose effectively the advance of Russia around the Black Sea had been proven false. Even the faith-healers must now concede the Sick Man to be in a perilous state, and that he must lose some limbs if he would avoid immediate dissolution. That England would pursue a more active policy in the Near East was symbolized by the purchase of an interest in the enterprise she so long had striven to prevent.

And it involved another momentous change. It made a foreign investment a veritable weapon of British foreign policy. It associated the British government with financial commitments which made it impossible for it to maintain its indifference to them. It symbolized the advent of foreign investments as one of the abiding interests of British foreign policy.

"The nation awakes this morning," said the *Times* in announcing the purchase, "to find that it has acquired a heavy stake in the security and well-being of another distant land, and that it will be held by all the world to have entered upon a new phase of Eastern policy." [55] After a lapse of half a century, the historian can find no truer word to say.

CHAPTER XI

AT THE END OF THE SURPLUS

"Blessed are the meek; for they shall inherit the earth."
Matthew, v, 5.

THE STOCK-AND-BOND ARISTOCRACY

The England that Disraeli electrified with his purchase of Canal shares was a different England from the one that muttered at Baring's dealings with the French.

That other England had been a landholding aristocracy, measuring income in rents and wealth in the value of the land. It had begun to make community with the "great commerce" of London and with the Manchester mill thru the increment of value which the industrial transformations were bringing to the land, thru joint proprietorship in the Funds, and thru joint recourse to the deposit banking system. These relations were those of an exceedingly loose partnership. And altho every effort was made to conciliate the City and the provinces, England was neither one. It was still the land, or the beneficiaries of land.

That England had all but been submerged in 1875. The landholding aristocrats had been absorbed in the growth of another society which now thought of itself as England. The "great commerce" had been welded into a continuous whole with the mill of Manchester, and that of Birmingham and Sheffield and Leeds, by the railway and the Stock Exchange. The sphere of their united action had spread thru the British Isles and overseas. The machine had by 1870 conquered industry. Business held the keys to the machine. And participation in industry and business was being extended thru the device of the joint-stock company into regions which the machine did not directly touch. England was now a stock-and-bondholding aristocracy, measuring income in dividends and wealth in the quotations of the Stock Exchange. It owned land and exploited it, and apportioned social esteem by its scale. Land was the conspicuous visible sign of the invisibly accumulating grace of successful business. But the real interests of the Forsytes and other men of property now lay in stocks and bonds.

These were the men who governed the British Isles, and felt no delicacy in regarding the pursuit of their interests as identical with pursuit of the interests of Great Britain. For that is the wont of those who govern. The region which they ruled was filled with a great many people, who had nothing to do with stocks and bonds, but on whose conduct in some vague way the regularity of dividends depended. These people had to be fed. There was also a large and growing population of machines. These too required food—materials for their subsistence. Thus the commerce whose expansion was largely a matter of habit and of the particular interests of the few men who drove it, was beginning to be of some importance to the way in which life and manufacture went on in the British Isles.

There was imported from willing markets abroad what England needed of cotton, silk, wood, sugar, tea and wines; and a portion of the requirements of wool, flax, copper, iron, zinc and foodstuffs. These importations were easily paid for in exports of manufactured goods, steadily augmenting in quantity at steadily decreasing prices; and paid for in the services of the merchant marine, also at declining freights.

And these exports of goods and services made possible the steady export of a capital surplus besides, whose story we have been narrating. Thus the machine brought to the people of stocks-and-bonds a healthy independence of the other people in the British Isles who were not England. At the same time in strict pursuit of their interests, the governing aristocrats assured the machine of materials and the masses of work and, if they were industrious, of food. For the harder men worked in the British Isles, the more manufactured goods there were to export, which could buy more tea and more cotton with which to make more calico, which would buy more tea; and there was always a surplus somewhere which could be left abroad to make more money for the stock-and-bondholding aristocracy who now were England. This was in 1870.

THE REVOLUTION IN FOOD SUPPLY

In a few brief years in the early seventies this comfortable situation swiftly altered. The new England found herself suddenly in a different relation to the world. The minor quantity of imported food products now became a necessary major quantity. The generous diversified activities of England abroad, spreading the spirit of commerce and industry indiscriminately into all parts of the world in the interest of the "great commerce" which was its ornament, must now be focussed on the problem of obtaining the very elements of life for the people living in the British Isles. The economic balance which had been maintained between industry and agriculture was definitely destroyed.

For twenty years following the repeal of the Corn Laws, English agriculture had continued to thrive.[1] The machine had indeed been efficient; but the land also was fruitful. Rents rose; produce kept pace fairly well with the increase of population. Capital was invested in the land, under business management, in the form of fertilizers. Guano, discovered off the coast of Peru, made her story a unique one in the history of South American finance, enabling her to pay off one public debt entirely, and to begin again upon a new and larger one. And it caused wheat and rye and oats and cattle to thrive thruout the British Isles in steadily increasing quantities. In 1868 the United Kingdom still produced four-fifths in value of what the inhabitants consumed of grain, meat, dairy produce and wool. She was still so nearly self-sufficing that in emergency she could be completely so without superhuman effort. Only a few areas, with respect to a few commodities, like the American South with cotton, were tied to Great Britain in close economic interdependence. The "great commerce" was still of the nature of adventure, the fruit of the superabundant energy of Great Britain more than the essential root of her economic existence.

Ten years were enough to effect a revolution. In 1878 the United Kingdom supplied her inhabitants with scarcely one-half of what they consumed of grain, meat, dairy produce and wool. One-fourth of all kinds of grain and one-third of the wheat had been drawn from foreign sources in 1868, which was not an unusual year. "In the past ten years." wrote James Caird in 1878, "there has been a gradual reduction of the acreage and produce of wheat in this country, and a more than corresponding increase in the foreign supply; the result of which is that we now receive our bread in smaller proportion from our own fields than those of the stranger. In regard to meat, and other animal products, ten years ago the proportion of the foreign was one-seventh of the whole. It has now risen to one-half." [2]

Climatic conditions were in part, no doubt, responsible for the rapidity with which England shifted her source of supply of agricultural products. From 1875 to 1879 the harvests were the worst in half a century. But the climatic conditions only made emphatic the influence of factors chiefly manifest at the market end of the agricultural process.

The population of the British Isles was increasing at the rate of ten per cent each decade. The standard of living of their inhabitants had been rising appreciably, especially in regard to articles of food.[3] And at the same time larger quantities of food were being made available for market in foreign countries. The migration of population and enterprise and capital which steam transport had encouraged were cooperating with the passing of feudalism in eastern Europe to bring great continental areas of grain and meat and wool production within the reach of the British market. The railway and cheap freights made it possible to bring wheat from the Mississippi valley to London at a lower price than that at which most British farmers could produce it. The increased demand at home, with an increasing facility of supply from abroad, definitely ended Great Britain's dependence upon the home supply and discouraged the extension of agricultural activities at home. For a quarter of a century after 1870 change in British farming consisted chiefly in a steady abandonment of wheat-raising and in specialization in such products as fresh meat and milk and vegetables in which foreign producers could less effectively compete. The provision of the staples of British diet, wheat and bacon, passed steadily into the province of foreign areas. And those areas became linked in an intimacy of new closeness with the economy of England.

Now to pay for all this wheat and bacon without disturbing the harmonies, it was necessary to export a great deal more manufactured goods or earn more in shipping freights. And precisely when she needed to do so, England found that she could not increase her exports. At the very time when British wheat-growers encountered the competition of Russia and the Prairie West, British manufacturers met reverses in markets which they formerly had completely dominated. For between 1870 and 1880 the United States and the Germanies —formerly the two greatest foreign markets for British goods—became almost self-sufficing industrially. British exports to the United States fell off abruptly in quantity and value. The movement of goods to Germany did not actually decline, but it ceased wholly to expand and it altered in character. At the same time Great Britain met the competition of German and American goods as well as French and Belgian in other markets.

For the new England existed in a new commercial world. The British Isles were now but one of many regions that had become industrialized, and that had become parts of organisms of commerce and finance that steadily grew. There was a world market, which British manufacturers no longer dominated, in which they must sell the produce of their mills. The stimulation of demand, by precept and example, no longer turned to the advantage alone of England's "great commerce." There were governments abroad with a more generous idea of their functions than she had entertained, ready to see to it that the development of market areas in various countries should bring business preferentially to their subjects. And in the competition for new markets, British manufacturers found the advantage of an early start a liability. In the iron and steel trades notably, plant was becoming antiquated. The shift from iron to steel as the basic metal for construction and machinery coincided with the rise of metal industry upon a large scale in other countries. They were able to profit by English processes. Some British steel manufacturers seriously considered abandoning production in England, and moving their business to Birmingham, Alabama.[4]

There was another revolution as well as those in agriculture, in industry and in technique. The secular trend of prices, which in response to the annual increments of gold supply had been steadily upward since 1850, turned downward in 1873. There had been a rise, according to Sauerbeck's index, from 74 to 111 since 1849. There now set in a fall which continued without interruption until a low point of 81 was reached in 1879. And there began the greatest depression trend of modern times, which was to reach its limit in 1896 with a price index of 61. Export values fell off dramatically, while quantities could with difficulty be increased. Great Britain could not get the world to pay more, for the goods and services that she had to sell, than the world had paid before.

But there was more food, and more copper, and more iron and wool for which to pay. Great Britain did it out of the surplus which had formerly been available for foreign investment. For the twenty years ending in 1874 Great Britain had been exporting an average surplus of capital of about fifteen million pounds.[5] She had done this in addition to re-investing abroad all of the earnings upon foreign investments already made. These by the seventies amounted to at least fifty million pounds a year. At this time the surplus capital exports above this ran well over thirty millions. Within the space of three years this item of the British balance of payments entirely disappeared, and became in fact reversed. In 1876 and 1877 Great Britain collected income from her foreign property for home consumption. She was at the end of an era. The balance of industry and agriculture at home had been destroyed. She could scarcely balance her requirements of food and raw materials, with the manufactures she could export and the freights her merchant marine could collect. The export of a capital surplus was over. Her further investments were to come for a generation from the accruing profits of those which had already been made. They were to consist in what a German writer has termed "the secondary export of capital." [6]

IN LIEU OF CONCLUSION

Thus the cosmopolitan endeavors of enterprising men in search of profit wrought the commercial world anew. Great Britain midwived a half dozen lusty rivals, whose vigorous growth could only damage her prestige, yet whose collapse must imperil her prosperity.

British investors exported between 1815 and 1875 a capital surplus amounting to about half a billion pounds. They did this chiefly during the years 1850–73 when the trend of prices was upwards, during the period of most marked prosperity in the century. To a considerable extent the surplus consisted in enterprise, in creations of credit, in capital goods, which might otherwise not have been employed at all. Foreign investment throve frequently as business at home was encouraging. It frequently supplied the weakest link in the chain of credit which at recurring intervals became overstrained in a greater degree than enterprise at home. It involved financing on a large scale. It gathered great resources under the control of bankers who were more interested in employing them abroad than at home. The business of issuing securities was almost exclusively a traffic in foreign bonds. The intermediaries had the most sure position for profiting largely from it. Even more than the inducement of higher interest rates, it was their access to loanable funds which impelled the migration of British capital. But each considerable movement of capital had a distinctive character of its own, arose from a particular set of circumstances, had its special group of advantages in view.

In the main the export of Britain's surplus was not waste, nor a drain upon the resources of the kingdom. It did not amount by a half to the export of iron and steel, machinery and other capital goods in the same period. And it was the superabundant energy of the metal industries that made the remunerative export of surplus capital possible.

It is in the socio-political, rather than the economic, sense, that the migration of British capital was harmful to the mass of British people. It fostered the growth of a rentier governing class, whose economic interests lay outside the community in which they lived and exerted influence. Their influence encouraged the illusion that Great Britain as a whole, not a few subjects of the Queen, drew tribute from foreign investments; that all would be injured if that tribute should cease.

However, during the period from 1815 to 1875, "imperialism" was not a prominent factor in the movement of British capital. Nor was political authority interposed to ensure its profits abroad. Only sporadically, in Canada, in India, in Turkey and Egypt, London capitalists showed a disposition to control the economic life of distant countries thru the action of their money market, or, less directly, thru the policy they could persuade statesmen to adopt.

British capitalists as a group did profit from investment

abroad, altho many individuals lost when recurring crises brought particular investment movements to an end. Thru regular reinvestment of the accruing interest abroad, the nominal value of Britain's foreign wealth had swelled by 1875 to about £1,200,000,000. This property was represented chiefly by the bonds of foreign governments and by railway shares and debentures. About half a billion pounds were invested in Europe, including Egypt; the remainder was distributed between the United States, India, South America and the Dominions, in that order. And from these countries, even from Egypt tho a peasantry groaned, there was punctually returned an interest which averaged in the seventies at least six per cent upon the British investment.[7]

This interest Englishmen had formed the habit of leaving abroad to earn fresh income. And the habit persisted. London was able to remain until 1914 the world's leading money market. In years of unusual depression, Great Britain was to bring home her dividends; but not her capital until the World War. British foreign investments did not, however, remain compounding income in just the countries in which they were placed in 1875. Foreign income and capital were incessantly withdrawn from Europe and put to work in South America, in the Dominions, in the United States, and finally in the development of the tropics and the Far East. They were put to work in the interest of binding markets to the British mill, and in developing sources of supply of foodstuffs and raw materials. They were engaged in cementing the new economic structure which grew about England's interdependence with the American West, with the Argentine, with Australia and Canada.

To manage this reinvestment and this redistribution there were still the agencies, the mechanisms which had impelled and directed the export of Britain's surplus. There were heirs to Baring and Rothschild, to Brassey and Gurney and Bischoffsheim. The commission merchant, the contractor, the bill-discounter, the cosmopolitan banker, were institutions that survived the wreckage of innumerable particular firms. Their activity was only partially diminished by the cessation of the surplus. To the new England whose industry and life always gave fresh hostages to the seas, they were the monarchs on whose word the defense and glory of all depended.

For the stock-and-bondholding aristocracy, which were England, ceased to think of themselves as settled only in the British Isles; they began to think of their geographical position as extending overseas. They achieved the idea of empire. There was a curious unreality in their conception. For while they spoke of an empire of fidelity to the Queen, and strove to bring new areas within its bounds, they lived their economic life in another empire, which did not, could not wholly coincide with the Queen's. The economy which owned London for a metropolis was at once more broad and more restricted than the empire which praised Victoria as the pattern of all the virtues. That economic empire was even more essential to the people of the stocks-and-bonds and to the people who earned them dividends. It did not yet in 1875 exist; but its elements were in being. And as the migration of British capital proceeded, and from the mechanisms that moved it, the structure of that other empire grew.

BIBLIOGRAPHICAL NOTES

NOTES TO CHAPTER ONE

The Literature of Foreign Investment.—The scientific literature dealing with foreign investment as an economic function is surprisingly small in quantity and narrow in range of interest. Hobson, C. K., *The Export of Capital* (London 1914) is the only volume in English devoted to the subject. Chapters 4 to 6 trace the historical growth of British investment abroad. But the claims of Mr. Hobson's book to distinction rest upon its efforts at statistical analysis of capital movements with reference to the balance of trade, from 1870 to 1914, and upon a vigorous introduction discussing the ethical aspects of capital export.

The economic aspects of foreign investment are considered more broadly and at length in Sartorius von Waltershausen, *Das Volkswirtschaftliche System der Kapitalanlage im Auslande* (Berlin 1907). J. H. Williams, *Argentine International Trade under Inconvertible Paper·Money* (Harvard Univ. Press 1922), Viner, Jacob, *Canada's Balance of International Indebtedness* (Harvard Univ. Press 1924) and Graham, F. D., in *Quarterly Journal of Economics* (1922), "International Trade under a Depreciated Paper Currency," examine the relation of foreign investments to particular exchange situations. Liefmann, Robert, in *Jahrbuch fuer Nationaloekonomie und Statistik,* third series, XXVII: 180, studies the relation of capital movements to crises.

Interpretations of the export of capital which have been influenced by the doctrines of Karl Marx are essayed in Hilferding, Rudolf, *Das Finanz-Kapital* (reprinted Vienna 1923) c. 22 and Hobson, J. A., *The Evolution of Modern Capitalism* (rev. edit. London 1917) pp. 262 ff.

Among the books illustrating the bearing of foreign investment upon what is frequently called "economic imperialism," may be mentioned:—Brailsford, *The War of Steel and Gold* (London 1913); Lippmann, Walter, *The Stakes of Diplomacy* (New York 1915); Woolf, Leonard, *Intervention and Commerce in Africa* (London 1919); Culbertson, W. S., *International Economic Policies* (New York 1925) ch. 10; Dunn, Robert, *American Foreign Investments* (New York 1925); Nearing, Scott, and Freeman, Joseph, *Dollar Diplomacy*

(New York 1925); "Lysis," *Politique et finance d'avant-guerre* (Paris 1920).

Criticism of the export of capital in the years 1909–12 gave rise in England, France and Germany to a considerable periodical polemic, and to some serious attempts to describe the existing state of affairs. The best introduction to these controversies and to the information collected may be secured from the following articles:—Paish, Sir George, *Journal Statist. Socy.* Sept. 1909 and Jan. 1911; Crammond, Edgar, *Quarterly Review*, 1911; Calmes, A., *Zeitschrift fuer Sozialwissenschaft*, 1915, nos. 11 and 12; Arndt, Paul, *ibid*, 1912, pp. 1–19, 99–110, 173–94; and 1915, nos. 3–8.

The Eighteenth Century Money Market.—The study of economic life in the eighteenth century has only in the last generation begun to shift its focus from the policies of contending statesmen to the conduct of business men. In this direction, Sombart, Werner, *Der Moderne Kapitalismus* (4th edit. Munich and Leipzig 1921) provides an indispensable analysis. Ehrenberg, Richard, *Das Zeitalter der Fugger* (3rd edit. Jena 1922) is the authoritative study of the rise of continental money markets. Appendices carry the development into the eighteenth century.

There is nothing comparable for the British Isles. The scholarly thoroness with which Usher and Bowden in the United States, and the Hammonds, Dr. Lillian Knowles, and the students of Professor Unwin at Manchester, have recently probed the industrial transformation of Great Britain in the eighteenth and early nineteenth centuries, has not been paralleled by studies of equal weight in her financial development.

Powell, Ellis T., *The Evolution of the Money Market* (London 1915) assembles much valuable material about a curiously overwrought series of theses borrowed from the Spencerian school of sociology. Andréades, *History of the Bank of England* (London 1909) has the limitations which its title suggests. Bouniatian, M., *Geschichte der Handelskrisen in England 1640–1840* (Munich 1908) together with Tugan Baranowsky, *Les Crises Industrielles en Angleterre* (Paris 1913) provides a succession of views of English economy at its moments of tension. However, the only survey of any adequacy of all aspects of English finance prior to 1815 is contained in Halévy, Élie, *Histoire du Peuple Anglais* (2nd edit. Paris 1913) I: 319–64. Halévy's book is now available in an English edition (New York and London 1924).

---

[1] The forms of foreign investment are manifold. The purchasing power may be metamorphosed into a mine, a factory, a stock farm

or a bank account. It may be lent to a government, a railway or a great corporation upon the security of its stocks or bonds. It may take the form of circulating capital in a carryng trade between foreign ports, or it may be represented by acceptances and discounted bills in payment for sales in the export trade. The essential factor is that the gain promised from these transactions arises beyond a national boundary.

It is somewhat arbitrarily, therefore, that this study makes no special attempt to consider investments in shipping enterprise between Great Britain and other countries, or investments by British merchants in carrying on their foreign trade. These uses of capital doubtless have some of the same political and social involvements as investments in industry, agriculture, public works and government securities. They in part function similarly in the international balance of payments. For investigation and report, however, they offer unusual difficulties, and they are knit up in a chain of events which makes their discussion seem more appropriate to a history of commerce than to one of finance. This discrimination, moreover, conforms to common use of the term "foreign investments."

[2] C. K. Hobson so defines it, page 1,—"Foreign investments consist of that part of the property of a country and its inhabitants, situated abroad, from which its owners expect to derive an income."

[3] Paish in supplement to *The Statist*, Feb. 14, 1914.

[4] Serionne (ed.), *Le commerce de Hollande* (3 vols. 1768) I: 223–27 deals explicitly with the point. For other dis-ussions of the position of Holland in the eighteenth century see Blok, *History of the People of the Netherlands* (New York 1912) V: 64–76, 186–88; Sombart, *op. cit.*, III: 953–58, 979–85, 1044; Ehrenberg, *op. cit.*, II: 291–300, 329–48; Sartorius von Waltershausen, pp. 367–80; Savary, P. L., *Dictionnaire Universelle de Commerce* (Copenhagen 1759–65) V: 810–849; Luzac, Elie, *Hollands Rijkdom* (Leyden 1780–83) esp. vol. IV; Alting Boesken, J. A., *Over Geldleenigen* (Utrecht 1864). On eighteenth century bourses, above all, Pinto, *Traité du circulation et crédit* (1772).

[5] Grossmann, Julius, *Die Amsterdamer Boerse vor zweihundert Jahren* (1876); Ehrenberg II: 296–97.

[6] Sinclair, Sir John, *History of the Public Revenue* (3rd edit. London 1803) III, App. p. 161, estimates the Dutch holdings in 1762 at £15,000,000 in consols and one million each in Bank and East India stock. Elsewhere (I:369–70) the same authority states that thirty millions of the English debt were held abroad. Postlethwait, *Dictionary of Commerce* (4th edit. London 1774), art. "Holland," reckons the annual interest payment due the Dutch at £1,000,000. Alting Boesken, *op. cit.*, speaks of 300 to 690 million gulden as esti-

mates of the maximum Dutch investments abroad in the eighteenth century. Ehrenberg and Sombart accept an estimate of 250 million gulden, originally made by the author of *Récherches sur le commerce* (1779). Hobson (p. 87) and Sartorius (pp. 374–75) cite larger estimates with favor. According to Savary (II: 686) it was commonly thought that one-fourth of the English National Debt was held abroad. Adam Smith, *Wealth of Nations* (Everyman ed. I, 82) cites an estimate of forty million pounds, considering it too high.

⁷ Steuart, Sir James, *Principles of Political Economy* (1772) II: 399; Hope, John, *Letters on Credit* (1784) pp. 21, 30, 36; Luzac, *op. cit.* IV: 190–235. Acceptances were current in Amsterdam at ½%. Luzac IV: 112–14.

⁸ West India Estates Bill. *Parl. Hist.* XVI: 686–90. In a petition of the sugar planters to the House of Commons in 1784, it was represented that £50,000,000 were invested in the settlement, cultivation and commerce of the West Indian colonies. Anderson, *History of Commerce,* IV: 548. This can only have been a capitalization of prospective income. Nothing like any such sum had ever been laid out either by British planters or their Dutch bankers. Slaves constituted the principal item of expense. The trouble of procuring them was the only real capital export. From the beginning of the sugar colonies in the seventeenth century, London and Liverpool merchants supplied the plantations with capital, an1 borrowed funds at lower rates in Amsterdam. Pitman, F. W., *The Development of the British West Indies* (New Haven 1919) ch. 6; Zook, *Company of Royal Adventurers Trading into Africa* (Lancaster, Pa. 1919) ch. 4. The episode in 1773 was part of an attempt to fund these credit relations in a form which would appeal to Dutch small investors.

⁹ "Early capitalistic" is here in the sense of Sombart II: 1–15.

¹⁰ Sombart II: 954–55. This situation altered rapidly in the eighties with the rise of the cotton industry and the Anglo-French Commercial Treaty of 1786.

¹¹ An exhaustive study of the importance of these "adventitious" sources for the accumulation of wealth in modern countries has been made by Sombart I: 680–714; II: 1071–75. His conclusion that "the European peoples became rich by the impoverishment of other parts of the world" seems to me to be inescapable for that period of which he speaks, namely, that preceding the Industrial Revolution. Botsford, J. B., *English Society in the Eighteenth Century* (New York 1924) ch. 5, assembles much material which verifies the view as for England. It is difficult to agree with Botsford, however, that the profits of the Liverpool slave-traders accrued from overseas trade and may therefore be set down as "honest." The Cunliffe and Earle

and Heywood fortunes were as parasitical as those of the nabobs. Cf. Fox Bourne, H. R., *English Merchants* (1886) 319–30, 324.

[12] Trevelyan, G. O., *George III and Charles James Fox* (1914) II: 327–33; Lecky, W. H. R., *England in the Eighteenth Century* (1892) V: 291–92.

[13] Botsford, esp. ch. 4, 7 and 10; Lecky, VII: 236–39.

[14] Serionne, II, 25–26. On the relative prevalence of the credit system in English trade as compared with the continental of the time, cf. Sombart, II: 514–16.

[15] Powell, E. T., *Evolution of the Money Market* (1915) ch. 2 and 3; Andréades, *History of the Bank of England* (1909) pp. 14–42; Macaulay, *History of England* (Everyman edit.) III: 289–91; Gilbart, J. W., *History and Principles of Banking* (2nd edit. London 1835); *The London Directory* (1676); Fox Bourne, p. 339; Bouniatian, *Geschichte der Handelskrisen* (1908) II: 4–8.

Palgrave, R. H. I., *Notes on Banking* (1873), citing a French government report of 1729, is authority for the statement that the Bank of Sweden (1657) was the first institution to issue banknotes. The goldsmiths appear to have used the device without public authorization before this date. More indisputable is their origination of the checking-account. By 1793 the London private bankers had abandoned note-issue entirely for this device, and check-books and a clearing-house (1773) flourished. Pownall, George H., *English Banking: Its Development* . . . (1914) p. 7.

On the Bank of England see, in addition to Andréades, Philippovich, Eugen, *History of the Bank of England and its Financial Services to the State* (Washington 1911) esp. 78–182: and Rogers, J. E. T., *The First Nine Years of the Bank of England*.

[16] Savary, II, 687–89. Cf. Malthus, *Essay on Population* (4th edit.) p. 437 as to importance of England's surplus agricultural production as a source of her wealth.

[17] Thornton, Henry, *An Inquiry into the Nature and Effects of the Paper Credit of Great Britain* (Am. edit. Phila. 1807) pp. 129–37; Smith's *Wealth of Nations* (Everyman) I: 261–94; Bagehot, Walter, *Lombard Street* (Withers ed. 1917) pp. 81–83; Powell, 116–23; Fox Bourne, 333–51; Halévy, *Hist. du Peuple Anglais,* I: 319–23.

[18] *Circular to Bankers* (London) 5 October, 1838. Most of the London private banks owed their rise to the grain trade, estate business or dealings with the government. Those which arose from manufacturers were exceptional. Barings arose from the manufacture of serges at Exeter. Denison & Co. originated in the middle of the eighteenth century when Joseph Denison was sent up to London as agent for a Wakefield firm of woolen manufacturers. Jones, Loyd & Co. grew out of a Manchester tea business which made

advances to cotton manufacturers and circulated notes as local currency at the beginning of Manchester's rapid rise. The Gurney banks developed out of a capitalistic connection with the domestic manufacture of worsted and linen, first in Norfolk and later in Yorkshire. Williams, Deacon & Co. began with the import trade in Swedish iron; Spooners and Attwoods in the steel monopoly of the latter family; Brown, Janson & Co. in the cloth trade of Leeds; and Praed & Co. in the Cornish mines. Of the famous country banks, many more were based upon industrial antecedents. Cf. Maberly Phillips, *History of Banks, Bankers and Banking in Northumberland* (1894). One, however, the firm of Davison-Bland & Co., later Lambton & Co., founded in 1788 at Newcastle-upon-Tyne, was known as the "Nabob Bank," because it was begun by men who had made their money in India. Phillips, p. 241.

[19] Sombart II, ch. 33. Defoe refers to the discounting of such bills as a "scandalous practice."

[20] Halévy, I: 338–44; Hamilton, Robert, *Inquiry concerning the National Debt* (3rd edit. Edinburgh 1818); Hume, "Of Public Credit," in *Essays Moral, Political and Literary* (London 1752).

[21] Francis, John, *Chronicles of the Stock Exchange;* Powell, ch. 5.

[22] *Circular to Bankers,* 5 Oct. 1838 and *passim;* Bowden, Witt, *Industrial Society in England* (New York 1925) pp. 139–40 and references cited.

[23] Steuart, Sir John, *Inquiry into the Principles of Political Economy* (1772) pp. 399–401; Smith's *Wealth of Nations* (Everyman) I: 81; *Cambridge History of British Foreign Policy* (New York 1922–23) I: 164–70.

[24] Hertslet, *Map of Europe by Treaty*, I: 398 ff.

[25] Alexander Hamilton's *Report on Manufactures;* Channing, Edward, *History of the United States,* IV, 95.

[26] Nolte, Vincent, *Fifty Years in Both Hemispheres* (New York 1854). At Hamburg in the seventeen-eighties another firm of British extraction rose to primacy. This was the house of John Parish & Co. In the early nineties the firms of Parish and Hope formed a consortium with Harman, Hoare & Co. of London and dealt with great success in *assignats* thru Boyd, Ker & Co., another English mercantile house, at Paris. John Parish claims in his memoirs that at one time almost the entire trade of the United States with Europe passed thru his hands. Ehrenberg, Richard, *Das Haus Parish in Hamburg (Grosse Vermoegen.* II. Jena. 1905). The Parish family became naturalized and ennobled in Germany.

[27] The position of the Dutch had been unprogressive for half a century. The first decisive blow was struck at the preeminence of Holland by the naval war with England, 1781–83, which ousted Dutch

vessels entirely from the Baltic carrying trade. Van Loon, *The Fall of the Dutch Republic* (New York 1913) ch. 2 and 7; Blok, *op. cit.*, V, ch. 11 and 18. Jacob, William, *View of the Agriculture . . . and state of Society of Germany and parts of Holland, France . . .* (London 1820) gives a good account of some of the continental effects of the Napoleonic wars. List, F., *National System* (1904 edition) p. 138.

[28] Silberling, Norman J., in *Quarterly Journ. of Economics*, February and May, 1924, is an excellent analysis of England's finance during the Napoleonic wars. Lowe, Joseph, *The Present State of England* (2nd edit. 1823) pp. 21–33 for the best contemporary explanation of how the war was paid for. On the incidence of taxation in 1815 see Dowell's *History of Taxation*, II : 249–72 ; Marshall, J., *Statistical Display of the Finances . . . of the United Kingdom* (1833) Tables I–IV and pp. 2–3, 14–15. On the effects of inflation and deflation on the fundholders see the curious *Series of Tables* by Robert Mushet (1821).

[29] Grellier, J. J., *Terms of all the Loans* (1st ed. 1797. 2nd ed. 1802). The loans raised in London for the allies were closely linked with the domestic loan business. Clapham, J. H. in *Economic Journal*, Dec. 1917. The first foreign government loan was offered in 1794 by Boyd, Benfield & Co. on behalf of Austria. A guarantee from the British government was necessary to secure a market for it; and the second loan in 1795 did not go off so well. Pitt found it more convenient, and with the present predicament of the United States in mind it must be pronounced wise policy, to give further financial aid to his allies by means of direct subsidies. *Accounts & Papers*, 1821 (520). *Correspondence and Contracts relating to the Austrian loans.*

[30] *Times*, 29 Sept. 1810.

[31] Halévy, I, Book II, ch. 3; Bagehot, *Lombard Street*, 253–54.

[32] Tierney in House of Commons, 3 Dec. 1798, *Annual Register*, 1799, pp. 177–78.

[33] *Public Characters of 1805* (London 1805) pp. 30 ff.

[34] *Public Characters of 1802–03* (London 1803) pp. 49–64.

[35] *Circular to Bankers* (1830) no. 48. "Every Administration has, for twenty years past, considered the Custom-House, the Excise, the merchants and manufacturers of Lancashire; the merchants, loan-contractors, and money dealers of London; as the whole of the political world. . . . The Government now watch the operations in London, of the great money machine, with as much solicitude as a projector watches the motion of the most essential parts of an ingenious invention, upon which he has staked his fame and fortune." Cf. Escott, T. H. S., *The Story of British Diplomacy* (London 1908) ch. 8.

³⁶ Tooke and Newmarch, *History of Prices* (1838 ff.) Vol. I; Smart, William, *Economic Annals, 1801–20* (1910); Bouniatian II; Sombart II, ch. 17; Bagehot, *Lombard Street*, ch. 6.

³⁷ The basis for all accounts of the early history of bill-broking is the testimony of Thomas Richardson before the Bullion Committee of 1810. *Minutes of Evidence*, pp. 177 ff. Bagehot, ch. 11 and Tooke & Newmarch, VI: 584–608 cover later developments. Cf. Fox Bourne, pp. 467–81, and the *Circular to Bankers*, passim.

³⁸ Spence, *Britain Independent of Commerce* (1807); Mill, James, *Commerce Defended* (1st ed. 1807). Cf. Seligman, E. R. A., "On Some Neglected British Economists," *Econ. Journ.* XIII: 336–39 for a description of two other anonymous works of this time, likewise of a physiocratic tendency.

NOTES TO CHAPTER TWO

Business Conditions in England.—The starting-point of any report of English business conditions in the first half of the nineteenth century is Tooke, Thomas and Newmarch, William, *History of Prices* . . . (6 vols. London 1837–58). Volumes I and II are relevant to this chapter. The price-tables presented by Tooke were unscientifically prepared. An independent series has been collected by Norman J. Silberling in *The Harvard Review of Economic Statistics*, Preliminary Volume for 1923, pp. 223–61. It is there made the basis for the best set of index numbers of prices in England before 1850. See also the same publication for 1919, pp. 282–97. The National Bureau of Economic Research is publishing a volume of *Business Annals*, by Willard L. Thorp, with an introductory chapter by Wesley C. Mitchell, which is an admirable guide to British business conditions since 1790. Palgrave, R. H. I., *Bank Rate and Money Market* (London 1903) begins with 1844. Tugan-Baranowsky, M. I., *Les Crises industrielles en Angleterre* (Paris 1913) is a helpful analysis of the critical periods in the nineteenth century.

An introduction to the economic material contained in *Hansard's Parliamentary Debates* and in parliamentary reports is available in Smart, William, *Economic Annals* (2 vols., extending to 1830. London 1910 ff.) and Page, William, *Commerce and Industry, 1815–1914* (2 vols. London 1919). The third edition of Porter, G. R., *The Progress of the Nation* (1851) is the most useful introduction to general economic statistics in the first part of the century. The first *Statistical Abstract of the United Kingdom* was published in 1853, covering the years 1842–52; it is now out of print. John Marshall's *Digest of all the Accounts* (1833)˙ is a somewhat chaotic summary of statistics officially published to about 1830.

For day-to-day market incidents, the *Times* and the *Morning Herald* are useful, especially from the beginning of their "City" articles in 1825. The weekly *Circular to Bankers*, from 1828 to 1846, is the most penetrating running commentary on the money market

[1] Cannan, Edwin, *The Paper Pound of 1797–1821* (London 1917); Acworth, A. W., *Financial Reconstruction in England, 1815–1822* (London 1925). A brilliant study, ascribing England's troubles chiefly to deflation); Silberling in *Q. J. Econ.* XXXVIII: 214–33, 397–439.

[2] Cf. articles "Gold v. Goldwährung," "Silber v. Silberwährung" by Lexis in *Handwörterbuch v. Staatswissenschaften* (Jena, 1910). The view here taken of the importance of the precious metals conforms to that of Cassel, G., *Theory of Social Economy* (London 1923) ch. 11. The correlation there established between secular price trends and the rate of increase in the stock of gold available for circulation seems inescapable. The mechanism by which this correlation operates is, however, debatable. Cf. Fisher, Irving, *The Purchasing Power of Money* (New York 1911) pp. 239–46.

[3] Del Mar, Alexander, *History of the Precious Metals* (London 1880) pp. 152, 203.

[4] Treaty of Paris, November 20, 1815, article 4 in Hertslet, *The Map of Europe by Treaty* (1875) I: 347, 351 ff. Cf. memorandum by Sir Charles Stuart in *F. O.* 27: 154–69.

[5] Report of finance commission headed by J. Laffitte, summarized in *Times*, 6 Oct. 1816. Dareste de Chavanne, A. E. C., *Histoire de la Restauration*, Vol. I (Paris, 1879). Nervo, G. de, *Les finances françaises sous la Restauration* (2 vols. Paris 1865–68). Bresson, Jacques, *Histoire financière de la France*, Vol. II (Paris, 1829).

[6] *Memoires de G. J. Ouvrard sur sa vie. et ses divers operations financières.* (3 vols. Paris, 1826–27) I: 226.

[7] Ouvrard, I, 216–17, claims credit for the idea, and his narrative checks in the main with the dispatches of Wellington and Stuart, English ambassador in Paris, where verification is possible. However, Capefigue, *Histoire des grandes operations financières*, T. III (Paris, 1858) pp. 63 ff., assigns credit to Wellington and Pozzo di Borgo.

[8] Nolte, Vincent, *Fifty Years in Both Hemispheres* (London 1854) pp. 254–55; Escott, T. H. S., *City Characters* (London 1921) ch. 11; *Journals and Correspondence of Miss Berry* (London 1865) II: 344; *Dictionary of National Biography.*

[9] Ouvrard, I: 238–44. Capefigue, III: 28–29. The connection seems

to have been not direct, but thru Hope & Co. This enabled Baring to deny flatly that Baring Brothers were concerned in army contracts. *F. O.* 92:32. Castlereagh to Wellington, 17 Jan. 1817. The situation seems to have been as follows. The army contractors were paid by France in rentes which they disposed of quietly upon the stock exchanges and among their friends. In the course of 1816 Barings had sold about five million pounds of them in England and had made plans to sell more. Meanwhile France was meeting her indemnity instalments with three-months bills, which she paid in specie at maturity. However the Powers had agreed to accept rentes instead of bills; and when crop failure forced her to suspend payment in December, 1816, the army contractors feared that she would pay in rentes, that they would be thrown upon the market without arrangement between the Powers and that heavy losses would be occasioned all round, not least to the contractors. This even more than the prospective profits of the loan business caused them to exert all their influence to bring all of the credit operations of France under unitary management in their own hands. Ouvrard and Castlereagh, *ut supra.* Vansittart in Commons, 9 Apr. 1818, *Parl. Dcb.* XXXVII: 1230 ff.

[10] *Memoirs and Correspondence of Robert Stewart, Viscount Castlereagh* (London 1848–53) XI: 22–3.

[11] *F. O.* 27:129. Castlereagh to Stuart, 7 Dec. 1816. The "neutrality" was purely official. *Baring discussed the proposition in detail with Liverpool, Castlereagh and Vansittart before going to Paris, and the government had both Wellington and Stuart reporting to it every stage of the negotiations. In the conference of ambassadors, Great Britain and Russia took the lead in making such arrangements as would facilitate unitary handling of French credit operations.

[12] *F. O.* 92:32. Wellington to Castlereagh, *passim. F. O.* 27:153. Stuart to Castlereagh, two letters dated 27 Jan. 1817. Ouvrard, *op. cit.* I: 247.

[13] Baring insisted that he be given the loan at five points below the market price, and was successful. *Supplementary Despatches of the Duke of Wellington* (London, 1864) XI: 619.

[14] The Austrian loans of 1794 and 1795, made thru Boyd, Benfield & Co., totalling £5,600,000, carried the guarantee of the British government and proved to be in fact British securities. *Accounts and Papers.* 1821 (11) and (520). British claims were composed for £2,500,000 under convention of November 17, 1823, which was raised in the following year by a loan in London. Lord Brougham stigmatized this arrangement as a settlement for half a crown in the pound.

In 1809 there had been a Portuguese loan for £600,000 privately arranged, with the guarantee of the British government. This loan was formally assumed by the government by treaty of January 22, 1815. In 1813 and 1814 there were two loans of £200,000 each, to the governments of Holland and France respectively, directly out of the British Treasury. These loans were repaid. These transactions were minor variations of the subsidy policy for carrying on the struggle with Napoleon. See the article by J. H. Clapham in *Economic Journal*, XXVII: 495–501, and parliamentary papers there cited.

¹⁵ A draft of this contract is in *F. O. 27*:154. The first loan was payable in twelve monthly instalments, the second in nine. Both were in 5% rentes. Baring refused to handle a special terminable security on the ground that in case of revolution it could be easily singled out for repudiation.

¹⁶ *Annuaire Historique*, 1818, pp. 193–94. *Supplementary Despatches of Wellington*, XII: 247–49, 353–55, 526–28, 540, 571–73. The convention of May 23, 1818, arranging the settlement of claims is in *F. O. 94*:88. Dareste, I, 316–17. *Times*, 17 Oct. 1818, 2c.

¹⁷ Vansittart in Commons, 9 Apr. 1818.

¹⁸ *Commercial Chronicle*, 16 Jan. 1817. *Times*, 17 Dec. 1816.

¹⁹ *Parl. Deb.* XXXV: 226–32, 428–35. "A" in *Times*. 27 Dec. 1817.

²⁰ *Morning Herald*, 9 Jan. 1822.

²¹ "I. A." in *Times*, 12 Feb. 1817. The coincidence of this article with the launching of the first Baring loan suggests its inspiration. At an earlier date the *Times* was quite indignant at the idea of helping so arbitrary a government as that of France. *Ibid.* 14 Dec. 1816, 2c.

²² *Report of Commons Committee of Secrecy on the State of the Bank*, 1819 (282). Testimony of N. M. Rothschild and of S. E. Holland, managing partner of Baring Brothers.

²³ France imported in 1817 an excess of 135 million francs over her exports. *Annuaire Historique*, 1818, p. 493. This corresponds very closely with the difference between the total amount of loans raised by her abroad and the amount of indemnity payable by her outside her borders. However no inferences may be based upon analysis of balance of trade returns, particularly for Great Britain before 1854, which are not capable of independent demonstration. We have no trustworthy account of bullion movements for that time. Moreover, the prevalence of shipment upon consignment and long-term credit renders the relations between exports and imports and the balance of payments quite incalculable, except for periods of time long enough to render the lapse between customs return and payment negligible. Statistical inquiry into quarterly and annual phases in these relations, not to speak of the incidence of particular transactions, is unfruitful. And this quite apart from the fact that

down to 1854 only "official" values are available of both imports and exports into Great Britain, based upon a price scale fixed in 1694, and that "real" values are to be found only by computation on the basis of declared values of British and Irish produce and manufactures exported. Porter, 355–57.

[24] The dispatches of Douglas and Rose to Castlereagh from Berlin—to be found at *F. O.* 64 : 113 and 115—form a curious commentary upon the negotiations which culminated in this loan. As was pointed out in the *Times*, 6 Apr. 1818, 2d, the loan was very advantageous to investors since it was offered at 70 to the public when similar securities of the Prussian government were selling in Amsterdam around 90. Rothschild got the securities at 68 with advantages in the exchange rates. It must be remembered that while Prussian ministers were thoroly corrupt (Rose to Castlereagh, *F. O.* 64 : 109 #98) money markets were ruthless, and the offering of a new loan gave an excellent opportunity to enemies of Prussia to raid her credit. Prussian ministers defended the loan against attacks at home on the ground that any attempt to raise the money in Prussia would have drained capital away from commerce and manufacture. Indirectly this foreign loan was regarded as a means of securing foreign capital to promote those branches of Prussian economy.

[25] *Reports of Committees on the State of the Bank,* 1819 (282), Testimony of A. L. Haldimand; Castlereagh in Commons, 2 Feb. 1819, *Parl. Deb.* LXXV : 246–48; Tooke, *History of Prices,* II : 95. About one-half of the Russian issue of 1818, or two million pounds, was subscribed in English names through the agents of Baring Brothers. The Austrian loan drew only about £100,000 from England. Upon public finance in Central Europe at this time, see Cohen, B., *Compendium of Finance* (London, 1822) ; Beer, Ad., *Die Finanzen Oesterreichs* (Wien. 1877) : Bender, J. H., *Die Verkehr mit Staatspapieren* (1830) ; Nebenius, Carl F. E., *Die Oeffentliche Credit dargestellt* (1820) ; von Goenner, N. T., *Von Staats-Schulden* (1826).

[26] In the *Jewish Encyclopaedia,* article *Rothschilds,* it is stated that the Rothschild ascendancy and in large part their fortune dated from successful bear operations upon this occasion. This may have taken place under cover of sales for Prussia of rentes in anticipation of her allotments for indemnity claims. *Annuaire Historique,* 1818, p. 391. The Rothschilds were agents for Prussia and smaller German states in remitting the indemnity, and had contracts which made those countries an exception to the arrangement to leave everything in the hands of Baring Brothers and Hope & Co. *F. O.* 27 : 139 #458, 470.

[27] *F. O. Protocols of Aix-la-Chappelle,* #36–38. Drafts of letters

to Corvetto and Wellington from Baring in *F. O.* 92:37, with the covering dispatch from Castlereagh to Liverpool. Protocol #36, which is accessible in *Ann. Hist.*, 1818, pp. 427–9, contains a full description of the financial situation in what appears to be Baring's own language. The rentes assigned to the Allies never were issued. Instead the private claims were disposed of by the issue of Treasury bills in 1820.

28 *Supplementary Despatches of Wellington*, XII: 864–68, 883–84.

29 Haldimand's testimony in *Reports of the Bank Committee*, 1819. England had supplied 32 million pounds out of 38 millions paid up on loans during 1817 and 1818. Thus two-thirds had been re-sold very quickly. Of the balance remaining in the hands of English purchasers, at least seven millions were in French rentes. This estimate apparently did not include rentes issued in 1819, of which very little had been paid up when Haldimand testified.

30 *Ibid*, page 158.

31 *Parl. Deb.* XLI: 906; *Cf. ibid,* 335, corroborated by Lord Grenville, *ibid.* 476.

32 A table which includes most of the foreign government loans from 1818 to 1827, is reprinted in Hobson, C. K., *The Export of Capital* (1914) p. 101 from the *Journal of the Statistical Society of London* (1827) p. 112. With this may be compared the data in English, Henry: *A Complete View of the English Joint-Stock Companies formed during the years 1824 and 1825* (London, 1827), Fortune's *Epitome of the Public Funds* (1833) and Spackman, W. F., *Statistical Tables* (1842). Cohen's *Compendium of Finance* gives ample details of all issued before 1822. The "City" article in the London press originated with the *Times* and the *Morning Herald* in 1825. Prior to that year reports of stock market activities are sparse, reflecting to some extent the social disesteem which tradition imputed to them. There are files of prospectuses of the period in the British Museum at 8223. e. 10 and 1881. b. 23. There are more voluminous files in the archives of the Stock Exchange, without arrangement or date.

33 The earliest reliable account of the Rothschild family is the article by Fr. von Gentz, "Biographische Nachrichten ueber das Haus Rothschild," written in 1826 for the Brockhaus *Conversationslexikon,* and reprinted in *Schriften von Friedrich* von Gentz, V: 113–23 (Mannheim 1840). The origin of the family fortune at Frankfurt has been lifted entirely out of the realm of myth and conjecture by the substantial monograph of Berghoeffer, C. W., *Meyer Amschel Rothschild* (Frankfurt 1923). Ehrenberg, Richard, *Grosse Vermoegen, ihre Entstehung und ihre Bedeutung. Fugger-Rothschild-Krupp* (Berlin 1905) follows the family fortunes through the first generation on the basis of documentary material and fairly reliable memoirs. Edward

Herries, *Memoirs of the Public Life of John S. Herries* (2 vols. London 1880) I, ch. 3, gives an account of the financing of the British armies on the Continent. Reeves, John, *The Rothschilds* (London 1887) is a biographical account of the Rothschild family. Francis, John, *Chronicles and Characters of the Stock Exchange* (New York 1850) contains a generous selection of anecdotes of the first London Rothschild.

[34] Capefigue, III:101–05.

[35] *Times,* 5 June 1830 (city article). Rothschilds made money scarce by cornering bills on German centers and presenting them simultaneously for discount.

[36] *Circular to Bankers,* 31 July, 7, 14 August, 1835. Rothschild controlled the London market for any object for which he needed money. *Ibid,* 9 Oct. 1835.

[37] For political reasons English and French bankers were associated in the contracts, but the bulk of the money came from England and Holland. Toward the end of 1823, Ferdinand VII was restored to an absolute throne by the aid of French arms, and refused to recognize the obligations which his governments had incurred while he had been constitutional sovereign. The solidarity of the London and Paris money markets upon this occasion is impressive by comparison with the conflicting policies of their governments. Neither would have anything to do with Ferdinand, except upon the condition that he recognize the usurious constitutional loans *in toto*. This was the origin of the Stock Exchange rule that no security of a defaulting state may be officially quoted. *Times,* 7 Jan. 1824, 4c; 18 and 21 Oct., 4 Nov. 1824; 26 Feb. 1825. The *Morning Herald,* 31 Aug. 1924 hooted at the suggestion that the attitude of the Stock Exchange should be in any way controlled by England's warm sympathies for South American independence. "John Bull would lend his money to any Government, if he could only be certain that his interest would be regularly paid; and as to his Patriotism, it is, on the Foreign Stock Exchange, supposed to be not worth a farthing." Nevertheless this consideration was actively exploited by Barings, who may be presumed to have understood their business. *Ibid.,* 1 Sept. 1824.

[38] Webster, C. K., "Castlereagh and the Spanish Colonies" in *English Historical Review,* January, 1912 and October, 1915.

[39] *The Present State of Colombia* . . . (by one of the British officers of the expeditions. London, 1827) pp. 85–115. *A Brief Review of a Pamphlet published at Popayan, under the Title of "Opinion of a Native of New Granada upon the Division of the Colombian Debt"* (London 1836). British aid was of course not limited to Colombia. Mulhall, M. G.: *The English in South America* (1877) indexes the activities of countless officers and merchants in South America dur-

ing the independence period. At Buenos Ayres at the end of 1823 half of a domestic debt of $2,500,000 and the "best part of the most valuable property in the city" was owned by British residents. Report of Woodbine Parish to Canning, 25 April, 1824, in *F. O. 6 : 3.*

40 Castlereagh's refusal is at *F. O. 97 : 114.*

41 *Colombia . . . a Geographical, Statistical, . . . and Political Account* (2 vols. 1822–23), pp. xcii–xciv, cxii. Besides six hundred thousand pounds in claims, debentures were issued to cover a tidy sum for the personal accommodation of the Vice-President. *The Contractor Unmasked* (1823).

42 The chief basis of this account is the voluminous pamphlet literature to which the controversies of contractors and bondholders and Colombian politicians gave rise. In addition to the titles cited may be mentioned *Statement presented to the meeting of the Holders of Colombian Bonds.* (1823), *Reply to the Letters to the Contractors* (1823), *Statement of some Circumstances connected with the Mode of Contracting the Colombian Loan in April, 1824.* (1825). The rivalry of Herring, Powles & Graham and B. A. Goldschmidt & Co. seems to have been behind much of the publicity. These anonymous pamphlets are indexed under "Colombian Loan" in the British Museum. Cf. also Comacho, Vicente O., *Resumen histórico sobre la Deuda Exterior de Colombia,* T. I. (Bogotá 1914).

43 *Colombia . . .* (2 vols. 1822–23) cited above is an excellent illustration. The connection with the contractors was distinctly avowed in the introduction. The book was intended to promote an elaborate scheme of colonization and development, as well as the loan. On the concoction of news, see *Morning Herald,* 29 Dec. 1825. On underwriting see J. S. Ricardo in *Times,* 28 Oct. 1826, 2e.

44 It was essential to the success of the loans that they run in sterling. They were thus rendered independent of currency manipulations on the part of the borrowing governments. The retention of the business of agents in remittance of dividends was important to the contractors, not only for the brokerage fees, but also for keeping them in contact with a clientele of investors, and providing them with increased exchange facilities arising from the monopoly of government remittances.

45 *Present State of Colombia,* pp. 237 ff.

46 Report of Committee of Greek Bondholders, *Times,* 24 October, 1826, pages 2 and 3. The issues of the *Times* for September, October and November of the same year contain numerous leading articles upon the scandal as well as letters from Bowring, Hume, Ellice, the Greek deputies and others involved in the transactions. There was also a large pamphlet literature. Palma: *Greece Vindicated* (1826). *Westminster Review,* July, 1826 (article by Bowring). *The Greek*

Loans of 1824 and 1825. How they were handled, and what the world thought of it (1877). Stefanos Xenos in *Times*, 3 Feb. 1864, 7a. Blaquière, *Narrative of a Second Visit to Greece* (1825). Finlay: *History of Greece* (2nd Edit. Oxford 1877) VI :328, 433–36. Duer, John and Sedgwick, Robert: *An Examination of the Controversy between the Greek Deputies and Two Mercantile Houses of New York* (New York, 1826) handle the American side of the matter. See also Cobbett's *Weekly Political Register* for Nov. and Dec. 1826.

[47] English, Henry, *A Complete View of the Joint Stock Companies formed during the years 1824 and 1825* (London 1827) is the most reliable authority. Other lists are contained in Secretan, J. J., *Epitome of the various Foreign Mining Companies* (1824) and in *The Monthly Repository* (issues from February, 1825). Brief accounts of the joint-stock mania are to be found in *Annual Register*, 1825, pp. 3 ff.; Martineau, Harriet, *History of England during the Thirty Years' Peace* (London 1849) and Walpole, Spencer, *A History of England from the Conclusion of the Great War* (London 1878–86). Wilks, John, *Six Letters on the Past Operations and Future Prospects of Joint Stock Companies* (London 1825). *Times*, 29 Dec. 1825.

[48] Canning's policy followed closely the action of France with reference to Spain, and became positive only after France invaded Spain in behalf of Ferdinand's absolutisms. In April, 1823 the French army crossed the Pyrenees; in October Canning accredited consuls to the principal South American cities. The French army lingered thru 1824; the Foreign office assisted in organizing a Mexican expedition and negotiated a commercial treaty with the provinces of the Plate. When it became certain that the French army would remain indefinitely at Ferdinand's service, Canning announced, January 1, 1825, definite recognition of all the revolting republics. The parallel with the movement of elation in the stock market is striking.

[49] It is piquant to discover these arguments set forth with skill by the future prime minister, Benjamin Disraeli, who made his debut upon this occasion by writing the publicity for a stockbroker interested in keeping up the price of mining stocks. Disraeli: *An Enquiry into the Plans, Progress and Policy of the American Mining Companies* (1825) and *Lawyers and Legislators* (1825). Cf. Rawson, Sir William: *The Present Prospects and Future Operations of the Mexican Mining Associations Analysed . . .* (1825).

[50] Alexander Baring denounced the joint-stock mania in the House of Commons in February, 1825. It interfered with "legitimate" government-loan making.

[51] *Quarterly Review* XXXI: 349. Tooke, *History of Prices,* II: 145.

[52] *The American Monitor, a Monthly Political, Historical and Commercial Magazine, particularly devoted to the Affairs of South America* (London, 1824–25) esp. I:136, 181, 366–7, 412. *The Present State of Colombia,* pp. 314–24. Report of Lieut.-Col. Campbell, 7 Nov. 1824, at *F. O.* 18:3.

[53] The authority for Stephenson's experience is Jeaffreson, J. C., *Life of Robert Stephenson* (London 1864) I, chapters 5 and 6. One project better than any other illustrates the blend of naïveté and enterprise which characterized the South American undertakings. It is the Churning Company formed to manufacture butter at Buenos Ayres. The capital was subscribed, a shipload of Scotch milkmaids sent out, and the wild cattle of the Plate led captive to the milking stools. The shops were filled with butter. Not until then was it discovered that the "guacho" had an unaccountable preference for oil. Head, Sir Francis, *Rough Notes of a Trip across the Pampas* (London, 1826) pp. 303–4.

[54] The city articles of the *Times* and *Morning Herald* for 1826 may be consulted for details. Ward, Henry G.: *Mexico in 1827* (2 vols. London 1828). *Times* 11 Sept. 1838. *Kinder vs. Taylor* in *3 Law Journal R.* ch. 68–84, reports a law-suit involving the Real del Monte company. In 1826, two million pounds additional capital was called up on the mining company shares; in 1827, £800,000; in 1828, over one million; and thereafter two or three hundred thousand a year until the revival of joint-stock enterprise about 1835. These figures are based upon computations derived from data in Wetenhall, J., *Course of the Exchange* and the *Financial and Commercial Record,* weekly precursors under private auspices of the Stock Exchange Daily Intelligence. These publications contain the amount paid up at any time upon shares in active trading. It has thus been possible to compute at least the nominal investment in the enterprises listed. To 1849 when the company sold out, the Real del Monte mine cost $15,000,000 for a return to the proprietors of $10,500,000. Hill, S. S., *Travels in Peru and Mexico* (2 vols. London 1860) II:308–10. Cf. Powles, Illingworth & Co., *Observaciones sobre la Mineria de la Nueva Granada* (Bogota, 1837). Head, F. B., *Reports relating to the Failure of the Rio Plata Mining Association* (London 1827); Dahlgren, C. B. *Historic Mines of Mexico* (N. Y. 1883).

[55] *Report of Committee on Renewal of Bank Charter,* 1831. *Annual Register,* 1825. Tugan-Baranowsky.

[56] *The Present State of Colombia,* 241–44. It did not promote the confidence of South Americans in British good faith for Barclay,

Herring, Richardson & Co., which succeeded Goldschmidts as agents for Colombia as well as for Mexico, to fail in 1828, also with government funds in their possession. Cf. comment in *Times,* 29 Jan. 1829.

[57] During the five years 1828–32, 8,894,424 quarters of foreign and colonial grain were imported into the British Isles, at an average price exceeding sixty shillings. Tooke, *History of Prices,* II: 204–5.

[58] *Times,* 2 and 15 Jan., 8 July 1829. *Circular to Bankers,* 19 Sept. 1828. A similar movement of securities was a prominent feature of the corn and currency crises of 1839–40 and of 1847. "Foreigners can wait for our manufactures till adverse times are over; they can go for six or eight months, wearing out their clothes, but we cannot wait for our corn." Adam Hodgson, before *Committee on Commercial Distress,* 1847–48 (395) #97. Salomons, David, *An Examination of the Causes of the Present Monetary Difficulties* (London, 1837).

[59] The value of machinery exported from Great Britain during the years 1822–29 inclusive was reported at £1,586,256. *Accounts and Papers, Machinery Account,* 6 May, 1830 (373). About one-half of this was to European countries, chiefly France and the Netherlands. About one-fourth went to the colonies.

[61] Cf. Parish, H. H., *Diplomatic History of the Monarchy of Greece* (London, 1838) pp. 366–67. "The evident political corruption, the constant agitation, the changes and insecurity which the best of these new states exhibits, may, in some degree, have been produced by the demoralizing effects of the capital which has been obtained under false pretences, which has been squandered for dishonest or for factious ends, and which consequently, as in Greece, has allowed those shortlived governments to run a career of reckless folly, indifferent alike to the support and the feelings of the masses of the people."

[62] A more precise quantitative summary is out of the question. A very large per cent of the investments, particularly to the Continent were made in securities which ran in foreign currencies, which were bought quietly abroad and could be disposed of as quietly. With respect to the more speculative loans, it was not infrequent for them to be offered to the public at one price and sold all down the line if they fell in price.

My own data show a net investment in European stocks the end of 1825 of 57 million pounds. I can trace £300,000 invested in companies of various kinds doing business in Europe. It would be sheer guess-work to make mention of purchases of canal bonds, mortgages and such industrial investments as the iron works of Manby, Wilson & Co. at Creusot. With these figures may be compared contemporary estimates. The *Times* for Oct. 14, 1824 finds that Great Britain had lent £47,815,000 to all foreign governments to that time. Marshall's *Digest of all the Accounts*, #20, presents a balance-sheet in which foreign loans to Europe between 1817 and 1830 are computed at 81 million pounds. Marshall allows no set-off for re-sales in 1828, 1829 and 1831 although he has 17 million returned to Europe from 1817 to 1824. He makes no statement of non-government loans. And I find nothing to corroborate his allowance of 20 millions for securities purchased in Great Britain after 1825. British investments on the Continent certainly did not exceed 60 millions at any time in the twenties.

According to a letter from William Thompson, chairman of the South American and Mexican Association to Lord Aberdeen, April 14, 1830, published in *Times*, 10 May, 1830, 5 million pounds of British capital were invested in trade with those countries in 1830, £4,800,000 in mines, chiefly in Mexico, and 17 millions in debts due by the governments. Marshall allows 17½ millions for American investments. My own data total nearly 18 million pounds realized upon government securities, assuming them to have sold at the price of issue. In the same time more than 6 millions had gone into mining companies.

NOTES TO CHAPTER THREE

The Literature of Anglo-American Finance in the Jackson Period.—The commerce and balance of payments between Great Britain and the United States have been studied by Chapman, S. J., *History of Trade between the United Kingdom and the United States* (London, 1899) and by Bullock, Williams and Tucker in *Harvard Review of Economic Statistics*, Prelim. Vol. I, 215–66.

Buck, N. S. *The Organization of Anglo-American Trade, 1815–50* (New Haven, 1925) is a welcome study, classificatory in method, of business institutions and technique. It has appeared too late to be drawn upon for the purposes of this chapter, which is based upon some of the same sources but which relies upon an apparently wider selection of British material. It is to be regretted that Professor Buck has limited himself to the direct trade between the United Kingdom and the United States, omitting the instructive and vital triangular relations by way of the Orient and tropical areas.

A clear narrative of American financial experience in the Jackson period is presented in Dewey, D. R., *Financial History of the United*

States (New York, 1922) ch. 9 and 10. Detailed and authoritative studies, based upon the *Biddle Papers* are Catterall, R. H. C., *The Second Bank of the United States,* (Chicago, 1903) and McGrane, R. C., *The Panic of 1837* (Chicago, 1925). To both of these writers the problems of government finance and their political involvements are central as they are to Bourne, E. G., *History of the Surplus Revenue of 1837* (1885).

Internal improvements have been treated by state and by enterprise in numerous monographs. Bishop, A. L., *The State Works of Pennsylvania* in *Transactions of the Conn. Acad. of Arts & Sciences* XIII : 149–297; Meyer, B. H., *History of Transportation in the United States before 1860* (Washington 1917) ; Gephart, W. F., *Transportation and Industrial Development in the Middle West* (New York 1909) esp. ch. 7 and 8; and Reizenstein, *Economic History of the Baltimore and Ohio Railroad,* 1827–53 in *JHU Studies,* XV, 7–8 are the most significant of these. The contemporary accounts of Chevalier, M., *Lettres sur l'Amerique du Nord* (Paris, 1836) and of von Gerstner, F. A., *Die innern Communicationen der Vereinigten Staaten* (2 vols. 1842–3) do not suffer by comparison. There are useful summaries in McGrane, ch. 1 and McMaster, *History of the People of the U. S.* (1910) ch. 63.

The only study of British investments in the United States during this period is by Callender, G. S., "*Early Transportation and Banking Enterprises of the States,*" *Q. J. Econ.* XVII, 111–62. A contemporary authority, Trotter, Alexander, *Observations upon the Debts of the North American States* (London, 1839) is of great value.

The primary source for this chapter has been the weekly letters of Henry Burgess, editor of the *Circular to Bankers* from 1828 to 1846, who was largely instrumental in developing the market for American stocks, and whose analyses of the London money market surpass anything of their time in cogency and insight. In handling them it must be borne in mind that Burgess was a protectionist and champion of bimetallism, allied to the Birmingham school of economists. The files of *Niles Register, The American Railroad Journal* (1832 ff.), and *Hunt's Merchants' Magazine* (1839 ff.) have also been used.

[1] *Report of Committee on the State of the Bank,* 1819 (282) p. 109.

[2] Channing, Edw., *History of the United States,* IV : 95.

[3] *Report on State of Bank,* 1819, testimony of S. C. Holland, managing partner of Barings, at p. 119. Holland considered that most of the coupons held in England were paid through his firm. Cf. Cohen, *Compendium of Finance,* p. 165.

[4] *Niles Register,* XLV : 178 : Gallatin, *Observations on the Currency*

(1831) p. 44. *Opinions respecting the Commercial Intercourse between Great Britain and the United States* (Boston, 1797) : Bayley, R. A., *History of the National Loans of the United States.*

[5] Catterall, *op. cit.*, pp. 108 ff. and 508. *Niles Reg.* XLI, 112, 113.

[6] *Report of Secretary of the Treasury*, Oct. 15, 1828. Cf. Seybert, *Statistical Annals*, p. 757. *H. R.* 121. 22 Cong. 2 Sess. p. 13. The estimate of £8,600,000 quoted in *Niles Reg.*, June 12, 1824 is certainly unfounded.

[7] Channing, *op. cit.*, IV: 111.

[8] *Niles Reg.* XLV:178; XLVIII:145. Caermarthen owned the bank "body and breeches" except about enough to form a board of directors from citizens of New York state.

[9] Porter, *Progress of the Nation* (1851) pp. 359–65: Pitkin, Timothy, *Statistical View of the Commerce of the United States* (2nd edit. New Haven, 1835) pp. 266–93: Marshall's *Digest of all the Accounts.* (1834).

[10] Smart, W., *Economic Annals*, 1820–30, pp. 329–30. *The Auction System* (Baltimore, 1824). *Circular to Bankers*, 14 March, 1834. This system is described in discriminating detail in Buck, *Organization of the Anglo-American Trade.* (1925).

[11] *Circular to Bankers*, 14 Mar. 1834, 15 Jan. 1836, 24 June 1837. *Edinburgh Review*, July 1837 (McCulloch) pp. 228–31. Buck, *op. cit.*, is certainly in error in deferring the development of this technique to 1830.

[12] Catterall, *op. cit.*, 111–12. Prime, Ward & King of New York also had an independent position in the exchange market. Agents of British and French houses took up most of the cotton bills not handled through the Bank. Samuel Ward of Boston was for a generation the American agent of Baring Brothers. S. V. S. Wilder of New York represented Hottinguers. The man who took the name of Auguste Belmont came to New York as agent for Rothschilds about 1837.

[13] Thomas Wilson & Co., Timothy Wiggin & Co., George Wilde & Co. (the three "W's" which failed in 1837), Morrison & Co., Lizardi & Co. and Rothschilds were the other firms engaged in this business in 1836. Rothschilds had only recently been drawn into it, possibly because they succeeded Baring Brothers in 1835 as agents abroad for the United States government. *Niles Reg.* XLVII: 234; *Circular to Bankers*, 13 Feb. 1835. They had houses in New York, Boston, Philadelphia and Baltimore within a year. *Niles Reg.* XLVIII: 250. After 1837, Palmer, Dent & Co. and Magniac, Jardine & Co., among others, were drawn into the business by the close connection of the American with the Chinese trade. Cf. *Circular to Bankers* 7 Oct. 1836, 25 Mar. 1837. The Liverpool firm of Brown

Brothers was in reality an off-shoot of an American mercantile house, Alexander Brown & Sons of Baltimore. Brown, J. C., *One Hundred Years of Merchant Banking* (N. Y. 1909). On the death of S. C. Holland in 1825 and the elevation of Alexander Baring to the peerage as Lord Ashburton in 1828, Barings had been reorganized. Humphrey Mildmay, Ashburton's son-in-law Thomas Baring, and Joshua Bates of Boston became active partners. Nolte, *Fifty Years*, pp. 277-79.

[14] *Report of Committee on Commerce, Shipping, etc.* 1833 (690)., testimony of Joshua Bates, managing partner of Barings, # 769, 867, 964-6, 1001.

[15] *Ibid*, testimony of Joshua Bates, # 744-1057. *Circular to Bankers*, 13 Jan. 1832. Fully one-half of the value carried by American vessels to China, for instance, in the thirties consisted in bills on London. These bills went from Hong Kong to India in payment for opium, and came to London in payment for the increasing exports of Manchester goods to the Orient or as part of the Indian revenue. The disruption of the opium traffic from 1838 to 1842 was no small factor in the breakdown of the commercial system of which it was an important part. Forbes, R. B., *Remarks on China and the China Trade* (New York 1844). Testimony of Sir George Larpent before *Committee on East Indian Trade*, 1840. Pitkin's *View*, 303. *Hunt's Merchants' Magazine*, VI :567-70; XII :44-52.

[16] Pitkin's *Statistical View*, pp. 189-213 contains a discussion from the New England standpoint of the effect of Jackson's diplomacy. Cf. Benns, F. Lee, *The American Struggle for the British West India Carrying Trade* (Bloomington, 1923) pp. 185-88.

[17] Porter, *op. cit.*, 391, 403.

[18] *Circular to Bankers*, 13 Jan. 1832.

[19] *Report of Committee on Commercial Distress* 1847-48, testimony of Samuel Gurney. *Times* 5 April, 17 May, 1830.

[20] *Circular to Bankers*, 14 and 21 December, 1832.

[21] *Ibid*, 13 Jan. 1832.

[22] The case of the Earl of Derby, with estates in Lancashire worth £14,000 a year before the rise of manufacturing centers raised his rent-roll to £180,000. *Money Market Review*, 10 Dec. 1864.

[23] Dewey, *op. cit.* 212-16; Callender's article is the best available summary.

[24] *New York Annual Register*, 1834, p. 176. *American Railroad Journal*, VI :37; Trotter, 127-57; Message of Gov. W. H. Seward, Jan. 1840, in Hazard, *U. S. Comm. & Stat. Reg.* II, 69-74.

[25] For financial details see Pitkin, p. 557; Chevalier II :40-106, 432-36; Trotter, *passim;* Report of Comptroller A. C. Flagg of New York, printed in *American Almanac*, 1840, pp. 103-11 and elsewhere;

H. R. 121, 21 Cong. 1 Sess. p. 13; Poor, H. V., *Sketch of the Rise and Progress of the Internal Improvements*, (New York, 1881). The first American state securities quoted in London were New York 6's, which made their appearance in 1817. In 1822, New York was borrowing at 5 %. In 1824, the first securities of Pennsylvania, Virginia and Louisiana were known in London. Very small sums had thus far been involved. In 1828 Ohio, in 1830 Maryland, in 1831 Mississippi, in 1832 Philadelphia and Baltimore, in 1833 Indiana and Alabama joined the lists. The City of Washington floated a loan in Amsterdam in 1830. The Louisiana loan of 1829 for the Planter's Association seems to have been the first to have been made payable in London at a fixed rate of exchange. Trotter, *passim; Financial & Commercial Record; Bankers' Magazine* (Baltimore) I:658–59. The bulk of the state and city securities made their appearance between 1835 and 1838.

The extent of the interest of London bankers in American finance is suggested by the distribution of the debt of Alabama at the end of the thirties. Hazard, *op. cit.*, III:334. Of a debt of $11½ millions, nearly $6 millions were payable in the first instance at one of the following London houses: Reid, Irving & Co., Rothschilds, Gowan & Marx, Magniac, Smiths & Co., Holford & Co., Prescott, Grote & Co., and Denison, Heywood & Co.

[26] Trotter, *op. cit.*, 290, 324–27 etc.; Callender, 160–62.

[27] *Times,* 27 April, 1829.

[28] *Times,* 5 Nov. 1842.

[29] *American Railroad Journal* (1839) pp. 30, 348.

[30] Quoted from *New York Express* in *National Daily Intelligencer,* 10 Sept. 1839.

[31] Mention has been found of the following private companies, part of whose shares or bonds were owned in England: Manhattan Banking Company; Girard Bank of Philadelphia (8,000 out of 30,000 shares. *Niles Reg.* XLVI:67); New York Life Insurance & Trust Co. (founded 1830, whose shares were first quoted in 1836); American Life Ins. & Trust Co. (advertising for deposit accounts in 1836); Ohio Life Ins. & Trust Co.; N. Y. Farmer's Loan & Trust Co.; North American Trust & Banking Co. (1838, ½ of 10 m. capital); Morris Canal & Banking Co.; Schuylkill Bank; Philadelphia & Reading Railway (shares and bonds); Iron Mountain Railroad (shares, by Rothschilds); bonds of numerous railways (Wilmington & Raleigh, Harrisburg & Lancaster, Camden & Amboy, Richmond); Union Gold Mining Co. (Va. $500,000 capital); Pa. Bituminous Coal, Land & Timber Co.; Hazleton (Pa.) Coal Co.; Lehigh Coal & Mining Co.; U. S. American Land Co. (£500,000 capital); Virginia Silk & Sugar Co. Considerable purchases of land were made, especially in

West Virginia, for re-sale to intending emigrants. There were also investments upon direct mortgage, specially thru New Orleans. John Wright & Co., which failed in 1840, had invested in New York mortgages. *Times*, 26 Nov. 1840.

[32] *Circular to Bankers*, 13 Jan. 1832.

[33] "Many English capitalists, who are habitually purchasers and holders of American stocks, will not touch an investment issued by a slave-holding state." *Circular to Bankers*, 8 Nov. 1839; *Westminster Review*, LII :213; *Am. Railroad Journal*, 25 June 1853, p. 401.

[34] Trotter complains of this difficulty. He was then or later member of Capel & Co., prominent stock-brokers of London.

[35] At least these were the circumstances dwelt upon by financial writers in recommending American securities for purchase. *Circular to Bankers*, 13 Jan., 5 Oct. 1832, 6 May 1837, 31 May 1839.

[36] The case of Sydney Smith is an example in point. See his *Letters on the American Debts* (London, 1843). The complaint of the injured bondholders for whom he wielded his brilliant pen was not that of disappointed investors but of liberals whose ideals had been betrayed as well as their pockets.

[37] *Circular to Bankers*, 23 Sept. 1842. *Niles Reg.* XLV: 179.

[38] An expression of the anticipated development of the Mississippi grain supply is in testimony of Joshua Bates, *Report of Committee on Commerce, Shipping, etc.* 1833 (690) # 896–905. Bates was advocating fixed grain duties. For an analysis of ultimate factors in the grain problem, see *Circular to Bankers*, 19 April 1839.

[39] See Wakefield, *England and America* (1833) and *The Art of Colonization* (1849). Considerations similar in some points are developed in the *Circular to Bankers*, 5 Oct. 1832, 12 Oct. 1838 and 31 May, 1839 and supplements to the issues of 27 Aug. and 24 Sept. 1840. The "decline of purchasing power" doctrine is here elaborated. "Water, steam and mechanism are creating goods and destroying customers."

[40] *London Shipping & Mercantile Gazette*, 2 Jan. 1840. Cf. *Circular to Bankers*, 16 Feb. 1838. £3,753,000 were invested in mills and machinery during 1834–36, with an estimated capacity of eighteen millions in value.

[41] Porter, *op. cit.* p. 327.

[42] This analysis is drawn chiefly from *Circular to Bankers*, 1 and 8 May, 3 July, 9 Oct., 6 and 20 Nov., 11 Dec. 1835.

[43] *Parl. Deb.* 33 : 688–91.

[44] Banks were opened in Australia, South Africa, Canada, Cuba and the Ionian Islands. Among the members of the group was Edward Blount, agent for the Duke of Norfolk. The same men were interested in the National Bank of Ireland founded in 1835. John

Wright & Co. failed in 1840. Two of the banks, the Bank of Australasia and the Ionian Bank, were still in existence in 1914.

[45] Isaac L. Goldsmid and Alderman W. Thompson were leading proprietors of the famous Royal Santiago (Cuba) mine. On the monopoly see *Hunt's Merch. Mag.* IX:143–46, 482. Prior to the development of the Lake Superior region which began in 1842, Cornwall, Cuba and Chili were the chief sources of copper supply.

[46] Palmer, J. Horsley, *Causes and Consequences of the Pressure in the Money Market* (London, 1837); Ricardo, Samson, *Observations on the recent Pamphlet of J. Horsley Palmer,* (1837); Duncan, Francis, *The English in Spain* (London, 1877).

[47] Nicolaï, Ldm., *Étude historique et critique sur la Dette Publique en Belgique* (Brux. 1921) ch. 2.

[48] Bullock, Williams & Tucker in *Harvard Rev. Econ. Stat.,* Prel. Vol. I: 217–19 display a balance-sheet of American trade for the "period" 1821–38. In main lines the discussion is sound. However, there is no sound basis for terminating a period in 1837. The $60,-000,000 (or $80,000,000, we are given two estimates in different places) allowed for accumulated interest by 1837 are simply grotesque. The amount can not have exceeded half the former sum. Contemporaries estimated the amount of specie carried by emigrants from Great Britain at £15 per head, instead of the $50 allowed. *Fin. Reg. of U. S.* I:59. And in the absence of any data at all upon tourist expenditure, the inclusion of an item of $11 millions respecting it seems to be a stroke of statistical genius. For a fuller analysis of the items in the balance of payments, contemporary and non-statistical, see article by A. B. J. in *Financial Register of U. S.* I, 304–14.

[49] These figures are taken from the report of Comptroller Flagg. In 1838 Garland estimated British investments in American stocks of all kinds at $110,000,000. *Niles Reg.* LIV:322. In 1843 a House Committee made an estimate of $150,000,000. *H. R. 296,* 27 Cong. 3 Sess. Callender computes a total of $300,000,000 loaned between 1815 and 1840, including mercantile credits. *op. cit.* 146. Bullock, Williams & Tucker allow only $125,000,000 for the period from 1821 to 1837, with an unsettled balance of payments against us of about $27,000,000. This is probably a slight understatement of both amounts.

[50] *Niles Reg.* XLVIII:74.

[51] *Hunt's Merch. Mag.* X:76–78; *Manchester Guardian,* 29 March, 1837.

[52] *Edinburgh Review,* LXV:235 (by J. R. McCulloch).

[53] *N. Y. American* 27 Nov. 1837; *Morning Chronicle* (London) 22 March 1837.

[54] *Circular to Bankers,* 27 May 1837. Testimony of William Ward, then governor of the Bank, *Report of Committee on Renewal of Bank Charter,* 1832, p. 2074. Testimony of J. Horsley Palmer, *Report of Committee upon Banking etc.,* 1838.

[55] *Circular to Bankers,* 23 Apr., 27 May, 1837. Tooke, *History of Prices,* II :264–73 argues that it was an oversupply of tea, cotton and silk that caused pressure upon overstrained credit relations. But it must be kept in mind that it was upon the trade in which those items figured prominently that the brunt of credit restriction fell. Silk declined in price from Dec. 1836, cotton from February; wool and iron were leading items in the subsequent slump.

[56] Besides the current comment in the *Circular to Bankers* for 1836 and 1837, the best contemporary accounts of the crisis are in Tooke, *op. cit.,* II : 279–345; *Edinburgh Review,* July 1837, LXV : 221–38; *U. S. Magazine & Democratic Review,* March 1838, pp. 383–402; and a speech by Samuel J. Tilden at New Lebanon, Oct. 3, 1840 (separately printed). The conduct of the Bank occasioned a pamphlet controversy in which J. Horsley Palmer, Samson Ricardo, David Salomons, Colonel Torrens and Thomas Tooke were leading contestants. McGrane, R. C., *The Panic of 1837,* is disappointing; it contributes to the reader's insight into nearly everything in the thirties except the panic itself.

[57] This relation is clearly analyzed in *Circular to Bankers,* 1 July 1837.

[58] The astute American minister in London, Andrew Stephenson of Virginia, is said to have reported that if the embarrassments continued, the Tories would be crushed, the money power crippled, democracy would triumph, and Ireland would be emancipated! *Niles Reg.* LII :82. If the State department files contain much of this sort of thing, it is readily understandable that national honor will dictate their continued suppression.

[59] Nicholas Biddle to John Quincy Adams, 10 Dec. 1838. *Niles Reg.* LV : 259.

[60] *Niles Reg.* LII : 65, 66, 81, 390; *Manchester Times,* 20.May, 1837.

[61] *Manchester Times* 29 Apr. 1837; *Circular to Bankers,* 28 April, 5 and 27 May, 1837.

[62] A rise of a penny in the pound on the 1837–38 crop, explains Vincent Nolte, *op. cit.,* p. 419, would make a difference of $11,500,000 in its market value.

[63] Report of Committee of Stockholders of the Bank of the United States, April 3, 1841 in Hazard, *op. cit.,* III :228–9 Letters of Biddle to J. Q. Adams, 10 Dec. 1838 and to J. M. Clayton, 8 April 1841, printed in Hazard, *op. cit.,* III :248–50. *Circular to Bankers* 15 June 1838. One of Biddle's operations is said to have involved the accept-

ance of champagne for cotton sold in France, and "Biddle champagne," labelled with the vignette of the Bank and the arms of Pennsylvania was on sale in Philadelphia at the end of 1837. *Times,* 1 Jan. 1838.

⁶⁴ *Morning Chronicle* (London) 11 Dec. 1838. That is to say, debts due within ninety days which could not be paid when due had been metamorphosed into debts due at longer dates whose payment it was not immediately necessary to think about.

⁶⁵ "American bills," i. e.—bills drawn upon houses in the United States or accepted by them. On Jaudon's agency, cf. *Circular to Bankers,* 11 Nov., 2 Dec. 1837, 16 Feb. 1838; *Morning Post* (London) 21 Nov. 1837. There had been earlier suggestions by American merchants that it was desirable to develop a market in London for American bills. See the letter of a merchant in *New York Express* 15 Oct. 1836, quoted in *Manchester Guardian,* 12 Nov. 1836. In defence of London exchange the following is worth quoting as representative:

"The distance which bills drawn on the U. S. have to travel, and the time that must of necessity elapse before the fate of them can be ascertained, is one great impediment to the negotiation of such bills (i. e. American bills) in Europe. The knowledge that the Americans have, in most cases, payments to provide for on this side of the water for manufactured articles also operates as an obstacle. The law of debtor and creditor in the U. S. is, moreover, said to be unfavorable to the recovery of debts in the part of the world by foreign claimants. Friendly assignments of property so as to evade payment are, we have been led to suppose, connived at by the civil authorities. . . . But the English merchant or manufacturer has another excellent reason for not departing from the present mode of settlement with his American debtor. The validity of a bill remitted to him from the U. S. is guaranteed by an ample re-exchange, in the event of dishonour. This is in the shape of damages which, in some parts of the Union, are upwards of 20 per cent." *Morning Post,* 21 Nov. 1837.

⁶⁶ *Morning Post,* 18 Nov. 1837; *Times,* 28 Jan., 9 Mar. 1838; *Circular to Bankers,* 23 Feb., 2 and 9 Mar. 1838; *Niles Reg.* LIV:161. The city articles of the *Times* for October and November, 1837 are full of ill-natured abuse of American credit, for which Jaudon is a frequent target. The *Post,* as organ of the Bank of England, had been very friendly to American securities, but became lukewarm if not hostile upon Jaudon's appearance. For a time the Bank refused to have anything to do with Jaudon or with Jaudon's paper. However Biddle forced the directors of the Bank to retire from this position by threatening to discredit the Bank's mercantile claims in

the United States. See Biddle's correspondence with Cowell, agent for the Bank in Philadelphia. *Circular to Bankers*, 28 May 1842. Possibly as a result of this contretemps, the Bank shipped one million pounds in gold to the United States in February, 1838 to facilitate resumption, an action which Tooke denounces as "mere quackery." *History of Prices*, III :79–81.

67 This system like that which preceded it was capable of a great deal of inflation. It was not long before bills were in circulation which had nothing to do with the cotton trade, but which formed a circuitous method of collecting the proceeds of security sales in London. Thus Biddle's paper reached London by way of Hong Kong and Bombay.

68 The Mississippi banks, for instance, held in 1839 but $109,791.17 in specie against liabilities in excess of $28,000,000. Hazard, III :173–75, 189.

69 Nolte, *Fifty Years* (1853) ch. 26.

70 The money articles in the *New York Herald* for 1837–40, written by Thomas P. Kettell, give the best account of these concerns. These were the first daily money articles published in the United States. Kettell continued with the *Herald* until Nov. 1843. Later he was proprietor of the *Democratic Review* and his monthly financial comment was a leading feature.

71 Quoted by *Daily Nat. Intelligencer* (Washington) March 9, 1839, from the *Richmond Enquirer*.

72 *Circular to Bankers*, 5 March 1841. Burgess refers in another connection to "that powerful money-sect, the Society of Friends, who may be said to be the leading operators, and most constant and extensive dealers in credit in both countries." *Ibid.*, 6 May, 1837.

73 Hazard, III :282.

74 This interest of course did not monopolize English opinion. The *Times* and the *Morning Herald* (Conservative) resisted the notion that any financial good could come out of the United States. But the jeremiads of the *Times* had begun as far back as 1832 and had pictured utter desolation in 1837. It never tired of berating that "nation of unprincipled blackguards and swindlers." The city columns of the *Morning Chronicle*, the *Courier* and the *Evening Sun* (all Whig) gave plenty of support in 1838 to those disposed to buy American stocks.

75 Tooke, III :73. *Circ. to Bankers*, 6 July, 26 Oct. 1838.

76 *Circular to Bankers*, 15 Nov. 1839. The refusal of China to receive opium coupled with the destruction of 2½ million pounds' worth of that commodity at Canton would have been enough in itself to cause high tension in the Anglo-American mercantile system.

77 News from Maine in March, 1839 suspended business in American

stocks. "They are all sellers and no buyers." *Circ. to Bankers,* 22 Mr. 1839; *Manchester Guardian,* 21 Mr. 1839; *Niles Reg.* LVI: 115–18. *Circ. to Bankers,* 23 Feb. 1838.

[78] Tooke, III:74. *Manchester Guardian,* 29 Dec. 1838, 3 July 1839.

[79] Report of Shareholders of Bank in Hazard III:228–29. The "cotton circular" issued by Biddle's group is printed in *National Intelligencer,* 15 June, 1839. Cf. *Ibid.,* 10, 13 June, 26 July 1839; *NY Express,* 7 June 1839; *NY American,* 11 June 1839; *Manch. Guard.,* 3 July 1839.

[80] *National Intelligencer,* 29 July, 6 Nov. 1839. This movement was associated with the Macon Convention called for October 22. Cf. Russel, R. R., *Economic Aspects of Southern Sectionalism* Urbana, 1922) ch. I. This was a more public expression of plans earlier considered to develop "direct trade." British consuls in the United States had wind of them in 1837, and exhorted Palmerston to give them encouragement. In August, 1837, James Baker, consul to Mobile, appeared in London as agent for the Planters' and Merchants' Bank of that city to open an account with the Bank of England. He assured Palmerston that if direct trade developed political separation would follow. It would be automatic and cost Palmerston nothing. "J. O. S." wrote repeatedly to the Foreign Office to the same effect from Philadelphia, and even considered that Jaudon would be helpful. The communications are at *F. O.* 5:316.

[81] The issues of *Circular to Bankers,* 13 Sept. to 18 Oct. and 13 Dec. 1839 give the arrangements made to carry the post-notes of the Bank.

[82] Hazard, III:228–29, 261–64.

NOTES TO CHAPTER FOUR

[1] *Cong. Globe* VIII:245. *Sen. Docs.* 26 Cong. I Sess. IV, 153. A last-minute clause in the resolutions disclaimed any desire to throw doubt upon the constitutional right of the states to get into debt, or upon their ability to fulfil their engagements. The tone of the debate, in which some speakers showed apprehension lest the American farmer be reduced to a serf grovelling under the whip of the foreign moneylender, was not so reassuring.

[2] Hazard, III, *passim.*

[3] Oberholtzer, E. P., *Jay Cooke, Financier of the Civil War* (Philadelphia 1907) I:67–8.

4 *Hunt's Merchants' Mag.*, X:78.

5 *H. R. 296. 27* Cong. 3 Sess. p. 117.

6 *North American Review*, LI :335.

7 The case of Pennsylvania is important and representative. Her public works cost $33,464,975 to build. During the years of their operation they earned a total revenue of only $32,505,563, with operating expenses of $24,471,225. Pennsylvania began borrowing to meet interest as early as 1829, and her total bill for dividends was $43,-675,034. The works when sold to private corporations brought $11,-281,000. Bishop, *The State Works of Pennsylvania*, p. 286. Pennsylvania's total indebtedness in July, 1842 was more than $34,-000,000, of which $23,738,000 were held abroad. *Ibid.*, 216.

8 Annual message of Governor Grayson of Maryland, *Niles Reg.*, March 28, 1840.

9 The message of Governor McNutt of Mississippi, February 5, 1841, vetoing legislative resolutions which recognized the validity of a certain bond issue, contains some memorable passages :

"The Bank (i. e.—of the United States) . . . has hypothecated these bonds, and borrowed money upon them of the Baron Rothschild. The blood of Judas and Shylock flows in his veins, and he unites the qualities of both his countrymen. He has mortgages on the silver mines of Mexico, and the quicksilver mines of Spain. He has advanced money to the Sublime Porte, and taken as security, a mortgage on the Holy City of Jerusalem, and the Sepulchre of our Saviour. It is for the people to say whether he shall have a mortgage on our cotton fields, and make serfs of our children." Hazard, III :273–77.

10 *Times*, 2 Jan. 1847, 5b : *Hunt's Merch. Mag.*, VI :478–79. B. R. Curtis in *North Am. Rev.*, LVIII :109–54; *U. S. Mag. & Dem. Rev.*, March, 1845. A detailed discussion of the "Debts and Finances of the States of the Union" is contained in a series of articles by Thomas P. Kettell which appeared in *Hunt's Merchants' Magazine*, XVII :466, 577; XVIII :243; XX :256, 481; XXI :148, 389; XXII : 131.

11 George Peabody in *Baltimore Patriot*, 26 Dec. 1842. While public investments in the U. S. ceased, investments in real estate and industrial undertakings continued. In 1844 Baring Brothers bought up at public sale the Merchants' Exchange in New York City for $900,000. *American Memoranda* (London, 1844) p. 9. The Mount Savage Iron Works (Md.) with a capital of $1,500,000, in which the manufacture of railway iron in the U. S. began in 1844 was mainly owned in Great Britain. *Shareholder* (London) Nov. 12, 1845. Two British packing houses were opened in Cincinnati in 1842, in anticipation of a relaxation in British tariffs. *Times*, 1 Dec. 1842.

[12] *Times,* 31 Oct. 1844.

[13] Smith, Sydney, *Letters on the American Debts* (2nd ed. London. 1844, first published in the *Morning Chronicle,* Nov. 1843).

[14] First printed in *Times,* 19 May 1843. An answer, *The Americans Defended, by an American* (London 1844) is not in the British Museum. Smith's investment was in fact made out of a legacy which had been recently acquired.

[15] *Bankers' Magazine* (Baltimore) II:201–05. *U. S. Economist* 14 Jan. 1854, p. 218.

[16] *Times,* May 5, 1842.

[17] Duff Green to John C. Calhoun, 24 Jan. 1842, in *The Correspondence of John C. Calhoun* (Washington 1900) 841–42.

[18] Overend, Gurney & Co. to Colonel Robinson, Oct. 3, 1842, printed in *Circular to Bankers,* Apr. 21, 1843. This was not a new suggestion. It had been contained in a famous circular of Baring Brothers, sent out in October, 1839, which featured as an issue in the campaign of 1840. Webster intimated publicly that credit for the idea belonged to Samuel Jaudon.

[19] *H. R.* 120, 27 Cong. 3 Sess. Jan. 30, 1843; *H. R.* 296, 27 Cong. 3 Sess., Mar. 3, 1843.

[20] *Times,* 20 Feb. 1843; *Hunt's Merch. Mag.* VIII:272. A story in the *New York Herald* for 15 Jan. 1845 relates that revival in American trade was initiated by a group of speculators of London, Liverpool and Havre. They exported specie to the United States, and used it in the American markets to corner cotton. The consequent rise in price stimulated a resumption of commercial activity in Atlantic port towns.

[21] *Times,* 12 Jan. 1843.

[22] *Times,* 16 May, 27 June, 11 July 1843; 20 July, 1844; *Hunt's Merch. Mag.* XII:279–81; XIV:177, 363; XV:508.

[23] *Times,* 28 June, 1843.

[24] The exception was constituted by the stocks and bonds of a few railways, notably the Erie and Illinois Central, in the fifties. Pennsylvania resumed payment of her dividends, at a discount, in February, 1845; other states followed. During 1846 and 1847 large quantities of American stocks were reabsorbed in the United States in payment for grain exports. In the two following years merchant-bankers recommenced their practice of accepting American stocks in settlement of balances. Thus the secondary finance of the Mexican war was performed by aid of British capital.

[25] Humboldt, Alexander, *Political Essay on the Kingdom of New Spain* (London 1811) Book VI.

[26] Humboldt, Books IV and V; Ward, T. H., *Mexico* (2nd edit. London. 1829) Book 3, sec. 5, esp. pp. 327, 336 and also pp. 392–404;

Bancroft, H. H., *History of Mexico* (San Francisco 1888) V:59–61, VI:505–06.

[27] Ward, pp. 267–304; Bancroft, VI:492–98; Prieto, G. *Indicaciones sobre el Origen, Vicisitudes y Estado que garden actualmente las Rentas Generales de la Federacion Mexicana* (Mexico. 1850). The introduction to this book stresses the social causes of Mexico's economic backwardness.

[28] *Bancroft*, VI:468.

[29] Ward, 291–92; Payno y Flores, Manuel: *Mexico y sus Cuestiones financieras* (Mexico 1862) p. 7. On the history of the debt there is a rich literature. Casasus, J. D., *Historia de la Deuda Contraida en Londres* (Mexico. 1885); Ramero, *Memoria de Hacienda y Credito Publico* (Mexico. 1870. official); McCaleb, W. F., *The Public Finances of Mexico* (NY 1921); *Fenn on the Funds; Times*, 19 Sept. 1843 (city articles).

[30] *Parl. Deb., N. S.*, 24:875–907.

[31] Casasus, *op. cit.*, pp. 141–72. Adams, E. D., *British Interests and Activities in Texas, 1838–1846* (Baltimore. 1910). Adams reaches the conclusion that the Texan policy of Palmerston and Aberdeen was not influenced by the bondholders. The Mexican correspondence of the *Times* during 1839 advocates repeatedly proposals to cede part of the territory outright to the creditors, who should organize a company on the model of the East India Company for its exploitation. Similar projects sponsored by the British, minister, Pakenham, and Barron, Forbes & Co., reached the Foreign Office in 1841 and were summarily disposed of by Aberdeen. Adams, 237–40.

[32] *Times*, 19, 23 Sept. 1843; Casasus, pp. 245–309; Murphy, C. Tómas, *Memoria sobre la Deuda Esterior de la Republica Mexicana* (Paris 1848).

[33] Payno, p. 49. The exact figures according to his accounting were $29,535,937.94.

[34] The city articles of the *Times* from 1840 to 1846 have been of assistance in making this synthesis.

[35] *F. O.* 18:2. J. Planta to Henry Hughes, 19 May 1823.

[36] *Ibid.*, J. Planta to Herring & Co., 24 Oct. 1823.

[37] *F. O.* 50:103. J. Backhouse to R. P. Staples, 18 June 1829 and Thomas Kinder to Palmerston, 23 Sept. 1836.

[38] *F. O.* 18:10. J. Planta to William Clarke, 27 April 1824.

[39] Temperley, H. W. V., "The Later American Policy of George Canning," *Am. Hist. Rev.* XI:780–81.

[40] *Correspondence on Foreign Loans*. 1847 (157) #156,157. *Correspondence on Foreign Loans*. 1854 (53) #94,103. These bluebooks contain numerous examples of the "unofficial representations" which the Foreign Office permitted itself to make freely.

⁴¹ *Times*, 23 April, 1829.

⁴² G. R. Robinson to Col. Ytterreguy, 26 Feb. 1847 in *Times*, 13 Mar. 1847. *Fenn on the Funds.*

⁴³ Parish, H. H., *Diplomatic and Financial History of Greece* (1838) pp. 204–08, chapters 7 and 8, and App. 65ff.

⁴³ᵃ Maxwell, Sir H. E., *Life and Letters of the Earl of Clarendon* (1913) I :184–98.

⁴⁴ *Times*, 4 Nov. 1842, 16–Mar. 1843.

⁴⁵ *Times*, 23 Apr. 1829 (edit.). "A British Minister can really take no official steps to enforce the settlement of claims which a subject of the empire may have upon the foreign Government," said the *Times* upon another occasion, adding that some of the South American states might have hazier notions as to the powers of British ministers, and that any wholesome illusion to that effect was to be encouraged. *Ibid.*, 31 Jan. 1845 (money art.). "The British Government does not interfere by any other than moral force to induce foreign Governments to fulfil their loan obligations, unless there is some absolute robbery of assigned property." *Ibid.*, 25 Jan. 1861, 5a.

⁴⁶ For instance, F. Warrington, chairman of a committee of Mexican bondholders asked Palmerston, Jan. 30, 1836, to intervene upon their behalf in Mexico or to permit reprisals. The reply, 24 Feb., was a flat refusal to use anything but "unofficial representations." *F. O.* 50:103. Ricardos urged 31 Dec. 1833 that an exception be made in the case of the Greek debt, without success. *F. O.* 32:40. The notion that the government owed a duty of protection to foreign investors was voiced very rarely. William Burge in *Times*, 10 June 1843; *Loans by Private Individuals to Foreign States entitled to Government Protection by the Fundamental Laws as a Branch of Trade* (London, 1842).

⁴⁷ The following are some of the materials used for the account of the Rio Plate intervention: Pfeil, A. R., *The Anglo-French Intervention in the River Plate* (London 1847); Idem, *Resumé des Affaires de la Plate* (Paris 1849); Baines, Thomas, *Observations on the Present State of Affairs in the Plate* (Liverpool 1845); Bourguignat, *La Question de la Plate* (Paris 1849); de Montrenal, L. T., *La Plate au point de vue des interêts commerciaux de la France* (Paris 1851); Parish, Woodbine, *Buenos Ayres and the Provinces of the Rio de la Plate* (2nd edit. London 1852); Shuttleworth, N. L. K., *Life of Woodbine Parish* (London 1910); Latham, W., *The States of the River Plate* (London 1868); *Edinburgh Review*, LXXXVII:564; *Economist*, 6 Nov. 1847, p. 1273.

⁴⁸ *Cambridge History of British Foreign Policy* (London 1920–22) II:185–98. A lively contemporary account of the feeling

created by the episode is Hughes, T. M., *An Overland Journey to Lisbon at the close of 1846* (2 vols. London 1847).

[49] *Times,* 17, 27 Oct., 3, 10 Nov. 1846.

[50] *Hansard's Parl. Deb.,* 3 ser. XCIII:1285–1307.

[51] *State Papers, British & Foreign,* XLII, 385.

NOTES TO CHAPTER FIVE

The Literature of the Railway History of Great Britain and the Continent.—The first important economic history of British railways was published in London as this work went to press, and was unavailable for reference. It constitutes Volume I of a *British Economic History in the Nineteenth Century* by Professor J. H. Clapham of Cambridge University. The early work of Francis, John, *History of the English Railway; its Social Relations and Revelations, 1820–1845* (London 1851) and the recent treatise of Jackman, W. T., *The Development of Transportation in Modern England* (2 vols. Toronto. 1916) stop short at 1845. Pratt, E. A., *History of Inland Transport and Communication in England* (London 1912) is fragmentary. The treatment in Knowles, L. C. A., *The Industrial and Commercial Revolutions* (London 1921) pp. 253–90 is built about the problem of state control. For an account of the financial aspects of the rise of the railway, one may go back to Tooke & Newmarch, V:348–90. Clarke, Hyde, *Theory of Railway Investment* (London 1846) discusses with a good deal of penetration the way in which capital was found for building railways. Cf. his articles in *Railway Register,* IV:163–77, 211–27, and 301 ff.

For English readers, Clapham, J. H., *The Economic Development of France and Germany 1815–1915* (London 1921) ch. 6 and 7 is the best introduction to the coming of the railway in France and Belgium. There are innumerable annalistic accounts in French of railway development, mostly concerned with the infinitely tangled relations with the government. Audiganne, A., *Les Chemins de Fer Aujourd'hui et dans Cent Ans* (2 vols. Paris 1858–62) is a curious work, nevertheless of merit. The *Œuvres de Isaac et Emile Pereire* (whose publication was suspended by the war) promises to be a mine of documentary source material.

Loisel, F., *Annuaire Spécial des Chemins de Fer Belges* (Bruxelles 1867) contains the annals of early railways in Belgium.

[1] *Economist*, 4 Oct. 1845, pp. 950–51. With this issue begins a railway supplement, and it contains the best contemporary analysis of the effects of the railway revolution upon the capital market.

[2] *Circular to Bankers*, 21 Oct. 1842.

[3] *Trueman & Cook's Overland Despatch*, 1 June, 1 Aug., 2 Oct., 2 Dec. 1843. For further details of the depression, cf. Page I: 141 ff. and *Parl. Deb.* LXIV: 861 ff.

[4] Scrivenor, Henry, *The Railways of the United Kingdom Statistically Considered* (London 1849) App. pp. 58 ff; Williams, F. S., *Our Iron Roads* (7th ed. London 1885) p. 39; *Herapath's Railway Journal*.

[5] Data from Porter, *Progress of the Nation* (1851) p. 327 and Tooke & Newmarch, V:352, which are in turn compiled from numerous parliamentary returns, made up from voluntary reports.

[6] Williams, F. S., pp. 138–51; Francis, John, *History of the English Railway*, (2 vols. 1851) II, ch. 3.

[7] Tooke & Newmarch, V:355–57.

[8] Porter, p. 336.

[9] Slosson, Preston, *The Decline of the Chartist Movement.* (New York, 1918).

[10] Disraeli, *Endymion*, (1881) chapter 58.

[11] At least not as directors of English railways. A number of these names turn up in shareholders' lists.

[12] Spackman, W. F., *Statistical Tables of the United Kingdom and its Dependencies* (London 1843) tabulates the nominal value of securities quoted at that time upon the Stock Exchange:

British and Irish funded debt	£773,000,000
Loans to foreign govts and Am. States	121,501,410
70 Railway companies	57,447,903
Banking interest	46,449,694
59 Canal companies	17,862,445
8 Dock companies	12,177,237
Turnpike Trusts	8,774,927
East India Company	6,000,000
South Sea Company	3,662,734
24 foreign mining companies	6,464,833
81 British mining companies	4,500,000
107 Assurance companies	26,000,000
27 gas, light and coke companies	4,326,870
11 water companies	2,536,122
5 bridge companies	2,123,874

4 Literary institutions	1,003,125
196 shipping, land, asphalte, loan etc., companies	25,000,000
Total 612 companies	£224,229,754.

Within the following ten years the volume of the public debt was surpassed by that of other securities quoted on the stock market.

[13] A parliamentary return supplies the most exact evidence. Of the capital promised upon subscription lists filed in the Private Bill Office during the session of Parliament in the spring of 1845, more than £21,000,000 had been subscribed in sums less than £2,000. These had been pledged by more than 20,000 people and the amounts ranged as low as one hundred pounds. During the same period sixty million pounds were subscribed in sums of more than £2000 each, by some 5000 gentlemen and merchants. *Railway Subscription Lists, Accounts & Papers.* 1845. #317 and 625.

[14] Tooke & Newmarch, V:234.

[15] **The Financial Press.** Financial news occupied special departments in the daily newspapers of London and leading provincial towns. There was a regular money article for which in the thirties material was written and gathered up at the North & South American Coffee House. Correspondence of *NY Commercial Advertiser,* quoted in *Daily Nat. Intell.* 27 Aug. 1839. See also *Tait's Edinburgh Rev.,* suppl., Dec. 1834. The scope of this article embraced trade and exchanges and everything else that to an informed person might have a bearing upon the markets for short-term loans or long investments. The first financial weekly was the *Circular to Bankers,* which existed in several forms from 1827 to 1860, but which is distinctly less forceful after 1846. The appeal of this sort of journalism, however, was to those who were professionally interested in the money market, at least until the rise of the *Daily News* and other penny journals in the fifties.

The first publication for the benefit of a wider public was the *Mining Journal,* begun by Henry English in 1834. It did not limit its attention to the numerous mines in which British capital was employed, their technical progress and business prospects. It carried news of other companies as well. In the same year a monthly *Railway Magazine* was started by George Walter, which later became a weekly. The *Railway Times* was the first weekly. *Herapath's Railway Journal,* founded in 1838, survived into the twentieth century with a high standard of journalistic excellence, and in the forties and fifties was freest from the taint of devotion to particular interests.

During the forties rivals multiplied rapidly. There was the *Railway Record*, begun in 1844 by John Robertson, an experienced railway journalist; the *Railway Chronicle*, more scientific, supposed to be devoted to Liverpool interests: an *Irish Railway Gazette*, concerned with Irish projects; the *Railway Herald*, specializing in foreign railway news. In December, 1844, Hyde Clarke founded the *Railway Register*, a monthly review which attempted for three years more serious journalistic work. At the height of the mania in 1845 there were 20 publications, weekly, semi-weekly, and a morning and an evening daily, exploiting the demand of company promoters for advertising and the curiosity of shareholders for news of their concerns. An Englishman crossed the Channel and founded a *Journal des Chemins de Fer* in Paris in 1842. And the *Economist*, founded in 1843 to champion the principles of free trade, was devoting an ever-increasing portion of its space to joint-stock company projects, and issued for a time in 1845 and 1846 its *Railway Monitor* as a weekly supplement. Evans, D. M., *The Commercial Crisis of 1847-48* (London, 1848) p. 10; Hyde Clarke in *Railway Register* (1845) Vol. I, intro.; *Tercentenary Hand-list of Newspapers . . .* (London 1920).

[16] Williams, F. S., *The Midland Railway, its Rise and Progress* (London, 1876) p. 25; *Journ. des Chemins de Fer*, 3 Jan. 1846.

[17] Francis, *Hist. of the Eng. Ry.* I :266–73, II :76–7.

[18] *Men of the Time* (London 1865) p. 320.

[19] Helps, Arthur, *The Life and Labours of Mr. Brassey* (London 1872).

[20] Galt, William, *Railway Reform* (London 1865) 348–50.

[21] Galt, p. 352; Francis, II : 83–4.

[22] Three small railways, operated partly by stationary engines, partly by horse-power, were built in the twenties in the vicinity of Lyons. One of these lines, the *St. Étienne-Lyons*, used a steam locomotive over part of its line for passengers, but it did not abandon horse-power until 1844. Audiganne, A., "Origine et periode d'invention des chemins de fer," *Rev. des Deux Mondes*, 15 Jan. 1855, pp. 354–64; Picard, A., *Les Chemins de Fer Françaises* (Paris, 1884) I :11; *Hommes & Choses de P.-L.-M.* (Paris, 1911 private) p. 28.

[23] *Bulletin des Lois*, 1835, 2nd sem., suppl. p. 845. for the articles of incorporation. Since these articles almost always contain in the allotment of shares and other financial arrangements, they are of great importance for the history of all French *sociétés anonymes* in the middle of the century. Baron Salomon von Rothschild at Vienna was similarly a pioneer in the financing of Austrian railways from 1836 when he organized the *Kaiser-Ferdinand Bahn* in Bo-

hemia. Czedek, A. Fr. v., *Der Weg von und zu den Oesterreichischen Staatsbahnen* (Wien, 1913) I:29–39.

24 According to Picard, I: 234, there were 569 kilometers in France in 1842, for which 179,000,000 francs had been expended. These were widely scattered. The most important line was from Strasburg to Basel, 140 kilometers, in charge of *Nicholas Koechlin et cie.* of Mulhouse. Audiganne, A., "Les chemins de fer sous le Gouvernement de juillet," *Rev. des Deux Mondes,* 15 Fev. 1855, pp. 825–36 is an excellent narrative of the government's attitude. Grippon-Lamotte, L., *Historique du réseau des chemins de fer de France,* (Issoudun, 1904) pp. 1–59, quotes relevant passages from speeches of Lamartine, Thiers and others.

25 The first steam railway opened in Europe, was the line from Brussels to Mechlin, May 5, 1835. In the Germanies, Bavaria (1835) and Saxony (1837) were ahead of Prussia (1838) in commencing railway operation.

26 *London Quarterly Review,* Oct. 1868, pp. 160 ff; Dobson, Edward, *An Historical, Statistical and Scientific Account of the Railways of Belgium from 1834 to 1842* (London 1843); Boulger, Demetrius, *History of Belgium,* (London 1910–25) II:276: Demarteau, L., *Histoire de la Dette Publique Belge.* (Bruxelles 1886) ch. 8–11.

27 *Railway Register,* II, 32–34. Belgium thus seems to have been the first modern country to construct public works in a deliberate attempt to relieve unemployment. She was three years in advance of New York state.

28 *Journ. des Chem. de Fer,* 13 Feb., 1 Mr., 1842; 1 Mr. 1843; On Cockerill's project, Picard, I:52–55 and *Biographie Nationale de Belgique; J. Chem. de Fer.,* 26 Nov. 1842.

29 The prospectus of this company is in *Times,* 13 Aug. 1836. The best guide to the legislative history of French companies is the six-volume work of Picard previously cited.

30 *Memoirs of Sir Edward Blount* (London 1902) ch. 4; Helps, *Life of Mr. Brassey,* ch. 4 and 5; Devey, Joseph, *Life of Joseph Locke* (London 1862); Fay, Sir Sam, *A Royal Road, being a History of the London & Southwestern* (London 1883); Testimony of Thomas Brassey and William Reed in *Second Report from the Select Committee on Railway Acts Enactments.* 1846 (687); *Bulletin des Lois,* 1840, suppl. 2nd. sem. p. 65; *Times,* 5 June 1840 (prospectus); *Journal des Chemins de Fer,* 3 and 10 Sept. 1842, 9 May 1843, etc.

31 It must be understood that the concession was not in perpetuity, but for a strictly limited term of years. The arrangements in this respect concluded by the governments of Louis Philippe were

generally made more liberal by reorganizations during the Second Empire.

[32] *Railway Register*, III:359. The promoters sold their *Paris-Rouen* shares at 100% profit. By the end of 1846 it was thought that the English had made at least five million pounds upon their original investment in French railways. *Ry. Register*, IV:259–61.

[33] For this report and current opinion see the issues of *Journ. Chem. de Fer*, 26 Nov. 1842 to 7 Jan. 1843.

[34] *Times*, 3 August, 1844. Stephenson had recommended the Calais route, as the company's English terminus was Dover. And with this in mind application was made for the "Nord" in 1843, and a concession was actually made by the ministry of public works. Boulogne interests were powerful in the Chambers, however, and the English were obliged to withdraw. *J. Chem. de Fer*, 11 Mr., 13 May, 1843. At that time the group had the support of Glyn, Halifax & Mills and of James de Rothschild. For subscription list, see *Bull. des Lois*, 1845, 2nd sem., suppl. pp. 779–815.

[35] *J. Chem. de Fer*, 7 Jan. 1843; *Times*, 28 Feb. 1843; *Pigot & Slater's Manchester Directory*. 1841. Barry proposed to get his capital and build the *Orléans-Tours* line within two years, if the French government would admit iron rails duty free. His mission appears to have been in the first instance that of business getter for iron manufacturers. However there were also iron manufacturers in France, and when the project got definitely under way in 1844, one of them appeared as a promoter, entitled to 10% of all the profits above 6%. The *Orléans-Tours* line was finally built by Mackenzie & Brassey, who employed American excavating machines, and laid a mile of track a day. Thirty locomotives were ordered in England; the balance of the rolling-stock was built in France. *Times*, 17 Aug. 1845.

[36] *Blount's Memoirs*, ch. 6. The details of this paragraph are drawn from innumerable references mainly in the *Times* and *Journal des Chemin de Fer*, and prospectuses there published. The Mackenzie group also associated themselves with companies formed in 1845 to bid for the *Paris-Strasburg, Paris-Lyons*, and *Lyons-Avignon* concessions, and shared in the allotment. After numerous reorganizations of the various companies in western France in which it had an interest, the group organized the "Compagnie de l'Ouest," which in 1855 took over all lines running west from Paris thru Brittany and Normandy, including the *Paris-St. Germain, Paris-Versailles, Paris-Havre* and lines terminating in Rennes and Cherbourg. Of this company, Blount was chairman until 1894 when a burst of patriotism forced his retirement. *Memoirs*, pp. 91–92. *Bull. des*

Lois, 1st ser. suppl. 1855, p. 1221. The property of the company was taken over by the French government upon the expiry of its concession in 1909. One of the Belgian lines, the *Tournay, Jurbise & Hasselt,* sold out to the Belgian government in 1900, but in 1914 there were still financial interests being handled in London thru the agency of Thomson, Bonar & Co.

[37] *Le Courrier de l'Europe,* 22 Mr. 1845. The shares of companies which won concessions were usually held pretty closely by promoters and their friends. However the *Bordeaux-Cette* company, awarded Sept. 24, 1846 to a coalition of the Mackenzie group with a Quaker-Jewish combination headed by David Salomons, had 13,000 original subscribers, most of whom were English. *Bull. des Lois,* 1846, 2nd sem., suppl. 233-362.

[38] According to *The Shareholder,* 8 Oct. 1845, up to the end of September there had appeared 66 foreign railway projects in London, calling for £190,010,000 in capital. These figures include capital offered for subscription in foreign money markets. And the companies include a number of "bubbles." My own computations are based upon the *Times* prospectuses, checked by such information respecting allotments, etc., as came to light in the financial publications which were handled. The figures are not necessarily exhaustive. On the French railway mania in general, cf. *Ann. de l'Économie Politique,* 1846, pp. 264-79.

[39] *Morning Post,* 11 Jan. 1843. Cf. *Times,* 12 Jan. 1846, 5b.

[40] *Circular to Bankers,* 2 Nov. 1844.

[41] *J. Chem. de Fer,* 4 Feb. 1843; *Times,* 19 Nov. 1845, 3b.

[42] *Blount's Memoirs,* p. 273.

[43] For instance, George R. Dawson, Peel's brother-in-law, was director in the company organized by Charles Laffitte to bid for the *Paris-Lyons* railway (*Times,* 10 Mr. 1845) and of the Lefebvre company seeking the *Tours-Nantes* concession (*Times,* 10 Feb. 1845).

[44] Reports of sessions of the *Chambre des Pairs,* 13 and 15 Feb. 1845; *Le Courrier de l'Europe,* 1 Mar. 1845, p. 140; *Times,* 17 Mar. 1845, 5d. As far as the railway promoters themselves were concerned they were the dove of peace. Engineers pressed upon France a choice between armed peace with policies of suspicion and provocation, and railway building with persuasion and economic expansion. Cf. Teisserenc, Ed., *De la Politique des Chemins des Fer* (Paris 1842).

[45] Audiganne, A., in *Rev. des Deux Mondes,* 15 Feb. 1855.

[46] *J. Chem. de Fer,* 30 Aug. 1845.

[47] Details of the fused company are in *Times,* 29 Aug. 1845 and *J. Chem. de Fer,* 30 Aug. 1845. The following are the English

allottees whose nationality is readily recognizable, with the number of shares assigned to each:

Baring Brothers	8000	J. D. Powles	2000
Denison, Heywood & Co.	8000	Joseph Esdaile	2000
Morris, Prevost & Co.	4400	Andr. Spottiswoode	2000
Morrison, Sons & Co.	4400	L. Murray	2000
I. L. Goldsmid	4400	Francis Mowat	5381
A. J. Paull	2000	T. M. Weguelin	5125
John Gattley	2000	Pratt Barlow	5125
Thomas Cooke	2000	W. Magnay	5125
John Shewell	2000	T. O. Powels	500
Francis Mills	1250	David Salomons	1250
J. Hopkinson	2000		

The shares distributed thru the London Rothschilds can not be distinguished. The English directors included Francis and Thomas Baring, John Moss, John Masterman, William Chaplin, Francis Mills, T. M. Weguelin and T. O. Powels. Probably about one-third of the shares, or two million pounds, were marketed in the first place in England. The management, however, was from the first in the hands of Baron James de Rothschild, the president, and his agents.

[48] "Fusions" worked to the disadvantage of English share in the original allotments, since frequently weak French companies were organized in order to make certain of participation in the allotment of shares that were certain to command a premium. However, no very exact computations can be based upon the shareholders' lists published in the *Bulletin des Lois,* in view of the cosmopolitan character of the clientele of firms like that of Edward Blount, which were prominent among the large subscribers.

[49] *Economist,* 23 Jan. 1847, p. 111.

[50] *Railway Register,* III:359. Cf. *Times,* 19 Nov. 1845.

[51] Guyot & Raffalovitch, *Dictionnaire du Commerce* (Paris 1898) II:254–55.

[52] The Queen Mother of Spain was one of the original subscribers to the Central Railway (Orléans-Vierzon), *Bull. des Lois,* 1845, 2d ser., suppl., 462–90. At the beginning of 1847 the Czar of Russia made large investments in gold in French rentes. *Morning Chronicle,* 20 and 22 Mar. 1847.

[53] *Shareholder,* 15 Oct. 1845.

[54] The companies were: Sambre & Meuse, West Flanders, Namur & Liege, Charleroi & Erquelines, Tournay, Jurbise, Landen & Hasselt, Anglo-Belgian, Belgian Grand Junction and Great Luxembourg.

For this period of Belgian railway history, see Laveleye, E de, *Histoire des vingt-cing ans* (Brussels). There were other companies formed, which did not survive.*

[55] Andrew Spottiswoode at first meeting of shareholders, *Railway Register,* III :412–13.

[56] *Railway Register,* II :296–98.

[57] *Ibid.,* III :207.

[57a] *Ibid.,* IV : 260 ff. There was no public quotation of railway shares in Belgium until 1847. *Moniteur Belge,* 30 Mar. 1847.

[58] James Wilson in *Economist,* 28 Mar. 1846, pp. 401–03; 1847, pp. 87–89, 143–44, 172–74 develops this theory of the causes of the panic at length. On the other hand, absolving the railways from blame, are Martin, R. M., *Railways—Past, Present and Prospective* (London 1849) pp. 42–56 and Clarke, Hyde, *Theory of Railway Investment.*

[59] *Economist,* 21 Oct. 1848.

[60] Galt, William, *Railway Reform* (1865); Smith, Arthur, *The Bubble of the Age* (London 3rd ed. 1848); "How we got up the Glenmutchkin Railway, and how we got out of it," *Blackwood's Mag.,* Oct. 1845; *Morning Chronicle,* 19 Jan. 1847, 2c.

[61] Evans, D. M., pp. 32, 51, 107.

[62] Tooke & Newmarch, V : 352.

[63] Lord Sandon in House of Commons, *Parl. Deb.,* 3rd ser. LXXXV : 891.

[64] Andréades, A., *History of the Bank of England,* pp. 331–42.

[65] Cf. Morrison, James, *The Influence of English Railway Legislation on Trade and Industry* (1848) p. 71. Morrison was himself a considerable investor in foreign rails.

[66] Hubbard, J. G., *Letter to Sir Charles Wood, Chancellor of the Exchequer* (1847) quoted by Morrison; *Economist,* 21 Aug. 1847, p. 954; Testimony of Joshua Bates, Samuel Gurney, J. Pears, James Morris and Adam Hodgson in *Report of Commons Committee on Commercial Distress* 1847–48, #605–8, 1927–29, 3502, 4589–91, 2458–60, 2579–80, 2614–31.

[67] According to the *Circular to Bankers,* 19 Nov. 1847, the balance of accounts against Great Britain for the current year had been 24 million pounds, which had been paid,—10 million in bullion, 6 million in securities sold to Europe, one million in securities sent to the United States, 4 million due Great Britain from old balances, and 3 million in defalcations and unpaid mercantile debt. Cf. *Economist,* 18 Mar. 1848.

[68] *J. Chem. de Fer* VI :811–16, 830–32, 848–50; *Railway Register,* III :425–46.

[69] Relief was not obtained until the fifties, for one from the Nord,

which wanted a connection to Brussels; for another from Mr. Brassey with his organization to keep employed; for others in a more enlightened policy upon the part of the Belgian government which guaranteed dividends upon the capital in order to get "feeder" lines constructed to enhance the revenues of the state railways. By this time the capital accounts of all were highly watered, and they never became high-class investments that had been anticipated.

[70] Normanby, *A Year of Revolution* (London 1850) pp. 262–65.

[71] *Ibid.*, pp. 178–79, 230–31, 266–67; *J. Chem. de Fer*, VI: 640; *Œuvres de Emile & Isaac Pereire.* . . . Series G. III (Paris 1913) pp. 2610–17.

NOTES TO CHAPTER SIX

Sources of Information for British Enterprise upon the Continent.—The activities of British enterprise upon the Continent during the conquest of the latter by industrialism form an almost forgotten chapter of history. Scholarship in France, Germany, Austria, Switzerland and Russia has been more attentive to the recent economic annals of those countries than British scholars have been even to their own. But this chapter may fairly claim to be the first attempt to show the influence of Great Britain upon the economic transformation of the Continent generally. It is to be hoped that it may harbinger a more exhaustive report. For such a purpose the existing secondary literature is of value only as a background.

The basis for this account consists mainly in the news columns and market reports of the financial press; reports of directors and of shareholders' meetings in the same; manuals, almanacs, directories, year-books and commercial dictionaries; the reports of British consuls and secretaries of embassy and legation; testimony taken by various parliamentary committees; contemporary periodical and pamphlet literature; and, in a few instances, the Foreign Office papers at the Public Record Office in London.

The prospectuses carried in the advertising pages of the *Times,* with accompanying comments in its City column and in the financial weeklies, provide the most comprehensive survey of British enterprise, so far as it assumed the form of public companies. Company meetings are most adequately reported in *Herapath's Railway Journal,* the most widely read railway weekly in the fifties, which also carries a partial list of "calls" on railway capital. Complete files of *Herapath's* (1836-1901) and of the *Railway Times* (1833-1914) are accessible to American students in the New York Public Library. *The Mining Journal, Railway and Commercial Gazette.* (London, 1830–date. Henry English, mine agent, editor during the fifties) also accessible at the NYPL, carries excellent weekly letters from the metal trades as well as reports of mine operations and companies. The *Economist* (complete files NYPL, Athenaeum, but not at Harvard) is not helpful as to continental investments. Its supplement, the *Investor's Monthly Manual,* commencing in 1863, gives relatively adequate tables of new issues and calls, excluding vendors' shares and conversions. Foreign issues may be distinguished without great difficulty from domestic. Hence statistical report of foreign capital issues is possible from 1863. Computations for earlier years may be made upon the basis of prospectuses and brokers' share lists, but they are too incomplete to be made the basis of comparison and correlation.

Of European financial publications, the *Journal des Chemins des Fer* (Paris) was in the fifties controlled by the promoter J. Mires, and was a combination of a brokerage house and newspaper. It is accessible in the NYPL (1842–date) and the BM. The entire French financial press in the middle of the century was merely the publicity department of various financial groups. I have not run across a file of any other of the numerous weeklies which flourished in connection with the Paris Bourse. The terms of concessions and shareholders' lists of the companies organized under French law in 1867 are contained in the *Bulletin des Lois* (Harvard). For international financial relations the *Moniteur des Intérêts Matériels* (Brussels) and *Der Aktionär* (Frankfurt) provide the most illuminating and uncolored reports from 1850 to 1875. Their correspondence from London, Paris, Vienna and other money markets is frequently superior to the news published in those centers. The *Moniteur* was published by the de Laveleye family, and its editorial articles are of a distinction fully equal to those of the *Economist* for the period. Files of both these periodicals were obtained in the library of the University of Heidelberg, which incidentally contains a voluminous and well-indexed collection of pamphlet material relating to British economic conditions in the early part of the nineteenth century.

The *Revue des Deux Mondes* is the contemporary general periodical containing the most suggestive articles upon social and economic affairs in Europe.

The following manuals, year-books, etc., have been of frequent service: *Bradshaw's Railway Guide* (London. annual. BM); *The British Almanac and Companion* (London. annual. BM. NYP. Amherst); *The Mining Manual and Almanack* (London. annual. 1851 in NYP); *Annuaire de l'Economie et la Statistique* (Paris.

annual. NYP); *Annuaire Historique* (Paris. ann. BM, Harvard, NYP); *Oesterreichisches Eisenbahn-Jahrbuch* (Vienna, from 1867. NYP); Courtois, M., *Manuel du Bourse* (in various editions under several titles); Vitu, Auguste, *Guide Financier* (Paris 1864); Mc-Culloch, J. R., *Dictionary of Commerce* (London 1854); Slaughter Mihill, *Railway Intelligence* (half-yearly 1849–52, yearly 1852–55. biennial–1879).

Abstracts of British consular reports were published regularly from 1854, and in greater fullness from 1862. A series of reports upon commerce and manufactures of leading countries prepared by secretaries of embassy and legation commenced in 1857 continuing until 1886, and includes some studies of real value. The *Statistical Abstract of the United Kingdom* began to appear annually in 1854 and to carry 15-year summaries in 1856. The *Statistical Abstract of Foreign Countries* began in 1860. It is necessary to employ the *Annual Reports of the Trade and Commerce of the United Kingdom* in order to trace the volume and value of the trade in particular products with particular countries. There are no official returns of British capital movements.

Other sources which have been used are in part referred to particularly in the ensuing notes.

1 Bancroft, H. H., *History of California* (San Francisco 1888) VI, ch. 2.

2 Soetbeer, Ad. in *U. S. Consular Reports* (1887) XXIV, pp. 435-663; *U. S. Mint returns;* Del Mar, *History of Precious Metals* (2nd edit) p. 449; Tooke & Newmarch, VI: 150–51; Sombart, I: 534–35.

3 Allsop, Robert, *California and its Gold Mines* (London 1853). Between October, 1851, and January, 1853, 32 mining companies were formed to take up claims in the United States and raised £2,440,-000 in capital; 42 were formed to work in Australia, with virtually three millions capital. Prospectuses in *Times;* reports of operations and failure in *Mining Journal.* A great many of the California companies were founded upon claims of uncertain validity sold by General John C. Fremont. The first gold shipment from a company was in 1853. *Herap. Ry. Journal* XV: 622.

4 Jevons' index numbers (1782 price levels taken as 100) show a rise from 64 in 1849 and 1850 to 85 in 1857, the level remaining around 78 until 65. *J. Stat. Socy. London,* XXVIII: 314–19. Sauerbeck (average for 1866–77 taken as base) shows a rise from 74 in 1849 to high points of 102 in 1854, 105 in 1857, 105 in 1864 and 111 in 1873. According to Sauerbeck, between 1853 and 1876 price levels fell below 95 only in the years 1858 and 1859, at which time there was a phenomenal movement of specie to the Orient, oc-

casioned by the Sepoy revolt. *J. Stat. Socy. London.* XLIX: 5G2-93.

⁵ For contemporary views of the relation of the gold discoveries to the business revival, see Tooke & Newmarch, VI, ch. 4; Newmarch, W., *The New Supplies of Gold* (London 1853) Hyde Clarke in *The Mining Manual and Almanack for 1851* (London) pp. 224-40; Patterson, R. H., *The New Golden Age* (London 1868 2 vols); Leon Faucher in *Rev. des deux Mondes,* Aug. 1852.

⁶ Michaelis, Otto, *Die Handelskrisen von 1857* (Berlin 1858, reprinted in *Volkswirtschaftliche Studien* (1873) 1:278-79.

⁷ October 9, 1852, to Bordeaux chamber of commerce, quoted in Aycard, *Histoire du Crédit Mobilier* (Paris 1867). The Paris chamber in an address, Oct. 25, 1852, declared, "c'est l'ordre, le travail, le crédit, l'essor imprimé à toutes les grandes entreprises publiques et privées; c'est le bienêtre, s'infiltrant dans toutes les classes de la sociéte; c'est la prosperité générale." (*ib.* 32-33). For a valuable contemporary survey of this aspect of the Second Empire, see *Ten Years of Imperialism in France: Impressions of a Flaneur* (London 1862), especially ch. 7. The "Flaneur" was the Earl of Clarendon, British Foreign Secretary, 1853–58, 1865–66, and 1868–70.

⁸ Full discussion in *Annuaire Historique,* 1852, pp. 125-37. The personnel of management was wholly French. Out of fifteen directors, three were English, Francis Baring, John Masterman, Jr. and J. P. Kennard. Baron Seillière is said to have represented the Peto, Brassey & Betts interests on the board. The leading English shareholders with the number of shares originally allotted were as follows:

Baring Brothers	14,868	J. P. Kennard	628
N. M. Rothschild & Co.	14,864	A. Devaux	600
Joseph Locke	3,080	Grisewood, Harman	600
Matthew Uzielli	2,355	W. J. Chaplin	554
Thomas Brassey	1,750	Jas. Morrison	450
S. M. Peto	1,750	Thomas Smith	442
E. L. Betts	1,750	John Masterman	400
Charles Devaux	1,605	B. E. Morrice	363
S. Hudson	900	A. A. Hogton	300
James Hutchinson	750	S. M. Murray	300
		Sir John Easthope	300

J. Chem de Fer (1852) pp. 237ff.

⁹ Meinadier, A., *La Compagnie du Chemin de fer de Paris à Lyon et à la Méditerranean* (Paris 1908) pp. 30-32; *Her. Ry. Journ.* XIII:1377. Opposition had come partly from anti-English in-

terests, partly from a rival English group, headed by Sir David Salomons, which was having difficulties in recovering deposits for concessions from which it withdrew in 1847.

¹⁰ Paris-Strasburg, Blêmes-Didier-Gray and West of France (originally Versailles to Rennes).

¹¹ *Bull des Lois.* 1852. 1st sem. suppl. 712; *J. des Chem. de Fer* 1852, pp. 249, 411, 494. There is an account of Laing in Escott, T. H. S., *City Characters* (London 1922) pp. 183-85. Masterman with Sir William Magnay and James Ashwell were given prison sentences for misuse of funds of the *Great Luxemburg.*

¹² *Bull. des Lois.* 1852. 1st sem. suppl. p. 171; *J. Chem. de Fer* 1852, pp. 74, 118, 206, 207, 218, 921–22, 137–38. The first general meeting of this great railway company was attended by only one Frenchmen not a director; and most of the English knew not a word of French (*ibid.,* pp. 388–89). *Herap. Ry. Journ.* XI:1222; XIII: 903, 1049; XIV: 279. In 1855 a consolidation of the railway systems of Normandy and Brittany was effected, including the pioneer Rouen, Havre and St. Germain lines with the new "Ouest" and Cherbourg. *J. Chem. de Fer,* 1855, pp. 68–69, 356, 634. Edward Blount, W. P. Chaplin and G. G. Glyn were the English directors. *Bull. des Lois.* 1855, 1st sec., suppl. 191, 1221.

¹³ There were English directors upon the Ardennes, Blême-St. Didier-Gray, Creil-Beauvais, Dijon-Besançon, Dôle-Salines, Grand Central, Graissessac-Béziers, Paris-Caen-Cherbourg, Paris-Lyon, Lyon-Genève, Lyon à la Méditerranean, Midi, Montluçon-Moulins, Nord, Ouest, Paris-Orléans, Paris-Rouen, Rheims-Mezières, Rouen-Havre. The consolidations of the later fifties merged most of these lines in the five great systems, Nord, Est, Ouest, Orléans and P-L-M, in each of which there was for a time at least one English director.

¹⁴ Edwin Chadwick in *Journal of Stat. Socy. of London.* Jan. 18, 1859. XXII:385.

¹⁵ R. Dudley Baxter in *ibid.,* Nov. 1866, XXIX:567–79 printed separately as *Results of Railway Extension,* (see pp. 21–26). Baxter found that the dividends of the large systems averaged above ten per cent, altho net profits were only five or six. The large subventions from the French government accounted for this situation, as well as the large bonded debt carried at three per cent. The high dividends enabled considerable amounts to be paid to the original promoters upon founders' shares.

¹⁶ *Memoirs of Sir Edward Blount,* p. 83.

¹⁷ *Herap. Ry. Journ.* XV: 766.

¹⁸ Nassau Senior, *Conversations with Thiers, etc.* (London 1878) I:161.

[19] Cochut, André, "Les Chemins de fer Autrichiens," *Rev. de Deux Mondes*, 2d ser. IX:1059. Frühling & Goschen, a firm of Leipsic Jews established in London about 1815, is said to have made the fortune of its members out of Hungarian mining property.

[20] *The British Almanac and Companion* (1853) contains an excellent review of the European railway situation at that time.

[21] Hedrich, O., *Die Entwicklung der schleswig-holsteinischer Eisenbahnwesens* (Kiel 1915).

[24] Bert, A., *Nouvelles Lettres du Comte de Cavour* (Paris 1889) contains Cavour's correspondence with his banker at Geneva. Dunand-Henry, A., *Les Doctrines et Politique Economique du comte de Cavour* (Paris 1902), esp. pp. 131–41 (a shallow piece of work); Ferri, C. E., *Il pensiero economico del Conte di Cavour* (Milan 1921) is abler if less comprehensive. White, A. J., *The Early Life and Letters of Cavour* (London 1925) is the first biography in English to emphasize Cavour's economic interests.

[25] Cavour, "Des chemins de fer en Italie," *Revue Nouvelle*, VIII, 1 Mai, 1846, is probably the most influential of Cavour's writings. Bert, letter dated 28 Oct. 1845.

[26] See despatches of Sir James Hudson to Palmerston, 23 March, 23 June, 7 Nov. 1852, at *F. O.* 67:184.

[27] A full discussion based upon contemporary newspapers is in Gubler, Ferd., *Die Anfänge der Schweizerischen Eisenbahnpolitik* (Zurich 1916), esp. pp. 137, 160, 319 ff., 330–31, 336. The West of Switzerland, the Southeastern Swiss, Lake Constance-Basel and Lausanne-Fribourg were the lines eventually promoted by the English.

[28] Memminger, A., *Die Alpenbahnen und deren Bedeutung für Deutschland und Oesterreich* (Zürich 1878) pp. 17–25; *Hunt's Merch. Mag.* XVII:255–57.

[29] Gubler, pp. 330–31.

[30] Chiala, Luigi, *Lettere Édite e Inédite de Cavour* (Turin 1883), esp. I, 185–226, 310–23; Bert, *op. cit.* 418–28; Dunand-Henry, pp. 38–52; Bianchi, N., *La Politique du Comte Camille de Cavour; Lettres inédites* (Turin. 1885) pp. 1–12; Thayer, W. R., *Life and Times of Cavour* (Boston 1911) I:135; *F. O.* 67:184, Sir James Hudson to Malmesbury, 14 July 1852. Cavour renewed cordial relations with Rothschilds in 1853. Chiala, II, 386; Bert, 451–53.

[31] Report by E. M. Erskine in *Reports of Secretaries of Embassy and Legation 1858*, pp. 29–33; M. de Lizaranzu, *La Compagnie du Chemin de Fer Victor-Emmanuel devant ses Actionnaires* (Paris 1867); *Herap. Ry. Journ.* XVI:536; *Times*, 6 Sept. 1852, 3c. Brassey built most of the line, including the Mont Cenis tunnel, a memorable engineering feat in its day, with the connecting sections,

Turin-Susa and Turin-Novara running thru Piedmont to the Lombardy frontier. Rothschilds also approved of this route across the Alps. Helps, ch. 13.

[32] *Der Aktionär*, 10 Sept. 1854.

[33] Thayer's *Cavour*, II :4–9; Pratt, E. A., *Rise of Rail Power in War and Conquest* (London 1915) pp. 9–13.

[34] *Oesterreichisches Eisenbahn-Jahrbuch, 1868*, pp. 80–116. Austria was moved to act, according to Sir James Hudson, out of rivalry to the proposals of English engineers in Sardinia and planned the original routes on the advice of Radetzky to "ensure the easiest military occupation of North and Central Italy." *F. O.* 67:184, 7 March 1852. £1,800,000 in shares and bonds were allotted to England on the sale to the Rothschild company in 1856. *Times*, 17 Apr. 1856, 4 f. No indication has been found as to the British share in later financing. In 1868, Lionel Rothschild was the only English director remaining at the board.

On English railway enterprise in central Italy, see *Herapath's Railway Journal*, XIII :1229; XIV :1177; XV :396. William Jackson and Thomas Brassey were contractors for several small lines in Tuscany, which completed the connection to Rome. Gandell Brothers had contracts in Parma. *Eisenbahn Zeitung* XI: 176.

Details of the fusion of 1856 in *Times* 18, 19 Mr., 26 Apr. 1856, 11c; *Herap. Ry. J.* XVIII :462.

[35] Nassau Senior, *op. cit.*, II :126; *Herap. Ry. Journ.*, XIII :1229; XIX :116, XVII :567; *Times*, 20 May 1855, 5 f.

[36] *Moniteur des Intérêts Matériels*, 2 May 1858, 8 Aug. 1858, 1 Jan. 1860.

[37] *Infra*, pages 244 and 297, n. 20.

[38] *Memoirs of Sir Edward Blount*, p. 47.

[39] *Bull. des Lois.* 1859, 1st sem., suppl. p. 972.

[40] Helps, *Life and Labours of Mr. Brassey; Herap. Ry. Journ.* XV :482.

[41] *Monit. des Int. Mat.*, 16 Sept. 1860, 24 Feb. 1861.

[42] *Monit. des Int. Mat.*, 18 Oct. 1857; *J. des Chem. de Fer, passim.*

[43] *Mont. des Int. Mat.*, 2 May 1858.

[44] *Monit. des Int. Mat.*, 29 Dec. 1867; 22 Nov. 1868.

[45] *Monit. des Int. Mat.*, 26 Jan. 1868; Dimchov, R. M., *Die Eisenbahnwesen auf der Balkan-Halbinsel* (Bamberg 1894).

[46] *Monit. des Int. Mat.*, 3 Jan. 1869. Schönberger, L., *Die Ungarische Ostbahn. Ein Eisenbahn-und Finanz-Scandal* (Wien 1873); *Der Aktionär*, 1873, *passim.*

[47] A list of leading iron and steel merchants published in the *Mining Manual and Almanack.* 1851, pp. 429–30, includes the following which appear frequently in lists of foreign shareholders:

Barlow, J., 32, Bucklersbury
Gandell, J., 11 Clement's Lane
Jackson, W., 59 Crown St.
Kennard, R. W. & Co., 67, Upper Thames St.
Mortimer, H. H. & Co., 10 and 25 Bush Lane
Pickering, T., 44 Narrow St., Limehouse
Thompson & Co., Dyers' hall Wharf, Upper Thames St.
Walmsley & Co., 3, Upper Thames St.

[48] For instance, the Dyer family owning patents for the manufacture of tube roving-frames and other cotton spinning machinery, carried on business at Gamaches, France as Dyer Frères, and were concerned in the firm of Escher, Wyss & Co. of Zurich. *Report of Select Committee on Exportation of Machinery*, 1841 (201) pp. 114–115.

[49] *Report of Select Committee on Artizans and Machinery*, 1824 (51) ; *Report from Sel. Comm. on the Laws relating to the Export of Tools and Machinery*, 1825 (504) ; Hobson, *Export of Capital.*

[50] From an address by the Rev. Charles Faulkner (1884) quoted in *Second Report of Royal Commission on Depression.* 1886. App. Pt. II. pp. 141–42.

[51] *Bull. des Lois* 1838, 2nd sem., suppl. pp. 553–75; *Rep. on Export. of Mach.*, 1841, p. 85.

[52] *F. O.* 83:111 and 115. Unpublished reports sent in to Palmerston in 1848 in answer to inquiries with regard to British, French and American mercantile houses abroad. Most of the consuls construed the questionnaire narrowly and made no report on industrial firms. The New York consul was entirely too busy to be troubled with making out the forms at all. The most valuable report is a description of the American trade at Buenos Ayres.

[53] *Rep. on Artizans and Machinery,* 1824, p. 6.

[54] *Men of the Time* (London 1805) p. 564; Reybaud, Louis, *Le Fer et la Houille* (Paris 1874) pp. 28 ff.

[55] *J. des Chem. de Fer* 1853, p. 808; *Bull. des Lois* 1853, suppl. 1st sem. 148.

[56] *Times,* 12 July, 1852, 3b; *Herap. Ry. J.* XIV:758.

[57] *Times,* 7 Apr., 1856, 5d.

[58] The account of the Cockerills is based upon Mahaim, E., "Les débuts de l'établissement John Cockerill à Seraing," *Vierteljahrschrift für Social- und Wirtschaftsgeschichte* (1905) III:627–48. Cf. Ed. Morrien in *Biographie Nationale de Belgique,* art. "Cockerill."

[59] For the expansion of Belgian industries in the thirties, see Briavionne, V., *De L'Industrie de la Belgique* (Brussels, 1839) ;

Dunn, Matthias, *View of the Coal Trade* (Newcastle-on-Tyne, 1844) pp. 157–201.

[60] Mavor, J., *Economic History of Russia* (London and Toronto 1914), esp. I, 522–55 and II, 368–89, provides an excellent general survey of Russian industry in the nineteenth century. Hammerschmidt, W., *Geschichte der Baumwollindustrie in Russland* (Strassburg 1906) is a voluminous monograph covering the economic conditions of cotton manufacture in Russia before the emancipation of the serfs. There are important materials in Schulze-Gaevernitz, *Volkswirtschaftliche Studien aus Russland* (Leipzig 1899) and Tegoborski, *Études sur les Forces Productives de la Russie* (Paris 1852)

[61] Lumley, J. S. in *Reports of Her Majesty's Secretaries of Embassy and Legation,* 1865; Ure, *Philosophy of the Cotton Manufacture* (London 1860) p. 491; *Rep. on Export. of Machinery,* 1841, pp. 115–17; *Report of Royal Commission on Depression in Trade,* 1886, 2nd report, App. Pt. II, p. 295; Ischchanian, *Die Ausländische Elemente in der Russischen Volkswirtschaft* (Berlin 1913) p. 177.

[62] Schulze-Gaevernitz, pp. 90–106; Mavor, II:378–80; Michell, T., "The Present State of Trade between Great Britain and Russia." 1866 (144), bound with *Reports of Secretaries of Embassy and Legation.*

[63] *Accounts & Papers* 1843 (515) pp. 271, 282. (Macgregor's compilation of commercial tariffs and regulations of various countries).

[64] Schulze-Gaevernitz, pp. 295 ff.; Ischchanian, pp. 146–47.

[65] *F. O.* 83:111 and 115; *Report on Export. of Machinery,* 1841, p. 77; *Bull. des Lois* 1842; *Times,* 25 Apr. 1853, p. 10; 6 Mar. 1856, 5d. There was also a European Gas Company, organized in 1835, which operated plants at Amiens, Boulogne, Caen, Rouen and Nantes in 1854, with property costing about £150,000. *Mining Journal* XXIV:772. It supplied eight French towns in 1914. In this latter year the Danish Gas Company supplied nine towns in Denmark and two in Schleswig with gas, and three Danish towns with water. And the Anglo-Romano Gas Co. had 80,000 shares of £20 each, fully paid, "a large number" of which were still held in Great Britain. *Stock Exchange Off. Intelligence.* 1914, pp. 1136, 1148, 1151.

[66] *Der Aktionär,* 1866, p. 316; Wygodzinski, *Die Nationalisierung des Volkswirtschaft* (Tubingen 1917) pp. 56–58. The Frankfurt property was not disposed of until 1909. And in 1914 it was a five million pound concern, supplying gas to Antwerp, Brussels, Bruges, Flushing, Graslitz, Hanover, Komotan, Prague,

Saag, besides having "important interests in other continental gas concerns." *St. Exch. Off. Int.* 1914, p. 1159. The company was founded by Barlow and Manby.

[67] This was a *société en commandite*, under French law. E. E. Goldsmid and W. B. Gregory were the managers.

[68] *Herap. Ry. Journ.* XV:366. William H. Goschen was the original chairman of the company.

[69] *Herap. Ry. Journ.* XIII:767. There was also a company for Madrid in 1852, capitalized at £800,000. *Ibid.,* XIV:214.

[70] *Bull. des Lois,* 1854, suppl., 1st. sem, p. 55.

[71] *Revelation of Spain in 1845 by an English Resident* (London 1845. By T. Hughes) II:121. Brown, N. and Turnbull, C. C., *A Century of Copper* (London 1906)

[72] *Moniteur Belge,* 1845, 1st sem., 589; *Times,* 19 May 1846; *Herap. Ry. Journ.* IX: 58.

[73] *Mining Journal,* May 5, 1855, p. 274.

[74] There were at least nineteen mining companies formed in England in the fifties to engage in mining along the Rhine. The Ruhrort Coal Mining company, formed by Durham agents in 1854 and the New Scotland Mining and Ironworking Company formed in 1857 were perhaps the largest. *Mining Journal,* XXIV:399, 400; XXVII:20. Frederic Huth & Co. owned an iron-works at Hagen. *Eisenbahn Zeitung,* 23 Oct. 1853. Most of the companies worked copper and lead concessions. An excellent series of articles upon mining conditions in Prussia in *Mining Journal,* XXVI:812, 833, 854, 890; XXVII:20, 32, 80.

[75] Consul Mulvany in *Second Report of Commission on Depression in Trade,* 1886, App. Pt. II:171–73.

[76] Bloemer, K., *William Thomas Mulvany. Ein Beitrag zur Geschichte der Rhenish-Westfalischen Grossindustrie* (Essen 1922) is a scholarly biography.

[77] *Bankers' Magazine* (Baltimore) I, 88–90.

[78] *Report of Select Committee on the Bank Acts,* 1857–58. Testimony of J. Ball, # 1671–77.

[79] Reports of Colonel Hedges, consul-general at Hamburg, 1856 and 1857 in *Abstracts of Reports . . . from Her Majesty's Ministers and Consuls,* No. 6, 1857–58. pp. 70–94; Sartorius von Waltershausen, A., *Deutsche Wirtschaftsgeschichte* (Jena 1920) pp. 153–92.

[80] *Monit. des Int. Mat.,* 13 Sept. 1857.

[81] *Monit. des Int. Mat.,* 3 Jan. 1858.

[82] *Rep. on Bank Acts,* pp. 112–42; Andréades pp. 343–52; Evans, D. M., *The Commercial Crisis of 1857* (1859).

[83] *Monit. des Int. Mat.,* 15, 22 Jan., 25 Sept. 1860; 13 Jan., 7

Apr. 1861. French competition in the export iron trade was made possible by provisions enabling English iron to be imported duty free ton for ton for iron exported. Nassau Senior's *Conversations with Thiers,* I:145.

NOTES TO CHAPTER SEVEN

[1] An essential feature of Wakefield's economic program was the control of colonial waste lands by the British government for "imperial purposes," i.e.,—to be handled by land companies at remunerative prices, and in such limited amount as to permit the British social system to be transported to the colonies without exposure to the democratic menace of free land. But land control had to be virtually surrendered to solve the Canadian problem in 1840. And in 1852 the waste lands in Australia were surrendered to local authorities. Cf. Bodelsen, *Studies in Mid-Victorian Imperialism* (N. Y. 1925) pp. 16–22.

[2] The chief companies formed to do business in Australia before the fifties were: Australian Agricultural (1825), South Australian Company (1836), Bank of Australasia (1840), Union Bank of Australia (1840), Royal Bank of Australia, and Scottish Australian Investment Co.

[3] The account of the Grand Trunk rests chiefly upon the following authorities: Skelton, O. D., *The Railway Builders* (Toronto 1916) ch. 4 and 5; Skelton, *The Life and Times of Sir A. T. Galt* (Toronto 1920) ch. 2 and 4; Myers, Gustavus, *History of Canadian Wealth* (Chicago 1914) I: chs. 10, 11; Brown, Thomas S., *A History of the Grand Trunk Railway* (Quebec 1864); Keefer, T. C., *Eighty Years' Progress of British North America* (Toronto 1863); Helps, *Life of Mr. Brassey,* ch. 14; *Report of the Commissioners appointed to inquire into the Affairs of the Grand Trunk Railway* (Quebec 1861); Trout, J. M. and Ed., *The Railways of Canada for 1870–71* (Toronto 1871); prospectuses and reports of directors and shareholders meetings from *Herapath's.*

[4] The Colonial Office correspondence on early Canadian railways is at *C. O.* 42: 540, 547, 556, 580 and 586, covering the years 1845–52. On the interests of Earl Grey, see Walpole's *Russell,* II: 78, 80.

[5] Francis Hincks was so embarrassed that he was constrained to publish a volume of *Reminiscences* by way of accounting for the matter.

⁶ Skelton, *Railway Builders,* pp. 81–82.

⁷ *Times,* 21 Feb. 1861, 5b, citing report of shareholders' investigating committee.

⁸ Company rule has been the object of a great deal of indiscriminate abuse. From 1834 this government was in reality a dual form. All important decisions had to be taken with the approval of a Board of Control, headed by a British minister responsible to Parliament, as well as with the approval of a Court of Directors responsible to the East India stockholders. The argument of John Stuart Mill that this scheme was preferable to despotic control by a British cabinet minister responsible to a British electorate deserves consideration. Certainly the conspicuous blunders of the Company, the Afghan wars and the Dalhousie annexations, were forced upon it by its Board of Control.

⁹ Seeley, J. R., *The Expansion of England* (1885); Wingate, George, *Our Financial Relations with India* (L. 1859) states: "Not a shilling from the revenues of Britain has ever been expended on the military defence of our Indian Empire."

¹⁰ The rupee debt of the Company amounted to 10 millions in 1799, 27 millions in 1807, at about which point it stood at the end of the administration of Lord William Bentinck as Governor-General in 1836. In the next twenty years it grew at an average rate of one million pounds a year, and an increasing proportion of the debt was registered in British names. Out of a rupee debt of £44,000,000 reported in 1858, two-thirds were registered in the names of European residents. *Stat. Abstr. for British India.*

¹¹ Cooke, C. R., *Rise, Progress, etc., of Banking in India* (L. 1863); *Report of Sel. Comm. on East India* 1833, III, Testimony of Thomas Bracken of Alexander & Co.

¹² Lees, W. Nassau, *Land & Labour in India* (1867) pp. 232–33. A writer in the *Westminster Review,* LXIX:202, estimates this unearned income at £10,000,000. So also "Anglo-Bengalese" in *Times,* 12 Aug. 1857, 12c. The latter computes his total as follows: £3,000,000 in pensions, interest, and salaries; £3,000,000 in family and partnership remittances; the balance in profits and freight upon an Anglo-Indian trade of £55,000,000 a year.

¹³ *Report of Sel. Comm. on Growth of Cotton in India.* 1847–48 (511) # 3668–80. Test. of Ross D. Mangles.

¹⁴ For economic effects of British rule generally, see from opposing points of view, Knowles, L. C. A., *Economic Development of the Overseas Empire 1763–1914* (1924) pp. 261–312 and Romesh Dutt, *India in the Victorian Age* (1904) Book I.

¹⁵ An important exception must be made as to plantation advances. The development of indigo, reaching a peak about 1833, was almost

wholly due to advances of British merchants accompanied by contracts to buy. Opium and sugar and to some extent cotton were similiarly promoted. The East India Company itself made advances of opium. The indigo contracts were by the fifties notoriously usurious. Cf. testimony of Prideaux et al. before Comm. on Growth of Cotton 1847–48.

[16] *Times,* 6 Jan. 1846, quoting *Friend of India,* 20 Nov. 1845.

[17] Davidson, Edward, *The Railways of India* (1868) is the most minute discussion of the early history of India railways. The *Report on railways in India to the end of 1859* by Juland Danvers, government director, reviews railway development to that time. Schulz, Ernst, *Die Ostindischen Eisenbahnen* (Berlin 1909) is a more general railway history.

[18] Cf. *Hansard Parl. Deb.* 92: 476–91 ; *Times,* 16 Feb. 1847; *Herapath's* IX:229, 741 ; X:1257–58.

[19] See note 13.

[20] *Correspondence relating to Railway Undertakings in India,* 1852–53 (787) On Dalhousie's policy cf. Arnold's *Dalhousie,* ch. 20.

[21] Duke of Argyll, *Parl. Deb.* 155: 1324.

[22] *Annual Register* 1858, p. 259.

[23] *Report of Select Committee on East Indian Finance.* 1872. Test. of Lt. Col. George Chesney.

[24] *Economist,* 25 July 1857, p. 810.

[25] Martineau, John, *The Life & Correspondence of Sir Bartle Frere* (1895) ; Smith, R. B., *Life of Lord Lawrence* (NY 1883) esp. II: 377–83 and ch. 12.

[26] The account of the Bombay boom is drawn from Martineau, ch. 11, 12, 14 and Wacha, (Sir) Dinsha E., *A Financial Chapter in the History of Bombay City* (2nd ed. Bombay 1910).

[27] Cf. statements of Lord Stanley, then Indian Secretary, 14 Feb. 1859, *Parl. Deb.* 152:367–68.

[28] *Economist,* 12 June 1858, p. 644.

[29] When Sir Charles Trevelyan proposed in 1865 to levy 3% export duties on jute, wool, tea and coffee, the *Economist* fairly screamed with anguish. "They are taxes on European, on English industry and capital. Sir Charles proposes to tax the exports which our capital and enterprise at considerable risk and at the cost of expatriation, send from India." (p. 558). The proposals were withdrawn in haste.

It is fair to say that penal clauses at first drawn for a new Law of Contracts were abandoned in 1863 after a powerful memorial had been circulated, supported by Lord Shaftesbury and other Tory humanitarians, among whom was Sir Morton Peto.

[30] Davidson, pp. 145–48, 159–61, 206, 218, 264, 306, and 315; Brassey

& Wythes and Hunt, Bray & Elmsley were the most active firms.

[31] *Parl. Deb.* 152:362; 153:792–93. Cf. also Lord Lyveden in *Parl. Deb.* 155:1331, who declared "no one would be bold enough in this country to repudiate the debt."

[32] Thornton, W. T., *Indian Public Works* (L. 1875) pp. 34–5. Thornton was at the time of publication Public Works Secretary at the Indian Office, and the book is dedicated to the Duke of Argyll, recently Indian Secretary.

[33] *Report on East Indian Finance* 1872. Test. of Rt. Hon. W. N. Massey, #8867.

[34] *Report on East Indian Finance* 1873. Test. of Lord Lawrence, #4589–93.

[35] *Annual Report on Railways in India,* 1881–82.

[36] Dilke, Charles, *Greater Britain* (1869) pp. 470–74.

[37] *Report of Select Committee on E. I. Finance.* 1871. Appendix. Petition of Members of the Bombay Association, pp. 513–16. Testimony of Sir Charles Trevelyan in 1873 report, #424–25.

[38] The following table summarizes the balance of trade between India and the British Isles.

Years	Av. Export Mdse.	Av. Import Bullion (in £ millions)	Av. Export Balance
1849–54	8.0	3.8	4.1
1854–59	9.4	10.3	—1.0
1859–64	18.2	16.1	2.1
1864–69	24.2	15.8	8.3
1869–74	24.0	6.7	17.3
1874–79	22.0	7.0	14.9

[39] Clarke, Hyde, *Practical and Theoretical Considerations on the Management of Railways in India* (1846).

[40] These data are taken from the annual reports of the Government Director of Indian Railways.

[41] Knowles, *op. cit.,* pp. 320–37. Cf. Stachey, Sir John, *Finances and Public Works of India 1869–81* (1882).

[42] Dutt., *op. cit.,* pref., xiv. Connell, A. K., *The Economic Revolution in India* (L. 1883) takes a similarly critical view. Cf. also the testimony of James Geddes before the Select Committee on E. Indian Finance, 1871.

[43] Dilke, *op. cit.,* p. 332; Cf. Arnold, Edwin, *The Marq. of Dalhousie's Administration of Brit. India* (1865) II:241–42.

[44] *Sel. Comm. on E. I. Fin.* 1873. # 5701.

[45] Smith, Goldwin, *The Empire* (1863) p. 270.

NOTES TO CHAPTER EIGHT

[1] Weber, Max, *Wirtschaftsgeschichte* (Muenchen 1924) pp. 238–46; Sombart, *Der Moderne Kapitalismus* (1921) II:110–65. The clear analysis of Robert Liefmann, *Die Unternehmungsformen* (Stuttgart 1921) has been useful for this section as well as his more detailed study, *Beteiligungs- und Finanzierungsgesellschaften* (3rd edit. Jena 1921). Scott, W. L., *Joint Stock Companies in England, Scotland and Ireland to 1720* (London 1914). The more general indebtedness to the writings of J. A. Hobson and Thorstein Veblen also deserves recognition. Cf. especially Veblen, *Absentee Proprietorship* (New York 1924).

[2] "Stock-and-bond capitalism" is an adaptation of the term "*Effekten-Kapitalismus*" employed by Liefmann to characterise the current stage of economic history.

[3] Under the terms of the Bubble Act, 1720, companies were definitely illegal. The Act remained in force until 1825. The following accounts of corporation history have been helpful:—Baldwin, Simeon E., *Modern Political Institutions* (Boston 1898) esp. pp. 182–83, 194–95, 207–10; Cohn, George, *Die Aktiengesellschaft* (Zurich 1921); Perry, S. E. "The History of Companies' Legislation in England," *Journal of the Institute of Bankers,* XXIX (1909) 475–512; Frank Evans, "The Evolution of the English Joint-Stock Limited Trading Company," *Columbia Law Review,* VIII (1909) 339–61, 461–80; Christie, J. R., "Joint Stock Enterprise in Scotland before the Companies' Acts," *Juridical Review,* XXI:128–47, Powell, *Evolution of the Money Market,* ch. 6.

[4] 21 & 22 George III, c. 46. 12 Irish Statutes-at-Large 547; *Code de Commerce,* 1807, #19, 29–37, 40. The Irish statute permitted companies upon registration to limit their liability for fifteen years at a time. The French code recognized two forms of association. The *société en commandite,* which has a continuous history as a business form running back into the Middle Ages, required only public registration. It was a partnership in which only the active managers were responsible beyond the amount of their invested capital, but it had social personality in the eyes of the law. The *société anonyme,* as spread widely from France over the Continent, required the approval of the local prefect and of the executive until 1867. Until then, therefore, incorporation was a special favor in countries under Napoleonic codes. Free incorporation was recognized in France in 1867, in Germany in 1870, and other European countries soon followed.

[5] Davis, J. S., *Essays in the Earlier History of American Cor-*

porations (Cambridge 1917) finds material for two volumes in the record of companies formed by special favor in the eighteenth century.

⁶ W. F. Spackman, *Statistical Tables of the United Kingdom and its Dependencies* (1843), lists 612 companies then known in London with a nominal capitalization of about 225 million pounds. Among them were 24 foreign mining companies, 81 British mining companies, and 196 shipping, land, asphalte, loan, etc., companies, which presumably did not have special sanction for their existence. The capital under these heads was, however, only about 35 million pounds. The mining companies were partnerships with transferable shares, run on the cost-book principle. Many of the others were organized abroad as *sociétés en commandite*.

⁷ *First and Second Reports of the Select Committee on Joint Stock Companies* 1836 and 1837 : *Report on the Law of Partnership* by Bellenden Ker. 1837 (530) ; *Report of the Select Committee on Joint Stock Companies* 1844 (119) ; *First Report of the Mercantile Law Commission*. 1854 (1791) ; McCulloch, J. S., *Dictionary of Commerce* (London, 1854) art. "Partnerships with Limited Liability." It may be mentioned that Lord Ashburton, J. L. Ricardo, Kirkman Hodgson, Richard Cobden, and Nassau Senior, equally representative persons, endorsed limited liability.

⁸ Mill, *Principles of Political Economy* V, ch. 9 #11.

⁹ *Hansard*, 134: 751–99; 139: 1378 ff, 1896; 140: 110–38.

¹⁰ 7 & 8 Vict. c. 110 & 111.

¹¹ 18 & 19 Vict. c. 133.

¹² 19 & 20 Vict. c. 47.

¹³ 21 & 22 Vict. c. 91.

¹⁴ 25 & 26 Vict. c. 89.

¹⁵ Leone Levi in *Journ. Stat. Socy.* XXXIII (1870) 1–41.

¹⁶ The extent of the movement must not be exaggerated, however. Partly as sequel to the panic of 1866 the mass of iron and textile manufacturers in Great Britain conducted their business until the twentieth century without resort to the form of a limited liability company. Cf. von Wieser, *Der Finanzielle Aufbau der Englischen Industrie* (Jena 1919) ch. 5 and 6.

¹⁷ The account of the Crédit Mobilier is based chiefly up on Plenge, J., *Grundung und Geschichte der Crédit Mobilier* (Tubingen 1903) ; Aycard, *Histoire du Crédit Mobilier* (Paris 1867. A well-documented attack, afflicted with the notion that anything that causes stocks to move up or down is essentially wicked) ; Vergeot, J. B., *Le Crédit comme stimulant et regulateur de l'Industrie* (Paris 1918) pp. 111–93, based upon the still unpublished Pereire manuscripts ; Eugen Forçade in *Revue des Deux Mondes*, 15 March, 1

April, 15 May, 1 June, 1856; Pierre Vosgien, "Les Banques Françaises" in *Le Correspondant* (1861) III: 459 ff; Horn, J. E., *Das Creditwesen in Frankreich* (Leipzig 1857); Steiner, F. G., *Die Entstehung des Mobilbankwesens in Oesterreich (Gruenberg's Studien.* Wien 1913) ch. 4; Hirschfeld, H. M. "Le Saint-simonisme dans le Pays-Bas," *Revue d'Economie Politique,* May–June 1923; annual reports in *Herapath's.* Zola's *L'Argent* is a graphic and detailed study of the Paris money market in the sixties, depicting the rise and fall of an emulator of the Pereires. Tooke & Newmarch, VI: 104–34 give a fair exhibit of the horror excited by the Crédit Mobilier in contemporary England.

[18] *Œuvres de Saint Simon de d'Enfantin* (Paris 1865–78), esp. XLI: 220–82.

[19] The Crédit Mobilier was of course not the first holding company. There had been at least two earlier investment companies. The *Société Générale de Belgique* dates back to 1824, when it was organized for the purpose of looking after the industrial and mining investments of King William IV of Holland. It came into the hands of private capitalists after the Belgian Revolution and engaged in rivalry with the *Banque de Belgique* in organizing mining and manufacturing and insurance concerns in the late thirties. Both institutions, were, however, highly select affairs. They were not issue houses. Nor did they engage in deposit banking in the English sense. They developed these traits after the advent of the Crédit Mobilier. The *Schaffhausenschen Bankverein* (Cologne 1848) and the *Diskonto-Gesellschaft* (Berlin 1851) were conceived as industrial banks from the beginning. But they lacked organizing and issue functions until later. The *Darmstaedter Bank fuer Handel und Industrie,* founded by Gustav von Mevissen in 1853 was the first German bank to be influenced by the gospel of Saint Simon according to Isaac Pereire. Riesser, *Die Deutschen Grossbanken* (4 Aufl. 1912); von Wieser, pp. 243–70 for pre-war bank concentration in Great Britain.

[20] *Herap. Ry. Journ.* XXVII: 832.

[21] Jannet, Cl., *Le Capital, la Speculation et la Finance au xix*ᵉ *Siècle* (Paris 1892).

[22] The Bank Act of 1844 terminated a prolonged controversy between the Bank of England and country banks by curtailing the privileges of the latter as to note-issue. Andréades, p. 292.

[23] Baxter, Robert, *The Panic of 1866* (London 1866) pp. 19–20.

[24] Sir John Lubbock to shareholders of Anglo-Italian Bank at London Tavern, 30 Jan. 1865. *Herap. Ry. Journ.* XXVII:293.

[25] *Times,* 23 April 1844.

[26] *Economist,* 20 Nov. 1847, pp. 1333–35.

[27] Palgrave, R. H. I., *Notes on Banking* (London 1873) pp. 34, 39.

[28] *Bankers' Magazine* (London) LVI:807.

[29] Xenos, Stefanos, *Depredations* (London 1869). Bagehot's *Lombard Street* (1873) is of course the authority upon financial London in this period. Cf. Tooke & Newmarch, VI:589–608; *City Men and City Manners* (London 1852).

[30] *Times,* 16 March, 1864.

[31] Advertised prospectus in *Money Market Review,* 16 May, 1863.

[32] Advertisements in *Her. Ry. Journ.* XXV:562; *MMR,* 23 May, 1863.

[33] The *Société Générale,* as this institution has always been briefly styled, centered about the private banking firm of Bischoffsheim & Goldsmidt, which operated under various names in London, Brussels, Paris, Amsterdam and Frankfurt. It included with a number of constant allies of that house, the industrialist Schneider of Creusot, the engineer-contractor Talabot, and Edward Blount. A system of interlocking companies was planned, extending to Austria, Italy, Switzerland and Scandinavia. *Mon. Int. Mat.* 3 May, 13 Sept., 15 Nov. 1863, 17 Jan. 1864.

[34] *Bankers' Mag.,* Jan. 1865, p. 96 lists 29 finance companies then actively selling shares and seeking business.

[35] R. A. Heath to the shareholders, 21 Jan. 1865, *Bankers' Mag.* XXV:197.

[36] H. Drummond Wolff's *Rambling Recollections* (2 vols. 1908) II:51–54; *Mon. des Int. Mat.* 1863 and 1864 *passim* and 3 Mar. 1867; *MMR,* 22 May, 1864.

[37] *Herap. Ry. J.* XXVI:136.

[38] For railway finance in the sixties see accounts given by Lord Redesdale in House of Lords, *Hansard* 284:818 ff; 285:859–60; A. de Laveleye in *Monit. des Int. Mat.* 1 Jan. 1865, 3 June 1866; *Her. Ry. J.* XXIV:1262, 1304; *Economist* 24 April 1866.
"'To finance a company,'" states Xenos, *op. cit.,* p. 47, "is a technical phrase in use amongst the great City capitalists, and means nothing more than raising money after a certain fashion. Some person connected with the company that is to be 'financed' draws bills either from abroad or in England upon said company. This paper is discounted by some bill-broker, and the money handed over to the company to meet urgent payments." "Finance bill," "accommodation bill," and "open credit" were virtually interchangeable terms. Powell, pp. 378–80.

[39] A. de Laveleye in *Mon. des Int. Mat.,* 23 June 1865. Cf. Sterling, James, *Practical Considerations on Banks* (Glasgow 1866).

[40] Sir Robert Giffen has pointed out that an outstanding factor in the crisis of 1866 was the remarkable decline in shipping freights

evident as early as 1857 and continuing unchecked to 1868. *Essays in Finance, Second Series* (London 1886) p. 192.

[41] Oberholtzer, E. P., *Jay Cooke, Financier of the Civil War* (New York, 1907 ff.) I: 391; II: 211.

[42] *Money Market Review,* 10 May 1862, pp. 412–13. The *Times'* City editor, Marmaduke B. Sampson, was a director in the *San Paulo Railway,* a Rothschild enterprise in Brazil. The *Times* boosted Brazilian and Russian stocks. It was sometimes called the "Jews'-harp." Sampson retired in some disgrace in 1874, following a libel suit, having saved a large fortune out of his salary as editor.

[43] *New York Assembly Documents* 96th Session (1873) vol. VI, no. 98, page 529. Testimony before Erie Investigating Committee.

[44] This story of McHenry, as of the other activities of railway finance, is drawn chiefly from the files of *Herapath's Railway Journal,* the *Money Market Review* and the *American Railroad Journal.* Portions of it are related in scattered form in Mott, Edward H., *Between the Ocean and the Lakes. The Story of Erie* (New York 1898). Train, George Henry, *My Life in Many States* (New York 1902) pp. 237–49 gives a racy version of the Spanish negotiations.

[45] Fite, E. D., *Social and Industrial Conditions in the North during the Civil War* (New York 1910) pp. 54–57.

[46] *Economist,* 9 December 1865, p. 1487.

[47] Peto, Sir S. Morton, *Resources and Prospects of the United States* (London 1866). Barry, Patrick, *Over the Atlantic and Great Western Railway.* (London 1866) is another piece of literature inspired by this junket.

[48] The meeting is reported in *Herapath's* XXVII:1303.

[49] Mastermans and Kennards manœuvered consolidations, becoming the Agra & Mastermans' Bank and the Consolidated Bank, respectively. The former attempted to do branch banking in France.

[50] The account of the Overend failure is based chiefly upon the report of the criminal proceedings in *Queen vs. Gurney et al.,* published in the 79-page supplement of the *Bankers' Magazine,* Jan. 1870; *In Re Overend Gurney & Co., Ltd.,* in House of Lords, 15 Aug. 1867; *Gray vs. Lewis,* Vice-Chancellor's Court, 17 Feb. 1869; *Overend Gurney & Co., Limited. Report of the Committee of Defence Association* (London 1867); Emmanuel, Joel, *In the Matter of "The Companies Act, 1862" and in the Matter of Barneds' Banking Corporation, Limited. Depositions of Witnesses* (Liverpool 1866); *Herapath's Ry. Journal,* XXVII:445, 1156, 1429; XXVIII: 128, 356, 383, 418, 466; and *Bankers' Mag.* (London) XXV:905, 1018; XXVI:668–70, 737–44, 848–63, 1132–38; XXVII:1069–73 LVI:807. There is an account of the matter in Powell, *Evolution of the Money Market,* ch. 14.

⁵¹ The note is published in *Bankers' Mag.* XXVI:668–70.

⁵² For other accounts of the panic, cf. Bagehot, *Lombard Street*, ch. 8; Andréades, pp. 353–61; Tugan-Baranowsky.

NOTES TO CHAPTER NINE

Public Finance about 1870.—The standard reference manual for public security issues is Fenn, Charles, *Compendium of the English and Foreign Funds.* The first edition appeared in 1837, and frequent revisions followed. In the sixties the work came under the editorship of Robert L. Nash, and became something of an institution with the short title, *Fenn on the Funds.* I have made particular use of the sixth edition (1860), the ninth (1867), the fifteenth (1893). The *Annual Reports of the Council of the Corporation of Foreign Bondholders* are indispensable, especially for the affairs of governments that were in chronic financial difficulties. They begin with the year 1873. Recent issues contain admirable historical summaries, with particular reference to dealings which involved the London money market. *The Stock Exchange Year Book* was published annually from 1874. *The Statesman's Year Book* commenced publication in 1864. R. Dudley Baxter, *On Public Debts* (London 1871); Nash, R. L., *A Short Enquiry into the Profitable Nature of our Investments* (London 1880); Hyde Clarke "On the Debts of Sovereign and Quasi-Sovereign States," *J. Stat. Socy.* XLI:299–347.

The *Report from the Select Committee on Loans to Foreign States,* 1875, is a storehouse of material upon the loan business. "A Sketch of the History of Foreign Loans," *Bank. Mag.* (London) 36:424–30, 517–22 has been drawn upon. However, the financial periodicals cited in connection with the two preceding chapters have been the chief sources of information with respect to the actors and activities of the public loan market.

¹ Cohn, Gustav, *The Science of Finance* (Chicago 1895) translation by Thorstein Veblen, pp. 691–726, contains a detailed historical account of public debt theory.

² Dietzel, Carl, *Das System der Staatsanleihen* (Heidelberg 1855) p. 200.

³ Stein, Lorenz, *Lehrbuch der Finanzwissenschaft* (Leipzig 1886, 5th edit.) II ³:1–17. The later classical economists arrived at much the same conclusion by observing the steady decline in the per capita

debt of Great Britain, while the whole remained constant. Consequently McCulloch, J. R., *On Taxation* (London 1845) reasoned that the progress of industry is the best sinking fund. Cf. Mill, J. S., *Principles of Political Economy*, Book V, ch. vii # 1. It was a fact that the per capita debt of the United Kingdom, which had been 41 % of the estimated per capita wealth in 1815, by 1878 had fallen to the proportion of 10 %. *J. Stat. Socy.* 1878, p. 21.

³ᵃ Some notion of the possible limits of this activity is supplied by the estimate of Ernest Seyd in *Journ. Socy. Arts*, 5 Apr. 1878, XXVI: 409, that there were 50 to 60 million pounds in acceptances continually oustanding in Europe against London.

⁴ The best source for the personal data respecting the Bischoffsheims and their affiliations, as for the other cosmopolitan bankers, has been the files of the *Moniteur des Intérêts Matériels*. Details have been drawn from Collas, Henry, *La Banque de Paris et des Pays-Bas et les emissions d'emprunts publies et privés*. (Dijon 1908) ; Chirac, Auguste, *L'Agiotage sous la troisième Republique* (Paris 1888) ; the *Jewish Encyclopædia;* and innumerable references in the periodical press.

⁵ *Report from the Select Committee on Loans to Foreign States,* 1875 (367) ; usually bound in vol. IX of Parliamentary Papers for 1875. Its full analytical index renders further documentation of the text discussion unnecessary.

⁶ Cf. Lotz, Walther, "Die Technik des deutschen Emissionsgeschaefts," *Schmoller's Jahrbuch*, 1890, Heft 2.

⁷ Drummond Wolff, II :56–66.

⁸ *Report of Foreign Loan Committee*, # 21 ff.

⁹ *Money Market Review*, 8 June 1872 ; Seyd, Ernest, in *Journ. Stat. Socy.* XXXIII :46–49.

¹⁰ Michaelis, Otto, *Volkswirtschaftliche Schriften* (Berlin 1873) II :198–235.

¹¹ *Fenn on the Funds* (London 1898) p. vii.

¹² Seyd, Ernest, "The Fall in the Price of Silver," *Journal of the Society of Arts*, XXIV :306–34, 345–66.

¹³ Moulton, H. G. and Lewis, C., *The French Debt Problem* (NY 1925) pp. 439–48 is a recent statement of these transactions. Cf. Giffen, Sir Robert, "The Cost of the Franco-German War" in *Economic Inquiries and Studies* (London 1904) I :1–74; Say, Leon, *Les finances de France sous la troisième Republique* (Paris 1898–01) ; *Blackwoods'* 110 :215.

¹⁴ The revival of British investment in American securities on a large scale at the close of the Civil War deserves chapters by itself in a volume dealing with the participation of European capital in the development of the United States. The purchase of "Five-

Twenties" after the Civil War, their rapid redemption, and the investment of the proceeds in American railways, form a story which must be told for its own sake, apart. It is of the greatest importance in the rise of the American economic system. It was of less significance in the history of the British money market before 1875. Here is an important thread in the warp of financial history that cannot be conveniently broken in 1875.

[15] Alvarez, F. A. . . . , *A La Nacion. Manifiesto de los senadores i representantes que votaron contra el contrato de emprestito de $7,500,000* (Bogota 1866). The terms of the contract are here set forth.

[16] *Testimony before Select Committee on East Indian Finance,* 1871 (363) # 9674.

[17] This was the case with Spanish banking and industrial securities. *Mon. des Int. Mat.* 21 Aug. 1864.

[18] Maxwell's *Clarendon,* II:107.

[19] See the article, "Loans and Standing Armaments" in *Westminster Review* LII:205, October, 1849. Samuel Gurney publicly predicted European bankruptcy unless war loans were stopped. A great meeting at London Tavern, Oct. 8, 1849, agreed to Cobden's resolutons, declaring that the Austrian loan offered no security for prudent investment, and that war and armament loans were "unsound in principle and injurious to the interests of nations." The *Economist* considered the 5¾ % offered a highly speculative rate. *Econ.,* 29 Sept. 1849, p. 1075; 13 Oct. 1849, p. 1129. When the Russian loan was launched in January, 1850, the Jewish community joined the Quakers in attack. James Mitchell, editor of the *Jewish Chronicle* occupied the platform with Cobden Jan. 18, 1850. The *Daily News* gave editorial support; the *Times* championing the loan.

[20] Address to his constituents. *Times,* 20 October 1856, 10d.

[21] *Bullionist,* 6 Jan. 1866; *Economist,* 9 Nov. 1867, p. 1267. The British government had missed other opportunities, however, to enforce the property right of bondholders in customs which had been assigned as security for their loan. Lord John Russell was censured for such negligence in the case of the Ecuador customs at Guayaquil, seized by General Franco in 1858. *Times,* 15 March, 1861, 10e.

[22] *Bullionist,* 2 November 1867.

[23] *Moniteur des Int. Mat.,* 15, 22 Nov., 6 Dec. 1868.

[24] *Economist,* 1868, p. 1300.

[25] Giffen, Sir Robert, "The Liquidations of 1873–76," *Economic Inquiries and Studies* (London 1904) I:98–120; current market reports.

[26] *Report on Loans to Foreign States,* 1875, p. xlvi.

[27] Giffen, p. 108.

NOTES TO CHAPTER TEN

[1] Lane Poole, S., *Life of Lord Stratford de Redcliffe* (London 1888) II : 78.

[2] *Report from the Select Committee on Steam Navigation to India.* 1834 (478) ; *Euphrates Expedition. Accounts & Papers.* 1837 (540).

[3] Kinglake, A. W., *The Invasion of the Crimea* (London 1863 ff) I : 34.

[4] Lane Poole, II : 79.

[5] Contemporary accounts of Turkish resources and of sporadic projects to exploit them prior to 1855: McFarlane, Charles, *Kismet, or the Doom of Turkey* (London 1853) pp. 317–21 ; Rolland, Charles, *La Turquie Contemporaine* (Paris 1854) ; Bouvet, Francisque, *La Turquie et les Cabinets de l'Europe* (Paris 1853) p. 145; Pierre de Tchihatcheff in *Rev. des Deux Mondes,* 15 May, 1850, pp. 716 ff. Rolland's book is in the form of a journal compiled in 1852 during a mission to Constantinople on behalf of a land company organized by Lamartine with the support of English capital. Lamartine had secured a concession to 22,000 hectares of land, with quasi-feudal rights over the inhabitants, in the vicinity of Burgas-Ova. His associates seized the opportunity to discuss vast projects with the grand vizier, a public loan, road-building, agricultural colonies, the recoinage of the currency, a bank, railways and mining enterprises.

[6] Farley, J. L., *Modern Turkey* (London 1872) p. 343.

[7] Nassau Senior, *Journal kept in Turkey* . . . (London pp. 206–07. A somewhat later conversation with Hugh Thurburn in Egypt preserves in excellent form the insight of Englishmen into the probable operations of western ideas about real property. Thurburn expressed delight at the clause of the Hatt-i-Humayoon authorizing Christians to purchase land. "It will be acted on extensively, for foreigners can afford to give more for land than natives can, as they can make more of it; a rich native is subject for plunder by every one in authority. . . . But a foreigner delights in a contest with the Government; he is sure to entrap the Turks into some illegality, and then he runs to his Consul, and gets 1000 per cent. indemnity. The Levant is full of Finlays and Pacificos. It is a regular trade. Then the Turks are borrowers: they never know what their incomes are, and always exceed them. Let a Turk once mortgage his land to a Christian protégé, and he will soon cease to have any property in it. In a very few years the mortgage money will exceed the value of the

fee simple." *Conversations and Journals in Egypt* (1882) II: 194–95.

[8] Du Velay, A., *Essai sur l'histoire financière de la Turquie* (Paris 1903) pp. 227–45; *British Foreign Office. Peace Handbooks* (1919) XVI: 92–97.

[9] As reported in the *Times,* 16 Nov. 1858.

[10] "If we wish for a canal, England opposes. If you wish for a telegraph, France opposes. If France and Russia wish the Principalities to be united, England and Austria require them to be separated. If you support Reschid Pasha, we support Fuad Pasha. If Russia builds at Pera a palace big enough for a king, so do we, and so do you. . . . At a great expense of talents, diligence, paper, ink, and diplomacy, we produce only negative results." French merchant at Galata quoted by Nassau Senior, *Journal kept in Turkey* . . . pp. 29–30.

[11] J. C. McCoan in *Fraser's Magazine,* Dec. 1878, pp. 701–03. One advantage possessed by the *Smyrna-Aidin* company was that the promoters stood very close to the Peto-Betts organization and secured the rails used by them in building the war railway at Balaclava. Kinglake, VI:385; *Monit. des Intérêts Matériels,* 17 May 1857.

On early Turkish railway projects, see further: Wilson, Thomas, *The Lowlands of the Danube* (London 1855); Forester, Thomas, *The Danube and the Black Sea, Memoir on their Junction by Railway* (London 1857); Stephenson, R. Macdonald, *Railways in Turkey* (London 1859); report of C. Alison on the commerce of Turkey in *Reports of Her Majesty's Secretaries,* etc., 1858; *Abstract of Reports of Her Majesty's Ministers and Consuls.* No. 6. 1858, pp. 219–26; Dimitschoff, R. M., *Zur Geschichte der Balkan-Eisenbahnen* (Wurzburg 1894. A brilliant study.) Dimitschoff supplies corroborating details for the statement of the *Levant Herald* (*Times,* 13 Feb. 1869, 6a) that to 1869 all railways in Turkey, except the *Smyrna-Cassaba* had been a "system of contractors' jobs."

[12] Andrews, W. P., *India and her Neighbours* (London 1878); Clemm, P. E., *Life of Lieutenant Waghorn* (London 1894); *Report from the Select Committee on Steam Navigation to India.* 1834 (478); *Report from the Select Committee on Steam Communication with India.* 1837 (539); *Papers relative to Steam Communication with India.* 1839 (431).

[13] Letter from Consul-General Campbell to John Bowring, 18 Jan. 1838 in *Report on Egypt and Canada. Accounts & Papers.* 1840. (277) p. 190; *Times,* 10 Oct. 1844.

[14] Lindsay, W. S., *The History of Merchant Shipping* (London 1876) pp. 378–83; Meeker, Royal, *History of Shipping Subsidies* (N. Y. 1905).

[15] Galloway, John Alexander, *Communication with India, China, etc. Observations on the Proposed Improvements in the Overland Route via Egypt.* (London 1844) ; *Times,* 1 and 5 Nov. 1844; *Journal des Débats,* 13 Nov. 1844; *Times,* 2 Jan. 1845.

[16] Palmerston to Murray, 8 Feb. 1847, *F. O.* 97:411. "It is certainly the wish of Her Majesty's Government to maintain as far as possible the employment of British Capital and Agency in carrying on the communications with India through Egypt"; *Times,* 9 Feb., 26 Oct. 1846.

[17] *Report from the Select Committee on Steam Navigation to India.* 1834.

[18] *F. O.* 97:411. The letter is dated Feb. 20, 1841.

[19] *F. O.* 97:411. Palmerston to Murray, 27 May 1847 (draft).

[20] *Herapath's Ry. Journ.* XIII: 1106–07, 1118; XIV: 1358; *Parl. Deb.* 118: 1858–59.

[21] Letters of George Crawshay and Ferdinand de Lesseps in *Newcastle Daily Journal,* 23 March, 12 June, 1868.

[22] *Parl. Deb.,* 3rd ser. 146: 1044, 7 July 1857. See also the debate of August 14, 1857 on the route to the East for the clash of opinion between Palmerston and Gladstone on this matter. *Parl. Deb.* 147: 1666–82.

[23] For instance, *Times,* 5 Jan. 1846; *Messrs. Waghorn & Co.'s Overland Guide to India by Three Routes to Egypt.* (London 1846).

[24] Article under heading, "The Direct Line to India," *Shareholder,* 29 Oct. 1845.

[25] Stephenson, R. M., *Railways: an Introductory Sketch, with Suggestions with Reference to their Extension to the British Colonies* (London 1850) ; Andrew, W. P., *Letter to Viscount Palmerston on the Political Importance of the Euphrates Valley Railway* (London 1857) ; and the writings of Andrew generally to the extent of some twenty-five press-marks in the British Museum.

The prospectus of the company (*Herapath's* XVIII: 614) stated its purpose to be "to connect the Mediterranean and the Persian gulf by a railway from the ancient port of Selucia by Antioch and Aleppo, to Ja'ber Castle on the Euphrates, of 80 miles in length, and afterwards from thence by other towns to Bagdad and on to the head of the Persian gulf." It was stated that the route had been surveyed by command of William IV, by Major General Chesney, R. A., F. R. S., and later by Captain Lynch, C. B., and Commander Campbell of the Indian navy. John Laird of Birkenhead had contracted to build river steamers for the company. Palmerston placed a warship and naval officers at the company's disposal to survey rivers and harbors. On June 22, 1857, a deputation waited upon Palmerston, headed by Lord Shaftesbury, the great Tory humanita-

rian peer, and included forty members of Parliament, not counting
peers temporal and spiritual, the Lord Mayor of London and a
spokesman for the Liverpool Chamber of Commerce. They desired the British government and the East India Company to
guarantee them 5% dividends for at least twenty-five years. The
argument presented by Andrew, the company's president, was summarized in the *Morning Herald,* June 23, as follows:

"The grand object was to connect England with the north-west
frontier of India, by steam transit thru the Euphrates and Indus
Valleys. The latter would render movable to either the Kyher or
the Bolan, the two gates of India, the flower of the British army
cantoned in the Punjab, and connected by the Euphrates line by
means of steamers, the flank and rear would be threatened of any
force advancing thru Persia towards India. So that the invasion
of India by this great scheme would be placed beyond even speculation; and it would be evident, by the great army of India of 300,000
men being united by this means to the army in England, the *mutual*
support they would render each other would quadruple the *power
and ascendancy of this country,* and promote powerfully the progress,
the freedom, and the peace of the world."

The *Times,* 10 Aug. 1857, 4 f. urged favorable action. The adverse decision of the government was announced in debate, August
14.

[26] *Memoirs of Sir Edward Blount,* pp. 108–09; *Cyprus, Historical,
Descriptive,* adapted from the German of Franz von Lueher with additional matter by Mrs. A. Batson Joyner (London 1878), last
chapter.

[27] Nassau Senior, *Journal kept in Turkey,* p. 84.

[28] See the admirable letter of Sir Henry Bulwer to Admiral Martin, Sept. 22, 1860, printed in Drummond Wolff, Sir Henry, *Rambling
Recollections,* II : 1–6.

[29] The structure of this narrative of the growth of the Turkish
debt is drawn from Du Velay, *op. cit.,* and Morawetz, Charles, *Les
Finances de la Turquie* (Paris 1902).

[30] Nassau Senior, p. 115.

[31] *Economist,* Sept. 4, 1858, p. 991. The *Bankers' Mag.* declared
in this year, pp. 724–25 that "scarcely any country possesses in a
greater degree the elements of financial prosperity."

[32] Du Velay, p. 154.

[33] Sir Henry Bulwer to Said Pasha, 6 Aug. 1860. *Papers relating
to Administrative and Financial Reforms in Turkey, 1858–61.* 1861.
pp. 44–48.

[34] Du Velay, pp. 164–65.

³⁵ *Reports of Mr. Foster and Lord Hobart on the Financial Condition of Turkey.* 1862 (475) ; 1863 (503).

³⁶ In House of Commons, 31 Mar. 1862, *Parl. Deb.* 166:298. *Ibid.*, pp. 289–90. Brokers' circulars advertised the loan as "under the direct cognizance and favour of the British Government" and the prospectus carried a letter from Earl Russell to A. Bruce expressing the "interest in this operation" taken by Her Majesty's Government, and announcing the designation of Lord Hobart, to administer the proceeds of the loan as "a further security against the misapplication of the present loan."

³⁷ Biliotti, A., *La Banque Imperiale Ottomane* (Paris 1909). The bank was to act as fiscal agent for the Turkish government and to engage in commercial banking. After 1866 it withdrew from active participation in the loan business and confined itself to banking until the crisis of 1875. Its early financial activity seems to have been upon the initiative of the *Crédit Mobilier* which was active in its formation. English interests well-disposed to the *Crédit Mobilier* were associated, Devaux, Grenfell, Baring, Glyn. *Mon. des Int. Mat.* 11 Jan. 1863.

³⁸ Newton, *Lord Lyons. A Record of British Diplomacy* (London 1913) I : 152; Farley, J. L., *Modern Turkey* (London 1872) pp. 134–49. Farley was the organizer of several companies to do commercial banking in Turkey, each of which to his disgust devoted himself to debt speculation.

³⁹ **The Literature of Egyptian Finance to 1875.**—The only adequate account of the early career of Egypt's debt is the *Histoire financière de l'Égypte depuis Said Pasha 1854–76* (Paris 1878) by "J. C." This book was written by a Frenchman who was in Alexandria in the sixties, in a position to know exactly what was going on, and who was later similarly situated in Paris. For confirmation of its interpretation and details, I have depended upon McCoan, J. C., *Egypt as it is* (London 1877) and *Egypt under Ismail,* by the same author (London 1889) ; Faucon, T., *La Ruine de l'Egypte* (Paris 1873) ; Genevois, Henri, *La verité sur les finances égyptiennes et le Crédit Foncier de France* (Paris 1876) ; De Leon, Edwin, *The Khedive's Egypt* (1st edit. 1877; 2nd. 1882. New York) ; Lokman el Hakim, Sidi, (pseudonym), *Les milles pertuis des finances du Khedive et les banques en Égypte* (Vienna 1873) ; various editions on *Fenn on the Funds* and current market reports in the *Economist.*

The bulk of the literature of Egypt in English dates from the formal British intervention in 1882, and discreetly is silent about the activity of bankers who depended upon British capital. Rothstein, Theodore, *Egypt's Ruin* (London 1910) is an exception. Cromer,

Modern Egypt (1908); Milner, *England in Egypt* (1893); and Blunt, Wilfrid S., *Secret History of the English Occupation of Egypt* (2nd edit. 1907) do not have anything to say of value on what happened before the later seventies. De Freycinet, C. L., *La Question d'Égypte* (Paris 1905) is the best proportioned history of Egypt in diplomacy, altho narrowly French in perspective. Daudet, Alphonse, *Le Nabab* (Paris 1877) is a realistic portrait of a Franco-African financier of the period.

[40] *Allgemeine Zeitung* 1862, pp. 372, 892.

[41] *Times*, 8, 9, 10 April, 1862.

[42] The English promoters included the Agra & Masterman's Bank and Samuel Laing's General Credit & Discount Co. *Mon. des Int. Mat.* 31 July, 1864.

[43] *Histoire financière*, pp. 37–40.

[44] *Economist*, 5 July 1873, p. 809.

[45] *Le Nil* (Alexandria) Dec. 17, 1872. The list was compiled by E. P. Mirzan, share-broker of Alexandria.

The income and expense account for Egypt from 1864 to 1875, drawn up by Stephen Cave in 1876, is instructive:

Receipts		Expenditures	
By Revenue	£94,281,401	Administration	£48,868,491
Loans	31,713,987	Tribute to Porte	7,592,872
Sale of Suez		Works of utility	30,240,058
Canal shares	3,976,583	Extraordinary expenses,	
Floating Debt	18,243,076	some of questionable	
		utility, others under	
	£148,215,047	pressure of interested	
		parties	10,539,545
		Interest and Sinking	
		Fund	34,898,962
		Suez Canal	16,075,119
			£148,215,047

Accounts & Papers 1876 (1425). There was only the Suez Canal to show for it, said Cave, "the whole proceeds of the Loans and Floating Debt having been absorbed in payment of interest and sinking funds, with the exception of the sum debited to that great work."

[46] *Hist. fin.*, p. 158.

[47] Cave report, *ut supra*, p. 8.

[48] *Hist. fin.*, p. 161.

[49] Boulger, D. C., *Life of General Gordon* (2 vols. London 1896); Mackay, T., *Life of Sir John Fowler* (London 1900).

[50] For **The Suez Canal Share Purchase.**—Chief reliance has been

placed, in addition to the *Histoire financière,* upon Lesage, Charles, *L'Achat des Actions de Suez* (Paris 1906); letter of Julien Wolf to the *Times,* 26 December, 1905, with subsequent correspondence running for a couple of months; Newton's *Lord Lyons,* II: 85–94; Moneypenny and Buckle, *Life of Benjamin Disraeli* (London 1920) V: 439–54; and *Correspondence respecting the Purchase by Her Majesty's Government of the Suez Canal Shares belonging to the Egyptian Government.* 1876 (C-1391). The narrative of W. H. Dawson in *The Cambridge History of British Foreign Policy* (1921–23) III: 154–58 shows no evidence of resting upon any materials that have been unpublished.

[51] There had been an earlier proposal for the British government to purchase the khedive's shares, first considered in December, 1870, which was allowed to pass without action. On both proposals and the controversy with de Lesseps, see Moneypenny and Buckle, V :411–13; *Parl. Deb.* 219: pp. 1032–37; *Correspondence relative to the Question of the Suez Canal Dues.* 1874 (455); *Correspondence respecting the Suez Canal.* 1876 (C-1392).

[52] The mystification which surrounded the purchase was largely the work of Disraeli's imagination; however, it may have been played upon. Thus Disraeli writes to Lady Bradford on November 25, 1875, "We have had all the gamblers, capitalists, financiers of the world, organised and platooned in bands of plunderers, arrayed against us, and secret emissaries in every corner, and have baffled them all and have never been suspected."

Now this is the legend in its rarest perfection, but it is almost wholly false. At least the Rothschilds and Oppenheims were working with Disraeli; altho he probably did not know all that they were doing. They were as anxious as Disraeli to bring off the coup, and not necessarily for the same reasons. At least one of the sets of proposals which reached Ismaïl from Paris was of Oppenheim's concoction. And the picture of England rescuing the canal at the last moment from a France eager to gobble it up will not bear the light of day. The materials thus far available do not show that the possibility of a French government purchase had any existence outside the mind of the British cabinet. Undoubtedly it was a material factor in enabling it to make up its mind. But France did not wish to make the purchase, (1) because to do so would definitely alienate England, whose friendship had recently been of notable assistance in the war scare of May, 1875, (2) because to alienate England would entirely neutralize any possible benefits to the price of Egyptian securities, and would thus not relieve the *Crédit Foncier.* This concern is said to have been expressed by Leon Say, Minister of Finances, who had the reputation of being "Rothschild's man."

Moreover, this legend is entirely irreconciliable with the cordial eagerness with which de Lesseps, and indeed the entire French press, congratulated Disraeli upon what he had done. It is noteworthy that this is almost the only step taken by Great Britain with reference to Egypt for a great many years that met with any such expressions.

[53] "What was, however, altogether creditable—and to a later generation, less squeamish in such matters of public duty, incredible—was the fact that no one in the secret used his knowledge for personal gain," comments W. H. Dawson in the *Cambridge History*, III : 158. What is incredible is that Mr. Dawson should commit himself to any such statement. The action of Egyptian securities in the stock market proves conclusively that some one made a great deal of money.

On November 15, the day on which the first despatch was sent to Cairo, the 1873 loan reached its low mark of 53½–54½. Thereafter it rose steadily a point or half a point a day, presumably under quiet buying. It was not until the 19th that there was a rumor abroad that Paris was trying to buy the canal shares. On the 20th the market stood at 59¾–60¼. In reporting the situation the following Monday morning, the *Times* city editor stated : "In Egyptians there is a very large account open for the fall and every variety of adverse rumor that could be concocted has been circulated, but the market notwithstanding is firm." Evidently some one was doing some consistent buying. The news of Disraeli's purchase reached the Stock Exchange at 1 : 35 P. M., November 26; and immediately the 1873 loan rose six points. The following day it rose four more, and on November 30 it stood at 73–75, remaining above 70 to the end of the year. Those who purchased at 55 had their reward. The quotations are taken from the *Times*. Other issues of Egyptian securities fluctuated sympathetically. However it was the 1873 loan which was chiefly in the market, and in which there was the largest swing.

[54] Lesage, p. 208.
[55] *Times,* 27 November, 1875.

NOTES TO CHAPTER ELEVEN

British Economic Conditions in the Seventies.—The principal source of information is the *Statistical Abstract of the United Kingdom.* In its analysis the papers of Sir Robert Giffen, collected in *Economic Inquiries and Studies* (2 vols. London 1904) are indispensable. Volume I deals principally with the economic trans-formations of the seventies. Stephen Bourne, *Trade, Population and Food. A Series of Papers on Economic Statistics* (London 1880) is less painstaking. However, the book is distinctly more helpful than Giffen's writings in giving an insight into the transformation of com-mercial liberalism under the stress of the depression. Bourne's paper on "The Growing Preponderance of Imports over Exports in the Foreign and Colonial Trade of the United Kingdom," *Journ. Statist. Socy.* March, 1877, was the starting-point of scientific discussion of the transformations. For other current discussions, see Caird, James. *The Landed Interest and the Supply of Food* (London 1880) ; New-march, William, "On the Progress of the Foreign Trade of the United Kingdom since 1856," *Journ. Stat. Socy.* XLI : 187–298; Mun-della, A. J., "The Conditions on which the Commercial and Manu-facturing Supremacy of Great Britain Depend," *ibid,* 87–134; Shaw-Lefevre, G. J., "The Depression of Trade," *ibid,* 573–96: Seyd, Ernest, *Journal Socy. of Arts,* 1878, pp. 401 ff.

[1] Prothero, R. E., *English Farming Past and Present* (London 1912) ; Knowles, L. C. A., *Industrial and Commercial Revolutions* (London 1921) pp. 361–74; W. Sturge before the Institute of Sur-veyors, summarized in *Economist,* 11 Jan. 1873, p. 15.

[2] Caird, p. 127.

[3] For instance, the importations of tea grew as follows:

1863	85	million lbs.
1868	106	" "
1873	131	" "
1878	157	" "

[4] Armes, Ethel, *The Story of Coal and Iron in Alabama* (Birming-ham, Ala. 1910) pp. 377–93; *The Hill Country of Alabama, U. S. A.* (undated. Found at BM, pressmark 10410. cc. 5).

[5] **Great Britain's Export of Surplus Capital.**

It must be flatly declared that all quantitative statements with re-spect to the export of capital, past and present, are estimates.

These estimates may have more or less of a basis in substantiating evidence. Prior to 1854 such a basis is lacking with respect to all estimates of the British balance of trade payments. Imports were reckoned in official values, based upon the scale of prices prevalent in 1696; while exports were reported in declared values. There are no statistics whatever of other items in the balance that deserve consideration. With a great deal of effort it has been possible to make a list of foreign security issues, which is fairly complete, but which is no real index to capital movement, for that period.

For the period from 1854 to 1875 (and we shall carry it to 1880) there is some evidence to go on. This is particularly true for the close of the period, when the balance of trade came to be the chief concern of statisticians for a time. On the basis of materials gathered and estimates made by Giffen, Bourne, Newmarch, Seyd, and others, a table of Great Britain's international accounts has been constructed, and is presented here.

The merchandise and bullion values are taken from the *Statistical Abstract*. With them have been included in the table the item of "ship sales." These values were computed by Bourne in 1877 on the basis of the annual tonnage officially reported. They range from one to three million pounds a year.

The net earnings of the British merchant marine are taken directly from the computations of Giffen. They are to be regarded as valuable estimates as it will ever be possible to make.

The items of insurance, brokerage, stamp duties, and shipping commissions have been computed from Giffen's estimated allowance of 2½% upon the entire volume of British foreign trade. Higher estimates have been made.

Then there are the profits upon England's foreign trade. Where imported goods were shipped by English firms residing abroad, or where exports were to be marketed abroad thru English houses, mercantile profit is an invisible item to be placed in the balance in England's favor. Bourne estimated trading profits for the twenty years ending in 1877 at an average of from 20 to 30 millions a year, with reference to an average total trade of 500 millions. In addition he allows 5 to 10 millions annually for ship earnings in the carrying trade abroad, besides recognizing the existence of profits from mercantile, industrial and agricultural establishments abroad. I have ignored these latter items and computed a flat 5% on the foreign trade as being a probable moderate estimate of foreign trade profits.

With reference to tourist expenditures, and absentee remittances there are no contemporary suggestions of any kind. They have consequently been ignored.

The available data thus make possible a highly tentative series of capital and interest balances. It shows a net export of capital from 1854 to 1874 inclusive of 332 million pounds. This total is about as close to a true quantitative statement of what happened as it is possible to secure. However, the annual variations shown are not to be taken too seriously. For it is precisely profits that are most likely to fluctuate from good year to bad. And any computation based upon an assumed average of profit necessarily eliminates part of the annual changes.

The total, however, may be checked against estimates of the

volume of Great Britain's foreign investments. Giffen in 1878 estimated this amount as at that time £1,300,000,000. Seyd in 1876 (*Journal of the Society of Arts*, XXIV: 309) considered it certainly more than one billion pounds in 1875; probably about £1,200,000,000. The data in Nash's *Short Enquiry* (1880) make possible the following estimates of it by classes:

Foreign Government Loans and Guarantees	£500,000,000
Railways in Europe, U.S. & South America	240,000,000
United States Debt	200,000,000
Indian Railways	90,000,000
Indian Debt	70,000,000
Colonial Government Loans	50,000,000

There is no basis for any sort of an estimate of the capital value of investments not represented by securities. The above estimates are all reckoned at face value.

Now this total of £1,200,000,000 would have been reached simply by annual reinvestment of interest and dividends arising abroad had in 1854 the volume of foreign investment amounted to £434,000,000. However I have found no grounds whatever for believing with Bowley, *England's Foreign Trade in the Nineteenth Century* (rev. edit. 1905) p. 75, that this volume was anywhere near so great. I am unable to account for a much larger volume of investment at that time than £200,000,000, distributed approximately as follows:

United States	50 to 60	million pounds
French, Belgian, Dutch and Russian govt. securities	45 to 55	" "
Spain and Portugal	35 to 45	" "
Latin America	35 to 40	" "
French Railways	25 to 30	" "
Belgian Railways	5	" "
Total	195 to 230	" "

Assuming this sum to have compounded by reinvestment at 5 %, and compounding the capital export balances in the same manner, a total is reached which bears comparison with the estimates of Giffen and Seyd.

Thus altho the estimates in the following table are incomplete, and altho the annual items in the Capital & Interest Balance column must be taken with great reservation, the data is sufficient to establish the sharp change in trend which took place under this head about 1875. It is adequate to support the modest inferences drawn from it in the text.

TABLE SHOWING THE BALANCE OF PAYMENTS OF THE UNITED KINGDOM, 1854–1880, AND THE NET MOVEMENTS OF CAPITAL

Year	Import Bal. incl. Bullion and Ship Sales (1)	Net Freight Earnings (2)	Foreign Trade Profits (3)	Insurance, Brokerage, etc. (4)	Capital and Interest Balance (5) [subtract (1) from (2), (3) and (4)]
	(in millions of pounds sterling)				
1854	40.6 a b	24.0	12.4	7.9	3.7
1855	34.0 a	25.2	11.9	7.7	10.8
1856	34.1 a	25.3	14.4	9.1	14.7
1857	33.5 a	26.6	15.5	9.9	18.5
1858	33.7	27.4	14.0	8.9	16.6
1859	17.0	27.3	14.4	10.2	34.9
1860	49.9	27.4	17.3	10.6	5.4
1861	55.5	28.7	17.1	10.4	.7
1862	61.1	29.6	17.4	11.3	− 2.8
1863	54.9	32.2	18.8	12.6	8.7
1864	66.1	34.6	21.7	13.5	3.7
1865	57.5	36.5	21.8	13.1	13.9
1866	67.8	37.2	24.2	14.7	3.6
1867	57.8	37.3	22.8	13.5	15.8
1868	70.1	37.5	23.6	14.2	5.2
1869	61.6	37.6	24.2	14.2	14.4
1870	68.0	39.2	25.1	14.9	11.2
1871	50.4	41.2	27.7	17.2	35.7
1872	36.1	43.7	30.5	18.2	56.3
1873	61.0	45.7	31.3	18.6	34.6
1874	70.6	48.2	30.4	18.0	26.6
1875	96.1	49.8	29.8	17.9	1.4
1876	125.4	51.0	28.7	17.4	− 28.3
1877	138.8	53.0	29.6	18.1	− 38.1
1878	127.5	55.5	28.0	16.8	− 27.3
1879	107.2	57.6	27.7	16.6	− 6.3
1880	119.5 b	59.8	31.7	18.3	− 10.2

a No official records were kept of bullion movements, 1854–57 inclusive. The estimates of Giffen have been used.

[5] There is no estimate of ship sales available for 1854. For 1880, to which Bourne's computations do not reach, I have assumed the same proportion of value to tonnage as prevailed in 1879.

[6] Grundherr zu Althenhaun u. Weyherhaus, Werner von, *Ueber die wirtschaftliche u. politische Bedeutung der Kapitalanlagen im Auslande* (Greifswald 1914).

[7] The following table compiled from Nash, R. I., *A Short Inquiry into the Profitable Nature of our Investments* (London 1880) indicates the annual average of earnings upon securities listed in the London Stock Exchange between 1870 and 1880, based upon the market value in January, 1870:

Securities	Profit in Dividends	Increase in Market Value of Principal	Total Profit
Foreign Government Stocks	5.9	0.3	6.2
Colonial Government Debentures	5.0	0.5	5.5
Indian Four Per Cents	4.0	0.3	4.3
Indian Railways	4.8	1.5	6.3
Canadian Railways	1.9	0.2	2.1
American Railways	5.7	3.6	9.3
U. S. Govt. Loans	6.1	1.4	7.5
Continental Railways	5.1	0.4	5.5
South American Railways	5.3	3.4	8.7
Indian Banks	5.1	− 2.0	3.1
Colonial Banks	8.4	4.3	12.7
Foreign Banks (chiefly Europe)	7.2	− 1.1	6.1
Land and Mortgage Companies	13.3	10.0	23.3
Steamship Companies	6.1	0.3	6.4
Cable Companies	6.6	− 1.3	5.3

And Egyptian securities, which fell heavily in market value as that country fell into receivers' hands, yielded an average of about 8% in dividends from 1870 to 1880, and had a total yield which varied upon different issues from 4.8% to 9.2% a year thruout that period.

APPENDICES

APPENDIX A

Year	Contract	Partners	Mileage
1841	Paris and Rouen	W. Mackenzie	82
1842	Orléans and Bordeaux	W. & E. Mackenzie	294
1843	Rouen and Havre	W. Mackenzie	58
1844	Amiens and Boulogne	E. & W. Mackenzie	53
1847	Rouen and Dieppe	W. Mackenzie	31
1848	Barcelona and Mataro	W. Mackenzie	18
1850	Prato and Pistoja		10
1851	Norwegian Railway	Peto & Betts	56
1852	Nantes and Caen		113
	Le Mans and Mezidon		84
	Lyons and Avignon	Peto & Betts	67
	Dutch Rhenish		43
	Grand Trunk of Canada	Peto, Betts & Jackson	539
1853	Sambre and Meuse		28
	Turin and Novara		60
	Hauenstein Tunnel		1½
	Royal Danish Railway	Peto & Betts	...
1854	Central Italian Railway	Jackson, Fell & Jopling	52
	Turin and Susa		34
	Bellegarde Tunnel	Parent & Buddicom	2½
1855	Caen and Cherbourg		94
1858	Bilbao and Miranda	Wythes, Paxton & Bartlett	66
	Eastern Bengal	Wythes, Paxton & Henfrey	112
1859	Victor Emmanuel Railway	Jackson & Henfrey	73
	Ivrea Railway	Henfrey	19
1860	Dieppe Railway	Buddicom	(second track)
	Maremma, Leghorn, etc.		138
	Jutland Railway	Peto & Betts	270
1862	Rio de Janeiro Drainage	Ogilvie	...
	Mauritius Railway	Wythes et al.	64

Year	Contract	Partners	Mileage
1863	Meridionale Railway	Parent & Buddicom	160
	Queensland Railway	Peto & Betts	78¼
	North Schleswig	Peto & Betts	70
1864	Central Argentine Railway	Wythes, Wheelwright & Ogilvie	247
	Lemberg-Czernowitz		165
	Viersen-Venlo Railway	Murton	11
	Delhi Railway	Wythes & Henfrey	304
1865	Boca and Barracas	Wythes & Wheelwright	3
	Warsaw and Terespol	Vignoles & Ogilvie	128
	Chord Line (India)	Wythes & Perry	147
1865	Calcutta Waterworks	Wythes & Aird	...
1867	Czernowitz-Suczawa Railway		60
	Kronprinz Rudolfsbahn	Klein & Schwarz	272
1869	Nepean Bridge	Peto & Betts	...
1870	Callao Docks		...
	Vorarlbergbahn	Klein & Schwarz	55
	Suczawa and Jassy		135

(abridged from Helps' *Life and Labours of Mr. Brassey*, pp. 161–66)

APPENDIX B

TABLE SHOWING VALUES OF PRINCIPAL ITEMS OF CAPITAL GOODS, PRODUCE OF THE U. K., EXPORTED 1846–76

Year	Iron and Steel [a]	(Railway Iron) [b]	Machinery	Hardwares and Cutlery	Copper	Tin [d]	Total
			(in millions of pounds sterling)				
1846	4.1		1.1	2.1	1.5 [c]	.7	9.5
1851	5.8		1.1	2.8	1.5	1.1	12.3
1856	13.0	(4.0)	2.7	3.7	2.5	1.6	23.5
1861	10.3	(2.9)	4.2	3.4	2.1	1.2	21.2
1866	14.8	(4.1)	4.7	4.3 [e]	2.5	2.2	28.5
1871	22.6	(8.0)	5.9	4.0	2.9	3.6	39.0
1873	34.1	(10.4)	10.0	4.9	3.2	4.7	56.9
1876	17.2	(3.7)	7.2	3.4	2.9	3.2	33.9
1846–76 inc.	432.0	(97.5)	127.6	108.8	75.0	63.7	806.3

ᵃ "Iron and Steel" includes the items under heading "Total of Iron and Steel" in the Trade and Navigation reports for 1850. At a later time, the items "Tinned Plates" and "Manufactures of Steel, or of Steel and Iron combined" were included in the total. They are here deducted. The latter item ranged from .4 to .7 million a year.

ᵇ "Railway Iron" is included under "Iron and Steel." No separate figures are available earlier than 1856.

ᶜ Including "Brass" 1846.

ᵈ Including Tinned Plates.

ᵉ After 1868 the figures under "Hardwares and Cutlery" are made up of a slightly smaller range of items than before that date.

APPENDIX C

TABLE OF FOREIGN GOVERNMENT LOAN ISSUES IN LONDON, 1860 TO 1876, INCLUSIVE

Year	Country or State	Issue Amount	Issue Price	Rate of Interest	Amorti- zation	Issue House
		mill.	%	%	%	
1860	Brazil	1.3	90	4½	1.65	Rothschild
	Russia	5.0	92	4½	1½	Baring; Hope
1861	Italy	conv.		4	perp.	Rothschild
	Denmark	conv.			1	Hambro
1862	Denmark	.6	91	4	none	Hambro
	Egypt	2.1	82½	7	1	Frühling & Goschen
	Egypt	1.0	84½	7	1	
	Italy	1.3	74	5	99-yr.	Hambro
	Morocco	.5	85	5	5	Robinson & Fleming
	Peru	5.5	93	4½	8	Heywood, Kennard
	Portugal	4.0	44	3	none	Knowles & Foster
	Russia	10.0	94	5	none	Rothschild
	Turkey	8.0	68	6	2	Ottoman Bank; C. De- vaux; Glyn, Mills & Co.
1863	Brazil	3.8	88	4½	1.65	Rothschild
	Colombia	.2	86	6		L. & County Bank
	Confederacy	3.0	90	7	20-yr.	J. H. Schroeder E. Erlanger
	Italy	3.0	71	5	perp.	Rothschild
	North Carolina	.3	par	7		Manchester & County Bank
	Portugal	1.2	48	3	none	Stern
	Venezuela	1.2	63	6	2	Baring
	Turkey	5.0	72	6	2	{ Ottoman Bank { Crédit Mobilier
	Tunis	1.5	96	7		Erlanger
1864	Danubian Prin- cipal	.9	86	7	2	Ottoman Bank Stern
	Denmark	1.2	9?	5	1	Hambro
	Denmark	.7	94½	5	13-yr.	Raphael
	Egypt	5.7	93	7	2	Fr. & Goschen

Year	Country or State	Issue Amount	Issue Price	Rate of Interest	Amorti-zation	Issue House
		mill.	%	%	%	
	Mexico	8.0	63	6	1	{ Glyn, Mills { Intern. Fin. Co. { Crédit Mobilier
	Mexico	arrears	60	3		Baring
	Russia	6.0	85	5	1	Baring; Hope
	Sweden	2.2	92½	4½	54-yr.	Schroeder
	Uruguay	1.0	60	6	1	Maua, Macgregor
	Venezuela	1.5	60	6	2	Gen. Fin. Co.
1865	Brazil	6.8	74	5	1	Rothschild
	Italy	2.5	77½	5	15-yr.	Gen. Credit & Fin. Co.
	Peru	9.0	83½	5	5	Thomson, Bonar
	Turkey	6.0	65½	6	2.44	Ottoman Bank
	Austria	?	66	5	37-yr.	Agra & Mastermans
	San Paulo	.4				
	Massachusetts	.4			3	Baring
	Turkey	3.6	50	5	1	Gen. Credit Co.; Er-langer
1866	Argentina	.5	75	6	2½	Baring; Hope
	Chili	.4	92½	6	2-yr.	Thomson, Bonar
	Chili	.6	92	7	2	Morgan
	Egypt	1.6	90	7	6⅔	Anglo-Egypt. Bank
	Egypt	3.0	92	7	3–8 yrs.	Frühling & Goschen
	Russia	6.0	86	5	1	Baring; Hope
	Massachusetts	.4			3	Baring
1867	Chili	2.0	84	6	2	Morgan
	Danubian Pr.	1.2	71	8	1.62	Frühling & Goschen
	Egypt	2.0	90	9	3½	{ Ottoman Bank { Oppenheim
	Honduras	1.0	80	10	3	Bischoffsheim
	Holland	.3	89	4½		Holstman & Co.
	Portugal	3.7	38½	3	none	Stern
	Russia	12.2	61	4	.15	Baring; Hope
	Russia	4.5	77½	5		Thomson, Bonar
	Russia (ry)	?		5		Baring, et al.
	Tunis	4.0	63	7	none	Erlanger
	Massachusetts	.4	77	5		Baring
1868	Argentina	1.9	72½	6	2½	Baring; Hope
	Egypt	11.8	75	7	1	Ottoman Bank
	Hungary	8.5	71.67	5	50-yr.	L. & County Bank
	Italy	9.4	81.35	6	15-yr.	Stern
	Russia	1.9	78	5		Baring
	Russia	2.0	80	5		Raphael
	Russia	1.3	80	5		Schroeder
	Sweden	1.1	90	5	¼	Raphael
	Massachusetts	.6		5		Baring
	France	....				
1869	Alabama	1.0	81	8		Schroeder
	Guatemala	.5	70½	6	3	Thomson, Bonar
	Holland	.4	91½	4½		Montagu
	Italy	5.2	73	5	(1876–81)	Anglo-Italian Bank
	Peru	.3	71	5	2	Thomson, Bonar
	Portugal	8.6	32½	3	none	Stern
	Roumania	.4	90	7	7-yr.	C. Devaux & Co.
	Roumania	1.5	71¾	7½		Anglo-Austrian Bank
	Russia	11.1	63	4	.15	Baring; Hope
	San Domingo	.7	70	6	1¾	Peter Lawson; Hart-mont

Year	Country or State	Issue Amount	Issue Price	Rate of Interest	Amortization	Issue House
		mill.	%	%	%	
	Spain	8.0	29½	3		Morgan
	Turkey	22.2	60½	6	I	{ Comptoir d'Escompte; { Louis Cohen & Co.
	Turkey	2.4	83	6	(1872–73)	Devaux
1870	Alabama	.4	94½	8		Schroeder
	Austria		conv.			
	Buenos Ayres	1.0	88	6	I	C. de Murrieta & Co.
	Chili	1.0	83	5	2, later I	Morgan
	Egypt	7.0	78½	7	2⅜	Bischoffsheim
	France	10.0	85	6		Morgan
	Honduras	2.5	80	10	3	Bischoffsheim
	Japan	1.0	98	9	(1873–82)	Schroeder
	Massachusetts	.6	87	5		Baring
	Peru	11.9	82½	6	2	Schroeder
	Roumania	.4	86	7		Devaux
	Roumania	.6	72	7½		Anglo-Austrian Bank
	Russia	12.0	80	5	.098	Rothschild
	Spain	2.3	80	5	30-yr.	Rothschild
	Spain		conv.			
1871	Argentine	6.1	88½	6	1½	Murrieta
	Brazil	3.4	89	5	I	Rothschild
	Costa Rica	1.0	73	6	2	Bischoffsheim
	France	?	82½	5		Rothschild; Baring
	Holland	.2	90½	5		Montagu
	Hungary	3.0	81	5	1½	Raphael
	Liberia	.1	85	7		Holderness, Nott
	Louisiana	.4	84.38	8		Robinson & Fleming
	Massachusetts	.6	91	5		Baring
	Paraguay	1.0	80	8	2	Rothschild
	Russia	12.0	81½	5	.098	Robinson & Fleming
	Spain	2.6	80	6		Stern
	Spain	6.3	31	3		(by govt. commission)
	Turkey	5.7	73	6	I	Dent, Palmer & Co.
	United States	40.0	102.38			
	Uruguay	3.5	72	6	2½	Thomson, Bonar
1872	Argentina	1.2	76	6	I	Stern
	Bolivia	1.7	68	6	2	Lumb, Wanklyn
	Costa Rica	1.5	82	7	I	Knowles & Foster
	Entre Rios	.2	90	7	2½	Murrieta
	France	?	84½	5		Baring; Rothschild McCalmont Bros.
	Massachusetts	.4	93	5		
	Paraguay	.5	85	8	2	Robinson & Fleming
	Peru	15.0	77½	5	2	Schroeder; Stern
	Russia	15.0	90	5	.098	Rothschild
	Russia	1.7	87½	5		Hambro
	Spain	9.0	28¾	3		(by govt. commission)
	Turkey	11.0	98½	9	(1876–78)	Raphael
	Washington and other American cities	4.60				Seligman, Rothschild, Barings
1873	Buenos Ayres	2.0	89½	6	I	Baring
	Chili	2.2	94	5	2	Oriental Bkg. Corp.
	Colombia		conv.			L. & County Bank
	Egypt	32.0	84¼	7	30-yr.	Bischoffsheim
	Hungary	5.4	80	5	1½	Raphael
	Hungary	7.5	89	6	(1878)	Rothschild
	Japan	2.4	92½	7	2	Oriental Bkg. Corp.

Year	Country or State	Issue Amount	Issue Price	Rate of Interest	Amorti- zation	Issue House
		mill.	%	%	%	
	Massachusetts	.1	91½	5		Baring
	Russia	15.0	93	5	.098	Rothschild
	Spain		conv.			
	Turkey	8.0	58½	6	1	Imp. Ottoman Bank
	United States	60.0	102.38	5		Baring; Rothschild;
	Spain	6.3				
1874	Argentina	.3	80	6	1	Stern
	Belgium	1.4	75½	3	⅙	Baring
	Hungary	7.5	91½	6	(1879)	Rothschild
	Santa Fe	.3	92	7	2½	Murrieta
	Turkey	15.9	43½	5	none	Imp. Ottoman Bank
	American cities	.7				Morgan & Co.
1875	Brazil	5.3	96½	5	1	Rothschild
	Chili	1.1	88¼	5	2	Oriental Bkg. Corp.
	Massachusetts	.3	98	5	(1895)	Baring
	Russia	15.0	92	5	.098	Rothschild
	Spain	13.0	coupon funding			
	Sweden	1.0	98¾	4½	.16⁷	Erlanger
	American cities	.6				Morton, Rose
1876	China	.2	100	8	5	Hong-Kong Bkg. Corp.
	Norway	1.3	96½	4½	39-yr.	Hambro
	Portugal	.3	83½	5		Soc. des Dépots
	Sweden	1.5	96½	4½	½	Hambro
	United States	60.0	103½	4½		Rothschild; Morgan
	Cincinnati	.3	96½	6		Alliance Bank

APPENDIX D

SUMMARY OF FOREIGN SECURITY ISSUES MADE IN LONDON, 1860–76

(The data here summarized includes only shares and debentures publicly issued. It excludes so far as possible conversions, vendor's shares, and discount. It includes calls where ascertainable as of the year in which they were actually paid up, not in the year of the original issue of the stock.)

Year	Foreign Government Loans	Colonial and Indian Loans (including Railway guarantees)	Foreign and Colonial Railways and Other Companies	Total
		(*in millions of pounds sterling*)		
1860	5.8	13.2	6.7	25.7
1861	.6	12.7	4.8	18.1
1862	22.5	12.4	7.4	42.3
1863	8.9	7.9	12.9	29.7
1864	13.5	5.4	14.2	33.1
1865	22.0	9.6	20.9	52.5
1866	8.0	11.6	11.0	30.6
1867	11.4	9.4	6.5	27.3
1868	22.1	11.9	9.7	43.7
1869	20.1	10.8	8.8	39.7
1870	35.0	6.4	9.8	51.2
1871	40.1	4.9	15.3	60.3
1872	43.3	2.6	31.2	77.1
1873	16.5	4.8	29.8	51.1
1874	27.0	17.7	26.0	70.7
1875	20.4	13.0	10.6	44.0
1876	3.5	7.6	6.4	17.5
Totals	320.7	161.9	232.0	714.6

The prevalence of simultaneous issues of government loans in several markets has caused special difficulty, since the amount allotted to each market was usually not formally announced. The figures under this heading are therefore estimates, checked by such contemporary reports as could be secured. The estimates for the peak years run below the probable totals.

APPENDIX E

SECURITIES OF PRIVATE COMPANIES OPERATING ABROAD, ISSUED IN
LONDON, 1860–76

Year	European Private Railways	Colonial Railways	United States Railways	South American Railways	Other Foreign Companies	Total
		(in millions of pounds sterling)				
1860	1.8	1.2	1.0	.9	1.8	6.7
1861	2.3	.1	..	1.3	1.1	4.8
1862	3.0	.3	..	.2	3.9	7.4
1863	4.0	..	.2	.4	8.3	12.9
1864	2.7	.3	1.3	.6	9.3	14.2
1865	4.6	..	2.7	1.0	12.7	20.9
1866	1.3	.1	2.0	.7	6.8	11.0
1867	2.2	..	1.0	.4	2.9	6.5
1868	5.2	..	1.6	1.1	1.7	9.7
1869	3.3	.3	1.8	.5	2.9	8.8
1870	.5	.5	3.9	.1	4.5	9.8
1871	.9	1.0	6.1	1.3	5.9	15.3
1872	1.1	1.2	12.0	3.2	13.7	31.2
1873	.2	2.7	14.3	3.2	9.2	29.8
1874	.8	2.4	14.3	2.8	5.6	26.0
1875	.4	1.1	4.7	1.3	3.4	10.6
1876	.1	.5	3.6	.1	2.0	6.4
Total	34.4	11.7	70.5	19.1	95.7	232.0

Of the "Other Foreign Companies" it may be noted that the bulk
of these were to do business in Europe or the Near East. However,
while in the sixties the remainder were mainly located in some part
of the British Empire, in the seventies it was the United States and
South America which ranked after Europe as a field of opportunity.

INDEX

INDEX

A

Abbas, 302
Abdul-Aziz, 309
Aberdeen, 50
Aberdeen, Lord, 119, 122, 301
Acton, Lord, 231
Adams, Charles Francis, 103
Afghan wars, 296
Afghanistan, 126
Africa, British economic domination of, 194
"Agricole," 314
Aix-la-Chapelle, Congress of, 42
Algiers, 168, 295
Alliance Assurance Company, 52
Alten copper mines, 186
America, Bank of, 90
Amiens-Boulogne company, 145, 156-157
Amsterdam, 6, 7, 10, 14, 16, 65, 185, 284; bourse, 6
Anderson, Arthur, 301
Andrews, W. P., 249
Anglo-American credit system, 86
Anglo-American trade, 84
Anglo-Austrian Bank, 177
Anglo-Egyptian Bank, Ltd., 315, 317
Anglo-Egyptian Banking Company, 319
Anglo-French Commercial Treaty (1786), 15
Anglo-French railway association, 156

Anglo-French railway coöperation, 165
Anglo-Italian Bank, 250
Anglo-Mexican Company, 56
Antwerp, 6, 279
Argentine Confederation, 122
Argyll, Duke of, 222, 231
Arkansas, banks in, 76, 93
Arkwright, 13
Asia Minor, 298; railways in, 168
Atlantic & Great Western Railway, 169, 256, 258
Atlantic & Saint Lawrence railroad, 198
Augsburg, 6
Australasia, British loans to, 231; British possessions in, 194
Australian Agricultural Company, 53
Australian colonies, 206
Austria, 7, 38, 42, 43, 50, 167, 172, 279; railway construction in, 172
Austro-Sardinian war, 172

B

Bagdad Railway, 294
Baker, Sir Samuel, 319-320
Baltic ports, 38
Baltimore, 74, 78
Baltimore & Ohio Railroad, 74, 78, 103, 169
Banda Oriental, 122
Bank, Anglo-Austrian, 177; An-

429